AMERICA'S SAINTS

The Rise of Mormon Power

Robert Gottlieb & Peter Wiley

A Harvest/HBJ Book

Harcourt Brace Jovanovich, Publishers

San Diego   New York   London

Requests for permission to make copies of any
part of the work should be mailed to:
Robert Cornfield Literary Agency,
Five West 73rd Street,
New York, New York 10023.
Library of Congress Cataloging in Publication Data
Gottlieb, Robert
America's saints.
Bibliography: p.
Includes index.
1. Church of Jesus Christ of Latter-Day Saints—
Political activity. 2. Mormon Church—Political
activity. 3. United States—Church history—20th
century. 4. United States—Politics and government—
20th century. I. Wiley, Peter II. Title.
BX8643.P6G57   1986   289.3'32   85-24879
ISBN 0-15-605658-5

Printed in the United States of America
First Harvest/HBJ edition 1986
A B C D E F G H I J

CONTENTS

To our families:
Marge, Casey; Julie,
Beau, Nathaniel, Jesse, and Celia

PREFACE TO THE PAPERBACK EDITION

One of our first encounters with a Mormon audience came soon after publication of the hardcover edition of *America's Saints* in September 1984. It was a cold winter evening, and the overheated auditorium at the University of Utah in Salt Lake City was packed. The audience of about five hundred, almost all Mormons and mostly independent types, had come to hear about our book, which was already controversial. Some in the audience were friendly, a few were hostile, but most were intensely curious about the authors of a book that had been openly attacked by the church leadership.

The panel moderator's first question summed up both the strong interest and the uneasiness the audience felt toward the authors: why, he asked, would two non-Mormons want to write about the church? It was an odd question, one that Mormons, always self-conscious about how they are viewed by the outside world, would bring up time and again. Why, we replied, would two non-Mormons *not* want to write about this powerful, compelling, culturally complex, and authoritarian church? It was the kind of story that interesting books are made of—filled with dramatic characters and events, conflict, a rich history, and contemporary significance. And this was a time when religious groups, including the Mormons, were making new forays into the secular world, particularly into the political arena.

The implicit assumption of the church hierarchy, and indeed of many in the audience, was that with regard to Mormonism there are two categories of people: insiders and outsiders. The two are separated by more than 150 years of doctrine, persecution, and family and institutional heritage which have led to a fundamental sense that to be a Mormon sets one apart from other Americans. We never accepted that distinction, at least insofar as we were determined to explore the inner workings of the church and its impact on its membership and the larger society.

Many observers of the Mormon church think it difficult, if not impossible, for an outsider to penetrate the walls of secrecy and the detailed internal structure and language of Mormonism. Interestingly, we found just the opposite: the outsider who has become enough of an insider to witness and recognize the various worlds of Mormonism also escapes the constant constraints that a Mormon insider feels and breathes, whether he or she is a historian, journalist, or novelist. For critical analysis of the church inevitably puts a Mormon in conflict with authority, a matter not taken lightly.

It was our ability to get beyond the veil of secrecy and public relations imagery, to get a handle on the varieties of Mormon experience and see how the church as an institution operates, that was most deeply disturbing to the church leadership and most appealing to Mormon readers. Prior to publication, the Public Communications Department, the public relations arm of the church, had monitored our research and scrutinized our earlier writings on the church. We never were subjected to the intense scrutiny, surveillance, and harassment experienced by Mormon dissidents such as Doug Wallace, who baptized a black man in a motel swimming pool before the 1978 revelation that permitted blacks to hold the priesthood. We were, however, frequently blocked by the church in attempts to secure interviews with church leaders and bureaucrats. When we made it clear, after three years of requests, that we would state in our book that the church would not cooperate with us, we were granted interviews with Apostles Boyd K. Packer and Neal M. Maxwell as spokesmen for the church's top leadership.

Our progress was carefully tracked. Files on us were established and meetings were held concerning our research. Finally, when *America's Saints* came out, the church established a large committee to examine the book's information in minute detail. Meetings were held and memos were prepared to enable church leaders, the General Authorities, to devise a strategy to deal with the publication of the book.

The reaction of the church leadership to the book was never in doubt. Gordon B. Hinckley, the most powerful figure within the church hierarchy, had set the tone a couple of years before when he declared that the press had become the contemporary equivalent of the anti-Mormon mobs of the nineteenth century. Dallin H. Oaks, a recent member of the Quorum of the Twelve, the leadership body that sits just below the Prophet, or president, was just as blunt in an August 1985 speech to students at the church's Brigham Young University. "Criticism is particularly objectionable when it is directed toward church authorities, general or local," Oaks declared in a speech that took aim at the press and historians, including Mormon historians, who had written about the church. "Evil speaking of the Lord's anointed is in a class by itself. It is one thing to depreciate a person who exercises corporate power or even government power. It is quite another thing to criticize or depreciate a person for the performance of an office to which he or she has been called of God. *It does not matter that the criticism is true* [emphasis added]." And this was from ostensibly the most progressive of the Quorum of the Twelve, a founder of *Dialogue* magazine (a critical magazine put out by a group of younger, more "liberal" Mormons), a former president of BYU, and a former Utah Supreme Court justice.

The question for church leaders was not whether to attack *America's Saints* but in what manner. We had looked behind the church's carefully constructed and screened images of unity and religiosity to describe the conflicts and personalities that shaped the modern church. We were offering to the outside world and the Mormons themselves a very different description of developments within the church.

The church moved quickly against the book. An early decision was made to send out instructions to seminary and institute teachers in the church's own elaborate educational system to make sure they did not use *America's Saints* as a text.

To alert the membership to the General Authorities' views, a statement by Richard P. Lindsay, the head of Public Communications and the Special Affairs Committee, was printed in the *Church News,* the weekly supplement put out by the church. "*America's Saints* by Robert Gottlieb and Peter Wiley," the statement declared, "is so preoccupied with politics, power, 'dirty linen,' and 'closet skeletons' that the book captures little of the real essence of its subject, the remarkable growth and dynamic influence of the Church of Jesus Christ of Latter-day Saints. This focus seems not to result from ignorance, but by design."

"Their indefatigable efforts," the statement went on, "have produced a book—in the contemporary tradition of ambitious journalistic exposés—which makes interesting reading, but widely misses the mark. Their examination of the church departs from the biblical injunction to judge a tree by what it produces; rather they have concentrated on what they could find in the dirt surrounding the roots. . . ."

Of course, thousands of Mormons, who know little but gossip about what is going on within their church, rushed to the nearest bookstore to find out what was so "interesting" about "the dirt surrounding the roots."

A statement of this kind, attacking a book written by non-Mormons, is unprecedented in the contemporary history of the church. The church, which operates so frequently through indirect signals and oblique allusions, was sending out a very direct message in our case. *America's Saints,* though not officially proscribed, was being judged inimical to the interests of the church and not in the tradition of the "faith-promoting" literature recommended by the church.

The statement was published September 2, 1984, nearly two weeks before publication of the book, presumably providing advance warning to Mormons. Yet in the first weeks after publication, *America's Saints* sold very well, moving to the top of the Utah best-seller list, where it stayed for more than six months.

To make the church's negative assessment even clearer to the Mormon public, Lindsay agreed to debate one of us on Salt Lake public television in November. The situation had now become quite extraordinary. The opportunities to question and debate an official spokesman of the church are few and far between, especially in a format not under church control. It was also curious that the church leadership had agreed to such a debate since the surrounding controversy would undoubtedly increase interest in the book.

From the remarks Lindsay offered during the debate, it became obvious that he and the church leadership assumed that by simply agreeing to appear on television and stating that *America's Saints* was disapproved for its "Watergate-style journalism," as Lindsay put it, the message would be received and accepted. Lindsay assumed that he was speaking to his constituency—the Mormon faithful, and especially the Mormon orthodox—and the message would be unambiguous: do not buy and be deceived by this book.

In some ways this strategy backfired and in some ways it did not. Many of those who watched the debate included less orthodox Mormons, those we call Tightrope Mormons and Autonomous Mormons. They are the insiders, believing Mormons, who do not always subscribe to the narrow definitions of Mormonism put forth by the church leadership. This part of the audience, we found out later, had problems with some of Lindsay's statements. They were particularly upset when Lindsay described Mormon historians Leonard J. Arrington and Davis Bitton—Lindsay called them Harry Arrington and Bitton Davis—as historians the church looked on with favor. In fact the shabby treatment, described in our book, of Arrington, Bitton, and several other Mormon historians who had worked in the church's Historical Department when Arrington was the official church historian was a major reason a number of Mormon professionals, academics, and other intellectuals had grown increasingly unhappy with the contemporary church.

Yet for all the controversy that the *Church News* statement and television debate generated, the church leadership—though awkwardly, and perhaps for certain Mormons unconvincingly—had made its point and thereby flexed its muscles. We met and heard of a number of Mormons who considered *America's Saints* taboo without having read a word of the book. Among them apparently was Lindsay, who admitted during the debate that he had not read the book which he had critiqued and was discussing.

In at least one other instance the church flexed its muscles. We were to discover later that a Salt Lake television station had contacted the church for assistance with a documentary on the church. The program was to end with a town-meeting discussion featuring a panel of experts. The church asked whom the station planned to invite on the panel. When the documentary makers mentioned one of us, the church indicated that it could not cooperate with a program in which we were to participate. The documentary was made, and neither of us was invited to sit on the panel.

The most substantial criticism of the book was that we failed to deal sufficiently with "the spiritual side of the church." We agree and disagree. We agree because we did not set out to write a book solely about Mormon doctrine and the uniqueness of the Mormon belief system. We set out to write a book about the church as an institution and its interaction with its own members and the larger non-Mormon world. We heartily disagree when the criticism is made in the context of arguing that the Mormon church is solely a spiritual institution that has little to do with the world of politics and business. To claim this is to either fundamentally misunderstand or want to obfuscate the church's history.

The church was founded to establish the Kingdom of God *on earth.* There was an immediacy to the church's millenarianism, an immediacy that was expressed in the struggle for political power in church-influenced areas and in numerous experiments with communalism, cooperatives, and a new family system based on polygamy. To early church leaders, such as founder Joseph Smith, and his successor, Brigham Young, there never could be a separation between political power, economic well-being, and spiritual triumph. They were part of building the kingdom. These aspects of Mormonism remain linked, albeit in very different ways, down to the present, making the contemporary Mormon church very different from any other American church. The church's involvement in business and political affairs has been a constant source of embarrassment to the church, and this is probably the main reason that church leaders try to deny that this involvement exists. Even as this preface is written, Mormon spokesmen have been forced to explain a statement by Gordon B. Hinckley that the church is 100 percent behind a controversial Utah water project and will aid in the effort to get financial backing for it.

The assessment of and attack on *America's Saints* by church leaders and its reception within the Mormon community are symbolic of the state of Mormonism today. The leadership remains secure in its ability to continue a type of orthodoxy and authoritarianism in the midst of expansion. It still seeks to protect its members from what it perceives as hostile outside forces. Yet Mormonism persists as a complex culture. Certain forms of independence survive, and a whole new breed of Mormon intellectuals is unwilling to suspend critical thinking at the behest of church leaders.

As the institutional power and outreach of the church expand, the church becomes more and more widely known and is increasingly subjected to examination and analysis from both insiders and outsiders. The bitter confrontation between the church and some Israeli religious leaders over the establishment of a Mormon religious center in Jerusalem is only one recent example. So, too, the recent bombing of church buildings in Chile highlights the controversy over the church's presence in the Third World. Such developments are inevitable, and the level of conflict within the church is directly related to how church leaders deal with such controversies.

In October and November 1985, the church underwent intense scrutiny in the national media in the wake of the so-called Mormon bombings and the death of Spencer W. Kimball, who had led the church since 1974.

On October 14, Steve Christensen, a former Mormon bishop, and Kathy Sheets, the wife of his business partner, were killed by package bombs. The next day Mark Hofmann, a young dealer in historical documents, was seriously injured by a bomb that was in his car. Hofmann was subsequently indicted on a weapons charge. Although the Salt Lake City Police Department had considered Hofmann a prime suspect in the bombings, on November 13 he passed a lie detector test showing he did not plant the explosives that killed Christensen and Sheets.

Earlier in the year, Christensen and his business partner had bought from Hofmann a controversial document known as the Salamander Letter and donated it to the church. The church later acknowledged at an extraordinary press conference that it had been dealing with Hofmann since 1980 to procure a number of other potentially controversial documents; many believe the church intended to place the documents in the closed section of the church archives before they could be examined by researchers.

The Salamander Letter, written in 1830 by Martin Harris, one of the first members of the church, gave an account of Joseph Smith's discovery of the Book of Mormon very different from the official church version. The letter revived and intensified the more than decade-long confrontation between the church (for which questions of history and doctrine are inextricably inter-twined) and its historians over the origins and development of Mormonism. The sale of the Salamander Letter also fueled a high-priced scramble to purchase and gain control of other recently discovered documents that describe the early activities of Joseph Smith—activities, such as Smith's first polyg-amous relationships, that the leadership has tried to deny.

Three weeks after the bombings, Spencer W. Kimball died at the age of ninety and was quickly succeeded as church president by the eighty-six-year-old Ezra Taft Benson. Many Mormons had dreaded a Benson succession, fearing that his conservative political sentiments and his attempts to link the church with the ultraright would lead to a major schism. But as it turned out, other, younger leaders, such as Gordon B. Hinckley, had worked carefully over the years to bring several more moderate figures into the Quorum of the Twelve Apostles. A schism was averted.

Since publication of *America's Saints* in hardcover, both of us have traveled across the country speaking to numerous Mormon groups. These meetings have always been dramatic, involving us in discussions with members who have never had the opportunity to speak so intimately with outsiders about their church. Many of these Mormons thanked us warmly for writing what they considered an informative and balanced—if at times critical—book about their church. They have reinforced our faith in the value of independent thought and the need for autonomy, not only in the church but throughout society. These encounters have also reinforced our assumption that critical thinking and analysis—what Antonio Gramsci called optimism of the spirit, pessimism of the mind—are fundamental values.

The Dallin Oakses of the Mormon church see criticism as a negative instrument that destroys. We have always assumed that critical thinking is an essential value, a value that allows one to learn and to change, to see the present as history and the future as possibility.

November 1985

PREFACE TO THE HARDCOVER EDITION

When the mayor of Salt Lake City got on the phone on a Sunday in May 1983, he knew where he needed to start—at the top. The strongly hierarchical, patriarchal, and intricately organized Church of Jesus Christ of Latter-day Saints, or Mormons, had already prepared for this crisis and was ready to mobilize its considerable forces.

The mayor's message was urgent. The record snowfall accumulated during the winter's storms was melting fast. At any time, water would begin to pour from the canyon streams into the city itself. The mayor wanted The Church, as it is called in Utah, to call out its army of volunteers to help control the anticipated deluge.

This was the Mormons' finest hour. In anticipation of the flooding, they had already contacted the civil authorities to let them know how to set the church's volunteers in motion. Now they went to work, businessmen side by side with auto mechanics, school teachers, and housewives, filling sandbags and building a number of artificial rivers that carried the raging flood through downtown Salt Lake City and out onto the alkaline flats near the Great Salt Lake.

The key to the Mormons' ability to mobilize is their top–down structure, or what they call the priesthood organization. At the top stand the General Authorities, the paid leadership aided by thousands of full-time employees and made up of the men who supervise the church's huge missionary program and the stakes (similar to a group of parishes), wards (similar to a parish), and branches that extend downward from the Prophet, Seer, and Revelator, the church's supreme authority, and the Quorum of the Twelve Apostles (see organization chart). Below the General Authorities are the hundreds and thousands of stake presidents and their counselors, bishops and their counselors, and members of the Melchizedek and Aaronic priesthoods. Each of these positions is basically unpaid. A male member of the church joins the priesthood at its lowest level, the Aaronic priesthood, at age twelve and then can proceed up the hierarchical ladder. A member in good standing is "called" to undertake the various decision-making posts throughout the church.

This lay priesthood is the backbone of the church—the key to its spiritual and social influence and its power. These men are more than dedicated, often spending almost as much time on church matters as on their jobs. When the word comes down, the priesthood can act immediately and effectively. Thousands of dollars can be raised at a moment's notice to provide earthquake relief in Guatemala, 14,000 Mormon women can mobilize to take over a state women's conference, or, as in the case of the 1983 flood, a disaster can be prevented.

During the flood, government officials worked with local church leaders. The local leader plugged into an already established phone tree that within one hour could alert every active member of the church in a given area. When the mayor realized that the city could be saved by building a series of levees through the streets, one single phone call brought 2,000 volunteers in an hour.

"I'll tell you why it works," proudly proclaimed Robert E. Wells, a General Authority and executive administrator for the Salt Lake region. "It works because of priesthood obedience. That is part of our normal church system. We have recognized leaders, and people respond to clear leadership. Why, we can field 200,000 people in thirty minutes in the middle of the night if we have to." And Wells, as most Mormon-watchers know, is not kidding.

The Salt Lake City Flood of 1983 is only one of many illustrations of the enormous organizational capacities of the Mormon church. With amazing discipline and control, the Mormons continue to demonstrate their ability to recruit new members and to mobilize and influence events around them. Understanding how the church operates and how it has extended its influence and power throughout this country and the world is the subject of *America's Saints*.

The story of the Mormons, who emerged in the 1830s—according to Ralph Waldo Emerson as an "afterclap of Puritanism"—is the story of a vision as old as America. Mormon founder Joseph Smith, Jr., claimed that he had founded the only true religion. He set out to build a model community—the City on the Hill, or what he called the Kingdom of God on earth—that would be both more righteous and more charitable and would serve as a shining example to the benighted peoples of the world. The Mormons became a rapidly growing religious force *and* a tight-knit community estranged from the larger society. Driven westward by mobs, attacked by their sectarian competitors and by those who were threatened by the accomplishments of the Mormon community, they chose in 1846 to move to what would become Utah, outside the confines of what was then the United States. They left their native country, which tolerated their persecutors, but they believed they would be back because the new Zion they were building in Utah would be the beginning of the millennium when the Saints would rule the world during the 1,000-year reign of Christ.

The Mormons, however, faced the same problems as their forebears, the Puritans: how to build a just society in an unjust world and, beyond that, how to keep their own members obedient to the principles that the Lord had personally revealed to Joseph Smith.

Their quest for a just society led them to embark on one of the most remarkable experiments in American history. With their own hands they built a unique community in the arid wastes of the Utah desert, based on economic cooperation and a new family structure—built on polygamy, or plural marriage. It was a radical and utopian response to the prevailing political, economic, and sexual order. This was their answer to an America plagued by violence, poverty, slavery, and civil war; their new theocracy would accomplish what the Puritans had failed to do.

Although the Mormons, as they like to say, were and are "a peculiar people," "in the world but not of the world," they were also in the path of Manifest Destiny as the country swept westward. Slowly in the 1850s their enemies in the Utah territory and Washington instigated a national campaign against the Mormons that was taken up by a federal government that was desperately trying to maintain national unity in the face of Southern secession. When the federal government came close to destroying the Mormon church in the 1880s, important church leaders recognized that the only way to save their religious order was to abandon polygamy, overt control of Utah politics, and their dreams of a cooperative commonwealth.

With the fervor of a new convert, the Mormons embraced the values of the society that they had formerly rejected. Still committed to building the true church through their missionary program, the Saints preached the virtues of the monogamous, patriarchal family where the mother stayed home and raised children, of hard work, laissez-faire capitalism, and political conservatism. As the Saints embraced American nationalism and the business ethic, the construction of a just society was postponed until the millennium.

The Great Accommodation, which commenced in 1890 with what appeared to be a church ban on polygamous marriages, also solved for a time the problem of how to be in the world but not of the world. The reformed Saints lived in anonymity for the first three decades of this century. With the advent of the New Deal, they began to sense that the outside world, in the form of federal programs to assist the poor and unemployed, was again threatening the Mormon ethic of self-containment and self-reliance. After World War II, the Saints found more serious threats in the rapid changes in social mores, particularly those affecting the patriarchal family, and in the upheavals of the 1960s. And still later, as Salt Lake City became a major energy capital during the post-OPEC energy boom, the Saints found the world pressing in on them, aided ironically by the church's own efforts to attract relocated corporations to Zion.

Always more theocratic in the Puritan mold than democratic, the Saints continued to assert their separateness from American society through increased centralization and greater insistence on obedience and conformity to church doctrines and procedures. This contemporary Mormonism, with its celebration of corporate power, identified with the most conservative aspects of American culture. The church has become worshipful of wealthy businessmen and professional male athletes, suspicious of artists and intellectuals, particularly its own artists and intellectuals, disdainful of welfare recipients, and increasingly homophobic.

"The tragedy here," University of Utah Professor Sterling M. McMurrin, a well-known church maverick, told the National Association for the Advancement of Colored People in 1968, "is that in its early decades the Mormon church was alive with social and moral reform. It had a vital, prophetic, revolutionary message that called for a just society and it was willing to run great risks in advocacy of its principles. Now it is quiescent and conservative and has lost much of its capacity to dream new dreams and chart new paths."

Conservative yes, but quiescent the Mormons are not.

When the New Right began to mobilize in reaction to what it perceived as the excesses of the 1960s, the church found its proper métier. The issues that most concerned Mormons, issues of the family, education, and sexuality, were at the forefront of the New Right political agenda. In a sense, the Mormons were ready for the New Right forty years before its arrival on the scene. The church has insisted on a high degree of involvement—a form of participation without democracy—that gives it the ability to mobilize its cadres as a political force. Building on their strength in the Intermountain West, the Saints' political impact is now felt from California to Florida, and, with the presidency of Ronald Reagan, in our nation's capital.

Once a cooperative experiment, the church, through the Great Accommodation, transformed its economic base into an empire that by the 1980s had become one of the largest and most closely held in the western United States and the largest of any church based in America. With income from investments and a ten percent tithe on all members, the church has built an economic presence that is shaping the skyline of Salt Lake City and providing for an international missionary program beyond the dreams of any other church in the world.

Almost overnight, this small Utah church became an international church, with missionary outposts throughout the world. Despite their claims to universality, the Saints have remained, nonetheless, a preeminently American church. Their missionary program has, in a sense, followed the flag, providing a spiritual dimension to the United States' political and economic influence abroad. In the process, the Saints serve as a conservative counterweight in the Third World to a changing and radicalizing Catholicism. As a critic of Catholicism's blend of religion and nationalism and as a friend of right-wing dictators, Mormonism, with its hybrid blend of church organization and American cultural values, has become a colonizing force in the Third World. The Mormons have, in effect, sought to integrate native peoples into its own uniquely American way of life.

At the heart of their international thrust lies a racial dynamic reminiscent of other Americans of European descent but doctrinally peculiar to Mormonism. That doctrine distinguishes between the righteous, or white-skinned, people of this hemisphere and the unrighteous, or dark-skinned, people. As a consequence, the church has developed an extensive Indian program based on a missionary effort directed at the native people of both North and South America. While the Book of Mormon taught that the Indian peoples of the Americas held a special place in church mythology, blacks were relegated to another, less desirable racial category and were banned from entering the Mormon priesthood. In recent years this ban has been lifted, mainly because it created enormous problems in the church's international missionary program.

If the male priesthood hierarchy is the key to the power and influence of the church, women are the key to its organization. Women are the most active members, the most visible participants, the truest believers. Yet doctrine and organization place men in charge from the wardhouse to the family. Women are denied both the priesthood and ultimate control over their own organizations. They are told to play a counselor's, or secondary, role to their husbands, who are providers, heads of the family, and the priesthood authority in the home. At the same time, they are under enormous pressure to fulfill their role as mothers, which, the church says, is the most crucial and doctrinally exalted role within the church belief system.

With the rise of the contemporary women's movement, the role of Mormon women has become increasingly problematic. Traditional patriarchy and its prerequisites have been challenged by women both inside and outside the church. At the same time, the church's involvement in the campaign against the Equal Rights Amendment has placed it in the forefront of the conservative response to feminism.

Ultimately, the Mormon church is a strikingly unique phenomenon, a culture within a culture, a society within a society, a demi-nation within a nation. As an authoritarian church that puts a premium on obedience, the Saints present an appearance of consensus and unity, enforced by an expanding bureaucracy that was reorganized and centralized through the Correlation movement of the 1960s in an attempt to isolate the Saints from the dangers of the outside world. Yet the Saints are not a monolithic people. If anything, the push to correlate has sharpened divisions within the church, whether over the issues of political involvement, business practices, or, most especially, the role of women.

This tension between the call to obedience and the desire to build a modern, liberal church—a conflict between the free agency that Mormons often speak of and priesthood authority—is coming to a head in the 1980s with the next change of leadership. The present Prophet, Spencer W. Kimball, now a very frail eighty-nine, is most likely to be followed by Ezra Taft Benson, the president of the Quorum of the Twelve Apostles and an archconservative who has stirred controversy in the church for two decades. There are indeed significant differences among the General Authorities—differences over the content of missionary programs, over political activities, investment strategies, and more. Still the church leadership moves slowly, resisting change in the larger society while inching toward new accommodations with the established order. The church, in the end, remains a deeply conservative institution with an incredibly powerful hold on its members, whether liberal or conservative, straight or gay, male or female.

It is unfashionable among the liberal intelligentsia to say anything positive about modern conservatism, and the rise of secularism has obscured the meaning of modern religions. But one must answer the question: Why does the church appeal to an increasing number of foreigners and Americans?

"People find," said a Mormon who was an associate solicitor in the U.S. Department of the Interior in Washington, "a loving religious community with a strong sense of values and a strong identity."

Another young Washington attorney put it this way, "Our theology is a complete theology to a person interested in who they are and where they are going. Is there a life after and a life before? The church has a straightforward answer that is readily understandable and comforting. That message is not conveyed in divinity school, but by missionaries who are twenty-five or younger, who are able to teach it."

There is a certain continuity in Mormonism that also helps explain its appeal. It has always provided a deep-searching critique of contemporary society, whether the society of the frontier or the society of corporate America. In the past the Saints rejected the anticommunitarian chaos, violence, and unfulfilled promises of the frontier. Today, even though they have embraced the corporate ethic, they reject modern liberalism and the decadence of the society that has grown out of political liberalism and the corporate state. In response, the Saints have created a working model for a separate society—whether it be the cooperatives and polygamy of the nineteenth century or the contemporary church, which goes a long way toward fulfilling all the needs, spiritual and material, of its members.

In their retreat from a flawed democracy toward a "safer," more structured, secure, and ultimately authoritarian way of life, the Saints have also provided an insight into what Americans in the nuclear age have increasingly found missing from their lives—a sense of community, of permanence in family relationships, of direction, spiritual values, economic security, and continuity into eternal life.

*   *   *

The interplay of Mormon influence and power and its organizational makeup intrigued us from the very outset of our research. We had previously explored the role of the Mormon church in the changing political and economic dynamics of Salt Lake City and the Intermountain West in our book, *Empires in the Sun: The Rise of the New American West*. We quickly learned there that to be interested in the West meant, ipso facto, to be interested in the Mormons—their history, their organizational dynamics, their power. We knew that the church had become in recent years a powerful institution, with its ability to influence events, to move large amounts of capital, to help elect candidates, and to orchestrate antifeminist campaigns.

We soon discovered that, despite the plethora of books about the Mormon experience, nothing comprehensive had been written about the contemporary church—the rapidly expanding, spiritually influential, politically and economically powerful organization that had emerged in the post–World War II period. Further, little had been written about the dynamics of church organization—how the business empire had evolved; the impact of the church's racial policies; the policies and operations of the international church. Nor had there been much analysis of the changing of the guard—the dynamics at the top, which to so many Mormons and outsiders alike seems inaccessible and monolithic.

As non-Mormons and transplanted Californians, we realized that undertaking a book on the contemporary church offered hazards as well as opportunities. We had to quickly master a whole language of doctrinal terms and everyday usage, intricate and highly bureaucratized organizational structures, a rich and varied history, and a cultural dynamic that did make the Mormon community something different.

We were fortunate in having already done extensive research for *Empires in the Sun* that gave us a head start in undertaking an effort of this magnitude. We had also developed many strong friendships and acquaintances with Mormons throughout the country, ranging from the excommunicated Mormon feminist Sonia Johnson to church press spokesman Jerry Cahill, who became our guides, offering their own experiences and insights into this highly textured world of the Saints.

There were also important advantages to not being Mormon. We could pursue information where many Mormons would fear to tread, given the concern about retribution. We could write directly without holding back, since as non-Mormons there was no threat of unemployment or excommunication, very real threats to Mormon writers who deal critically with their church.

We also had to contend with the deep penchant among Mormon leaders for secrecy. Church financial records are never made public and haven't been since 1958. The deliberations of the General Authorities are a closely guarded affair. The involvement of the church in politics occurs behind closed doors. The church encourages an internal spying system so that documents and information do not get leaked to the outside world.

For those journalists who attempt in a limited time to do a story on the church, research and investigation can be a frustrating affair. We also initially experienced some of the same frustrations. Over time, however, we discovered that an extraordinary amount of information, including "secret" information, could be obtained.

We were also fortunate in being able to interview a wide range of sources: secretaries, bureaucrats, church leaders who spoke on a background basis, other church leaders we contacted outside official channels, politicians, businessmen, academics, feminists, bishops, ordinary members, right-wingers, liberals, gays, mothers of twelve, singles, Mormon Indians, Latinos, members from El Salvador, Japan, Mexico, and England. We attended numerous Sunday services, an essential component of the Mormon experience. We visited a young couples' ward, suburban wards, inner-city wards, wealthy wards, poor wards, university wards, a Tongan ward, a ward in England, and one in Mexico. We met members in small towns in Utah, Arizona, California, Virginia, and Idaho, in Salt Lake City, Las Vegas, Washington, D.C., New York, and Los Angeles.

We attended Family Home Evening in a friend's home and at the home of a Salt Lake City family selected for us by the church. We went to Mormon parties, receptions, and symposia, to family gatherings, the Pioneer Day parade (bigger than the Fourth of July in Utah), annual conference, and press conferences. We toured a new temple in the Salt Lake suburbs, watched church movies, and went to both of the visitors centers in Salt Lake City. We experienced the dual worlds of Mormon and Gentile (their term for everyone who is not a Mormon). Information gathering became in part a process of living and breathing the culture.

To get interviews, we met people in remote and obscure settings. We scouted President Kimball's modest home in Salt Lake City, knocked on Ezra Taft Benson's door, and prayed around the coffee table with the church's highest official in Las Vegas.

Not all our research methods were that unusual. Several months were spent systematically digging through church archives, BYU library files, and similar sources. Most important, we were researchers trying to absorb a culture while, at the same time, looking into the power and impact of the church. What we found was a complex and important story.

The Mormon church is an institution that in the coming decades will more and more occupy center stage in American society. It will be important as this country's fastest-growing religion, a growing economic power, and a political influence. In the coming years, the church will be facing its greatest challenges, its greatest opportunities to expand its influence, and its greatest problems in holding together in the face of a difficult leadership transition and a potentially diverging membership. It is an institution that is confident, even smug, convinced that it has, with its doctrine, the most compelling message around. It is also an institution that sees itself under attack. A siege mentality prevails, which forces the church to use even more heavy-handed methods to protect its members from what it perceives as the evil influences of the outside world.

For the leaders of the church, the issues are joined: continue and intensify the expansion while shielding Zion from the evils of Babylon. Mormonism can then become, in effect, America's dominant religion, a religion that is at once a civil society and a theocratic empire.

For the 1980s, the Mormon church stands at a crossroads. Its contemporary history tells us what that future might have in store both for those who are Saints and for the rest of us who are or will soon become aware that this is a force to contend with.

The Organization of the Mormon Church

The President of the Church
(The Prophet, Seer, and Revelator)

The First Presidency
(The Prophet and his Counselors)

Quorum of the Twelve (Apostles)
(Headed by the President of the Twelve, the
next in line as Prophet)

The Presidency of the First Quorum of the Seventy

Quorum of the Seventies

Regional Representatives

Stake Presidents

Temple Presidents

Mission Presidents

The Presiding Bishopric

(All persons from the Prophet to the Quorum of the Seventies are known as General Authorities)

CHAPTER ONE

THE CHURCH AT 150 YEARS: APRIL 6, 1980

COMING HOME

They call themselves Latter-day Saints or Mormons, members of the Church of Jesus Christ of Latter-day Saints. On a spring day in 1980, they came to Salt Lake City, Utah, from far and wide—from Buddhist Japan, from Tonga, Samoa, and the islands of the Pacific, from Catholic Central and South America, from England, Germany, and South Africa—to attend the annual spring conference of their church and to celebrate its 150th anniversary.

And there was much to celebrate. The Mormon church in 1980 was the only church in America to claim significant growth in membership in recent years. Small in comparison to almost 50 million American Catholics, but decidedly larger than the Episcopal church's almost 3 million members, Mormon church membership reached 4,638,000 in 1980 and would pass 5 million two years later. Church membership has grown because of the Saints' remarkable birthrate—double the national average—and because of thousands of converts, many from Latin America, brought into the church by the more than 29,000 missionaries who roamed the world in 1980 as part of the most ambitious missionary program of any church at the time.

Added to this, the church exerted a degree of influence from Utah to Washington well beyond its numbers. In the past two decades, the church had gained an unwanted notoriety as one of the wealthiest but most secretive churches in the world. Its multibillion-dollar holdings made it a major economic power in the rapidly growing Intermountain West and the caretaker of a private welfare system that was the delight of antigovernment politicians and the envy of the great corporate powers.

For years an established power in the Republican party from southern California to Idaho, Mormons were playing a major role in the defeat of the Equal Rights Amendment by merely flexing their considerable organizational muscle. Numerous influential church members had already joined Ronald Reagan's presidential campaign. And in less than a year, they would nail down important positions in the new administration in Washington, bringing to the Reagan coalition close ties to one of the wealthiest and best-organized conservative political forces in America.

The Saints were coming home to Zion, the city in the desert to which their forebears had fled, hundreds dying in the long flight from persecution along the American frontier. The ancestors of the American Saints had lived their lives against the American grain, as religious revolutionaries who were determined to build the Kingdom of God on earth and to usher in the millennial reign of Jesus Christ. Now the newest generation of Saints had come home to reaffirm their commitment to the virtues of the family, religious obedience, and hard work in the midst of a society that threatened, as they perceived it, to wash them from this island of stability into a vast and raging sea of sloth, godlessness, and rampant sexuality.

From the spot where Brigham Young called a halt to their exodus in 1847, the gathered Saints could look out across the Valley of the Great Salt Lake at one of the fastest-growing and most prosperous cities of the West. In Young's day, the Saints spoke of building their own Kingdom of Deseret, a nation beyond the persecution and corruption of American society. It was to be a great theocratic empire based on economic cooperation and polygamy that would fill the Great Basin between the Rocky Mountains and California's Sierra Nevada and would reach the sea by way of the Colorado River and a corridor of influence that stretched through Las Vegas, Nevada, to the port of San Diego, California.

The Salt Lake Valley, hedged off by the Wasatch Mountains to the east and the Oquirrhs to the west and fading into the alkaline haze of the Great Salt Lake, had all the appearances of any western community on the build. New highrises, including those financed by an unlikely alliance of Arab, Mormon and federal money, pushed skyward from the downtown center, and sprawling suburbs spread along the alluvial benches into the mountain coves and across the valley floor.

A closer look revealed that this was a very different community. The glistening white, twenty-eight-story office-building headquarters of the Saints dominated the downtown skyline, towering over the two central blocks that contain the Temple, the Tabernacle, Visitors Centers, and the church-owned Hotel Utah. And the city itself, laid out according to Joseph Smith's vision of the New Jerusalem, contained wide spacious streets numbered according to their distance from the Temple.

After even a brief stay, one senses that something culturally unique lurks beneath the surface of everyday life. At first, one focuses on the superficial differences, those differences best known to tourists who pass through the state. One must belong to a private club to buy a drink in a bar. In a restaurant, the customer must purchase wine or a drink, which comes in an airlines-type minibottle, at the cash register and bring it to his or her own table.

The local citizenry appears overwhelmingly blonde, blue-eyed, and disproportionately white. While people are gracious and warm in the friendly western manner, shopkeepers, particularly in the vicinity of Temple Square, ask you where you come from and often inquire about your knowledge of Mormonism. In short, the presence of The Church, as it is known, is overwhelming and all-pervasive.

Beyond the awesome beauty of canyonland and desert, there is something in the clear mountain air—or is it in the mind of the outsider who knows Utah only through the mythology of Mormonism?—the stories of angels and visions, of assassinations and secret avengers, of polygamy and blood atonement.

In *Roughing It*, Mark Twain, one of a long line of literary sojourners who passed through the valley, wrote, "This was a fairyland to us, to all intents and purposes—a land of enchantment, and goblins, and awful mystery." More recently a young man wrote in *National Geographic* of his experiences walking across the country, and how, when he entered Utah, he felt as if he had entered a foreign country. And a *Denver Post* reporter described the state as "a land where everything seems just a few degrees out of plumb."

To the Saints in April 1980, Zion was as it should be, but the rest of the world was a few degrees out of plumb. Thousands crowded into the Tabernacle, that remarkable turtle-domed structure built in the days of Brother Brigham. Those who could not squeeze into the Tabernacle hurried along South Temple through the city to hear the proceedings at the Salt Palace, a centerpiece of the new Salt Lake City and itself a monument to the profound but subtle influence of the modern church.

Inside the Tabernacle, the Saints, closely supervised by numerous ushers and security personnel, quickly took their seats. In the central part of the auditorium, surrounded by wooden pillars painted in exquisite detail to resemble colorful marble, men in standard missionary attire—blue, black, or brown suits, white shirt, and dark tie—were seated. This is the sacred priesthood, the lay leaders of this tightly organized hierarchy, Zion's devoted and obedient cadre. These are the regional representatives, stake presidents, bishops, high priests, and their counselors, who supervise the lives of the faithful and teach obedience to the will of the Lord as revealed to their leader, the Prophet, Spencer W. Kimball.

To the right under the overhanging balcony, the leadership of the women's organization was seated in its own separate section. Not too long ago, women leaders and members sat where they chose along with everyone else. But, on this great occasion as in other recent conferences, women remained segregated, symbolic of the growing problems defined by the "women's issue," an ever-contentious issue in this avowedly patriarchal church. Meanwhile, a small plane circled above Temple Square towing a banner that read:

MOTHER IN HEAVEN SUPPORTS THE ERA

the only public sign of the tensions that lurked below the surface.

The front rows of the auditorium were reserved for visiting dignitaries, including members of the Utah congressional delegation, all of whom are members of the church. Seated there were Congressmen K. Gunn McKay (a distant cousin of the late Prophet, David O. McKay) and Dan Marriott and Senators Jake Garn and Orrin G. Hatch.

In front of them, facing the audience beneath a bank of organ pipes and below the seats of the Mormon Tabernacle Choir, sat the General Authorities, the upper ranks of church leadership. First, on the lower level, were members of the First Quorum of the Seventy. Drawing on vague biblical references, Joseph Smith, the founder of the church, created the Seventies to build the church, especially in the missionary field. In the 1970s, they were given additional responsibilities to cope with the tremendous international expansion of the church. Among the Seventies sat a small handful of foreigners, four from Western Europe and one from Japan, a symbolic contrast to a church elite that is overwhelmingly American, Utahn, and quite often connected by descent or intermarriage to the original leaders of the church.

Interspersed throughout the Tabernacle were members of church security, a fairly recent arrangement and symptomatic of the increasing notoriety of this controversial church. In the 1960s, there were bomb scares provoked by the church's racial policies, including a bomb planted at the front door of the Temple. In the 1970s, members of a small polygamous cult threatened to kill the Prophet. Another conference was picketed by members of the American Indian Movement, who were demanding reparations from a church that prides itself on its work with its lost brothers, the American Indians.

This time there were no incidents. Conference was proceeding serenely, barely disrupting the squirming and whispering of the young couples in the balcony. Above the Seventies, ranged on either side of the single pulpit in large comfortable chairs, sat the members of the Quorum of the Twelve Apostles. The Saints believe their church is a restoration of the primitive Christian church after hundreds of years of the Great Apostasy, as the period of their Christian forebears is sometimes described. The Mormon organization, though bureaucratized to a degree that could only have been conceived in the modern world, is supposed to be modeled on that early brotherhood.

In the midst of the Twelve sat the three members of the First Presidency. In the middle was the supreme leader. Called the Prophet, Seer, and Revelator, Spencer Woolley Kimball is the man who, through direct and personal contact with their Heavenly Father, guides the destiny of Zion by means of prayer, inspiration, visions, and revelations. On either side sat his two counselors, President Nathan Eldon Tanner and President Marion G. Romney. Nearby sat Ezra Taft Benson, president of the Quorum of the Twelve and the man who by the established order of succession was a heartbeat away from being the next Prophet.

A SMALL-TOWN BURGHER

Kimball, the twelfth Prophet in the church's history, is, like so many of the church's leaders, descended from two families with long and distinguished ties to the church hierarchy. On the Kimball side, he is the grandson of Heber C. Kimball, the scion of an old New England family who had joined the church in 1832 with his neighbor Brigham Young, the man who would succeed Joseph Smith and lead the Saints to Utah. Spencer Kimball's father, Andrew, was Heber's thirty-fifth of fifty-two sons, and was born of his seventeenth of forty-five wives. On his maternal side, Spencer Kimball is the descendant of the manager of Brigham Young's extensive private business empire.

Kimball was born on March 28, 1895, into a church that, in the aftermath of the polygamy crisis of the 1880s, was in the process of ending future polygamous marriages. This crisis had led to the confiscation of church property, the disenfranchisement of thousands of Mormons, and the imprisonment of most of their leaders. Kimball's father, like many of his peers who had grown up in polygamous families, chose not to enter polygamy, and Spencer Kimball would grow up in a church significantly different from the one his parents knew.

Kimball was raised in Thatcher, Arizona, an irrigated oasis in the Gila River Valley, where his father had been sent as part of Young's strategy to extend the Mormon sphere of influence into Arizona and northern Mexico. His father farmed, ran a store, sold insurance, and spent many hours on church business traveling the wastes and oases of Arizona. His mother, Olive Woolley, described in a newspaper story as "an enthusiastic woman suffragist [who] fully understands the meaning of equal rights," became "a church widow" in charge of running the farm and caring for her growing family during her husband's frequent absences on church business. When Spencer was eleven, his mother died during her twelfth pregnancy in twenty-four years.

Kimball lived at first in a tent connected to a small adobe house and grew up good-natured, friendly, poor, and hardworking in this small, isolated town where the social atmosphere was totally dominated by the church. Like his father, he worked at a variety of jobs to bring in enough income for his small family. He inherited his father's franchise to sell laxative pills, worked in local banks, played the piano at local dances, and wrote social notices for the newspaper.

Upon the death of his father, Kimball moved up in the local church hierarchy, eventually becoming stake president. Kimball grew up, according to his son and nephew, with the feeling that his grandfather, whom he had never known, was watching his advancement in the church and "that in some measure the callings could be attributed to the merit and influence of Heber C. Kimball."

After a rocky start in the business world, which included employment at two banks that failed and the collapse of plans to develop a subdivision near Safford, Arizona, Kimball became a successful insurance salesman and supplemented his income with real estate dealings.

Kimball's comfortable but busy existence as a small-town burgher was interrupted when he received a telephone call from Salt Lake City on July 8, 1943. It was his cousin J. Reuben Clark. Clark, a former undersecretary in the U.S. State Department and ambassador to Mexico, was President Heber J. Grant's First Counselor. Clark was phoning to inform Kimball that he was being called to serve as an Apostle of the church.

Although Kimball was the first General Authority in the twentieth century to be called from outside the state of Utah, itself symptomatic of the growth of church membership in Arizona and California in the past decades, he was still connected by family ties to the small number of first families that dominated the church. Having abandoned one career as a small businessman, Kimball's life was now dominated by the exhaustive demands of church work. "Every Thursday," wrote his biographers, "the Council of Twelve met in a room on the Temple's fourth floor. The Apostles sat by seniority in the twelve large oak chairs, in a crescent around an upholstered altar. Harold B. Lee played a small organ in the corner as they opened with a hymn. Then all twelve, dressed in temple clothes, formed a prayer circle around the altar. The prayer completed, they changed back to street clothes to handle the Quorum's business."

Kimball's responsibilities were extensive. He traveled frequently to oversee and report on missionary work. He spoke to numerous church audiences. He dealt with members who came to him for personal advice and counseling. But he became best known for his work among Indians. Eventually Kimball would play a major role in the establishment of the Indian Placement Service, a church program that brought thousands of Indian children into the homes of church members.

As the church grew overseas, Kimball was placed in charge of much of the new missionary work in Latin America, where he ran seven South American missions and later presided over the establishment of the first church stake in Latin America, in São Paulo, Brazil. Kimball also hammered away at a favorite church theme—what one church history described as "the vital importance of moral cleanliness and chastity"—and was eventually placed in charge of counseling homosexual members.

While Kimball advanced in seniority in the ranks of the Quorum of the Twelve, he sensed that he would never be confronted with a call to the highest office because of his health problems. But in the early 1970s, Prophets David O. McKay and, then, Joseph Fielding Smith died, and Kimball became president of the Twelve making him next in line as Prophet.

This eventuality seemed far off. Harold B. Lee, Smith's successor, was a vigorous church leader who had spent more than a decade reorganizing the church from top to bottom and was a youthful (by Mormon standards) seventy-three. A year and a half later, Lee was dead of a heart attack, and on December 30, 1973, Spencer W. Kimball, at age seventy-eight, was ordained as the new Prophet.

The new Prophet had been born on a remote western frontier in a world totally different from the America of the 1970s. Kimball had been born before the automobile, rural electrification, jazz, corporate capitalism's war with the trustbusters, before the airplane, atomic weapons, and rock and roll, before secular humanism, existentialism, and born-again Christianity. His church, in those days, was primarily rural, and its leaders knew most of the Saints, or at least one of their relatives, personally.

To a remarkable degree, the church was still a face-to-face organization, even after a half century of bureaucratization had insulated leaders from followers. And Salt Lake City was still known as the city of brothers-in-law because of the complex interrelationships among the huge Mormon extended families. But the aging leaders of the church were victims of a triple generation gap, their lives spanning social changes almost beyond comprehension.

Kimball was being called to head a worldwide church that then had 3 million members and billions of dollars in assets and that was administered by thousands of paid employees from the church's twenty-eight-story office building. The man who was raised in a crude adobe house had ended up at the head of a church that kept its accounts by computer, stored its genealogical records in a mountain tunnel to protect them from nuclear attack, and communicated with its members by satellite.

Above all, Kimball was known and revered for his 1978 revelation granting the priesthood to black members of the church. This one change in church policy erased more than a decade of controversy that had surrounded the church during the civil rights era.

With tensions growing inside the church over the new quest for orthodoxy and the increasingly political direction of the leadership, the Kimball era would become one of the most turbulent since the polygamy crisis of the 1880s and 1890s.

CONFERENCE WATCHING

At the 150th anniversary conference, there was a sense of uneasiness, a sense of a crisis impending, a crisis beyond any the church had experienced in modern times. This vast, carefully crafted empire, still appeared to be resting on shaky ground.

Barely four months earlier, ERA activist Sonia Johnson had been excommunicated for allegedly teaching false doctrine and for challenging the authority of the church's male leaders. The media had swarmed over the church, finding irregularities in the church's lobbying activities in Virginia, where Johnson lived, and the secret transfer of funds from California to Florida to finance an anti-ERA campaign there. Some church leaders, equating media scrutiny with a renewal of the old persecutions that had cost the church so dearly, were more than nervous over their newfound notoriety.

Liberal critics within the church, pacified earlier by Kimball's black priesthood revelation, had resurfaced during the Johnson affair, and the church was in the midst of a prolonged internal debate over the ERA and the church's role in politics. This debate was inevitably linked to the question of who would succeed the ailing Prophet. By previous practice, the president of the Quorum of the Twelve would be elected to be Prophet by his fellow members of the Quorum. But Ezra Taft Benson was the president of the Quorum, and his virulent right-wing political stances and use of the pulpit to make political pronouncements had brought controversy to the church since the early 1960s.

Then, too, despite all appearances, this wealthy church was starting to experience an economic crunch that was threatening to curtail its missionary program and undermine its major source of new recruits. Beyond this, unknown to all but a handful of leaders, the church had become embroiled in the volatile politics of Latin America and was beginning to suffer the consequences of its fondness for right-wing military regimes.

In this atmosphere of restrained contention, the Prophet, after the opening hymn, moved slowly to the pulpit. A small, almost gnomish man with a round benign face, large ears, and a steady, kindly gaze, he was to the members a living proof of divine intervention. At eighty-five, he had survived a major heart attack, open heart surgery, a brain operation, two operations for cancer of the throat that led to the removal of part of his larynx, leaving his voice a low gravelly whisper, and repeated threats by a crazed polygamous cult to kill him.

Several days earlier, the Prophet and his two physically ailing counselors had stood before a ghostly statue of Jesus in the church Visitors Center, surrounded by the inevitable aides and public relations men, some with stern demeanor, others with tight beatific smiles, to announce with great fanfare that the church would build seven new temples, initiating the greatest period of temple building in its history. Six of these new temples were to be built abroad: in Argentina, Australia, Chile, Tahiti, Tonga, and Western Samoa.

At conference, the Prophet opened his remarks by saying that he was "grateful, as always, just to be with you and to be near you," and turned quickly to his concern about family life. For the church, more than anything, is a family church, a church where man's spiritual progress from prelife to birth, death, and ascension into the heavenly order is tied inexorably to the fate of the patriarchal family, a church where membership in the traditional nuclear family is the *only* passport to the highest level of the Celestial Kingdom. "The family," Kimball has said repeatedly, "is the basic unit of the Kingdom of God on earth."

As the conference droned on for two days through numerous sermons and sessions, the faithful watched for their particular favorites among the leadership or listened intently to the words of the more influential leaders, such as Kimball, Benson, and Tanner. More astute Mormon-watchers examined each phrase and sentence for signs of significant differences that reflected clashes of approach and style within the apparently unified leadership, for some indication of the clandestine debates and rumors that swirled through the nearby church offices, and for signs of younger, more dynamic leaders working their way up through the hierarchy.

Apostle LeGrand Richards, who would be dead in three years, a great favorite among the rank and file, hobbled to the pulpit and delivered a rousing sermon in the style of a Bible-thumping tent preacher. Richards, then ninety-three, had witnessed the dedication of the Salt Lake Temple in 1893. When his time was up, President Benson hooked Richards's leg with a cane, a prearranged signal, and Richards hobbled back to his seat.

Nathan Eldon Tanner, Kimball's First Counselor and the member of the First Presidency in charge of the church's business affairs, chose to advise the members on the subject of marriage. (Tanner, afflicted with Parkinson's disease, died in November 1982.) A former Canadian citizen, Tanner had been something of a prairie populist as an Alberta politician. After serving in the provincial government, he went into the oil and gas business. Eventually his business successes drew the attention of the church leadership. A dour man with an almost Manchurian look, he was known for his subtle style of leadership. He had done more than any man to reorganize and extend the church's business empire.

The Mormon form of marriage, Tanner explained in his speech, "is eternal, and couples so united are sealed for time and all eternity, and their children are born in the covenant of the everlasting gospel. They will be an eternal family according to their faithfulness. . . . Someone has said that a man breeding livestock is very careful about what he allows in the pasture with his prize animals, but he lets his son or daughter go with anyone without checking on their credentials." Referring to the Mormon beliefs about the nature of life before death and the principal reason for the Saints' soaring birthrate, Tanner explained that parents "have the responsibility to provide mortal bodies" for spirits still caught in the preexistence and then went on to say that limiting the size of families through birth control was "contrary to the laws of God."

Kimball's message of forgiveness and tolerance and Tanner's quiet, practical moralism and quaint agrarian ideas about proper breeding contrasted with the fire-breathing fundamentalism and sweeping apocalyptic visions of Apostle Bruce R. McConkie. McConkie is the son-in-law and former protégé of the tenth Prophet, Joseph Fielding Smith, grandson of Joseph Smith's martyred brother, Hyrum. Smith, who died in 1972, was known as a champion of orthodoxy and a critic of such pernicious doctrines as evolution. McConkie, a prolific author, has taken up the sword of his deceased mentor.

"We stand on a mountain peak, on a majestic, glorious peak in the midst of the mountains of Israel," McConkie intoned. "Below us lie the deserts of sin and the forests of evil, below us stretch the swamps of carnality and the plains of passion; below us rage the roaring rivers of war and hate and crime—through all of which we have struggled to reach this summit . . .

"Along the way, we shall yet climb, hidden in the underbrush, is the lair of the lion and hole of the asp. Venomous serpents are coiled on ledges beside the path and jackals lurk in dark caves by the wayside.

"Our onward course will not be easy. The Way ahead will be blocked by landslides of lasciviousness; an avalanche of evil will bury the trail."

McConkie's imagery evoked the fears of the nineteenth-century Saints of a Zion surrounded and besieged by its enemies while awaiting the imminent return of Jesus Christ and his millennial reign among men. McConkie, the protector of orthodoxy, the disciple of obedience, and the scourge of heretics, was preparing the Saints for Armageddon. "Liars and thieves and adulterers and homosexuals and murderers," McConkie went on, "scarcely seek to hide their abominations from our view. Satan reigns in the hearts of men; it is the great day of his power." The church, McConkie warned, faces the apocalypse, a time of war, plagues, and pestilence when it will suffer greater trials and tribulations than in its early history of flight and persecution. But ahead he saw a great vision of expansion, a time when "the Lord [will] break down the barriers so that the world of Islam and the world of Communism [will] hear the message of the restoration," ushering in the 1,000-year reign of the Saints. To achieve this, he emphasized, the Saints must "take the side of the Church on all issues, both religious and political . . . then all things will work together for our good."

After McConkie's stirring performance, the words of Ezra Taft Benson seemed pale by comparison. Building on John Taylor's cry, "The Kingdom of God or nothing," Benson warned critics of the church that the day had come "to stand firm and demonstrate their allegiance." He appealed to the numerous priesthood members who had fallen away from the church to resolve their differences and "to put aside habits that prevent you from affiliating with your brethren."

Missing from his sermon were the usual warnings about Godless communism and the invocations to the membership to follow the political leadership of the church. Was Benson, asked Mormon-watchers, giving a sign that if he became the new Prophet, he would eschew his pursuit of right-wing politics? Or were his carefully chosen words a stern warning to those who were straying from the fold that they should renounce their differences with the hierarchy or suffer the consequences?

The crowning event of conference came on Easter Sunday, April 6. When the Saints gathered in the Tabernacle, they sat before a giant television screen suspended above the pulpit or before numerous television monitors placed strategically around the room. The day before, the Prophet had left Salt Lake City flying to the town of Fayette in western New York where he was to dedicate a restoration of the Peter Whitmer farmhouse, a simple one-room log house where Joseph Smith and five men had gathered on April 6, 1830, to form the Church of Jesus Christ.

The giant screen showed the prophet inside the farmhouse accompanied by Gordon B. Hinckley, an Apostle, who some suspected was playing the major role, in light of the Prophet's weakened condition, in directing the day-to-day activities of the church and leading the campaign against the ERA. In a brief statement, the Prophet marveled at his six-hour plane flight in contrast to the Saints' long and painful westward trek "in search of a place where they could be free of persecution and could worship God according to the dictates of their own conscience."

"The church is stronger and growing more rapidly than at any time in its history," Hinckley proclaimed. He testified that God and Jesus Christ had appeared to Joseph Smith to proclaim the restoration of the church and that the priesthood was restored through the appearance to Smith of the ancient apostles, John the Baptist, Peter, James, and John. "We declare," he went on, "that the Book of Mormon was brought forth by the gift and power of God and that it stands beside the Bible as another witness of Jesus Christ, the Savior and Redeemer of mankind." Hinckley reaffirmed the sanctity of the family, declared that the Saints' lives were part of "an eternal plan," and testified that "the spirit of prophecy and revelation is among us." Next came a warning to the rebellious that they "shall be pierced with much sorrow; for their iniquities shall be spoken upon the housetops, and their secret acts shall be revealed." Hinckley concluded, "This is God's work. It is his kingdom we are building."

That night Hinckley packed his bags and headed for New York City, where he and J. Willard Marriott, Jr., the head of the huge Marriott Corporation, were scheduled to confront the media on Tom Brokaw's *Today Show*. When Brokaw asked if the church was a major force behind the defeat of the ERA in some western states, the man who had engineered the excommunication of Sonia Johnson from behind the scenes and had played a central role in rallying the Saints against the ERA paused and then responded, "I don't know that we have done that."

From a simple cabin in western New York to *The Today Show*, the church had evolved from a homespun frontier church to a vast bureaucratic institution extending to the four corners of the earth. Although church leaders repeatedly insisted that the church of the 1980s was the same church as that of the restoration proclaimed by their first Prophet, Joseph Smith, Jr., it was indeed very different. It had grown from a successful but tormented experimental community believing in the imminence of the Second Coming into a church unlike any other in the history of American religion.

CHAPTER TWO

THE TRANSFORMATION: BUILDING THE KINGDOM OF GOD ON EARTH

JOSEPH THE PROPHET

On a spring day in 1844, less than three months before he would be killed by a mob, Joseph Smith, in a moment of candor, told thousands of followers gathered in a grove outside the Mormon city of Nauvoo, Illinois, "You can't know me, you never knew my heart. No man knows my history. I cannot tell it; I shall never undertake it. I don't blame anyone for not believing in my history. If I had not experienced what I have, I could not have believed it myself."

A century and a half later, the mystical experiences and striking religious views of this modest son of a poor itinerant New England family still arouse fierce loyalties and equally fierce hostilities. While historians and theologians continue to debate whether Smith was a con man, a radical visionary, or the greatest religious leader since Jesus Christ, the church is still surrounded by the kind of controversy that in earlier, more violently sectarian times carried Smith and dozens of his followers to premature graves.

A vital communitarian experiment in the midst of a society that increasingly emphasized individual effort, Smith's church was a radical challenge to the whole chaotic drift of America's westward expansion. Through repeated conflict—headlong flight from mob persecution and armed confrontations, a minor guerrilla war with the U.S. army, and the futile effort to set up a separate nation-state in the West—the church was ultimately transformed into a demi-nation within a nation, an economy within an economy, a culture apart. Today, church leaders are still wrestling with their past, which is a source of never-ending embarrassment to these upright patriarchs. Key doctrines and practices, such as the church's communitarian experiments and polygamy, have been obscured or denied, but the Saints remain and want to remain a people apart.

Shortly before Smith's death, Josiah Quincy, scion of a prominent Boston family and son of the president of Harvard University, visited

Smith in Nauvoo. In his middle thirties, Smith was a large, handsome man, six feet tall, over two hundred pounds, with light brown hair, blue eyes, and a penetrating look accentuated by his deep-set eyes and long nose. Far from a somber preacher, he was known for his love of merriment, his eye for young ladies, and a fondness for physical sports, particularly wrestling.

Quincy met a man "clad in the costume of a journeyman carpenter, wearing striped pants, a dirty linen jacket, and three day growth of beard." In Smith, Quincy felt "a certain moral stress and compulsion that I have never felt in the presence of others."

A woman who attended a meeting at the Smith home at about the same time described his eyes as "expressing great shrewdness," and wrote of his loud voice and coarse manner, calling him "a great egoist and boaster," who enjoyed amusing his followers. Another non-Mormon found Smith "an awkward but vehement speaker. In conversation he was slow and used too many words to express his ideas, and would not generally go directly to a point."

From a very early age, this handsome young man seemed destined to lead a life of brilliant inspiration and bitter confrontation. His ideas blazed across the advancing frontier until his quest for the true religion and a new social order led to his final demise.

Smith was born in Sharon, Vermont, on December 23, 1805. On both sides, his ancestors had reached the shores of New England in the seventeenth century. As a member of a family that had broken free from the confines of a Puritan village, Smith inherited from both of his grandfathers a devout spiritual nature coupled with a skepticism about all organized religions. Smith's family, it is thought, was part of the seeker tradition, those who looked for the restoration of the true church and for the safety of an ordered community reminiscent of the coastal villages they had left.

Moving from farm to farm, the Smith family led a hard life, plagued by crop failure, business collapse, disease, and poverty. Finally in 1815, Smith's father took his family to western New York, where he heard there was an abundance of fertile farmland. At age ten Joseph Smith, now living amid the crude cabins of Palmyra, hired out as a farmhand.

The Smiths had moved into the eye of a spiritual storm, known as the Second Great Awakening. Starting about 1800, a great religious revival had swept the western border from Kentucky to Vermont. Part of a general reaction to the rationalism and deism of the revolutionary period, these revivals took a particularly frenzied form on the frontier. At camp meetings and smaller gatherings, people spoke of visions, talked in tongues, danced wildly, fell to the ground jerking spasmodically, barked, chanted, and laughed uncontrollably.

Caught between the promise of this new and abundant Eden and the harsh realities of frontier life, some sought personal religious exaltation. Others joined communitarian groups that talked of creating heaven on earth while preparing for the Second Coming. Isaac Bullard, wrapped in a bearskin, preached free love and communism and denounced washing. Both Ann Lee, the founder of the Shakers, and Jemima Wilkinson claimed to be Christ reincarnated. And later John Humphrey Noyes advocated communalism, free love, and *coitus reservatus*.

Revivalism became particularly intense in western New York at about the time of the Smiths' arrival, leading the area to be called the "burned-over" or infected district. Members of the Smith family were no strangers to religious exaltation and intense spiritual experiences. Both of Joseph's grandfathers had written long narratives about their religious beliefs for the benefit of their descendants, and Joseph's mother, Lucy, wrote that his father had had a series of seven visions.

New England migrants brought with them tales of buried treasure, rods with magic powers, and peepstones that were used to locate gold and lost objects. The new settlers' curiosity was fanned by the numerous Indian relics found in the area and by tales of epic battles between lost peoples. As a young man, Joseph gained a reputation as a seer and a gold miner, although he was never to find any treasure. He was also known for his ability to spin an elaborate tale.

Joseph sought his own religious testimony, but found the contending sects more confusing than enlightening. "My mind was greatly excited, the cry was so great and incessant," he wrote many years later. Having gone often to the woods to pray, he experienced his first vision probably at the age of fourteen. Thick darkness gathered around him, and then he "saw a pillar of light exactly over my head, above the brightness of the sun, which descended gradually until it fell upon me." In the light he saw two personages; "one of them spake unto me, calling me by name and said, pointing to the other—This is my beloved Son, Hear Him!" The person in the vision told Smith not to join any of the contending sects because all of them were corrupt and "an abomination in my sight."

Three years later Smith was visited by a messenger from God. The messenger, an angel Smith called Moroni, told Smith of certain gold plates that were buried in a nearby hill. These plates, the angel said, held "an account of the former inhabitants of this continent, and the sources from whence they sprang." With the plates would be two stones—set in silver bows, attached to a breastplate, and known as the Urim and Thummim—that would allow Smith to translate the ancient writings. Smith rushed to find the plates the next day, but Moroni appeared again and told him that he was not yet ready to translate them.

After three annual visits, Moroni again appeared to Smith and told him that it was time to translate the plates. Smith sat for the better part of a year with his face buried in his hat or behind a curtain dictating to a scribe what he claimed was a translation from the plates. The plates, said Smith, told the story of the flight from Jerusalem of two families under the leadership of a man named Lehi to the shores of the Red Sea some 600 years before Christ. Here Lehi built a boat and sailed eastward until he reached the shores of "the promised land." Even before Lehi and his followers left for the new world, a dispute arose between his sons. One, Nephi, was his father's loyal supporter, while two other sons, Laman and Lemuel, questioned their father's plans and prophecies. In the new world, the followers of Laman and Lemuel, who became known as Lamanites, broke with their brother after Lehi's death and came under a curse of God that had been predicted by their father.

Ten centuries of conflict followed between the Lamanites, who were said to be the progenitors of the American Indians, and the offspring of Nephi. When the Lord instructed the Nephites to send missionaries among their enemies the Lamanites, they met with great success. Then for a time, the Nephites were afflicted with wickedness while the Lamanites were blessed in the eyes of the Lord, and for a time, the two people lived in harmony. But the conflict resumed, and finally the Lamanites overwhelmed the Nephites in one great battle that took place near the Hill of Cumorah, where the plates were hidden. Only Moroni, the son of Mormon, survived to bury the record of the lost peoples of the Americas.

Critics of the Book of Mormon have dismissed it as a crude and turgid account filled with laughable names such as Shiz, Ethem, and Ahah. Mark Twain, calling it "an insipid mess of inspiration" and "chloroform in print," devoted a chapter in *Roughing It* to poking fun at the author's awkward imitation of the King James style. But to Joseph's followers, the Book of Mormon was both inspirational religious teaching and exciting reading, full of treachery, exaltation, flight, visions, prophecies, miraculous conversions, and great bloody battles.

In his inspiration, Smith had taken the folklore of the Bible and combined it with the primitive archeology of the frontier to create a native Christian church. It placed Christ in the new world—Christ came to visit the Nephites soon after the Resurrection, Smith proclaimed—and linked the immigrants from Europe with the original people of the continent. In the Book of Mormon, America is described as "a land of promise, which was choice above all other lands, which the Lord God had preserved for a righteous people." In time, Smith, in calling his followers to gather in Missouri, would reveal that the Garden of Eden was, in fact, located in that state and that Adam and Eve, after their expulsion from the garden, dwelt nearby in the land of Adam-ondi-Ahman. "For by modifying the Judaeo-Christian heritage and providing American church history with pre-Columbian native roots through the Book of Mormon," wrote historian Klaus Hansen, "Smith, in a sense, had produced America's religious declaration of independence."

Smith had not only written a truly American sequel to the Bible, he had done this by reestablishing a direct link through revelation to God, the highest authority. And in this way Smith solved the problem of which sect should be recognized as the one true church. Joseph's answer was that he was personally called upon by God in his visions to establish a new church, the one, true church, and to guide it by revelation.

By restoring the primitive church, Mormonism was meant to be both a repudiation of all existing sects and a final, joyous escape from the dismal confines of Calvinism. The Puritan followers of John Calvin taught the doctrine of original sin, emphasizing that only a select few would make it to the heavenly kingdom while most of mankind, no matter how righteous, was condemned to the agonies of hell. Smith, in contrast, undercut the notion of original sin by teaching that man would be judged by his works on earth and that ultimately man himself could aspire to godhood. Free agency, not predestination, became the watchword of the Saints—with the important and contradictory proviso of total obedience to their leader, who alone guided the church by revelation.

Further, Smith's church was conceived as a total response to the instability and hardships of the frontier. The Saints were not only called to gather in a new Zion in America, but were also encouraged to use all means, including political power and economic cooperation, to build the Kingdom of God on earth. For Smith, like many other frontier preachers, anticipated the coming of the millennium and the beginning of the 1,000-year rule of Christ.

THE SEARCH FOR ZION

By April 6, 1830, when Smith and six of his followers met in the Peter Whitmer home in Fayette, Smith had put together the outlines of a new church, which he called the Church of Christ, later the Church of Jesus Christ of Latter-day Saints. Joseph announced to his followers that he was to be called "a seer, a translator, a prophet, an apostle of Jesus Christ, an elder of the church through the will of God the Father, and the grace of your Lord Jesus Christ."

Smith and his followers quickly spread his new gospel to the towns of western New York. No sooner had Smith sent his book to press than opposition began. During the first printing, in fact, some citizens of Palmyra, where it was published, organized a boycott against the book. Smith was hounded into court, pursued by mobs, and taunted as a false prophet.

In time, Smith was introduced to a Campbellite preacher named Sidney Rigdon, who had formed a small communistic society in Kirtland, Ohio, where his followers awaited the millennium. After Rigdon visited Smith in New York and was converted by him, Smith called upon his followers to move to Ohio. After moving his family to the vicinity of Kirtland, Smith himself hurried on to Missouri.

Smith had had a new revelation that told how "There also came up a land out of the sea" that was the new world. The Lord revealed to Joseph that the final gathering place would be in western Missouri and that in due time the city of his vision, virtually the New Jerusalem, would be built in this area. In this land, Enoch, an ancient prophet, had built a great City of Holiness called Zion, where the people were "of one heart and one mind, and dwelt in righteousness; and there was no poor among them." In time Zion "was taken up into heaven where it became the city of the Lord." This city of Enoch, the longed-for city on the hill, would be the capital city of a great new empire of God, the harbinger of the millennial reign of Christ.

Smith's plan for a new economic community, which grew out of his intense identification with the plight of the poor, was called the United Order, or Order of Enoch, after the prophet of the great city. It is not clear whether Smith took his inspiration for his economic ideas from Rigdon's experimental community or whether they came from his study of primitive Christianity. What is clear is that Smith saw his new religion as a total response to all aspects, spiritual and material, of frontier life.

Smith's ideas, which appear to balance the rampant economic individualism of the land-thirsty frontiersmen with the demands of an ordered community, may have been a reaction to the excesses of Rigdon's communitarian experiment where "they would take each other's clothes and other property and use it without leave, which brought on confusion and disappointment," as one Saint wrote to Smith. "Order, unity, and community," wrote Mormon historians Leonard J. Arrington and Dean L. May, "were the supreme values of the Prophet's ideal society—values strikingly at odds with those characteristic of antebellum America."

As before, Smith set forth his ideas in a revelation that came to be known as the Law of Consecration and Stewardship. Smith called on his followers to consecrate their property to the church, that is, to turn title over to the church. Then each member would be made a steward over his property. Any surplus produced would be turned over to the church for the benefit of the poor.

Although its origins are still veiled in obscurity, Smith is thought to have begun to practice polygamy, or celestial marriage, in Kirtland with his secret marriage in 1835 to seventeen-year-old Fannie Alger, who lived in the Prophet's home. Whispered rumors about this new practice were part of the campaign against the church that soon developed in Ohio. Smith's response was to deny the practice. For proof, he pointed to the Book of Mormon, which denounces polygamy as "fornication" and "abominable."

These two new concepts, celestial marriage and communitarianism, fanned the flames of sectarian discontent that eventually drove the Saints from their second home in Ohio. No sooner had Smith moved to Kirtland than local newspaper editors and rival preachers picked up his scent and hounded him again with cries of imposter and false prophet. At one point, he and Sidney Rigdon were set upon by a mob. Smith was stripped, tarred,

and feathered, and had a vial of nitric acid forced between his lips, breaking a front tooth.

Joseph, however, would not relent. Missionaries were dispatched in all
directions, reaching Canada and Great Britain. Church membership grew
from about 150 at the time of Joseph's arrival in Ohio to several thousand.
Smith also worked at developing the organizational framework for his
church, creating a bishopric charged with dealing with temporal or worldly
affairs, a Quorum of the Twelve Apostles mirroring the primitive church of
Jesus, and a First Council of the Seventy charged with furthering the
missionary work of "the traveling councilors," as the Twelve were known.
Earlier Smith had set up the First Presidency with himself as president and
two counselors to assist him.

Smith's organizational plan unfortunately sowed the seeds of later dis-
sension. He had created no less than five organizational bodies with equal
authority. It would take his successor, Brigham Young, to impose a tightly
disciplined organizational structure on the church.

Smith also began to preach what he called the Word of Wisdom. "Strong
drinks," he explained, "are not for the belly, but for washing your bodies,"
although drinking of alcohol, particularly wine, was common among
church leaders, including Smith, throughout the nineteenth century. Hot
drinks, later interpreted as tea and coffee, and tobacco were also proscribed.

In Kirtland, Smith put new arrivals to work building a temple, but the
City of Enoch in Missouri, designed to accommodate 15,000 to 20,000
Saints, was to be the first of a whole series of cities that would stretch
westward across the continent. While Zion would be the center pole of the
new Kingdom of God, Kirtland and future Mormon settlements would be
the stakes of this vast tent of the Lord. The dedication of the first temple in
Kirtland in March 1836 was a joyous moment for the beleaguered Saints
and was attended by great spiritual manifestations. Jesus and the prophets
of old were seen in the building, which was lighted by a pillar of fire and
filled with the sounds of a rushing wind, and members of the priesthood
spoke in tongues.

While the situation in Kirtland remained tense but generally peaceful,
Smith's plans for Missouri, particularly when he spoke of consecrating "the
riches of the Gentiles unto my people," had made the non-Mormon population feel that they were being pushed from their lands by the hundreds of
Mormons moving into the state.

The Gentiles were also suspicious that the Saints were stirring up the
Indians with their talk of the Lamanites as part of the chosen people. And
when a church newspaper warned free black members of the church that
they needed a certificate of citizenship from another state to enter Missouri, the Gentiles charged that the Saints, many of whom came from
abolitionist areas, were interfering with slavery.

The Gentile residents of Jackson County had met as early as 1833 to denounce the Saints and to call for an end to Mormon immigration and even for their expulsion from the state. Mob attacks followed while both sides armed themselves. The Saints found themselves in the midst of a border war. Under increasingly vicious attack by mobs and night riders, the Saints abandoned the site of the future city of Zion and retreated north and eastward across the Missouri River.

In Kirtland, Joseph organized a military expedition in 1834, known in Mormon lore as Zion's Camp, to protect the Missouri Saints. When he reached Missouri, he decided not to attempt a military reoccupation of Jackson County. Instead, Smith disbanded his forces and returned to Kirtland.

While the Missouri Saints continued to lead an unsettled existence, Smith and Sidney Rigdon were forced to flee Kirtland in January 1838, for the embattled settlements of Missouri after a number of scandals involving the collapse of a banking scheme and real estate speculation. Two months later, half the Mormon community picked up again and followed their leader to Missouri.

The situation there was no better. The Mormons were still being pressed by their neighbors, and a secret Mormon organization, known as the Danites, had been formed and was beginning to retaliate. At the 1838 Fourth of July celebration at the Mormon town of Far West, Rigdon warned that any mob "that comes on to us to disturb us, it shall be between us and them a war of extermination; for we will follow him, till the last drop of blood is spilled, or else they will have to exterminate us: for we will carry the seat of war to their own houses, and their own families, and one party or the other shall be utterly destroyed." After a riot broke out during a heated election, the governor called out the militia and issued his infamous "Order of Extermination" directed at the Saints.

After a number of skirmishes and an attack on Mormons at Haun's Mill that left seventeen dead, Smith and church leaders Rigdon, Parley Pratt, and Hyrum Smith were arrested when they were betrayed by a Mormon member of the militia. Smith and the other church leaders were court-martialed and ordered to be shot the next morning, but the head of the militia refused to carry out the order.

As their leader languished in jail, the Saints, who now numbered some 5,000, were unable to reach accommodation with their neighbors and once again fled for places unknown. After they gathered in Quincy, Illinois, during the winter of 1838–39, they were joined by Smith and his fellow prisoners. Their guards had allowed them, the most wanted men in Missouri, to escape.

NAUVOO: THE CITY ON THE HILL

Since the founding of Mormonism, the exodus, the flight of the chosen people from the land of the oppressor, was the most significant and devastating part of the Mormon experience. After Missouri, the citizens of Illinois had expressed sympathy for the Saints and encouraged them to settle in Illinois, and now Joseph made plans to establish a permanent settlement there. With a charter from the legislature that gave Nauvoo many of the rights of an independent city-state, the Saints began to build a new city. The new charter legalized the Mormons' military forces. (Smith, who took the rank of lieutenant general, a higher rank than George Washington's, became fond of parading his troops while dressed in an immaculate uniform.) The new charter also allowed Smith and his followers to dominate the city government and gave major powers to the local courts, effectively putting the Saints outside the reach of Gentile law.

In 1841, Smith received a revelation to build another temple. As the temple was being built on a bluff above the Mississippi, surrounded by comfortable brick and frame houses, paved streets, stores, stables, small manufactories, and a cooperative farm, the population grew in this city of considerable splendor (at least compared to most crude frontier villages), swelled by hundreds of new recruits baptized by missionaries, particularly in England.

Finally able to demonstrate his powers as the leader of a great and productive city-building people, Joseph began to refine and elaborate on the doctrines that he had been teaching since his translation of the Book of Mormon. "In Nauvoo," wrote James B. Allen and Glen M. Leonard in *The Story of the Latter-day Saints,* "the teachings of the Latter-day Saints assumed the distinctive qualities that set them apart more clearly than before from other religions." Smith's new doctrines reflected his own sense of command and power, the immediacy of death, and the continuing belief that the Chosen People stood on the brink of the 1,000-year reign of Christ.

Death surrounded the Saints. Hardly a family escaped death from disease, infant mortality, and border warfare. Smith and his wife Emma alone lost five of nine children in childbirth or soon after, while two of Smith's brothers died at an early age. To reconcile his followers to the loss of their dear ones and to assure entrance into the Celestial Kingdom to those who had not received church ordinances, Smith taught the doctrine of salvation for the dead. The dead, Smith explained, could still enter the Celestial Kingdom without the benefits of a church baptism on earth. To prepare for their entry, it was necessary for a worthy Saint to undergo a proxy baptism for the departed person.

To explain the true nature of the universe, Smith began in his sermons to describe what he called the Divine Plan. In Kirtland, Joseph had bought some Egyptian artifacts, including several mummies and papyrus scrolls. Bolstered by his success with his translation of the Book of Mormon, he created a "reformed Egyptian" alphabet and began translating the scrolls.

In Nauvoo, Smith revealed that the scrolls, which some modern scholars have identified as common funerary writings mostly from the Book of the Dead, were lost writings of the prophet Abraham. In these writings, Smith claimed, Abraham described how God had held council in heaven to draw up a plan for the creation of earth and for the peopling of earth with spirits or intelligences who were with him in heaven.

Once on earth, a person's obligation was to marry and bear children. In this way, the Saints would free the spirits from the prelife, give them bodily form, and start them on their way toward the Celestial Kingdom. Propagation was doubly important to a people constantly threatened with extinction.

After death, Smith had revealed earlier, man moved on to greater things. In the Kingdom of God there were three different degrees of glory. Telestial glory was for those who had not denied the Holy Spirit, "but shall not be redeemed until the last resurrection" because they "are liars, and sorcerers, and adulterers, and whoremongers." Next came terrestrial glory, reserved for those who were honorable but "not valiant in the testimony of Jesus." Finally there was the Celestial Kingdom, which was reserved for worthy members of the church. They would be the first resurrected and would be brought back by God "when he shall come in the clouds of heaven to reign on earth over his people."

In his scheme of things, Smith vastly reduced the dimensions of the hell where the souls of most Puritans had languished for centuries. "Our heavenly Father," Smith wrote in one letter, "is more liberal in His views, and boundless in His mercies and blessings, than we are ready to believe or receive." In his famous funeral sermon for a member named King Follett, Smith proclaimed, "All sins, and all blasphemies, and every transgression, except one, that man be guilty of, may be forgiven; and there is a salvation for all men, either in this world or the world to come who have not committed the unpardonable sin."

Smith's God was a unique being. In the same King Follett sermon, Smith explained, "God himself was once as we are now, and is an exalted man, and sits enthroned in yonder heavens! That is the great secret." Indeed, Smith promised that as man moved through life and then through the three levels of glory, he would become a god himself and "inherit thrones, kingdoms, principalities, and powers, dominions." Smith's views were based on the philosophical proposition that there was a continuum between matter and spirit. "All spirit is matter, but it is more fine and pure, and can only be discerned by purer eyes." As historian Lawrence Foster has pointed out, Smith's views meant that the distance between God and man had been sharply reduced. The Celestial Kingdom was not a remote hereafter. It was coming, and soon, for both the living and the dead.

Smith's most controversial teachings and the ones that would cause irreconcilable conflict between the Saints and the outside world for another half century were his teachings on the nature of marriage. Smith chose Nauvoo as the place to reveal the principles that he had been pondering and practicing ever since his study of the Old Testament. First, he taught that there was a major difference between properly sanctified Mormon marriage and a conventional marriage, which one Mormon theologian described as "a bill of divorcement" because of the familiar words "until death do us part." The Saints were married "for time and all eternity." And the kingdoms over which they would rule as they achieved godhood in the hereafter would be ruled by the Mormon patriarch and his faithful wives. The patriarchal family, Smith taught, was the very center of Mormonism. Beyond this, Smith revealed to a select group of church elders that they could marry more than one wife, patterning their lives on the prophets of old.

For a decade, Smith had explored the thin line between power and sexuality. Now he was ready to bind his closest supporters in the priesthood to him and extend their own power through celestial marriage. Foster also suggests, after examining the one existing defense of polygamy produced by the church during the Nauvoo period, that Smith saw this new marital form as a further defense against the social chaos of the frontier. Polygamy, according to a pamphlet printed by a "J. Smith," but allegedly written by a non-Mormon, was the best way to reassert patriarchal authority in families that were threatened by the usurpation of power by women. Smith dared to practice his religio-sexual beliefs, but not to admit them. It was hard enough to survive in the shadow of the rumors about them.

Finally, Smith completed his most creative period with the elaboration of new rituals that would eventually become the mainstay of the Saints' most important religious ceremonies. Smith derived most of these rituals from the Masonic order, which he and many others had joined at the time.

A fatal mixture of marital experimentation and politics led eventually to Smith's demise and the abandonment of Nauvoo. In 1842, John Bennett, the mayor of Nauvoo, general in the Nauvoo Legion, and a close but recent associate of Smith's in the church presidency, defected from the church to write a lurid exposé of the goings-on in Nauvoo. At about the same time, Smith formed a new organization, the Council of Fifty, that was meant to extend the political power of the Saints and eventually to carry Smith to the presidency of the country. "I calculate to be one of the instruments of setting up the kingdom of Daniel by word of the Lord," Smith told his followers, "and I intend to lay a foundation that will revolutionize the whole world."

As tensions between the Saints and their neighbors grew, opposition began to develop within the church itself. In April 1844, a number of Saints, led by William Law of the First Presidency, left the Saints and set up their own church. When Law and his followers founded a newspaper to denounce Smith from inside the holy city itself, Smith took the fatal step of ordering the press destroyed. Two weeks later Smith, who had predicted his demise, was jailed in nearby Carthage along with his brother Hyrum and two other Saints. The jail was soon attacked by a mob, and Smith and his brother were shot to death.

ONE GREAT FAMILY OF HEAVEN

Smith died at thirty-eight, the victim of his own soaring visions. With Smith gone, it soon became apparent that the Saints' days in Illinois were numbered. But the immediate question was who would take up the mantle of the fallen Prophet.

From the day of its formation until his assassination, Smith's new church was overshadowed by his formidable personality, driven by his visions, and ultimately kept off balance by his grandiose schemes and unpredictable responses to adversity. Under Smith, the complex organization that he created meant little because he could appeal directly to the Saints, change his counselors, which he did frequently, and dispatch his opposition to the far corners of the earth.

Brigham Young was quite unlike Smith, except that once he became the new Prophet, he too ruled with a personal power that was as extensive, if not more so, than Smith's. Young was born, like Smith, in Vermont, and by his own account enjoyed only eleven days of formal education. His daughter Susa Young Gates, who was both a prominent suffragist and a Mormon, described her father as "a Puritan of the Puritans," who was brought up in a family that stressed hard work, obedience to the patriarch, and the absolute sanctity of the Sabbath. Apprenticed out to learn a trade at fourteen, he became a farmer and also a painter, glazier, carpenter, and cabinetmaker.

Neither a visionary nor a theologian, Young was an earthy and practical man, often blunt and profane. Significantly, Young's only published revelation had to do with the organization of the western exodus. "The most important element in the preservation of the Church," wrote Bernard DeVoto, "was Young's conversion of the dizzy sacerdotal system which Joseph Smith had created into a system of fiscal administration and control." Ultimately, Young, whom DeVoto described "as one of the foremost intelligences of the time" and "the first American who learned how to colonize the desert," became a masterful statesman and adroit nation-builder.

As vandalism increased and remote farmhouses were torched in Illinois, Young and the Saints rushed to complete the temple and to prepare for yet another exodus, this time to a location outside the boundaries of the United States, where they hoped to establish a separate kingdom. At the urging of Young, the Saints gave up their city, although reluctantly. For they felt, as Brigham Young said, that "Nauvoo was like a foretaste of Celestial enjoyment and Millennial glory."

Under the leadership of Young, the Saints set up an elaborate organizational scheme to provide for the orderly removal of some 10,000 members of the church. Advance parties planted crops so that later contingents would have food on the march. The Saints moved along the north side of the Platte River to avoid contact with other immigrants who used the trail on the south side of the river. After horrible privations, particularly during the winter of 1846–47, the first party of Saints emerged from Emigration Canyon onto the gently rolling benches that fell away to the chalky white floor of the Valley of the Great Salt Lake. Here Young called a halt. Another party of Saints under Samuel Brannan had reached the fertile valleys of California by ship some time earlier, but Young wanted to settle a remote area far from the possibility of further conflicts with the Gentile world. The carefully organized migration of the Saints to the Great Basin was one of the great achievements in the history of the westward trek.

In the West, the new arrivals, denizens of the rain-abundant woodlands of the East, were faced with the prospect of building a new life in a totally different environment. Always a tightly organized community, the westward trek had tested and hardened the followers of Joseph Smith.

In the splendid but short-lived isolation of the high mountain desert, the Saints at first faced little opposition to building the kind of society that they had experimented with with such disastrous results in Ohio, Missouri, and Illinois. A site for a new temple was selected. A new city following the plan of the city of Enoch was laid out on the valley floor. Adobe and log cabins were rushed to completion while fields were plowed and irrigation ditches laid out.

Young, who increasingly held sway over all church affairs, dispatched settlers in all directions. This new nation, which came to be known as Deseret or the Great Basin Kingdom, filled the vast expanses of mountain and desert between the Rocky Mountains on the east, California's Sierra Nevada to the west, and the Snake River in southern Idaho to the north. While most Mormons arrived from the east, others came by ship and by a new wagon road built to connect a line of Mormon settlements that stretched from southern Utah to Las Vegas, Nevada, to the Mormon-established town of San Bernardino, California. Ultimately, the Saints hoped that their new kingdom would include a corridor to the sea, either via steamboat traffic up the turbulent Colorado River from the Gulf of California or through the port of San Diego.

The Saints were not destined to remain alone with the Indians in the desert, however. The United States' successful war of conquest against Mexico, aided by a Mormon battalion anxious to earn some cash, and the discovery of gold in California once again brought the Saints under the sway of the federal government. Although a territorial government had been set up and the Saints applied for statehood by 1850, they were determined to build their own kind of society. "I have looked upon the community of the Latter-day Saints in vision and beheld them organized as one great family of heaven," Young proclaimed, "each person performing his several duties in his line of industry, working for the good of the whole rather than individual aggrandizement." In line with this cooperative vision, Young declared that the Saints would build an economy "independent of the Gentile nations." The Council of Fifty, created as the political arm of the church by Smith in Nauvoo, now became the real government of the new territory, with Young as governor and with a Mormon-dominated legislature. The Saints were so confident in their new situation away from the non-Mormon world that the church finally acknowledged in 1852 what so many had known for so long: Select members of the church were practicing polygamy.

Despite their isolation, the issues of polygamy and political control again drew attention to the Mormon community. Perhaps it was inevitable that the ideas of patriarchal theocracy would ultimately come in conflict with the attempts of the federal government to maintain its sway over the increasingly fragmented nation of the 1850s. While the Mormon political apparatus contested with federal appointees for control of the new territory, polygamy became joined with slavery as "twin relics of barbarism" that had to be eliminated.

There had been conflicts between the Saints and federal political appointees, particularly over land ownership and control of the judicial system. For a time, tensions subsided, but in 1857 they were renewed after an associate justice of the territorial government claimed that he feared for his life and fled Utah. In a letter to Washington he said that the Saints were bent on destroying the power of the federal government by any means, fair or foul.

In response, President James Buchanan sent 2,500 soldiers to escort a new governor to Utah. The so-called Utah War was a fiasco from beginning to end. When the invading army reached Wyoming, where it bogged down for the winter, their supply trains were harassed by Mormon guerrillas, who undertook a scorched-earth campaign. Ultimately, the military was persuaded to set up an encampment a goodly distance from the city.

Young had handled this new threat skillfully, avoiding the kind of confrontation for which the Saints had paid so dearly in Missouri and Illinois. Young had prepared his followers to resist and flee—Salt Lake City was actually abandoned—but he used just the right combination of resistance and diplomacy to head off a bloodbath.

The Utah War had brought out the Saints' ambivalence about the United States government. Although they had suffered at the hands of the state governments of Missouri and Illinois, they had never been able, despite repeated attempts, to get the government in Washington to intervene to protect their rights. Once in Utah, the nature of territorial government, with its arbitrary appointees, made Washington seem like the seat of an oppressive foreign nation. When the Civil War broke out, the Saints appeared to welcome the impending collapse of the central government. One observer quoted Young as saying, "We are bound to become a sovereign state in the union or an independent nation by ourselves." But when the Civil War ended with the triumph of the federal government, the Saints faced a new and dismaying eventuality: their reconnection to the outside world via the transcontinental railroad. This eventuality led Brigham Young to redouble his efforts to build the cooperative commonwealth, one of the most remarkable experiments in the history of the West. Joseph Smith had abandoned his effort to institute the Law of Consecration and Stewardship in 1834, claiming that "the people had polluted their inheritance." Young's limited effort to reinstitute the principle in the 1850s was cut short by the Utah War. Now recognizing that they no longer could separate themselves from the outside world, the Saints prepared to make a new bid for economic independence.

This new departure was announced by President Young in 1865 in a call for Mormons to undercut the profiteering of both Gentile and Mormon merchants by setting up their own cooperative merchandising arrangements. The church leadership responded by opening a cooperative store and wholesale marketing operation. Six weeks after the opening of the first cooperative in Salt Lake City, eighty-one cooperative stores had sprung up. It was relatively easy for the Saints to move into a wholehearted experiment with cooperatives and other communitarian forms since so much of their effort in building up the kingdom in Utah—the construction of church buildings, irrigation systems, roads and so forth—was basically communal in nature.

Under the leadership of Lorenzo Snow, who would become the fifth Prophet, Brigham City, the Saints' most striking cooperative experiment, served as a model for the cooperative campaign launched by Young in 1865. The first settlers were carefully selected to provide the wide range of skills needed in the community. The new Saints formed a cooperative retail outlet and then went on to build a tannery and a wool factory, which employed thirty-two people. "By 1874," wrote Leonard J. Arrington, Feramorz Y. Fox, and Dean L. May in *Building the City of God*, "virtually the entire economic life of this community of 400 families was owned and directed by the cooperative association. Some fifteen departments, later to be expanded to forty, produced the goods and services needed by the community and each household obtained its food, clothing, furniture, and other necessities from these departments. Almost complete self-sufficiency had been attained, and some textile products, leather, furniture, and dairy products were 'exported' to other northern Utah settlements." For thirty years, Brigham City existed as another foretaste of the Celestial Kingdom.

Young emphasized that the cooperative movement was "only the stepping stone to what is called the Order of Enoch, but which is in reality the order of Heaven." It was also the way in which the Saints could draw in upon themselves to resist the growing attacks on their religion and their communities. In 1862, the first national antipolygamy law, the Morrill Anti-Bigamy Act, had been passed. It called for penalties against those practicing polygamy, disincorporation of the church, and a limitation on the value of the real estate owned by the church to $50,000. In the early 1870s, a group of disaffected Mormons, known as the Godbeites after one of their leaders, William S. Godbe, formed an opposition party, started a bitterly critical publication, which later became the *Salt Lake Tribune*, and began to call for competition in trade and more outside investment— demands that were diametrically opposed to Young's strategy of economic self-determination.

In the midst of this turmoil, Young and other church leaders renewed their call for the establishment of the Order of Enoch. Their plea fell on particularly fertile ground in the Mormon communities of southern Utah, where the Saints faced a competing economic system in the new silver mining boom towns of Nevada. After Young and other church leaders toured the southern frontier to extol the virtues of cooperation, cooperative organizations called United Orders were formed in Saint George, Beaver, Kanab, and Richfield. They soon spread throughout the state to both urban and rural areas, to Idaho, and to a new line of Mormon communities being built in Arizona with an eye to extending the Saints' influence into Mexico.

One of the most impressive experiments was carried out by a group of settlers who retreated to Utah after abandoning efforts to grow cotton along the Muddy River in Nevada. This group of some 200 people planned and laid out the community of Orderville, dedicated to a communal form of living. Members retained ownership of their clothing and personal property; all else was owned by the community.

One visitor said that at first sight the community "looks like factory [sic]. The wooden shedlike buildings built in continuous rows, the adjacent mills, the bare ugly patch of hillside beyond it, give the actual settlement an uninviting aspect." On closer examination, the visitor was impressed by the intermingling of working and living space, the broad sidewalks, plentiful trees, experimental gardens, a museum, and a well-constructed schoolhouse.

Orderville suffered from invidious comparisons between its austere standard of living—self-sufficient though it was—and the relatively more prosperous life of surrounding towns. After six years, the inhabitants gave up the communal dining hall and then divided up some of the land into small home and garden lots. Unequal wages were introduced to increase productivity. The community continued to struggle along until federal posses drove most of the leaders, who were polygamists, underground in 1885. On the advice of church leadership in Salt Lake City, this experiment with the Order of Enoch was finally abandoned.

In other communities, the United Orders were dominated by the largest property owners. Some were hindered by the slovenly work habits of some of their members. Participants fell to fighting over pay and the distribution of goods. In urban areas, such as Salt Lake City, the experiment really never took hold because of the opposition of many of the church's leading businessmen. Some people even questioned why it was that Brigham Young's considerable business holdings and those of other prominent Mormon businessmen did not come under the United Order.

When Young died in 1877, the United Order lost its greatest advocate. The new prophet, John Taylor, had been an early proponent of cooperatives but regarded the more communally oriented United Orders as "visionary and impractical schemes." Taylor organized instead the Zion's Central Board of Trade. A regional rather than a localized approach to church direction of economic development, "it represented a type of mild economic planning and social experimentation consistent with prevailing capitalistic tendencies," according to Arrington et al. The new organization pushed for the development of more ambitious, large-scale, capital-intensive projects, such as the development of iron manufacturing, the construction of railroads, and the establishment of the sugar beet industry.

In 1882, five years after Young's death, the church circulated a letter that marked the end of this fascinating experiment. "Our relations with the world and our own imperfections prevent the establishment of this system at the present time and therefore, as was stated by Joseph in an early day, it cannot yet be carried out." The United Orders receded into memory like minute particles swept from the desert floor by a dust devil. The spirit of cooperation, the idea of providing for the Saints' worldly needs, would resurface in a very different form many years later during the Great Depression.

Brother Brigham Young left an ambivalent legacy upon his death in 1877. His major achievements were as a colonizer, statesman, and organization-builder. His leadership in establishing some 350 Mormon communities in the Great Basin was tied intimately to his promotion of cooperatives and the United Order. Like Joseph Smith, he championed the cause of the poorer Saints and inveighed tirelessly against domination by outside economic forces and against what one church epistle described as "the growth of riches in the hands of a few at the expense of many." At the same time, he himself became one of the territory's wealthiest businessmen, casually intermingling his own business affairs with those of the church and keeping them apart from the affairs of the cooperatives and the United Orders. Life among the Mormon elite in Salt Lake City in the time of Young took on the grand style he followed with his fancy homes, carriages, and entourage of bodyguards and attendants. He also seems to have recognized the patterns of inevitability in the larger economic development of the West. The railroad could not be stopped. So Young, rebuffed in his efforts to get it to pass through Salt Lake City, arranged for the Saints to get a number of contracts to grade the roadbed.

Under Young, the organizational framework devised for the westward trek was redefined to become the foundation for the creation of the Mormon village and for the domination and control of every aspect of a member's life. No detail was too small for Young's attention. He lectured female members on their housekeeping, arranged marriages, and personally dispatched missionaries and colonizers far and wide. On the local level, the bishops became his surrogates and local arbiters of their people's fate, acting as judges, counselors, and taskmakers. Under Young, the church took major steps to intervene in and control the everyday life of its members.

THE GREAT ACCOMMODATION

Even before Young's death, the campaign against the church picked up in intensity, aided now by the growth of the non-Mormon community in Utah due to the opening of the mining frontier. Polygamy was the battle cry, but an end to the Saints' control of the territory was the objective. "We care nothing for your polygamy," said a federal judge. "It's a good war-cry and serves our purpose by enlisting the sympathy for our cause. What we most object to is your unity; your political and commercial solidarity; the obedience you render to your spiritual leaders in temporal affairs. We want you to throw off the yoke of the Priesthood, to do as we do, and be Americans in deed as well as name."

A year after Brigham's death, the U.S. Supreme Court upheld the 1862 antipolygamy statute. The Mormon issue became a national issue addressed by the president, and thousands of Saints were disenfranchised in Idaho and Utah. When the anti-Mormon Edmunds Act was passed in 1882, the federal courts moved to prosecute polygamists, sending federal deputies to raid nearly every Mormon community.

Panic threatened to sweep the Mormon community as dozens of leading Mormons were jailed and others went underground or suddenly left the country on missions or for the sanctuary of the Mexican and Canadian colonies.

The church, now headed by John Taylor, advised its polygamist members to go underground to avoid arrest and imprisonment. Taylor, moving from house to house in Utah, urged the Saints to maintain discipline and to not retaliate in any way.

In 1887, Taylor died at the very moment when the federal government was taking its most drastic steps to destroy the church. Taylor, who had been critically wounded during the assassination of Joseph Smith, was an unrelenting proponent of celestial marriage and a bitter defender of republican principles against what he considered the arbitrary actions of the federal government and the "carpetbagger" territorial government. Taylor often defended polygamy by contrasting it to the double standard of marriage and prostitution or mistresses condoned in the "Christian" world. Polygamy, the Saints and Taylor insisted, was not an invitation to sexual license. Celestial marriage was a central part of the divine order, and sex was a means to procreation not pleasure.

During the debates just before Taylor's death over how to deal with the federal campaign against the church, a number of prominent church leaders began to urge an accommodation. As time went by, it became clear that the abolition of polygamy was the key to a settlement with the federal government and the means by which the Utah territory could become a state. Polygamy, never widely practiced, had been restricted to an elite group that could afford plural wives and had the approval of Brigham Young. Many of the younger generation also refused to take up the practice. As the country around them developed, the Saints realized they would never again live in the isolation of their first five years in the Great Basin. Indeed, by 1889, Gentiles controlled the city governments of Salt Lake City and Ogden, and the mining economy that dominated the state.

On September 25, 1890, Wilford Woodruff, the new president of the church, issued a manifesto saying, "We are not teaching polygamy or plural marriage, nor permitting any person to enter into its practice." He concluded that it was his advice to the Latter-day Saints "to refrain from contracting any marriage forbidden by the law of the land." The Manifesto of 1890, as it came to be known, was a shocking reversal of church doctrine, although it was accepted by most Saints as the sole means to achieve peace with the outside world. Plural marriages continued to be solemnized by a handful of church leaders for more than a decade. Some claimed that the practice had merely been driven underground as it had been in Nauvoo and that Woodruff's statement was called a manifesto to indicate to the Saints that it was not a revelation and therefore not doctrine.

Eighteen-ninety proved to be the most dramatic watershed in the history of the church, although it took another six years for Utah to gain statehood. Some historians would later argue that the history of the original Mormon church came to an end at this time. Others would refer to the Manifesto of 1890 as the great capitulation or, simply, the surrender. The attempt to build a separate nation ended with the Utah War and the triumph of the federal government in the Civil War. Joseph Smith's call to revolutionize the world through the establishment of the Kingdom of God by means of the secret Council of Fifty gradually gave way to pleas for statehood and John Taylor's defense of republican principles. The great cooperative experiments championed by Brigham Young as a means to economic independence collapsed of internal discord and external pressure. And now the Saints were being called upon to give up celestial marriage. The Saints no longer anxiously awaited the millennium. Surely, it would come, someday, according to the mysterious workings of the Heavenly Father.

Mormonism's most distinctive features gradually faded into the past and became the stuff of history. Henceforth, the Saints would concentrate on building up their church as a purely religious body as they came to identify more and more with the America of Main Street and the Model T.

It would take another fifteen years after the Manifesto of 1890 to reach a political accommodation with Washington. These years were the years in which Brigham H. Roberts was denied a seat in the House of Representatives because of his plural wives (1898) and Apostle Reed Smoot was subjected to a three-year-long investigation before he was seated in the U.S. Senate in 1907. Economic accommodation, the seeds of which were planted during Brigham Young's dealings with the Union Pacific Railroad and nurtured by the first generation of Mormon entrepreneurs even during the height of the United Orders, came much easier. The fevered negotiations to save the church that took place among leading Mormons, eastern politicians, and some of the country's most powerful business interests played a formative role in the development of the modern church.

During the press hysteria that attended the Smoot investigation, the church redoubled its efforts to make clear to the watching world that it was no longer the church of radical millennialism and polygamy. In 1903, the First Presidency redefined the meaning of the Kingdom of God. The next year, the current Prophet, Joseph F. Smith, the son of Hyrum, and Joseph's nephew, issued an official statement prohibiting plural marriage and making it an offense punishable by excommunication. To show that they meant business, John W. Taylor, the late Prophet's son, was first removed from the Quorum of the Twelve and later excommunicated for refusing to give up the principle. "With the official pronouncement," wrote his son, Samuel Woolley Taylor, in a memoir of his father, *Family Kingdom*, "the Church entered actively into a campaign to clear its skirts of the last vestige of the old order."

THE NEW THEOCRACY AND THE NEW LEADERS

With the advent of the Great Accommodation, the church enjoyed a period of noninterference from the world outside the Great Basin. The church continued to put its greatest emphasis on "proselyting," or missionary work, but grew very little outside the Intermountain West. During the nineteenth century, a steady stream of converts had poured in, particularly from Great Britain and the Scandinavian countries. In the decade between the arrival of the Saints in Utah and the Utah War, some 15,000 new members were recruited in England and shipped mainly in steerage to America. Some 3,000 of these *walked* to the Great Basin, pushing handcarts before them.

When the federal government intensified its campaign against the Saints in the 1880s, one of its major targets was the Perpetual Emigration Fund, which financed the gathering of new members and brought over 100,000 foreign Saints to Utah. The attack on the church cut down the immigration of new members. In time there were fundamental changes in the whole concept of the gathering. Although Utah was Zion, at least until the construction of the New Jerusalem in Missouri, new recruits were encouraged to stay where they were. At the same time, young men were recruited as missionaries, and the missionary experience became an important rite of passage in the church. Gone were the days of the famous missionary orators, who traveled at the Prophet's bidding "without scrip and purse," addressing street corner meetings and competing with other sects and political groups for the attention of England's disaffected proletariat.

The Great Depression struck Utah prematurely in the 1920s and many Saints were forced to look for work outside the state, which had become dependent on the eastern-based mining industry. This threatening outmigration would eventually work to the advantage of the church, as new groups of Saints banded together in places like Arizona and California, where the first stake outside the Great Basin was created in 1923. A decade later, stake missionary programs focused on recruiting new members in the areas where church organizational structures already existed.

As the visions of the millennium grew dimmer, the church for a time gave up the idea of building a parallel society that would fulfill all the spiritual and temporal needs of its members. Instead, it focused on building an autonomous religious culture that would involve its members in a spiritual life on a daily basis and touch all aspects of their lives. Over time, the church's elaborate organizational structure came to exert a degree of discipline and control that was foreign to all other American churches and secular organizations. From the ashes of the old cooperative commonwealth, a new theocracy rose.

Education provides a good example. Most of the early leaders of the church, such as Joseph Smith and Brigham Young, were self-educated. Like many self-taught people, they put tremendous emphasis on institutional education for their children. They remained suspicious of the public school system and put much of their effort into setting up a parallel course of religious and secular instruction. John Taylor, who served as territorial superintendent of education just before he became Prophet, once said, "We do not want men and women to teach the children of Latter-day Saints who are not Latter-day Saints themselves." Soon after it was established, Brigham Young Academy (later Brigham Young University) became a training institute for Mormon teachers.

When the government used funds confiscated from the church to support public education, the church extended its educational apparatus to supplement the course of instruction at public schools. Church academies and seminaries were set up in most Mormon communities. As late as 1910, half the students in Utah attended church academies instead of public high school.

In 1916, the church reached an accommodation with the public school establishment. In exchange for credit for work done at church seminaries, the church began to withdraw from secondary education while establishing a number of teachers colleges. Within eight years, it had closed all of its academies except one in Mexico. In 1930, after the state high school inspector challenged the church role in education for infringing upon the separation between church and state, the state board of education compelled the church to separate the seminaries from public schools. In the 1950s, the church set up a new seminary program that was to be attended by young members in the morning *before* going to school.

Brigham Young University eventually became the largest private religious university in the world, and a number of Mormons became prominent educators on the national scene. Sterling M. McMurrin served as Commissioner of Education in the presidency of John Kennedy. T.H. Bell joined the Reagan cabinet as Secretary of Education, and David Gardner, who headed a major educational commission for Reagan and Bell, went from president of the University of Utah to head of the prestigious University of California.

While the church's educational system was designed to buffer the Saints from the influence of the outside world, the church auxiliaries, more than any other organization, were used to increase the daily participation of the members and to bring the church into their everyday lives. The auxiliaries included the Relief Society for Women, the Young Men's Mutual Improvement Association, and the Young Women's Mutual Improvement Association. Later they were supplemented by church involvement in the Scouting program.

The death of Brigham Young marked the end of the period in which church affairs were dominated by a Mormon version of the cult of personality. Under the new leaders the various levels of the hierarchy grew and became more significant. At the same time, these leaders constantly tinkered with the increasingly unwieldy bureaucracy to extend it while making it responsive to centralized control.

Joseph Smith and Brigham Young had looked to different aspects of Smith's sweeping visions for inspiration about how to build the Kingdom of God on earth. The new leaders were concerned more with taking the conflicting and overlapping organizational structure bequeathed by Smith and making it work. While Smith and Young fought against the drift and patterns of western history, the new leaders were more responsive to the lessons that could be learned from the Gentile world. Young, though a capitalist in his own right, resisted the onslaught of youthful capitalism in the West. The new leaders, many of them successful businessmen, turned to the world of business for ideas about how to build their church.

In the modern church, there was little room for doctrinal innovation. There was no room for new visions. Instead, the teachings of Joseph Smith were being systematized by such theologians as James E. Talmage, while some of the rough edges were pared away and cleaned up for public presentation. Innovative theologians, such as B.H. Roberts, the same man barred from Congress, clashed head on with the hierarchy.

Roberts's greatest work, *The Way, Truth, and Light*, was never published because of his alleged lack of orthodoxy, while his official history of the church was revised repeatedly before it satisfied the church leadership. Smith's statement that "no man knows my history" now became a prediction, as the custodians of his legacy surrounded the real man with myth while codifying, some would say censoring, his writings.

When Heber Jeddy Grant became the seventh Prophet in 1918, he represented the second generation of church leaders. Grant was born in Utah nine years after the arrival of the Saints, and though he was a polygamist and lived through the United Orders and the last Great confrontation with the federal government, his attitudes were formed by the Great Accommodation and by the church's greater emphasis on building a parallel religious order.

Grant, who served as Prophet from 1918 until 1945, had participated in the Great Accommodation as a successful young Salt Lake businessman who went to New York to arrange a number of loans for church-related businesses. Grant was also well-traveled, having set up the church's first mission in Japan.

In the Grant era, the church was still treated as a curiosity and even became an important western tourist attraction, but it no longer inspired the rancorous animosity of its first century. Left alone, the church began to grow into the forerunner of the labrynthine bureaucracy that it is today. Most of the new leaders, unlike their predecessors who kept one foot in the world outside the church while serving the Saints, were increasingly full-time employees who spent all their time on church affairs once they were called to office.

Church leaders championed progress, technological innovation, and scientific achievement. The church started one of the first radio stations in the country and soon recognized that medium would help take their message to the world. Their constant concern about what the outside world thought of the church and the disappearance of the robust evangelism of the nineteenth century made for a more timid presentation of their religion.

This effort to appear presentable affected minor things, such as the nature of conferences. During one radio broadcast, President Grant even went so far as to stop General Authority J. Golden Kimball, who was known for his dynamic if profane oratory. At the next conference, a seemingly chastened Kimball got up and pulled out a typed version of his speech. He explained to the audience, many of whom had come just to hear him, that the brethren had thought it would be better if he would write out his speech so that they could censor it. After stumbling through the reading of his speech for a few sentences, he turned to the Prophet and said, "Hell, Heber, I can't read this damn thing."

J. Golden Kimball was a popular figure and much in demand as a speaker at local church meetings. But he was increasingly a figure from the past. Although the church was still based to a remarkable degree on the Mormon village and although members still had direct access to their leaders, these circumstances were slowly passing from the scene along with the likes of Kimball.

A major force in the modernization of the church was J. Reuben Clark, whom Grant called as his Second Counselor in 1932. Though Grant and Clark had known each other since childhood, their paths had diverged soon after. Grant moved into leadership of the emerging church bureaucracy, and Clark, seeking to make his way in the world, went to law school at Columbia University and then took a job in the solicitor's office at the State Department.

Clark emerged as a major force in the State Department in the presidency of William Howard Taft after writing a memorandum that presented a legal justification for U.S. intervention in Nicaragua. Later, when he returned to the State Department as an undersecretary in the Coolidge and Hoover administrations, he became a leading conservative voice calling for restraint and *non*intervention in the turbulent affairs of postrevolution Mexico.

While serving as ambassador to Mexico, he received a letter from Grant asking him to join the First Presidency. The request was unprecedented since Clark was a man of the world, relatively inactive in the church, and not a member of the Salt Lake church establishment. After Clark reluctantly acquiesced, he and Grant collaborated on a major innovation, the church welfare program, which reflected the stolidly conservative nature of the new theocracy.

When the Depression hit Utah harder and longer than most states, the resourceful Saints, drawing on the spirit of the departed United Orders, began to take local measures, such as community gardens and cooperatives, to deal with hard times. Early relief programs were turned over to local church units by local governments. With the advice of Clark, Grant developed a churchwide self-help program involving thousands of acres of farms, dairies, grain storage, canneries, meat-packing plants, and the like.

Both Grant, a nominal but conservative Democrat, and Clark, an active Republican with ambitions for higher office, described the program as a response to Roosevelt's social programs, which they saw as an attack on traditional Mormon self-reliance and as an effort to make the Saints dependent on the federal government. Grant and other church leaders emphasized that this new program was not related to the earlier United Orders, which were again exciting interest among the Saints. It was an antidote to the threat of communism, not a prelude to the Christian communalism of the vision of Enoch.

Church membership grew steadily during the Grant years from close to 500,000 in 1918 to almost 1 million in 1945. Almost half the membership, however, remained inactive; only seventeen percent of the Saints attended sacrament meeting on Sunday, the principal weekly worship service. The Saints were younger than the average Americans, better educated, and had a higher percentage of home ownership. The largest occupational group was farmers, followed by craftsmen, foremen, and clerical and sales workers. "The values associated with the yeoman farmer—hard work, thrift, stability, reward for individual effort, home ownership, avoidance of debt, and private ownership of property," wrote James B. Allen and Glen M. Leonard, "were still Mormon ideals." One could add that the Saints were generally healthier because of observance of the church ban on tobacco, caffeine and alcohol, which was increasingly emphasized as an integral part of the faith. They also lived longer and found productive and rewarding forms of activity for their older members. Typically leaders of the church, such as Grant and Clark, maintained full, active lives, complete with a regular day at the office and a full round of meetings, well into their eighties.

THE POSTWAR EXPANSION

During the postwar period, the church experienced the most spectacular expansion in its history. The war had had a decidedly dampening effect on the church. Overseas missions were shut down and missionaries called home. Some semiannual conferences were closed to the general public to discourage the Saints from traveling due to wartime shortages. Once the missionary program was reestablished overseas after the war and expanded, an effort that took some three years, the church moved from triumph to triumph.

David O. McKay, who became Prophet in 1951, was the central figure in this dramatic expansion. After Heber Grant died in 1945, George Albert Smith became the new Prophet. He was the great-grandson of Joseph's uncle and the grandson of an Apostle in the days of Brigham Young. Smith was the victim of a serious nervous condition that had led to one nervous breakdown and another near collapse. During his brief term as Prophet, the church leadership continued to be dominated by Clark, who had also run the church during the war because of Grant's poor health. Critics of Clark (and there were many), such as Mormon historian Juanita Brooks, used the term "Reubenization" to describe the conservative direction of the church during the Clark years.

When McKay came to office, he demoted Clark, whose conservatism many Saints considered out of step with the advancing church, to Second Counselor and called his close friend, Stephen L. Richards, to be his First Counselor. McKay, with a full head of wavy white hair and rugged good looks, looked like a modern American leader. His three immediate predecessors had all sported beards, Joseph F. Smith's having reached down his front like Methuselah, and somehow looked like the leaders of an exotic, not quite American religious cult.

Under McKay, the church embarked on a massive building program reflective of its rapid growth and expanding wealth. The centerpiece of the church's new building program was the construction of four new temples. One was built in Los Angeles; three others were built overseas, in England, New Zealand, and Switzerland. In the decade after the war, the church built 1,350 new buildings, and in one year alone (1955), $18.7 million was spent on new construction.

Rapid growth brought new problems for the church. There was increasing concern that the church's building program was outstripping its economic resources. Others were troubled by the growing impersonality of this vast bureaucratic network, where the work of the Lord was regularly tabulated in the cold statistics of new conversions, baptisms for the dead, and so on. In 1948, President Clark asked in his diary, "Can spiritual development and achievement be measured statistically, or will the use of statistical measures of success and failure in Church activities actually undermine spirituality by glorifying external piety? . . . Could efficiency become the end rather than spirituality?"

The church began to attract favorable publicity in the Gentile world. With Apostle Ezra Taft Benson leading prayers as Secretary of Agriculture in the Eisenhower cabinet, the church was finally being recognized by the conservative mainstream.

The 1960s changed all that. With the advent of this turbulent new decade, church leaders became alarmed at what they perceived as the impending collapse of the social order. Revolutions abroad, demonstrations at home, strange new behavior among young people—all were viewed as a direct threat to the church. This sense was heightened when civil rights activists began to take note of the church's restrictions against blacks entering the priesthood. When Benson and his son Reed began to draw press attention to their work for the John Birch Society, the polarizations of the outside world appeared to have come to Zion.

While the 1950s were a period of heady expansion, the 1960s became a period of reexamination and reorganization in response to changes in the social order. Efforts were made to evaluate and reorganize virtually every aspect of church life, from the church's huge but unwieldy business empire to the content of lesson material for Sunday School and other programs.

No issue was of greater concern to church leaders than the fundamental threat to family life posed by the social trends of the modern world. Themes of family breakdown and the threat of the outside world began to appear more frequently in conference speeches at the end of World War II. David O. McKay excoriated "the ill-advised suggestion of 'companionate marriage' and 'the ready-made divorce courts'" in a 1945 speech. He went on to say that "an ever-decreasing birth rate and an increasing divorce rate are ominous signs threatening the stability of the American home, and the perpetuity of our present form of constitutional government." The next year, he turned to the dangers of juvenile delinquency, suggesting that one of its causes was "a letdown in home ideals. . . . The exigencies of war," he continued, "induced many mothers to take up war work, and to leave their children in the care of others, or, too often, to let them shift for themselves."

By the 1960s there was a growing sense within the church that things were out of control. As McKay grew older, tensions among the Apostles increased. "It's a time of lack of top leadership in the Church which causes no end of problems," wrote BYU President Ernest L. Wilkinson in his diary. Benson appeared to have gone off on his own purely political tangent and was resisting attempts by other Apostles to control him. Rapid growth, particularly in the international arena, was turning out to be a mixed blessing. Many church leaders began to fear a possible dilution of doctrine. With the church spreading to Third World countries that were locked in a struggle for national identity, the ever-present danger of nationalism—the creation of semiautonomous national churches—began to preoccupy the church hierarchy.

Earlier attempts to bring the bureaucracy under control had fallen short of the mark. J. Reuben Clark had laid out a plan for reorganization twenty years earlier, but it had been lost in the dust of the expansionary drive. The timing was urgent, with such issues as Vietnam, civil rights, and, later, sexual discrimination beginning to polarize the country and further tear at the weakened social fabric.

THE LEE REVOLUTION

McKay and Clark had sounded the alarms, but they were quickly passing from the scene. In 1960, McKay was eighty-seven years old and losing his grip on the church. Clark was more a memory than a real force in church life. Into this vacuum stepped Harold B. Lee, a strong-willed, stern, and organizationally oriented General Authority, whose earlier work had been the model for the Church Welfare Program. Under Lee, the church would experience a major overhaul, a little understood and obscure revolution called Correlation. It would never again be the same.

More than any other church leader, Harold B. Lee grew into the quintessential organization man, intellectually rigorous and intimately acquainted with the often unwieldy church bureaucracy. Born on a small farm in Idaho, he began his career as a school principal, an insurance salesman, and a Salt Lake City commissioner, but soon entered church work full time.

Lee's rise in the church was rapid. In the mid-1930s, when he served as stake president in Salt Lake City, his effort to create a welfare farm among his unemployed members immediately drew the attention of the General Authorities and served as a model for the overall Church Welfare Program. Lee soon became a J. Reuben Clark protégé and was consequently named the welfare program's first managing director. A few years later, he became an Apostle and immediately immersed himself in a variety of church functions, including international work and overall church governmental matters.

Lee's style was both vigorous and methodical, and his forceful and often irascible personality made him a leader to reckon with among the Quorum of the Twelve. By the late 1950s, he had become preoccupied with the issue of rapid growth and was the first church leader to link the problem of growth with loss of control and possible doctrinal dilution. Lee was equally worried about how changes in the larger society, particularly those threatening the sanctity of the family, would soon tear at the church.

"There was the certainty at the beginning of correlation," said Apostle Boyd K. Packer in 1983, "that we were moving into some major social changes and that the institution of the family would be under attack, and that the vulnerability of our people related to weakness in the family institution. . . . But we were tooled up in anticipation of that, and correlation was putting the institutionalized church as a servant of the doctrine of the church."

Lee, who believed that "the most important of the Lord's work that you will ever do will be the work you do within your own home," knew that action had to be taken. He began maneuvering within the church bureaucracy to establish a new program aimed at strengthening and centralizing church organization and reinforcing its doctrinal core. Lee knew that previous attempts at reorganization had collapsed when groups within the bureaucracy, particularly those associated with the auxiliaries, such as the Women's Relief Society, had prevented any attempt to move onto their turf.

Lee had a plan. In 1960, he got church president McKay to establish a new committee called the Correlation Committee to evaluate the curriculum of all church programs. Lee became the head of the committee and immediately made it an instrument for his far-reaching goals.

Lee's master stroke was turning a limited goal, such as revising and correlating, that is unifying church curriculum, into a major and prolonged effort to reorganize the church. His ultimate aim was to protect the sacred family unit from the outside world and to maintain doctrinal purity.

By the mid-1960s, Lee's Correlation Committee had developed into a major center of power in the church. Lee reached down into the church bureaucracy to select as key aides some younger, ambitious individuals, including Neal A. Maxwell and Boyd K. Packer, who became Lee's troubleshooters in what was now becoming the reorganization of the entire church. Lee could also count on key General Authorities, such as Marion G. Romney (the first cousin of then Michigan Governor George Romney) and the newest member of the Quorum, Gordon B. Hinckley.

Lee made a point of promoting young, professionally trained men, according to Maxwell, who became an Apostle in 1982. "He wasn't inclined to be overly taken in by the church's own bureaucracy."

To deal with rapid expansion, Lee called for a major revamping of all church programs, and eventually of all church organizational structures, in order to simplify, economize, and centralize church efforts. Simultaneously, Lee called for a strengthening of church doctrine, enabling the Saints not only to deal with and offset potential diversity caused by growth, but also to insulate members from the evils of the outside world.

To strengthen the family, Lee called for the reestablishment of the priesthood as the center of power in the church. Lee told his co-workers in the Correlation movement that he wanted to "bring the priesthood back where it should be, according to revelations, and then determine the relationship of the auxiliaries to the priesthood."

The call to "bring the priesthood back to where it should be" required that "the family unit should be considered the integral unit in the church." To strengthen the priesthood and protect the family, the father, said Lee, must be seen as the representative of the priesthood in each family. Taking the church directly into the home, via the "the pipeline of authority," became Correlation's first priority. As an initial step, Lee called for a new home teacher program. In this program, members of the priesthood visited every family in their ward on a monthly basis to become personally acquainted with them and to check on their spiritual and material welfare. This gave the church the opportunity to better examine the daily lives of its members outside the context of their regular church activities, to serve their needs, and to reinforce its sense of control and authority.

Next came the reestablishment of Family Home Evening. Monday evening was set aside for this activity, and all other church activities were called off. Parents were to meet with their family. Using a series of manuals prepared by the church, they would combine discussion of family problems with doctrinal instruction and ideas for other activities, such as games.

Participation and obedience were major themes of the Lee effort. "An uninvolved member with no office and no calling and no opportunity to serve," Lee told a church seminar in 1971, "only shrinks in his own strength . . . We need appropriate involvement for every individual because there is little individual progress without participation, for it is participation by everyone which permits us to apply the principles of the gospel."

Lee and his staff worked out of a new Correlation Board Room, where only he and committee members were permitted and all changes were charted on a giant board. "It was like a road map of where we were going," recalled committee member Ruth Funk. By 1970, with the larger society in the midst of the most violent upheavals since the 1930s, Lee's Correlation revolution had swept through the church, reducing the power of the auxiliaries, radically restructuring the organization and content of church programs, and intensifying a process of desecularization that he hoped would cut Mormons off from the threat of the outside world.

Lee emphasized that the reforms had nothing to do with changes in doctrine. "The principles and doctrines of the Church are divine," he explained. "No one changes them except by revelation."

The Correlation Board Room also served as the training ground for a new generation of church leaders. More and more of Lee's men were entering the ranks of the Quorum of the Twelve, men such as Gordon B. Hinckley, Thomas A. Monson, Boyd K. Packer, and Neal A. Maxwell, who had all cut their teeth on Correlation.

When David O. McKay died and Joseph Fielding Smith became the new Prophet in 1970 at the age of ninety-three, many feared that the momentum toward modernization would be lost. Smith was an archconservative, a man from a different era, with quaint ideas on such matters as race and evolution. He had gained a reputation as a petty tyrant while he ran the church historian's office, just the kind of bureaucratic fiefdom that Lee was adept at outflanking. Age, however, had reduced Smith to pleasant amenability. Harold B. Lee and his young turks were able to press on with their plans.

Two consulting firms were hired to look at administrative procedures. They both recommended further reforms. The first result was the creation of a Department of External Communication, which later became the Public Communications Department, the public relations arm of the church. Next the Correlation Committee became the Division of Internal Communications and was put in charge of producing and reviewing all instructional material and all communications from church headquarters to members. To relieve church leaders of much of their burden, professional managers were placed in charge of most administrative functions.

Lee also played a major role in the creation of a new church Historical Department under the direction of the well-known historian Leonard J. Arrington, a startling development given President Smith's reputation as a champion of orthodoxy. Arrington provided greater access to material that had been kept hidden in the archives and embarked on a sixteen-volume history of the church, the first official history since that of B.H. Roberts. The early days of the Historical Department became known as the Arrington spring.

When Smith died two years after becoming Prophet, Lee took over at the age of seventy-three, the youngest Prophet since Heber J. Grant. Lee, despite all that he had done already, was just beginning to make major changes in the church. In a series of sweeping moves, he put an end to the autonomy of the auxiliaries and brought them under centralized control. Their lesson material was rewritten, and a new, permanent Correlation Review committee was established with sweeping and often arbitrary powers of censorship over the doctrinal content of written materials. The priesthood was finally and definitely in charge.

Lee's work since the beginning of the Correlation movement was paralleled by Nathan Eldon Tanner's successful efforts to untangle the church's complicated finances and rebuild its economic base. With a new corporate structure, a centralized bureaucracy, a revitalized priesthood, and other modern amenities, such as the new public relations arm, the church was poised for another burst of expansion.

Then, in late 1973, Lee, having driven himself in his efforts to reform the church, collapsed and died. "I suspect there has never been a man among the General Authorities," said one General Authority of Lee, "that has exercised such a predominant influence over church affairs as President Lee has done . . . [prior to] being President of the church."

Lee liked to describe Correlation as "the culmination of a life-long dream," but Correlation neither alleviated the problems gnawing at the vitals of the church nor arrested the ever-present threat of secular influences. Ten years after the Correlation effort began, Lee had asked his top troubleshooter, Neal A. Maxwell, to make a presentation to some high church officials about attendance at sacrament meetings, considered an important index of participation. Maxwell noted that attendance had climbed to thirty-seven percent in sixty years, but temple marriages had fallen off to forty percent. He also noted that there were 137 positions in a typical ward. Despite the effort to create positions of responsibility for young people, almost half of the members of the Aaronic priesthood were inactive.

Next Maxwell noted that there were 500,000 inactive fathers. Lee interjected to say this this meant that 2 million members out of a church membership of just under 3 million were living in homes where fathers were not members or were inactive. "This is another way of saying," Lee concluded, "that unless somebody wakes up, we'll have two-thirds of the church membership that will not be together in family relationships in the hereafter." Both men agreed that the church was losing ground every year, despite its carefully cultivated reputation as the fastest-growing church in America.

The Lee revolution was a major step in the quest for a modern church that could enforce a sense of orthodoxy and obedience and keep the world at bay. The new Historical Department was the obvious exception, but the new historians would soon come in conflict with the champions of orthodoxy. Correlation definitely tightened the screws on a potentially errant membership. Participation meant control, which led to a new kind of authoritarianism. Centralized control, the major aim of the Correlation movement, caused many members to question whether there was any room for tolerance and autonomy. Members of the international church wondered if they were really part of a solely American church, or more specifically a Salt Lake church, run by a small group of men from the

Intermountain West. Women, in particular, bore the brunt of Lee's centralization since their organization, the Relief Society, lost the autonomy that it had cherished during its long history, subjecting them more than ever to the male priesthood.

When Spencer W. Kimball succeeded Lee as the new Prophet, the church appeared from the outside ready to move smoothly ahead. The black priesthood issue no longer drew national attention after the decline of the civil rights movement. Kimball, who had never been expected to be Prophet, had not been as central a figure as Harold B. Lee in the modern church. He had pioneered the church's new Indian programs. And although Indians were central to the doctrine of the church and a concern of missionaries in Latin America, they were less important than Correlation.

The new Prophet, the stern moralist and gentle critic of racism, adopted the slogan "Lengthen Your Stride," quickly setting out to push the church into another expansionary drive. He called for the recruitment of more missionaries and for the construction of new temples. He oversaw the constant organizational fine-tuning that was necessary to keep the sometimes unwieldy bureaucracy functioning smoothly. Under his leadership, the church also embarked on its most controversial political campaign in years, setting out to play a major role in the defeat of the ERA.

Kimball turned out to be a surprisingly strong administrator. More important, the church was ready, thanks to the changes inspired by Lee and Eldon Tanner, to run on the strength of its reorganized and professionalized bureaucracy. The church under Kimball moved on regardless of the precarious state of his health.

The reform process continued. In 1974, the Special Affairs Committee was formed to provide the church with the capability of surveying important social and political trends in Utah, the nation, and the world. Special Affairs also became the focal point for all church contact with politicians. The most significant change, which was very much in line with Lee's modernization, was Kimball's 1978 revelation admitting blacks to the priesthood. Under Kimball, the modern church, with its professional bureaucracy, political specialists, and money managers, would emerge from the anonymity of the Great Basin to become a major spiritual, political, and economic power.

These changes, however, came in the context of the quest for the new orthodoxy. In reality, the church under Kimball was entering one of the most turbulent eras since the Great Accommodation. By the 1980s, it was clear that many young members of the church had internalized doctrine and organizational procedure to the extent that there was a new orthodoxy in the ranks of the church. At the same time, the church, through its emphasis on education, was spawning a whole new generation of young professionals and intellectuals who were uneasy with the emphasis on unquestioning obedience and an inflexible and ossified doctrine. Beginning in the late 1960s, they launched an intellectual movement within the church the likes of which, despite its timidity, had not been seen in years. Spearheading the new movement were women members of the church, the group most directly and negatively affected by Correlation.

While the church continued to battle internal critics of the new regime, it launched a whole new series of efforts to protect Zion from the dubious morality of Babylon. In the 1970s, politics became the new leaders' chosen instrument in their campaigns against abortion, pornography, and the dangers to the patriarchal order represented by the Equal Rights Amendment. Still, the church, with its rich and variegated traditions, remained unpredictable. The pronouncements of Ezra Taft Benson, Kimball's likely successor, continued to strike fear in the hearts of church liberals and modernizers. At the same time, the church chose to make a major statement in 1981 against the basing of the MX missile system in the desert of Nevada and Utah.

The new church of the 1970s was a far cry from the theocratic commonwealth conceived by Joseph Smith and brought to its highest level of development by Brigham Young. Mormonism remained a subculture within the larger culture, a nation within a nation. It had now absorbed the ideals of the moralistic, small-town, laissez-faire capitalism of an earlier era and fused them with the doctrines of Smith, the economics of Wall Street, and the politics of a resurgent conservatism and was using them all to fight the modern world. The church was still dedicated to expansion through missionary work and temple building, but in the absence of the millennium, building the Kingdom of God on earth had given way to a constant preoccupation with internal reorganization, control of its members, and keeping the world at bay.

CHAPTER THREE

POLITICS:
THE SECULAR COMPULSION

A YEARNING FOR AUTHORITY

Though a Republican, Richard Wirthlin, the son of a former Presiding Bishop and brother of a member of the Quorum of the Seventy, was not originally a Ronald Reagan supporter. He believed the popular characterization of Reagan as the actor-turned-politician. "I thought all the charges about learning lines were true," he said in a January 1983 interview in his Washington office. In 1969 a friend, who was a Reagan aide, took Wirthlin to visit Reagan at his home in Pacific Palisades without telling Wirthlin whom he was going to see. Reagan, during a two-and-a-half-hour conversation, won Wirthlin to his side. Wirthlin, one of the four pollsters who do close to seventy percent of the polling for top political candidates, has been his pollster and close adviser ever since. Many Mormons share Wirthlin's awe and respect for Reagan. When eight Apostles, including Ezra Taft Benson, met with Reagan in 1974, they were, as former BYU President Ernest L. Wilkinson wrote in his diary, "unanimously delighted with his philosophy of government." "I am completely sure," he went on, "they will speak very favorably of his candidacy for the Presidency when it is announced."

Over seventy percent of Utah's electorate voted for Reagan in 1980. Utah County, the home of Brigham Young University and the center of Mormon orthodoxy, led all counties in the country in its support for Reagan. "People in the church office building seemed pleased as punch," one Salt Lake City journalist noted the day after Reagan's election. "You could just taste their anticipation, their sense that they too were now ready to share in his power."

"After the decade of the me-generation," said Wirthlin, discussing why Mormons are attracted to Reagan, "the bloom is off the rose of the ego-centricity of the 1960s and 1970s. There is more focus on the family and the need for reinforcing networks of the extended family." The church emphasizes that, said Wirthlin, and so does Reagan.

Reagan, Wirthlin said, believes strongly in "a set of well-articulated values." During polling of "soft blue collar Democratic voters" in 1979 to develop themes for the Reagan campaign, Wirthlin found that they supported traditional values, such as family, authority, and patriotism. "These values are quite parallel to LDS ethics," concluded Wirthlin. "There was a yearning for a strong leader."

With the election of Ronald Reagan, the church's quest for authority in a chaotic world had brought it to the peak of national political influence. The Saints had emerged from a shadowy existence to become a major political force in the Intermountain West, a major factor in the national political scene, and an integral part of the ruling coalition. Richard Wirthlin was among the president's closest advisers. Utah educator T.H. Bell had been appointed to the Reagan cabinet as Secretary of Education. Mormon Rex E. Lee was arguing for the government before the Supreme Court as Solicitor General. Utah Senators Jake Garn and Orrin G. Hatch were powerful committee chairmen in the Republican-dominated U.S. Senate. Mormon power extended downward through the Washington bureaucracy and outward across the country to such places as Florida, Georgia, and southern California, where the church had never been influential before.

In recent years, church spokesmen have responded to all questions about the church's political activities by saying that the church only involves itself in moral issues. History, however, demonstrates that the church's working definition of a moral issue is conveniently flexible, and that the thin line between moral and political issues is often hard to discern. Above all, church leaders, despite constitutional provisions about the separation of church and state, cannot leave politics alone. Whether directly or indirectly, the church has felt compelled to increase its political activities to protect Zion from the dangers of the outside world. Politics, beyond the making of money, is perhaps the Saints' most obsessive secular compulsion, and one that originated with the church itself.

POLITICS: THE COMPULSION

Joseph Smith, in his vision of the city of Enoch and in his quest for a just society, made no distinctions between the religious, the political, and the economic. To him such distinctions were totally artificial. He called upon his followers to build the Kingdom of God on earth in all spheres of human activity. His vision, though, was an atavistic one. It harked back to the days of the Puritan village of New England, where the clergy ruled both the temporal and spiritual life of the community with an iron hand, and beyond that to the Old Testament and Mosaic law, in which, as Smith explained, "the government was a theocracy" and where God's anointed ruled "in both civil and ecclesiastical affairs."

As part of their apocalyptic vision, Smith and his followers believed that all churches and governments would soon fall in a mighty conflagration and that the new government of the priesthood created by the Prophet would come to fill the void, literally revolutionizing the world. For this reason, Smith, and later Brigham Young and John Taylor, were anointed "Prophet, Priest, and King" of the new Kingdom of God on Earth.

In 1842, Smith formed the Council of Fifty as part of his plan to build the Kingdom of God on earth. Under Smith, the council was assigned the task of exploring the possibilities of westward migration and working on his 1844 presidential campaign. Once the Saints had arrived in the Great Basin, the council, now under Brigham Young, served for a brief time as the real government of the new state of Deseret. Then it met as "a ghost legislature" on the day following regular sessions until 1870. "We are called the State Legislature," Young wrote to the council in 1863, "but when the time comes, we shall be called the Kingdom of God. Our government is going to pieces and it will be like water that is spilt upon the ground that cannot be gathered up."

After 1870, Young, with his dream of a separate nation fading fast, no longer convened the council. John Taylor revived the organization for a time during the persecutions of the 1880s. His grandson, Samuel Woolley Taylor, suggests that this might have been part of a larger strategy to take the church and polygamy underground. Whether the council was largely symbolic or the means to establish the political Kingdom of God, the church dominated state politics until the opening of the mining frontier brought an influx of Gentiles. In 1870, after a group of maverick Mormons, the Godbeites, allied with leading Gentiles to form the Liberal Party, the Mormons formed their own People's Party.

Even before the Manifesto of 1890, church leaders sent a clear message to the federal government that the church intended to accept the separation of church and state in the future. "This church," declared the First Presidency in 1889, "does not claim to be an independent, temporal kingdom of God, or to be an *Imperium in imperio* aiming to overthrow the United States or any other civil government."

During the Senate investigation of Reed Smoot, the church publicly bade farewell to the millennial era. To meet the charge that the priesthood of the church was "the supreme authority in all things temporal and spiritual," church leaders asked James E. Talmage to refute earlier church statements on the Kingdom of God. Talmage argued that the expression was "metaphorical or figurative," that the Kingdom of God would only be established "when Christ, who is scripturally designated King of Kings, shall come to rule in person upon the earth." Until that time the church "does not interfere with any earthly government," Talmage declared.

The change in church attitudes toward the Kingdom of God not only reflected the dwindling of millennial sentiment, it also reflected the Saints' ambivalent attitude toward the American nation. Smith had been a fervent nationalist born between the Revolution and the War of 1812. A central argument of the Book of Mormon was that America was the chosen land.

The Mormons came to believe that the Constitution was a divinely inspired document. Further, many Mormons believed a statement ascribed to Smith that at some future time the Constitution "would hang by a thread" and be saved by the Saints. Disgusted by a federal government that refused to intervene to protect their rights and buffeted by Missouri and Illinois politicians who wanted their votes but were suspicious of their independence, the Saints under Brigham Young hoped to build a new nation. With the arrival of the railroad their dreams were crushed, and from then on church leaders made statehood their major objective.

Despite the disclaimers of political involvement by church leaders during the Smoot investigation, the Great Accommodation and the achievement of statehood did not end church involvement in politics. The compulsion was still there. It simply took other, more complex forms.

To prepare for statehood, church leaders had dissolved the Mormon-dominated People's Party in 1891. At some stake conferences, the Saints were evenly and often arbitrarily divided between Republicans and Democrats. Since the Republicans had been responsible for most of the anti-Mormon legislation, the Saints were sympathetic to the Democratic party. Church leaders, however, feared that a rush to the Democratic party would continue to stir charges of church domination of politics.

More important, Republican leaders were actively courting church patriarchs and were working with their emissaries to bring Utah into the union and the Saints into the GOP. In the 1890s, Mormon leaders contacted eastern financial interests for loans and investments to keep the church and its enterprises afloat. Out of these negotiations came a series of business alliances that tied the church to a number of leading eastern financiers and businessmen and ultimately to the political party that they supported—the Republican party. "The Republican leaders and the business interests with which they were in relation," wrote Frank J. Cannon, then an insurgent Republican senator from Utah, "had their eyes on a distant prospect of fabulous financial schemes in which the secret funds of the Church were to help in building railroads and the promoting of other enterprises of associated capital." Cannon, who won the enmity of church leaders because of his independence and his opposition to their friends in eastern business circles, lamented that "the Mormon experiment in communism" had given way to an alliance with "the financial and commercial Plunderbund."

When Apostle Reed Smoot finally took his seat in the Senate, he formalized the emerging ties between certain prominent Mormons and the Republican party. Smoot had helped to sell the church's sugar operations to the sugar trust dominated by Henry O. Havemeyer's American Sugar Refining Company. He was now ready to take up the fight in Congress for higher tariffs that would protect the domestic sugar producers and other industries. Smoot dominated state politics for more than two decades and established the first church presence in Washington. Under Smoot, more and more young Mormons followed the church's counsel that political activity was an important civic responsibility and flocked to Washington to join his circle.

Although Smoot was supported in the Republican party by church president Joseph F. Smith until Smith's death in 1918, the church was no longer able or eager to control the political activities of its members. Church leaders, nevertheless, were increasingly conservative and pro-business in their outlook and more often tended toward Republican candidates whether members of the church or not. The Prophet and the Apostles could not give up the idea that politics was a prerogative of the priesthood.

THE CAMPAIGN AGAINST THE NEW DEAL

With the decline of a cooperative theocratic state after the Manifesto of 1890, a gap opened between the church leaders, with their preferences for the business elite and their political retainers, and the rank-and-file Saints. Some of the latter went into the Democratic party, quite a number became socialists or even members of the Industrial Workers of the World, who had their own millennial vision. This gap widened dramatically with the onset of the Depression and the rise of Franklin Delano Roosevelt.

J. Reuben Clark was the church's emissary to the Republican party during the New Deal. Clark, who had served two Republican administrations in the State Department, wanted to represent Utah in the U.S. Senate but had been passed over in 1922. Never close to Reed Smoot, he was also an early critic of the church's involvement in politics, offering the opinion that it was "un-American."

In 1934, a campaign was mounted by influential Republicans, including Harry Chandler, owner of the *Los Angeles Times* and the chairman of Bankers Trust in New York, to get Clark to accept a senatorial nomination. (Chandler even wanted Clark to run for president of the United States.) When Clark consulted with Heber J. Grant, Grant gave a number of reasons for opposing his candidacy, including possible charges of "Church influence." Finally, according to Clark's biographer D. Michael Quinn, Grant gave his approval for Clark to run, but Clark declined at the last moment, citing his responsibilities to the church. Clark still had serious reservations about whether church leaders should be politically active.

Grant said little about the New Deal during its first years but soon came to believe that it was "one of the most serious conditions that has confronted me since I became President of the Church." Church leadership, though, was far from unanimous in its hostility to the New Deal. First Counselor Anthony W. Ivins, until his death in 1934, was an enthusiastic supporter of Roosevelt. Through his influence, the *Deseret News* was also pro–New Deal.

Grant's opposition to the New Deal, like Clark's, grew out of historical antipathy toward the federal government but was intensified by their new-found devotion to laissez-faire economics. Grant feared that the Saints were coming under the control of a government that knew no limits to its intervention in people's lives. He expressed the belief, which was a measure of the distance between his own relative wealth and the situation of his impoverished followers, that "the evils of the dole" contributed to "the curse of idleness." Clark thought that the dole was a threat to "the old time virtues."

Beyond this, Grant began to feel a personal antipathy for Roosevelt. Half the Saints "almost worship him," he complained. That kind of loyalty, Grant implied, should be reserved for church leaders. Grant's feelings about Roosevelt became so intense that when his son-in-law, future Senator Wallace F. Bennett, once tried at Grant's home to turn up a radio broadcast of a Roosevelt fireside chat, Grant burst out, "My boy, I will not allow that man's voice to come into my house. He's a liar and a cheat."

Eager to do something about the New Deal, Grant increased his pressure on Clark to become active in Alfred Landon's 1936 campaign against Roosevelt. Clark agreed to campaign for Landon but restricted his appearances because he feared that he would encourage the opposition. Grant finally came out publicly against Roosevelt and for Landon in an unsigned *Deseret News* editorial that stated the issue crudely as a choice between the Constitution and communism. The editorial caused a furor among the Saints, most of whom were supporters of Roosevelt. Despite the editorial, the state went overwhelmingly for Roosevelt in the election.

In time, Clark's reservations about church involvement in politics were weakened. In 1940, Clark, who was now the de facto leader of the church due to Grant's poor health, prepared a *Deseret News* editorial attacking Roosevelt's bid for a third term and arguing that church leaders had "a civil right" to speak out on political issues. Not even J. Reuben Clark could resist the compulsion.

More important, Grant and Clark began as early as 1933 to devise a positive response to the New Deal and the growing dependency of their followers on its programs. This new Church Welfare Program grew out of a number of local initiatives, particularly one undertaken in Salt Lake's Pioneer Stake by its young president, Harold B. Lee. In Lee's stake, where the unemployment rate was over fifty percent, the Saints bought a farm, employed stake members in exchange for food, and branched off into operating a bishop's storehouse and a cannery. Inspired by the efforts of the Pioneer Stake, Clark undertook a campaign to convince a reticent church bureaucracy to launch the church's own relief program.

Prior to the Clark campaign, the church had instructed its local leaders to send members to governmental agencies for relief *before* sending them to the church. Church officials had worked closely with all levels of government. When Clark began pushing the Lee model of welfare, church leaders

feared that a public announcement of a new churchwide program would
lead to opposition among members who had become dependent on government programs and supported Roosevelt at the ballot box. Clark, in turn,
fretted over the fact that Utah was one of the largest recipients of federal
welfare funds. Finally, in 1936, after three years of internal debate, the
church announced that it was establishing the welfare plan.

This new church program took off quickly, with 200 projects set up
within six weeks of the official announcement. In 1938, the church formed
Deseret Industries, which was modeled after Goodwill Industries, and a
huge warehouse complex was set up in Salt Lake City to store food and
other supplies. In 1939, the church was providing some kind of relief for
155,460 Saints.

Clark, normally cautious in his public remarks, claimed in a speech that
the church program would remove 88,000 Saints from the relief roles and
make them self-sufficient. But Utah remained a leading recipient of federal
aid and continued to be dependent on government programs for employment.

Clark was particularly eager to disabuse the Saints of the idea that the
welfare plan was a revival of the United Order. "The Welfare Plan is not
the United Order and was not intended to be," he told a conference.
"However . . . when the Welfare Plan gets thoroughly into operation . . .
we shall not be so far from carrying out the great fundamentals of the
United Order." At one conference, Clark referred to "a whispering campaign" against the plan, which he thought came from some Saints who
thought that it was a "deep-laid political scheme," ostensibly to undermine
the New Deal in Utah.

The welfare plan was a major departure for church leaders. It was their
first effort since the Great Accommodation to reassert their independence
of the federal government. It was also a program directed at their own
members in an effort to weaken the growing support for the New Deal and
revive the Saints' own brand of provincial conservatism.

Despite the welfare plan, the overwhelming majority of the Saints continued to support Roosevelt. The New Deal brought more civic-minded
Saints to Washington than the entire twenty-five-year Smoot period had.
Prominent Mormons, led by Marriner Eccles, the Ogden banker who converted Roosevelt to deficit spending and became head of the Federal Reserve, rose to important positions in a number of New Deal agencies. The
church gained national recognition both for its anti–New Deal welfare plan
and for the number of worthy Saints who worked for the administration.

REPUBLICAN ASCENDANCY

In the postwar period, the long campaign against the New Deal led by
President Grant and First Counselor Clark began to pay off, although
Grant did not survive to see the results. The first sign that Utah voters were

being slowly weaned away from the Democratic party was the election of J. Bracken Lee as governor in 1948.

Lee became the enfant terrible of Utah conservatism and, because of his non-Mormon background and independence, an uneasy ally of the Republican establishment within the church. Born in the central Utah coal-mining town of Price, he represented the brawling Gentile culture of Utah's mining towns but shared the Mormons' hatred of the federal government. In 1935, Lee was elected mayor of Price, a wide-open town where gambling, booze, and prostitution flourished. As mayor of Price, Lee established a reputation as an antitax crusader, a budget-cutter, and a bitter opponent of the state's liquor laws, which were the product of the church's prohibition against the use of alcohol. Lee's antigovernment stance led him to oppose the activities of state liquor agents and to favor the controlling of prostitution rather than its elimination.

In 1944, Lee was nominated by the Republican party to run against incumbent Democratic governor Herbert B. Maw. Maw, although a Mormon, was none too popular with the church. Lee was supported by Apostle Ezra Taft Benson, who preferred "a nonMormon with high principles to a Jack Mormon," despite Lee's attitudes toward local vice, which were shocking to the Mormon population of Price.

In the 1944 election, the church, through the *Deseret News*, attacked the pro–New Deal Maw and dismissed Maw's efforts to smear Lee by accusing him of running a wide-open town in Price. The church, under the de facto leadership of J. Reuben Clark, was on the lookout for ways to weaken the New Deal in Utah. Maw nevertheless won by a narrow margin, and Lee prepared to face him again in 1948.

Despite their support of Lee in 1944, some church leaders, still concerned about Lee's position on the liquor issue, met with him. At the meeting, Lee later recalled, he was "raked over the coals" and told by one Apostle that he would not be elected unless he signed a letter that reflected the church's position. "You're going to sign it or I'm going to send out a letter to vote against you," Lee remembered the Apostle saying. Lee told them that he would be grateful if they sent the letter because he didn't want the job anyhow.

After the meeting, he went to see Clark, who was viewed by many as the de facto head of the Republican party in Utah. Clark, Lee said, was impressed by his performance in the meeting. "I want to tell you," Lee remembered Clark saying, "if anything made me proud of you, it was what you told those men in their office." The church decided not to oppose Lee. Maw, however, wrote a "Dear Brother" letter to 1,000 leaders of the church to tell them that he was an active member and that he feared that Lee would open Utah to the underworld. The Republicans countered with an advertisement from the Law Observance and Enforcement Committee that endorsed Lee after studying both candidates' positions on various "vices." The LOEC, made up of representatives of Salt Lake City stake presidencies, was run from a church-owned building, and its leaders reported regularly to Apostle Spencer W. Kimball.

Lee swept Maw out of office in the 1948 election, the only Republican in the country to defeat a Democratic governor and the first Republican governor in Utah in twenty-five years. Lee later credited Clark with getting him elected, noting that at least one stake president checked with Clark to see if Lee was "all right." Clark wrote in his diary that Lee told other politicians, "You are never going to have any success in Utah unless you let the leaders of the Church give you some advice. You better make it a point to talk with the Church officials to find out if they are going along with it or not." Lee made it a point to talk with Clark often, but rarely at Clark's request. "Though not by official endorsement," concluded Lee's biographer Dennis Lythgoe, "the Mormon church undoubtedly helped elect Lee governor in 1948. Moreover, in the ensuing eight years, he and the church would establish a mutually beneficial relationship that was essential to the success of his governorship."

Lee embarked on a career as a ferocious budget-cutter. His fulminations against government spending, income taxes, the dangers of dictatorial government, and the threat of the United Nations placed him in the forefront of the postwar reaction against the New Deal, endeared him to the national media and a growing number of Utah voters (both Mormon and Gentile), and proved a godsend to the church leaders in their long war on the New Deal.

Although Clark continued to be recognized as the de facto head of the Republican party, by the early 1950s he was referring all political inquiries to Harold B. Lee for Republicans and Henry D. Moyle for Democrats, two General Authorities who were the heads of the church's Political Committee. During the war, Clark began to include attacks on communism in his major addresses. He was particularly concerned that the Saints not see communism as "merely the forerunner, so to speak, of a reestablishment of the United Order. Communism," he explained, "is Satan's counterfeit for the United Order, that is all there is to it." Clark in his later years became enamored with the far right. Mormon columnist Jack Anderson revealed that Clark at one point was funneling funds from church-owned corporations to a right-wing organization called Irvington-on-the-Hudson.

When Clark became less prominent in church affairs, Thorpe B. Isaacson from the Office of the Presiding Bishopric kept in regular contact with Governor Lee. Isaacson, in a series of suggestions about legislation and requests for appointments of prominent Mormons, implied that he was writing after consulting with church leaders.

In the 1950 election, one of the dirtiest in Utah politics, communism became the major issue as the church joined the Republican party in a campaign that they hoped would rid the state of the New Deal. The Republicans picked Wallace F. Bennett to run against Senator Elbert Thomas, a New Dealer who had defeated Reed Smoot in 1932. From the church's perspective, Bennett was an ideal candidate. He was head of the National Association of Manufacturers and a son-in-law of the late Prophet Heber J.Grant, whose third wife was Bennett's mother-in-law.

The enigmatic Law Observance and Enforcement Committee, which had surfaced to support Bracken Lee in the 1948 gubernatorial election, now took after Thomas. Thomas, said the committee, had "red tendencies and socialistic ideas." The committee sent out two letters endorsing Bennett, which were used by local church officials.

The church openly joined the campaign through a *Deseret News* editorial that identified Bennett with "faith and freedom" and Thomas with atheistic communism. Apostle Henry D. Moyle, of the Political Committee and the church's "official Democrat," worked stake conferences, telling members that Thomas was not in good standing with the church leadership.

When a number of prominent Democrats protested to church authorities and asked the church to deny in the *Deseret News* that it supported the LOEC campaign, they were at first given the runaround. Finally, one of the candidates appealed directly to the Prophet, George Albert Smith. The problem was that Smith barely functioned as Prophet because of a nervous condition. Smith rose from his sickbed and ordered Apostle Mark E. Petersen, the Republican publisher of the *News*, to print a statement from Smith denying church involvement with the LOEC campaign. Petersen simply dragged his feet until Smith, in an unprecedented act, arranged for the rival *Tribune*, a Gentile paper, to print Smith's denial. The damage, however, had already been done. Bennett narrowly edged Thomas in the election.

Two years later, church leaders committed themselves even more openly to the Republican party. Members were urged from the pulpit to attend district meetings and elect Mormon delegates to the state convention. The church, wrote political scientist Frank Jonas, "for all intents and purposes 'controlled' Republican convention politics."

The 1954 reapportionment fight marked the last, blatant involvement by the highest levels of the church leadership in an overtly political confrontation. The church, led by Harold B. Lee's and Henry D. Moyle's Political Committee, pulled out all the stops in an attempt to influence the outcome. Moyle and Lee supported a plan that would give each county a senator regardless of its population. This would mean that the legislature would remain permanently in the hands of the rural areas, where the Mormons were very much in control. "They made it clear to me," said one state senator, "that the whole idea of one senator per county in Utah would prevent control of the government by the Gentiles—Catholics, Jews, Masons, and labor unions." Moyle calculated that the church would automatically get twenty-six out of twenty-nine votes in every session.

The Church Welfare Program's trucks were used to distribute bundles of leaflets to church members, who then passed them out at ward meetings. Local church leaders campaigned openly for the measure from the pulpit. And Moyle put pressure on the *Deseret News* to editorialize on behalf of the plan. When the inevitable protests were brought to President McKay, and the Internal Revenue Service warned church leaders about problems with their tax exempt status, McKay was forced at the last minute to state that the church was not taking a position on reapportionment. The plan was overwhelmingly defeated at the ballot box, indicating that the Mormons and Gentiles still cherished their political independence.

THE RISE OF EZRA TAFT BENSON

With the advent of the Eisenhower administration, the long campaign of most of the church's leaders on behalf of the Republican party paid off. Apostle Ezra Taft Benson was appointed to the cabinet as Secretary of Agriculture, bringing the church to national attention.

Benson, like most church leaders, came from old Mormon stock, including a grandfather who was an Apostle. He was raised in a two-room farmhouse with ten brothers and sisters in the Cache Valley in southern Idaho. As a young man, Benson worked on the family farm and went to the local agricultural college. After a brief stint as a farmer, Benson became the county extension agent.

Although Benson often spoke of the virtues of farm life, his rise in the Washington farm establishment was more closely associated with the origins of modern agribusiness. As agribusiness developed in the postwar period, it came to mean the domination or elimination of family farms by corporate farms and the growing political and economic influence of middlemen, processors, and financiers.

Benson went to Washington during the New Deal to work for the National Council of Farmer Cooperatives and soon rose to be its executive director and lobbyist. During World War II, he was a leader in the fight waged by the conservative wing of the farm movement in alliance with the U.S. Chamber of Commerce against price controls. Among his associates at the council was Charles C. Teague. Teague was a banker, a Chamber of Commerce official, head of two big California marketing cooperatives, and a fundraiser for the Associated Farmers of California, the violence-prone vigilante group that had fought the organization of farmworkers during the Depression. Together Benson and Teague continued to fight unionization of farmworkers and challenged government efforts to improve the conditions of Mexican farm labor in the U.S. during the war.

Benson saw his appointment to Eisenhower's cabinet in millennial terms. "This appointment," he told a BYU audience, "means that the world has come to recognize the Church for what it is [and] is the fulfillment of a prophecy of Joseph Smith, who said the Church would one day assume leadership in Washington."

Although Benson from his first press conference attacked what he called "a completely planned and subsidized economy," Eisenhower had promised farmers that he would continue the price supports implemented by the Democrats during the New Deal in his preelection bid for the farm vote. Benson surrounded himself with representatives of the emerging order in agriculture: bankers, conservative agriculture school professors, such as Earl Butz, who would become Nixon's controversial Secretary of Agriculture, and representatives of the new food corporations. They agreed with Benson's assessment that there were simply too many farmers in the agricultural system.

While working to lower price supports, Benson went after those elements of the New Deal–initiated programs that benefited the small farmer. He restricted rural credit, raised interest rates, cut back the Rural Electrical Association cooperatives and access to public power, and broke up the farmer-elected committees that supervised certain government programs. Eisenhower liked to attack the "Agricats," as he called the USDA employees in Washington, but Benson replaced farmers on crucial committees with government employees. The results were increased profit margins for processors and a decline in farm income and the number of family farms.

Benson chose not to tamper with those programs in wool and sugar that benefited his Utah constituents. After attacking government price supports for three years, Benson arranged to have them *increased* just before the 1956 election. They were reduced after Eisenhower won. BYU President Ernest L. Wilkinson, a protégé of Clark's who was eager to run for the U.S. Senate himself, complained in his diary, "I do not think the decision of the brethren in advising people whether they should run or should not run are [sic] consistent. They have advised me not to run and yet at the same time they allowed Ezra T. Benson, a General Authority, to be Secretary of Agriculture and espouse certain principles which are utterly inconsistent with the feeling of the brethren."

Although Benson saw his appointment in terms of national recognition for his church, he soon brought it some unfortunate notoriety. One enterprising reporter found out that this vocal opponent of government subsidies was vacationing at a government cabin that he had had fixed up at government expense. In 1955, Benson made the mistake of sending a letter to *Harper's* magazine praising an article entitled "The Country Slicker Takes Us Again," which stated that "the ordinary Iowa farmer . . . has a minimum of two new cars and they usually are brand-new Buicks or Oldsmobiles or Cadillacs."

His advisers also had a way of getting him in trouble. First there was a scandal involving insider dealing in government-owned commodities at discount prices. Next, three corporations, whose heads sat on Benson's advisory committee, were indicted for tampering with the government cotton-disposal program. The Republican National Committee had to hire a public relations firm to polish the secretary's image.

In Utah, Benson and other mainline Republicans were having increasing problems with the unpredictable J. Bracken Lee. Lee, who was running in 1958 for a third term as governor, was attacking the Eisenhower administration as a dictatorship, supporting Joe McCarthy, who was now a pariah in his own party, and suggesting that there was a need for a third party. Benson and Senator Bennett considered Lee a threat to their carefully crafted relationship with the national Republican establishment and worked to defeat Lee. Where Lee had been the champion of the conservative wing of the Republican party during the 1950s, Benson became the major exponent of the centrist Eisenhower administration.

Benson also used his position to equate Mormonism with Republicanism, which alarmed some church leaders. President McKay, in particular, was concerned that the church appear more evenhanded and more removed from politics. In this context, Hugh B. Brown was called as an Apostle in 1958. Brown was a Democrat who had worked for the government during the New Deal and also for J. Reuben Clark's law firm. Brown had a golden voice, a flair for the political platform, and tremendous charisma. With McKay's blessing, Brown addressed the 1958 Democratic state convention in a speech that "was frankly calculated to underscore the importance of Mormon participation in both major parties," according to his biographers.

Brown became a counterforce to Benson within the hierarchy, particularly after Benson left the Eisenhower administration and moved quickly to the right. Before long Benson and Brown were openly feuding. At a 1961 meeting with BYU President Wilkinson, for example, Benson lashed out at Brown's "socialistic tendencies." At a conference speech a couple of years later, Benson, in a veiled attack on Brown, who was then President McKay's Second Counselor, warned that Joseph Smith had excommunicated half of his original Apostles, implying that the Saints would have to be very careful in differentiating truth from error in these latter days. When Wilkinson approached Brown after the speech, Brown, clearly irritated, declared, "I don't think I'm going to be excommunicated."

Benson, like Harold B. Lee and other church leaders, was responding to what they perceived as the imminent breakdown of American society, caused, according to Benson, by seditious forces within the country. Harold B. Lee opted for strengthening the priesthood in the church; Benson for building a new political alliance between church members and the anticommunist right, particularly the John Birch Society.

In the early 1960s, the Birch Society, with the assistance of Benson and his son Reed, began to focus its recruiting efforts on the Mormon church.

In 1963, Washington columnist Drew Pearson reported that Reed Benson was circulating a letter written by Birch Society leader Robert Welch that accused Eisenhower of being a communist dupe. At the same time, the Birch Society *Bulletin* urged Mormon members of the society to write personal and confidential letters to the Prophet, David O. McKay, explaining why they had joined and asking if membership was acceptable to the church.

Benson, meanwhile, was becoming increasingly vitriolic in his warnings about the dangers of communism. Welch was also trying to get McKay to attend a Birch Society meeting in Salt Lake City. The Birchers thought that McKay's own attacks on communism mirrored their views. McKay had compared "the secret, seditious scheming of an enemy in our own ranks" to the "fault-finders, shirkers, commandment breakers, and apostate cliques" within the church itself, warning that it was "the enemy from within that is most menacing."

Instead of bringing the Prophet into an alliance with the Birchers, Benson's activities set off alarm bells in church headquarters. In 1963, Apostle Joseph Fielding Smith wrote a letter to an Idaho congressman who had been attacked by Benson: "I think it is time that Brother Benson forgot all about politics and settled down to his duties as a member of the Council of Twelve." Two months later, Smith again wrote to the congressman: "I am glad to report to you that it will be some time before we hear anything from Brother Benson, who is now on his way to Great Britain where I suppose he will be, at least for the next two years. When he returns, I hope his blood will be purified."

Smith was wrong. Less than two years later, Benson was back in Salt Lake City warning the faithful at a conference that there were traitors inside the church. As civil rights protesters picketed outside the Temple grounds, Benson charged that communists were "using the civil rights movement to promote revolution and eventual takeover of this country."

At the next conference, in the spring of 1966, the Birchers organized a major dinner to coincide with the church gathering, and Benson was asked to introduce Welch. Under pressure from the church, Benson merely attended the dinner, at which Welch described the church as "a very good recruiting ground." While Birch Society organizers sent a letter to church bishops, the church, through the *Deseret News*, warned its members that it was not involved in the right-wing organization.

Benson continued to work with the Birchers without becoming a member. When his son Reed became the Utah coordinator of the John Birch Society, his father called it "probably the most effective nonchurch group in the United States in the fight against galloping socialism and godless communism." Using his position in the church to imply that church leaders supported his views, he worked to create the impression that church leaders, particularly the increasingly frail McKay, endorsed his activities. Just before the spring 1966 conference, Benson circulated the story that President McKay's picture would be on the cover of *American Opinion*, the Birch Society magazine. When a delegation of church leaders got McKay to protest, *American Opinion* ran a picture of the late J. Reuben Clark on the cover.

Benson's political ambitions eventually brought him into conflict with another prominent Mormon Republican, George Romney, the automobile executive and governor of Michigan. In 1967, a campaign was started to draft Benson as a presidential candidate and to recruit Strom Thurmond as his running mate or to run Benson for vice president with George Wallace on the American Independent Party ticket. Romney, a liberal Republican, was also preparing to run. Benson pointed out that Romney supported positions, such as federal aid to education and opposition to right-to-work laws, that were in conflict with positions taken by the church presidency. When George Wallace wrote Church President David O. McKay formally requesting Benson as his running mate, the church leadership refused to let Benson run.

As a political spokesman, Benson was irrepressible. He would make a public statement that raised the ire of church leaders and would be called on the carpet. In no time, he would be at it again. As Benson hammered away with his hardline anticommunism, the church was moving toward more subtle and indirect ways of influencing the political process—with the notable exception of their campaign against the Equal Rights Amendment. When Benson appeared poised to become the next Prophet in the late 1970s, the whole issue of his political activities was revived, casting a shadow of fear across the face of the church.

FROM POLITICAL MACHINE TO SPECIAL AFFAIRS

As the church began to modernize in the 1960s through the organizational campaigns of Harold B. Lee and Nathan Eldon Tanner, church leaders also sought more subtle, nonpartisan ways to influence the political process. While President McKay's personal style of handling Salt Lake politics was coming to an end with his physical decline, the church was also giving up its role as a political machine supporting the Republican party.

The church during the 1950s used personal contacts as well as informal ties with Salt Lake establishment figures to influence local developments. L. C. Romney, a former city commissioner and unsuccessful gubernatorial candidate in the three-way 1956 election, tells one story about Political Committee member Henry D. Moyle. Romney and a Democratic committeeman went to Moyle to get his assistance in persuading a church leader to run for the legislature in a Republican district. "We knew he didn't have a chance," said Romney, "but we wanted a respectable candidate." Moyle listened and then went to a globe in his office, spun it around, and put his finger on a small island in the Pacific. "If he doesn't run," said Moyle, "he'll be mission president here in thirty days." The Democrats got their candidate.

In order for the city government to get things done or find out where the church stood on certain issues, it went to Gus Backman, the head of the Chamber of Commerce. Backman would then talk it over with President McKay and John Fitzpatrick, the publisher of the *Salt Lake Tribune*, at their regular breakfast at Lamb's Cafe on Main Street. "It was a way to go to the church without going directly to the church," said Romney.

The relationship between Salt Lake's Gentile and Mormon business elites had been buttressed by the formation in 1950 of a joint corporation to handle the printing, advertising, and distribution for the church's *Deseret News* and the Gentile *Salt Lake Tribune*. In the 1960s, the relationship was extended in numerous campaigns for the renewal of downtown Salt Lake City, where the church was buying up more and more real estate. The church had come a long way in the urban renewal fight, abandoning its opposition to big government and subsidization of the economy, heretofore viewed as socialistic. It broke with J. Bracken Lee, who had been elected mayor in 1959, over the question of urban-renewal funds and was now an advocate of federal subsidies for the redevelopment of the downtown area. Lee's attitudes, though remarkably consistent, were increasingly out of line with the modernizing church and the Gentile business establishment, both of which had earlier welcomed his taxation policies because they provided significant tax breaks for major corporations. Now the church and the Salt Lake business community had big plans for the downtown area and were looking for federal funds to finance them. They supported urban renewal as necessary to these plans. Lee opposed it, and the voters defeated it at the polls in 1965, making Salt Lake City the largest city in the country without urban-renewal funds.

The church and the business elite were also pushing for funds for construction of a new civic auditorium, later known as the Salt Palace. Lee opposed this too. He participated in a campaign to put the issue on the ballot and then delayed construction in the courts.

Inevitably, the church and the business community bested Lee in their campaigns to rebuild downtown Salt Lake City. In the process, church leaders, particularly Nathan Eldon Tanner, worked closely with Democratic Governor Calvin Rampton, who dominated state politics from 1964 to 1976.

The 1954 reapportionment fight turned out to be the beginning of a long process of distancing the church from its allies in the Republican party. In a sense the protracted campaign against the New Deal and its legacies was too successful. Too many church leaders (and opponents) had come to identify the church with the GOP.

For this reason, Hugh B. Brown's appointment as an Apostle proved to be fortuitous. In the 1958 elections, the Republicans suffered a major setback when Democrat Frank Moss defeated Senator Arthur V. Watkins and J. Bracken Lee, running as an independent, in a three-way race for Watkins's seat in the U.S. Senate. Brown proved helpful to Moss in his reelection campaign against Ernest L. Wilkinson, the president of BYU, six years later. Wilkinson was well regarded in high church circles, but Moss got Brown to talk to President McKay to see that the *Deseret News* was evenhanded in its treatment of the two candidates. Brown also became the major spokesman for the church while it was under attack from the civil rights movement for refusing to grant the priesthood to blacks.

The compulsion to intervene in politics was simply too great, despite the church leaders' newfound restraint and their eagerness to disassociate themselves from both the mainstream Republican party and Benson's brand of politics. In the 1960s, the church was active in two campaigns. One involved Sunday closing laws and another, led by Harold B. Lee, concerned the sale of liquor by the drink, the major issue in Utah while the rest of the country agonized over U.S. involvement in Vietnam. These campaigns were more in line with the church's claim that it only acted on moral issues. They allowed church leaders to revert to the old machine style of politics and for a time heightened tensions with the Gentile community because Jack Gallivan, Fitzpatrick's successor as publisher of the *Tribune*, was supporting the initiative.

In 1965, the church came out against the repeal of Section 14b of the Taft-Hartley Act, which sanctioned state right-to-work laws. Historically, the church had opposed labor unions, first as a Gentile phenomenon unnecessary in the cooperative commonwealth, then as competitors for the loyalty of their members and as avenues to radical politics.

In 1965, the First Presidency sent a letter to all Mormons in Congress, Utah's two senators and ten Mormon congressmen throughout the country, asking them to oppose the repeal in order to keep state right-to-work laws "inviolate" and to maintain "free agency to the greatest extent possible." Church leaders did not mention that a low-wage strategy was one of the inducements being held out to corporations looking to relocate along the Wasatch Front, a development that the church very much favored. This clumsy attempt to influence Mormons in Congress backfired, leading to another well-publicized outcry against church intervention in politics.

With the reorganization of the church initiated by Harold B. Lee's Correlation Committee in 1961, the church devised a new way of dealing with political issues. In 1974, the Special Affairs Committee was formed as part of the reorganization. Special Affairs, which was originally run by General Authorities Gordon B. Hinckley, James E. Faust, and David B. Haight, served as the intelligence arm of the church, with a staff that gathered information on social trends that affected the church. It also acted as a contact point for politicians. Politicians regarded Hinckley, before he joined the First Presidency in 1981, as the most important overseer of politics in the hierarchy.

The indirect way of dealing with the church described by L. C. Romney and numerous other politicians became the rule in the era of the Special Affairs Committee. The church only took the initiative in politics on carefully chosen issues, such as the campaign against the ERA. Instead, politicians seeking office or wanting to know how the church viewed a certain issue followed the advice given by J. Bracken Lee and went to the church to confer.

One political figure from a well-connected church family recalled how Special Affairs member Faust offered to intervene to back a political appointment. "I can't call the governor," Faust explained, "but if you get the governor to call me, then I can act on it."

Numerous candidates said that they contacted the church via Special Affairs to let church leaders know that they were entering a race. Salt Lake Mayor Ted Wilson, after the standard lecture on how the church only involves itself in moral issues, explained that he was going to meet with Special Affairs to discuss a parks bond issue.

While the church's influence over the legislature is both profound and subtle, Special Affairs is the contact point when necessary. The legislature in 1983 was ninety percent Mormon, with a large number of church officials, such as stake presidents and bishops, holding seats. In this situation, the church need not pull any wires. Lorin Pace, a veteran member of the Utah House of Representatives, a former Speaker of the House, and a former stake president, noted that the church never contacts the legislature about its wishes and desires. Only those legislators who are trying to curry favor with high church officials contact the brethren to ask for advice on how to vote. "The Mormon community is a pretty closely structured community," said Pace. "It starts with Primary [similar to Sunday School in Protestant churches] and most of these people have grown up in this environment."

Pace, however, has worked with Special Affairs on issues that affect the church. Hinckley used to be "the person to deal with," according to Pace, "although they never really told you who it was." Recently Special Affairs director Dr. Richard P. Lindsay has dealt with the legislature. Pace found that Hinckley "really didn't know a lot about it," but Lindsay, who served in both the Utah house and senate and is the brother-in-law of the powerful Republican senate leader Norman Bangerter, "has the ability to perceive the unanticipated consequences of a political action."

ZION VS. GOMORRAH

The church continues to insist that it is only interested in moral issues, and in fact, the main thrust of its political activities since the formation of the Special Affairs Committee does involve moral issues. Since the late 1950s, church leaders have imbued the Saints with a strong sense of the social and moral breakdown in the larger non-Mormon society. As Utah grew, bringing a larger Gentile population into the state, and as the Saints themselves were dispersed around the country, the church increased its efforts, through programs such as Correlation, to isolate the Saints from the temptations of Babylon by building an insulated Mormon culture.

Correlation brought the church's views into every active home and increased the sense of obedience to authority. At every opportunity, with increasing frequency during the 1970s, church leaders reiterated the theme that there was a real and immediate threat to the family and the church lurking just beyond the fringes of the Mormon community. When the historic themes of self-reliance, hard work, and disdain for government handouts, which were revived and reinforced during the campaign against the New Deal, were added to this sense of impending doom, the church had succeeded in creating an ideological predisposition toward conservative politics.

The revolt of the Mormon wards during the New Deal had frightened church leaders, such as J. Reuben Clark and Heber J. Grant. For once, the rank-and-file Saints appeared to be seriously out of step with their leaders. When the political insurrections and youth revolt of the 1960s knocked at the doors of Zion, the brethren were ready to lead a revolt of their own. This time it would be a revolt of the right, not the left.

In this sense, the Mormons were the forerunners of the Moral Majority and other church groups that brought the great moral issues, such as abortion, school prayer, and pornography, before the public during the rise of the New Right in the 1970s. The moral issues of the 1960s became the political issues of the 1970s, part of the social agenda of the New Right and its religious allies. And the Saints, having been spiritually mobilized through Correlation, were ready to go to war for the cause.

On numerous occasions in the 1970s and 1980s, the brethren preached political activism to the Saints. Every election is accompanied by a statement from the First Presidency to all stake and mission presidents reminding them to tell their members "to be actively involved in the political process." When mass meetings were scheduled by Utah parties in May 1976 at the same time as Family Home Evening, the First Presidency sent a letter instructing all families to reschedule Family Home Evening to allow adults to participate in the mass meetings.

The brethren also instructed their followers not to use church buildings to distribute literature or political announcements, to campaign for candidates or issues, or to solicit funds, all of which have been done at one time or another with and without approval of high church authorities. It is no longer always necessary, however, for the brethren to use the church as a political machine as they did in the 1940s and 1950s. Often they concentrate on setting a general political direction and then let the rank and file take the initiative. At other times, particularly in relation to moral issues, the leadership feels compelled to use the church's formidable organizational power to mobilize the membership.

In either situation, the Saints respond. For one, they are trained from an early age in such skills as public speaking and organizational procedures. Second, their worshipful and obedient attitude toward their leaders, particularly the Prophet, makes them susceptible to subtle initiatives from the top of the church hierarchy. "One of the big problems of a church with the principle of modern-day revelation," University of Utah political scientist J. D. Williams told a *Denver Post* reporter, "is Mormon voters' unconsciously making the transfer from inspired advice on spiritual matters over into the area of political matters and then their thinking comes to a halt."

The church-inspired campaign against pornography, for instance, grew in intensity during the 1970s, reaching a peak by 1983. In 1972, church ward and stake organizations helped gather 325,000 signatures to place an antipornography measure on the California ballot. The measure was formally endorsed by the First Presidency. In numerous speeches, General Authorities cited pornography as a major threat to the church and the family and urged "Latter-day Saints as citizens to exert every effort to fight the inroads of pornography in their communities." In 1982, a speech by Special Affairs Committee director Dr. Richard P. Lindsay appeared in the *Church News* supplement to the *Deseret News*. Lindsay stated that "the war against smut must be waged in many quarters besides the federal government level."

If this message was not clear enough—Lindsay was addressing a non-Mormon audience, but the speech was included in the *Church News*—three months later, the publication ran a one-page spread titled "How to Battle Porn on City, State Levels." It included an account of how a campaign was organized in suburban Pittsburgh, Pennsylvania, a "how-to checklist," and the address and phone number of an Arizona organization called Citizens for Decency Through Law. It also suggested that each church member "become involved as a private citizen without representing the church." Just so nobody missed the point, on the next page there was an editorial stating that "never in our day has sin been so rampant" and concluding that "Latter-day Saints cannot change the whole world but we can stand our own ground and influence as many as we can."

In 1983, the campaign against pornography was showing definite results throughout Utah and Arizona. Two antipornography rallies in Salt Lake City in 1976 and 1977 had drawn more than 10,000 people. (Organizers noted that these rallies, which coincided with *Deseret News* editorials against pornography, drew well while other political events did not.) An adult book store was closed in Ogden. A strong "community standards" amendment had been added to the state pornography law. Two X-rated movie houses were run out of the Salt Lake City area. Smut fighters gained control of the Davis County (Utah) Library Board after they lost a fight to remove from library shelves a novel found acceptable by professional librarians but deemed pornographic by the smut fighters. A citizens group successfully campaigned to get two laws banning cable television through the legislature. The first was found unconstitutional. The second, still thought to be unconstitutional, was passed over the governor's veto.

LAS VEGAS: "A GROUP TO PUT OUR HANDS ON"

Although there are frequent complaints about "a Mormon voting bloc," in states where the Saints have long been established, such blocs do not exist in an organized sense. It also should be noted that non-Mormon politicians have a long history, stretching back to the Great Accommodation, of trying to get church leaders to swing the Saints behind political efforts. The temptation, however, among local Mormon leaders to use the church organization as a political machine has, on occasion, been hard to overcome. This temptation proved too strong for church leaders in Las Vegas, a Mormon outpost since the days of Brigham Young's corridor to the sea and the present-day home of some 25,000 Mormons.

In 1974, Paul Laxalt decided to run for the U.S. Senate after retiring from politics at the end of one term as governor in 1970. Laxalt, a conservative Catholic, was opposed by Lieutenant Governor Harry Reid, a moderate Democrat and Mormon convert. Reid's problem in conservative Nevada was that he had taken liberal positions on issues such as abortion and the state's right-to-work law.

Laxalt gave Mormon Ashley Hall, who would later become Las Vegas assistant city manager, the job of targeting certain interest groups, particularly the religious community and especially Mormon voters. "We knew," Hall commented, "that the LDS people were a group that we could put our hands on."

Laxalt and his top aides, which included former Clark County Commissioner Robert Broadbent (a Mormon who became director of Ronald Reagan's Bureau of Reclamation and then Assistant Secretary of the Interior), decided that it was imperative to force Reid to restate his opposition to right-to-work publicly. If Reid was forced to go public on this issue, Hall and his associates would then have a basis for campaigning against Reid in the Mormon community, particularly since the church had taken a strong stand on behalf of right-to-work and was known to oppose abortion.

As the campaign progressed, Laxalt and Hall sat down with top Mormons in the Laxalt camp, including church regional representative Dr. Samuel Davis, Gaming Control Board chairman Richard Bunker, and North Las Vegas councilman Wendell Waite. The group decided to organize a meeting of about 110 Mormon business, political, and educational figures—Mormon "opinion leaders," Hall called them—to hear both candidates. Laxalt spoke at the first meeting and was well received. A number of leaders continued to lean toward Reid, because, as they put it, Reid "is one of us."

At the second meeting, a stake president, by previous agreement, confronted Reid about his right-to-work stand. Reid hedged, but the Mormon leader continued to press the candidate until he was forced to state his position. Hall's group now had an issue. How, suggested the group, could a true Mormon support a candidate who opposed right-to-work and, by extension, questioned the authority of the church?

The Hall group quickly moved to mobilize support for Laxalt in the Mormon community. Laxalt continued to meet with the select group of "opinion leaders." Here, Laxalt faced the problem that was as old as Mormonism: "How do you capitalize with the LDS community," as Hall put it, while creating the appearance that the church is not involved? "The worst thing a Mormon can do," Hall explained, "is to try to use the church in this town. At the same time, you've got some very effective leaders and you recognize that if you get the opinion leaders, you can influence church members."

Hall and his staff set out to find three or four couples in each ward who were opinion leaders. Hall explained that he was careful to avoid bishops, who are the most influential church officials at this level of the hierarchy, to eliminate any charges of "church lobbying."

Hall wanted each opinion-leader couple to send a letter or postcard to every member in the ward. The problem, according to Hall, was how to get a church membership list without procuring it directly from the church. Church membership lists were reconstructed by members of his committee, said Hall. According to others, including Mormons who worked on the campaign, Hall used official church ward maps that were mounted on the walls of his office.

When election day rolled around, Hall's campaign proved successful. A significant number of church members had been convinced that Reid had betrayed the principles of his church and its conservative members, and Laxalt was elected.

Hall and his fellow Mormon politicians had mobilized the Mormon community without directly involving the church itself. No one had actually gotten up in sacrament meeting and told the Saints to vote for Paul Laxalt. Other accounts of politics in Las Vegas show that local church leaders have a distinct affinity for the old Tammany Hall techniques of ward heeling.

In the spring of 1980, politically active Mormon leaders decided to mobilize the brethren for Democratic party precinct meetings. It was not necessary to mobilize for the Republican party, they concluded, since it was already considered well within the Mormon camp. From the pulpit in ward houses across the city, it was announced that there would be fireside meetings to discuss the candidates and find out how the precinct meetings work. The meetings, which were held in private homes, were opened with a prayer. Then the chairperson asked if there were any non-Mormons present. When no one raised a hand at one meeting, the chairperson exclaimed, "That makes things easier."

The participants were handed a list of the church's position on a number of issues, including parent control of sex education, opposition to abortion, child abuse, homosexuality, and the ERA. Having communicated the church's position on these issues, the ground was prepared for the precinct meetings. At each precinct meeting, a well-known Mormon woman wearing a white corsage to signal the membership took up a visible position in the room. As each issue came up to a vote, the woman with the white corsage took the lead in voting.

Using these methods, the Las Vegas Mormon community has been able to exert a degree of political influence well beyond its numbers. Mormons played a significant role in Laxalt's election and reelection, tying them to Ronald Reagan's closest adviser on Capitol Hill.

THE SAINTS MARCH ON WASHINGTON

With the rise of Ronald Reagan, the Saints' loyalty to the GOP has brought the Mormons to the peak of their influence in Washington. The Washington area is also home for the largest concentration of Mormons east of the Mississippi, a direct result of the tremendous emphasis placed by the church on public service.

"There was a religious concept of service," said Robert Barker, a Washington attorney who has represented the church on numerous occasions. "A lot of our people have been ingrained with the idea that if they could serve the country, they should."

The roots of the Mormon community in Washington can be traced to the arrival of Apostle Reed Smoot in 1903. Smoot rose to be a powerful and influential Republican through ties that he developed with major industrialists as a champion of high tariffs. Senator William King, a Utah Democrat who served in the Senate from 1917 to 1941, came to be known as the unofficial mayor of Washington because of his leadership of the committee that oversaw the District of Columbia. Both Smoot and King encouraged young Mormons to come to Washington, and many of them, including BYU president Ernest L. Wilkinson and his law partner Robert Barker, attended law school there.

In the early years, the social and religious life of the Mormon community centered around the Smoot home since the community was too small to have a church building. Noticeable because of his absence was J. Reuben Clark, who remained cool to Smoot, perhaps because Smoot turned down his church-supported request for a job as Smoot's private secretary.

The New Deal, though bitterly opposed by most church leaders, brought a major influx of Utah Mormons. Many of them entered government service. Marriner Eccles headed the Federal Reserve System. Franklin D.

Richards, later a General Authority, became head of the Federal Housing Authority. Gene Merrill chaired the Federal Communications Commission. And numerous others served in lesser posts. Many Saints came in private capacities, including Ezra Taft Benson to work for the National Council of Farmer Cooperatives, and George Romney to lobby for the automobile industry. For or against, the New Deal proved to be an important testing ground for later leaders of the church.

In the postwar period, there were three Mormon networks that radiated through Congress and the bureaucracy. The most important of these was headed by Senator Wallace F. Bennett. Bennett, according to his son Robert, emulated Smoot and "quite deliberately set out to tie in all these bright young men coming east. Any church member who had problems could call Wallace Bennett's office to get help." Bennett was well enough connected with Eisenhower and Senate leader Everett Dirksen that he was able to get a Utahn appointed as head of the Federal Deposit Insurance Corporation, despite attempts by Senator Jacob Javits of New York to place a Rockefeller man in the position. In time, Bennett's administrative assistants, among them Barker and Neal A. Maxwell, either became influential Washington insiders or went on to major positions in the church.

The second network was built by Ezra Taft Benson at the Department of Agriculture. Benson not only crafted ties with the agribusiness establishment, he also picked as assistants a number of Saints who had risen through the merit system and were actually Democrats. Benson dominated the religious community at the same time, becoming stake president in 1940. His successor, J. Willard Marriott, began his business career as the owner of Washington's Hot Shoppes and later rose to be one of the major business advisers of the church.

The third network centered around the offices of the law firm of Wilkinson, Cragun, and Barker. Wilkinson had worked under Felix Frankfurter at Harvard before Frankfurter became a justice of the Supreme Court and had joined the law firm of prominent Republican Charles Evans Hughes. The Wilkinson firm carved out its niche in Washington by representing more Indian tribes than any other firm. It also represented the Saints before the church had its own legal department and continued to deal with church matters after the church established formal ties with a Salt Lake firm.

Church public relations were handled for a time by a Washington-based firm headed by Robert Mullen. Mullen was a non-Mormon, but he was joined at his firm by Bennett's son Robert. Mullen dealt directly with the Prophet, David O. McKay, filling an important void in the church's relations with the outside world before the advent of the Public Communications Department. "If a reporter from the *New York Times* were to call Salt Lake and ask for something as simple as membership statistics," said Robert Bennett, "they wouldn't know at the switchboard how to deal with him."

By the time they left church service, Mullen and Bennett had gained a degree of notoriety. Mullen Associates served as a front for the Central Intelligence Agency and was heavily involved in the Watergate scandal through E. Howard Hunt's work for Mullen Associates. Young Mormons from BYU, in fact, were recruited to do some spying for Nixon's plumbers group.

Mormons, because of their overseas experience as missionaries, their language skills, and their willingness to respect authority, have found careers in the CIA and the Federal Bureau of Investigation. Apostle Neal A. Maxwell worked for a brief period for the CIA. According to Dale Van Atta, a former *Deseret News* reporter and an associate of columnist Jack Anderson, Mormons are represented disproportionately in the CIA and the FBI because "they're trusted and there's a lot to be said for trust." One Mormon in the CIA, assistant general counsel Michael J. Barrett, has written that the Bible could be read as "a classic treatise on espionage," and that spying has the blessings of God.

By the late 1960s, the Mormon community in Washington was so large that not everyone knew everyone else personally, and social contacts diminished. Prior to this time, Mormons as diverse in their political attitudes as Ezra Taft Benson and Utah Congressman Frank Moss had enjoyed a harmonious religious life by agreeing not to discuss politics within the church. "We almost kept blinders on," said Bennett, "and talked instead about church programs and problems." By 1983, the Mormon community had grown to 35,000, with thirteen stakes spread throughout the suburbs of Maryland and Virginia. Unlike the old face-to-face community of the 1950s and 1960s with its ties to native Utah, at least half of these new members were converts.

Mormon influence fell to an all-time low during the Carter administration. "Carter had suffered a great defeat in Utah," said Jack Anderson, perhaps Washington's best-known Mormon, "and Carter was the kind of person who remembers who his friends are." But under his successor, Ronald Reagan, Utah's Mormon Republicans reestablished their role by being part of the western-based national coalition that carried him into the White House. "The LDS church," said Anderson, "has disproportionate representation under Reagan."

Under Reagan, Mormons seemed to be everywhere in Washington. Richard Wirthlin could be found in and about the Oval Office. T. H. Bell, former U.S. Commissioner of Education and Utah Commissioner of Education, joined the cabinet as Secretary of Education. Richard Richards, for a time, was chairman of the Republican National Committee. Rex E. Lee, the founding dean of the BYU Law School, was Solicitor General, while Mark Cannon was administrative assistant to Chief Justice Warren Burger. Robert Broadbent, as Commissioner of Reclamation, controlled the vast, publicly funded water system that keeps the West alive and booming and was in a position to distribute pork-barrel funds in those states. And on and on, from the office of the President, through the higher and lower reaches of the bureaucracy.

The entire Utah congressional delegation was Mormon, as well as a good part of Idaho's. Other prominent Mormon politicians included Senator Paula Hawkins of Florida and Congressmen Ronald Packard from southern California and Harry Reid from Nevada, who had finally turned his Mormonism to his advantage in his quest for higher office.

Orrin G. Hatch and Jake Garn were particularly influential among Senate conservatives. Hatch chaired the Labor Committee, where he continued the anti-union traditions of the church, and the constitutional subcommittee that would deal with the resurrected ERA, while Garn was chairman of the Committee on Banking, Housing, and Urban Affairs. Garn in particular had helped the church by providing federal funds for the huge Triad office development in Salt Lake City, which brought together Arab money, church real estate, and the church's media corporation, Bonneville International. After the resurrection of the ERA in 1983 (its defeat had been a major church goal), Hatch boasted to the *Deseret News* that "no member of Congress will have a greater ability to defeat the ERA than I."

Given his support among Mormons, Reagan was eager to reciprocate by calling attention to the Church Welfare Program, which he called a model of private initiative. "Today we are returning to the principle of that cannery," said Reagan after visiting a welfare cannery in Ogden, Utah, "and that is the principle of reward for honest toil, living within our means—and paying heed to the spiritual values that have always been the inner strength of America."

A HOUSE DIVIDED

Reagan, through his skillful appeals to these values and his rabid anticommunism, satisfied the Saints' yearning for authority and stability in a chaotic world. Ezra Taft Benson's suggestion, when he was appointed secretary of Agriculture, that the growing influence of the Saints in Washington somehow fulfilled one of Joseph Smith's prophecies was a preposterous fantasy. The Republican Saints are, however, part of a national conservative coalition that is both an important base of the Republican party and a faction that has often been manipulated by Reagan and his advisers to gain him popular support.

Utah Republicans, like the Reagan coalition, are split between conservative and centrist factions, and this split reflects the divisions within the church community over how to carry on the fight to protect Zion. Organizations, such as the Utah-based Freemen Institute and the various Utah groups fighting pornography, are the real grassroots of the conservative wing of the GOP. They are also eager to use the church ambience to mobilize their followers.

W. Cleon Skousen, the founder of the Freemen Institute, is a politician in what sociologist and historian Richard Hofstadter called the paranoid style. In his book *The Naked Capitalist*, which he describes as a study of The World's Secret Power Structure, Skousen wrote, "The world hierarchy of the dynastic super-rich is out to take over the entire planet, doing it with socialistic legislation where possible, but having no reluctance to use Communist revolution where necessary." In Skousen's view, the international bankers, politicians such as Dwight Eisenhower and Richard Nixon, and elite organizations, such as the Council on Foreign Relations, have worked together to carry out this master plan.

Skousen started his career as an FBI agent and rose to be an assistant to J. Edgar Hoover and head of a special project in the 1940s to identify subversives. At the urging of Ernest L. Wilkinson, he left the FBI to teach and work as an administrator at BYU and then served as police chief of Salt Lake City until he was fired after a dispute about department budget cuts with Mayor J. Bracken Lee. As police chief, he was known for running a model department, for his officers' arrest of people caught smoking on the street, and for a raid on the Alta Club that netted Lee himself in the midst of a card game.

The principal objective of the Freemen Institute is to restore the Constitution, which, according to Skousen, has been subverted by the rise of the socialistic welfare state and its intervention in the lives of its citizens. Skousen would like to see a strictly limited government, with no farm subsidies, no aid to education, no public transportation, no public lands or national parks, no Indian reservations, no regulatory agencies. To Skousen the original Constitution is close to perfect.

The institute's main program is a course of study on the Constitution. The institute also holds regular "Candidate Nights," an obligatory appearance for conservative politicians in Utah. The institute's California-based political arm, the Informed Voters League (IVL), involves itself in political campaigns.

The institute is most influential in Utah, where an estimated twenty-five members of the 1981 legislature were in some way affiliated with the Freemen or had gone through its training courses. Skousen also serves as a local contact for national conservative organizations, such as the National Conservative Political Action Committee and the Committee for the Survival of a Free Congress, and has ties with the Moral Majority, some of whose members are taking his course. The Freemen and the IVL are also active in Arizona and California, and Skousen sees himself building a national and international network of constitutionalists.

Skousen makes much of the fact that he founded the Freemen Institute at the urging of the late David O. McKay. Indeed the suggestion of church approval is integral to the work of the Freemen, and much of its work uses the church vernacular. Skousen sees American history as the fulfillment of prophecy and as part of the "pre-Millennial preparation of the earth." Like other Mormons, he believes that the Constitution is a divinely inspired instrument and that it will be saved after "hanging by a thread." Joseph Smith's picture has been used on Freemen literature. Members speak of being "called" to work with the institute and of their "testimony" about the Constitution. The institute has used church buildings, its meetings have been announced from the pulpit, and its literature has been used by church groups. Skousen's greatest coup in relation to the church is the regular appearance of Apostle Ezra Taft Benson at institute events and the presence of his son Mark as an institute vice president.

This attempt to use the church led the First Presidency to write a letter in 1979 warning members not to announce meetings of the Freemen Institute from the pulpit. Unlike the earlier warning about the John Birch Society, the church did not caution its members about the organization. Skousen, however, remained a controversial figure linked as he was to the pro-Benson forces within the church.

The Freemen Institute is much more effective than the Birch Society because it is based in Utah and its politics are dressed in the trappings of the church. Skousen and his institute, as heirs to the J. Bracken Lee tradition, are provincial populists sharing with many Mormons a sense of being buffeted about by national and international forces beyond their control and comprehension.

The Freemen, said David Irvine, Utah public utilities commissioner in 1980, are "without a doubt the most significant, influential force within the Utah Republican party." It would be a mistake, however, to see the Freemen as the only political trend among the Saints. Utah voters still show a great degree of independence. While generally voting Republican, they have elected Democratic governors since 1968 and the right wing of the Republican party suffered some serious setbacks in the 1982 election.

The more sophisticated members of the church hierarchy see both the Freemen and Benson's politics as fringe phenomena that detract from the carefully constructed image of the church as a conservative but forward-looking religious organization. These leaders, such as Gordon B. Hinckley, Neal A. Maxwell, and the members of the Special Affairs Committee, see the church's MX statement as conforming to the way in which they would like the church to be perceived.

The church's announcement in May 1981 that it opposed the basing of the MX missile system in the Utah-Nevada desert was a shock to the Gentile world. One national columnist called the church hypocritical, and the *New York Times* referred to the statement as "disturbingly sanctimonious." It was, however, a logical extension of the Saints' fight to protect Zion from the outside world. The Special Affairs Committee played the major role in making the decision to oppose the basing system. Previously, the church had made a number of general statements denouncing the arms race and deploring the possible use of nuclear weapons, but it had never specifically criticized a defense system. The plan to base the MX in the desert had raised a popular outcry against the missile system in the Great Basin. Utahns had become increasingly hostile to the military since a growing number of residents of southern Utah had contracted cancer, a phenomenon that they linked to the venting of radioactive material during the testing of nuclear weapons in nearby Nevada.

One Mormon who presented a convincing case against the MX to the Special Affairs Committee was Professor Edwin B. Firmage. Firmage, a law professor at the University of Utah and a former Hubert Humphrey aide, had participated in the Geneva disarmament talks of the 1960s. Firmage argued that opposition to the arms race was a part of both biblical and Mormon tradition. To prove this, he cited remarks by Brigham Young, but dwelt more on the attacks on militarism by that remarkable conservative, J. Reuben Clark.

During the New Deal, Clark, a major architect of U.S. intervention in Latin America before World War I, became an isolationist and later a critic of World War II. After the war, despite his virulent anticommunism, he became a full-blown pacifist, an opponent of placing military installations in Utah, a critic of the United States' nuclear attacks on Japan and was instrumental in getting the church to come out against a peacetime draft in 1945.

After Clark, there is a noticeable lack of continuity in the Saints' anti-militarist tradition until the MX statement. The key to understanding the church's position on the MX lies in their statement: "Our fathers came to this western area to establish a base from which to carry the gospel of peace to the peoples of the earth." With the MX acting as a giant sponge to absorb a Soviet nuclear attack, beloved Zion, presently the center of the Saints' universe, would be a major target, and the Saints would be the victims of genocide. Reagan's decision to move the MX to Wyoming was a measure of his respect for the views of the church.

In 1984, Ezra Taft Benson loomed in the Saints' future as the likely next Prophet. Church leaders grew increasingly alarmed that his brand of right-wing conservatism would come to overshadow the modernizing forces within the church as exemplified by the MX statement. Their fears were intensified when Benson told a BYU audience in 1980, "Those who would remove prophets from politics would take God out of government," and when he said of the Freemen, "I don't think there is any power on earth that can stop this work because it's right and it has the Lord's approval." Despite his views, many argued that Benson would respect the calling of Prophet and would be tempered by his new office. Jack Anderson offered the opposite opinion. "My reports from friends in the Twelve," he said in 1983, "is that he isn't tempered."

Benson and Skousen are also the connection to the pre-1890 tradition in church political thought. Benson spelled this out in his 1952 speech at BYU when he described his appointment to the Eisenhower cabinet as the fulfillment of Joseph Smith's prophecy that the Saints would assume leadership in Washington. Ernest L. Wilkinson expressed the same idea when he wrote in his diary in 1958 about "the belief that I have that eventually the Mormon Church will mean more to the world than the American Congress or the American Government." And Professor J. D. Williams found the same attitude in his high priest's quorum in 1980 when its members said that they were looking forward to the establishment of a theocracy that would "lay down the law."

There is nothing monolithic about the political conservatism of the Saints. Like the national Republican coalition, they are torn between an activist right and a more worldly and sophisticated center. The Democrats too can claim their fair share of loyal followers in Utah, including Governor Scott M. Matheson, Salt Lake City Mayor Ted Wilson, former congressman Wayne Owens, and law professor Ed Firmage. Despite the hierarchy's repeated insistence that the church only involves itself with moral issues, the Saints cannot leave politics alone. It is a compulsion they cannot resist. Besides making the Republican Saints a force in Washington and increasingly in states where their membership is growing, that compulsion is threatening to become a major factor in contributing to splits within the church in the post-Kimball era.

CHAPTER FOUR

THE RISE OF THE MONEY MANAGERS: ECONOMIC POWER IN THE SERVICE OF THE LORD

When the short, pleasant-looking, conservatively dressed man entered the twenty-eight-story highrise in downtown Salt Lake City in the summer of 1982 to go to his modestly furnished office on the eleventh floor, he faced a full schedule of committee meetings, budget conferences, and staff discussions. He was a church money manager, an accountant with as solid a grounding in profit-and-loss statements as in the Doctrines and Covenants.

There would be the Budget Committee, the Investment Advisory Committee, a discussion with some staff from the Presiding Bishopric's Office, the Business Committee of the Deseret Management Corporation, some informal staff meetings on a new Kansas City investment, another on tax considerations regarding other property, an unscheduled phone call to check on the health of one of the General Authorities, and so on and so forth.

The First Counselor in the First Presidency, N. Eldon Tanner, was, of course, present at several of the sessions, frequently quiet for most of the meetings, occasionally asking some clarifying questions, only intervening over some important issue. Many of the committee meetings were pro forma. "Like most boards of directors," the money manager had commented, "decisions are somewhat perfunctory." Anything controversial had to be decided higher up, outside the meetings, in the more rarefied, less defined reaches of the Quorum of the Seventy.

Yet there was not exactly a direction, a strategy per se, handed down from the top. Tanner was far less active because of his Parkinson's disease (and would pass away within the year). Franklin D. Richards was still important and jealously guarded his investment domain, but he too was getting on in years, and would eventually be relieved of his role. The top management at Zions Securities and Beneficial Development Corporation never operated as full, autonomous policymakers, the way their counterparts did at the other holding companies and real estate groups in the city.

Several of the junior members of the Quorum, among them Marvin J. Ashton, L. Tom Perry, and even Thomas S. Monson, the chairman of the board at the *Deseret News*, sat in on these meetings, and vied for the extraordinarily important and powerful role of top church financial officer and money man, now that Tanner's time was passing. But nobody could fill the presidential counselor's shoes, and even Tanner had recognized the limits of what he alone could do and had accomplished.

"We're getting to be like a corporation more and more each day," the money man, a Tanner protégé, had remarked several months earlier, but this was not an ordinary bureaucracy.

The office building looked like an office building—some even called it the Power Tower—filled, as it was, with conservatively dressed men, sitting at their modest desks, exchanging interoffice memos like other corporation men would do. But there were differences. "Elevate Your Thoughts," read the signs in the elevators; dress codes were strict and pervasive; and the paintings in the main lobby and throughout the building included New Testament scenes and portraits of church Prophets.

If the church were a multinational, the money men knew, not everything could be kept secret. A story had circulated within the bureaucracy about how the state of Utah, in preparing a prospectus for the bond market, wanted to include a section on the largest employers in the state. They called over to the personnel department and asked how many people the church employed in Utah. Personnel then went to the General Authorities and the word came back: no figures. The state was then obliged to put in a footnote saying that the church was "believed to be" one of the largest employers in the state of Utah.

Then, there were the AP reporters who tried to put together an estimate of what the church was worth. Others have tried also, and they have all been somewhat off base. They say the church is big—like a Fortune 500 company with $2 billion in assets. And the church *is* big, but not in the way it has usually been presented.

There are, of course, the thirteen radio and TV stations, the four insurance companies, the hotel, the newspaper, the big farms in Florida (with 300,000 acres of land near Disney World), Georgia, and California, the real estate companies (which control four square blocks of prime real estate in the center of Salt Lake City), the clothing mills, the book company, all the schools, the welfare farms and industries, the big department store downtown, the investment portfolio. And it's true the church could tomorrow divest its stock holdings, say, in Utah and Idaho Inc., the big farm processor and distributor, and sell it on the open market. And if it was sold for the approximately $16 a share that it had been trading at during 1983, why the church might get about $30 million from that alone. But the church was not about to do that. U-I was one of the church's oldest companies. In fact, the church was continually putting money into U-I, $10 million more, in one instance, rather than divest what it had.

No, the real story was not the companies and investments, big as they might be. It was the income *within* the church that was so impressive. And the money managers now controlled it because of the policies that Tanner had implemented. That was where a lot of the wealth of the church could be found.

Also there were the land holdings from the wards and the stakes, and the welfare farms. One member pointed out how his stake a number of years ago purchased a farm for $150,000 that by 1980 was worth $1.5 million. In California alone, the figures from a few years back were impressive: In Los Angeles County, land holdings were worth $84 million and 84 percent tax exempt; Orange County $36 million, 45 percent tax exempt; Alameda County $14 million, 82.5 percent tax exempt; Santa Clara County $13 million, and 94 percent exempt, and the list went on county by county.

And then, of course, there are the tithes, the ten percent of a member's income that goes to the church. "The Lord, to whom one owes tithing, is in a position of a preferred creditor. If there is not enough to pay all creditors, He would be paid first," Second Counselor Marion G. Romney had said.

As part of its modernization effort, the church in 1983 created a computerized system for tithing. Members would get a tithing slip that they would fill out, place the white original in the envelope with their donation, then give the envelope to their bishop. The member would keep the yellow copy for his records. Then, once those slips went into the computer, the member could receive an itemized "year-to-date Tithing and Donations Record," as the church called it, in July and November. Once established, the money would come in right on schedule.

The money man remarked how members had been financially pinched lately. The Reagan recession had taken its toll, and some of the other contributions had been off. But not tithing. About forty percent continued to tithe, as the money man pointed out. Now, not everybody tithed the ten percent, and of course it would vary from place to place, but when you added it up, then you were talking about annual tithing income in the high hundreds of millions of dollars. And if the church continues to grow, it wouldn't be long before it reached $1 billion a year in tithing income alone.

Yes, the church is big, and its corporate revolution appears complete. It was Tanner's greatest achievement. Still, in the end, one had to come back to the fact that this is a bureaucracy of a church, not a corporation. These are money managers, but unlike any other kind of money managers. The church office building from the outside looks like any other nondescript highrise that now graces the Salt Lake skyline. But inside, things *are* different. The wealth and power, in the end, come down to the essentials: The church is in the business of expanding the church.

And today, as the money manager and his colleagues enter the building that dwarfs the Temple to the east and the church's spiffy new malls to the south, it is clear that these offices at 50 East North Temple have become the headquarters for the much-vaunted and poorly understood economic arm of the church.

THE AUTONOMOUS COMMONWEALTH

The complex and distinctive history of the Church of Jesus Christ of Latter-day Saints is most striking in its changing economic institutions and policies. Over the last two decades, in particular, the Mormon church has gained a reputation as a wealthy and powerful organization. More than other areas, the economic and investment activities of the church appear to be a mystery, particularly since the church eliminated its annual financial report after 1958.

Journalists, critics both inside and outside the church, and many of the church's own loyal members have puzzled over the "real" worth of the church and have attempted to develop an "educated" guesstimate. The actual figure is a jealously guarded secret, as N. Eldon Tanner demonstrated in an interesting exchange with California reporter Jeffrey Kaye in 1976. Kaye asked the church's economic leader what the church owned, how much it invested, and its income. Tanner replied, "We don't care how many people or who knows what we have," declaring that income and expenditures were "never disclosed."

"But you stopped doing that [disclosing income and expenditures]," Kaye went on.

"Yes, years ago," Tanner replied.

"For what reason?" Kaye asked.

"We just didn't think it was necessary," Tanner curtly replied.

"But how do you respond to critics who suggest. . . ," Kaye pressed.

Tanner, interrupting, declared, "We don't respond!"

"You don't respond?" Kaye asked.

"We respond by silence," Tanner concluded.

This interplay of silence and mystery has whetted the appetite of many an investigative journalist. In the process, a key element gets lost regarding not just how much income the church receives, but how it's spent and how the decisions are made about both the generation and expenditure of Mormon revenues and assets. Those processes, far more than the dollar value of the church, tell us about the changes taking place in contemporary Mormonism and the problems the church will face in the coming years.

The fear of Mormon economic power has been a significant element in the history of the church, though for substantially different reasons, during the nineteenth and twentieth centuries. Joseph Smith's experiments with the Law of Consecration and Stewardship and the United Order were at once social and economic, combining communitarian with theocratic impulses, as the Saints attempted to create a viable economic and political base in the middle border area.

In Utah, the cooperative movement and attempts to develop industries and relatively diverse agriculture, ranging from sugar beet to cotton production, were crucial in the attempt to establish both an *independent* commonwealth and the beginnings of the Kingdom of God on earth. Even after Utah became a territory and the laying of the railroads ended the Mormon's comparative isolation in the West, the church leadership still strove for near nation-state status, with Brigham Young's last experiments with United Orders a final, futile attempt to preserve the economic and social uniqueness of the Mormon state.

In several ways, the nineteenth-century Mormon experiment resembled an undeveloped nation seeking self-sufficiency, subject as it was to economic and political forces (such as the advent of the mining economy) beyond its control. Leonard J. Arrington's monumental *Great Basin Kingdom*, the most comprehensive analysis of this period, has been studied by Third World students as a way to look at the development of their own countries.

The Mormon economic experiment really never had a chance. As early as 1862, with the passage of the Morrill Anti-Bigamy Act, which limited the value of property the church could hold in its own name, the Mormon commonwealth came under siege, whipsawed between eastern capital and the federal government. The economic attacks culminated with the passage of the Edmunds-Tucker Act in 1887, which formally dissolved the Corporation of the Church of Jesus Christ of Latter-day Saints, the formal entity holding title to most church-run businesses and properties, such as their banks, their cooperative store, their industries, and land holdings. A series of economic raids followed, and though the church leadership maintained a short-lived resistance (organized in part through the transferal of church property into individual Mormon hands), accommodation and eventual integration seemed inevitable.

By the 1890s, a series of trade-offs was established: for the Mormons, the granting of statehood to Utah in 1896, amnesty for previously persecuted Mormon polygamists, and most important in the economic sphere, the restoration of church property. In exchange, the church abandoned polygamy and dissolved its political arm, the People's Party. In the economic sphere, the crippled church was hard pressed to compete with Gentile businessmen. "The Raid had finally culminated in the long-sought goal of statehoood," Leonard Arrington wrote, "but had produced capitulation in many areas of Mormon uniqueness, not the least of which was the decline in economic power and influence of the church. The temporal Kingdom, for all practical purposes, was dead—slain by the dragon of Edmunds-Tucker."

The economic accommodation was, in many ways, the most far reaching. When church leader Heber J. Grant traveled to Wall Street in 1890 to deal with the church's mounting deficits and loss of economic control due to Edmunds-Tucker, he began a process of linking the church to Wall

Street and the centers of economic power in the East that continues to this day. Grant arranged loans from the New York banks, but he, in effect, mortgaged the church. Several of the church-owned or -controlled companies such as Utah Power and Light or Utah-Idaho Sugar passed into the hands of Eastern financiers, such as E. H. Harriman and Henry O. Havermeyer, in the next two decades, and other properties were heavily mortgaged. By the turn of the century, Grant biographer Ronald Walter wrote, Grant's "New York loans wrapped the cords of American finance around the Utah Zion as surely as a Lilliputian net fastening Gulliver. Hereafter Church leaders would not only feel increasingly at ease with the ways of American capitalists, but they would be beholden, at least for the short run, for their services."

By 1918, when Heber J. Grant assumed the presidency of the church, Utah had already evolved into a more dependent—and integrated—economy.

In the 1920s and 1930s, the Mormon West witnessed a protracted decline in both its agricultural activities and the commerce of its towns and cities. Without a strong industrial base and with the mining economy in the hands of Gentiles and Easterners, the church's economic activities in this period were largely defensive in nature. Some assets were sold, such as an insolvent bank in Salt Lake City, and income came largely from tithing. The Grant generation, as they entered the world of private enterprise, demonstrated a new attitude toward the larger national economy, but Mormon businessmen were still part of a local economy that was vastly overshadowed by the East.

THE DEFICIT SPENDER

When J. Reuben Clark presented the church's financial report for 1945 at the Spring 1946 conference, the church appeared to be in sound financial health. Tithing income over the past decade had kept pace with state and national personal income levels, and there had been no significant percentage rise in the level of church spending. The church-owned businesses were, by and large, operating in the black, and if any fear existed for Clark, it was that profit levels would grow *too high*. "There is no difficulty making money," Clark told a meeting of the Quorum, "the question is making too much."

For Clark, the purpose of the church's business activities was to "help stabilize the financial and industrial conditions to the direct benefit of all our people in the areas affected," and not "for the mere purpose of making money." During the war, Clark had pared down church expenditures to twenty-seven percent of annual revenues, keeping the huge reserve as a means of coping with what he anticipated would be a postwar recession.

During the war, church activities, particularly outside the United States, had been severely circumscribed. Construction activities, such as the building of chapels and schools, and educational efforts, such as the printing and dissemination of materials, had been postponed. In contrast, the land values of long-term church properties in such areas as Utah, California, Mexico, England, and Canada had heavily inflated, providing a valuable base for any future activities.

After the war, spending levels began to increase, with Clark complaining that such increases were occurring "at a dizzying rate." In 1948, Clark declared, "I should like to urge the people to cease building cathedrals for ward meetinghouses, and to stop furnishing them as if they were palaces."

Though the postwar recession never did develop, Clark up until 1951 had managed to slow the long-anticipated expansion of church projects and increase in overall expenditures.

That year, however, a church financial officer reported to the recently installed President David O. McKay that a new dawn in the financial history of the church had begun. A financial turnaround would indeed occur during the David O. McKay presidency, with its dramatic increase in missionary activity, particularly outside the United States. With new counselors Stephen L. Richards and then Henry D. Moyle providing direction, the McKay presidency, particularly during the 1950s and early 1960s, marked a dramatic upsurge in church spending and overall economic activities as the church threw its resources into its missionary program.

The key to this change was Moyle, who burst on the scene in the 1950s, first as a member of the Twelve and then as Second and later First Counselor to McKay (1959 and 1961, respectively). Moyle, the son of a former assistant treasury secretary during the Woodrow Wilson administration was a conservative Democrat. He had been a lawyer and an oil man (he owned Wasatch Oil in the speculative postwar energy and mineral boom period).

Moyle quickly made his presence felt inside church councils. He was an aggressive personality with, as his daughter put it, "a sense of mission." Moyle immediately embraced McKay's missionary thrust, and as he gained control over the church's financial areas, he pushed strongly for the use of funds for expansionary purposes.

Moyle became the church's first deficit spender. His attitude was summed up by the principle of Spend Now, Tithe Later. He felt the financial reserves were far too high, and that by spending the funds now for new buildings and increased missionary programs, the payback would be realized later. As church membership grew, Moyle thought tithing income would undoubtedly increase; "When my father had money, he would spend it," was the way one of Moyle's daughters put it.

During the Moyle period the church established its current reputation as a wealthy and powerful institution. A 1962 article by Neil Morgan in *Esquire* cited the figure of $1 million a day in church income, a figure supplied by Moyle to Salt Lake Mayor J. Bracken Lee, who then passed it on to Morgan. That figure soon became a standard reference point since the church had stopped reporting income and expenditures in 1959, though later accounts also failed to pick up on Moyle's statement that the money was being spent as fast as it was coming in.

In fact, reserves were declining. In order to maintain the level of spending, Moyle began to dispose of long-standing church assets. In 1960, for example, Zions Bank was sold to a local Mormon financier. Rather than reduce expenditures, Moyle only seemed to step up his activities, as if his personal financial mission had now become coincidental with the church's overall objectives. As a church leader, he had a sense of urgency about him, and, as his daughter recalled, felt he had a certain amount of work to perform before Judgment Day.

While at the peak of his power in the early 1960s, Moyle began to run into serious opposition from church leaders. Moyle's main antagonist was Harold B. Lee, the leader of the Correlation movement, then just taking hold. Lee and Moyle were an interesting contrast in both personality and perspective, and they provided two key poles in the church. Lee was circumspect where Moyle was voluble, disciplined where Moyle was expansive, a formulator of bureaucracy where Moyle was a man of action. Where Moyle's dictum was spend and expand, Lee's was centralize and control. "Moyle was a generalist who liked to get things done," remarked church financial figure J. Alan Blodgett. "Lee, on the other hand, was a detail man who liked to keep things in order."

With support from church bureaucrats, some of whom felt that Moyle had brought the church to the breaking point, Lee and others in the Twelve attempted to reduce Moyle's power base. Moyle's opponents had a formidable ally in a new member of the Twelve—Moyle's obvious replacement in the financial sphere—Canadian businessman Nathan Eldon Tanner. Apostle Hugh B. Brown was another of Moyle's antagonists, and he played a role in bringing Tanner, who was his nephew, into the hierarchy to help guide the church's business activities. Tanner never directly contested Moyle and his activities, but when Moyle, under the strain of his whirlwind of activities, had a heart attack in early 1963, Tanner, was the man on the spot. When Moyle died several months later, a new First Presidency was organized with Tanner as Second Counselor and his uncle, Hugh B. Brown, as First Counselor. The deficit spending days were over, and a new, more corporatelike era for the church had begun.

THE NEW MANAGERS

Like his uncle, Nathan Eldon Tanner grew up in the Mormon colony of Cardston in Alberta, a colony established in the late 1880s as a refuge from the antipolygamy raids. Though various attempts to create major economic enterprises in the Canadian colony had failed or achieved only limited success, Mormon influence in the province was strong. When the newly

formed Social Credit party was organized in 1935, several Mormons became candidates, including Tanner, who was then the principal of the local
high school.

The Social Credit party was a populist farmers' movement that called for
new forms of government spending. Though not socialist in its orientation,
the Social Creditors were hostile to the traditional forces of capital, such as
the eastern banks, because of their control of the western Canadian economy.

Years later, when Tanner became the financial leader of the church and
counselor to four church presidents, questions were raised about Tanner's
political philosophy. Known for his occasional support for liberal positions
within the church on such matters as civil rights and opposition to the John
Birch Society, Tanner, many of his liberal supporters had assumed, was
something of a "socialist" in his early years. The socialist bugaboo had in
fact been a concern of the Salt Lake leadership in the years that Tanner
served in the Social Credit government. In one famous encounter in 1953,
a group of Salt Lake leaders, led by Harold B. Lee, sought out Tanner to
see if he was worthy. They directly confronted Tanner as to whether he and
his Social Credit allies were socialists. Tanner reassured Lee that he wasn't
and pointed to the fact that the Social Credit party had dropped much of its
radical program.

Tanner's early engagement in politics and ultimately business matters
was more a reflection of circumstances than choice. With no real experience in either political or economic matters, Tanner, like other Social
Credit candidates, was drawn into a social movement that looked outside
the traditional power centers for its leadership. When Social Credit swept
into office in a landslide victory in 1935, Tanner was no more or less
qualified than the other newcomers to lead his party in the legislature. Yet
his organizational skills and modest personality made him an attractive
figure to the party leadership, and he was chosen to be the speaker of the
Alberta house. Within a couple of years he would become Minister of
Lands and Mines.

Tanner quickly established himself as the leading figure within the government regarding natural-resource policy. He opposed the programs of
the more radical wing of the party, which emphasized confiscating oil
property and nationalizing oil companies. "Minister Tanner," his biographers noted, "felt that appropriate regulations and incentives in a free-
market system would accomplish greater good than under any other type
of economy."

The Tanner approach toward development of Alberta's oil and gas properties soon became the centerpiece of the overall Social Credit program,
which, by the end of the war, spoke in terms of "sensible free enterprise."
To Tanner, that meant incentives for exploration, an active search for new
sources of capital outside the province (including investors from England

and America), and a system of regulated production to allow for a degree of conservation of the area's overall resources. Tanner worked closely with oil men throughout the world who saw the development of the Alberta fields as a major new source of energy in the 1940s. One of the most important of these companies was Imperial Oil Limited, owned by a Canadian Mormon whose firm's exploration activities helped bring Alberta's fields to the attention of the industry.

Within a few months after Tanner stepped down from his government post, he was reenlisted by the provincial and central government to be the chairman and chief executive officer of a newly formed company, the Trans-Canada Pipe Lines Company Limited. Trans-Canada had been established to build a distribution system to send Alberta's natural gas eastward. Tanner was selected in part because of his negotiating skills and acceptability to both industry and government interests. Though he never became the most important figure in the pipeline development, he remained in the thick of the action for more than three years, achieving public recognition as well as occasional criticism.

Through his experience both as minister and as chairman of Trans-Canada, Tanner had become a person who understood economic power. He had gained respect in the corporate community, despite his populist background. He had become a man of business, an approach defined and framed by corporate influences, while at the same time he continued to convey the image of a modest, rather self-effacing bureaucrat.

After he resigned from Trans-Canada in 1957, Tanner remained active in the corporate world, joining the boards of several companies with which he had done business either through his work on the pipeline or as Minister of Lands and Mines. Then, suddenly, as he prepared to retire in 1960, he was called to Salt Lake to be an assistant to the Twelve, setting out at the age of sixty-two on an entirely new career.

When Tanner arrived in Salt Lake, the church under Moyle was in the midst of extremely ambitious expansion plans. Prior to 1960, the church had maintained a modest investment program centered around Zions Bank, which owned a great deal of land and held substantial cash reserves. But with Moyle's spending strategy and the rapid increase in building activities under a new program headed by Moyle ally Wendell Mendenhall, the reserves were drying up quickly, even after the sale of Zions Bank.

When Tanner became Second Counselor in 1963, he quickly moved to establish a new direction in the financial area. Within a couple of years, the powerful Church Building Committee would be dissolved and a new method of contracting and accounting established for future projects. Many construction projects were suspended, including plans to build a massive downtown skyscraper to serve as the new church headquarters.

Via a new budgeting approach, local funds gathered at the stake and ward level were now sent to Salt Lake, where they were to be handled by

Tanner's newly reorganized bureaucracy. Previously, those funds were simply deposited in local banks and savings and loans. Now, under Tanner's new system, funds would be invested at higher interest. That way, funds would be returned to the local organizations at a higher yield, while at the same time the new, centralized accounts helped reestablish the church's overall reserves and provided, for the first time since the sale of the bank, a new pool of investment capital.

By the mid-1960s, the Tanner approach meant a more conservative spending policy and a new, more expansive investment strategy. Tanner's first major initiative was in the area of broadcasting. In 1964, Mormon media provided a substantial and lucrative income base. It included the afternoon *Deseret News* daily newspaper, which operated primarily in the black, a book publishing and distribution operation for church books and other materials, and a broadcast arm that included KSL radio (AM and FM) and KSL-TV, Salt Lake's CBS outlet, and the CBS radio and TV outlets in Seattle, KIRO-TV, KIRO radio (AM), and KSEA radio (FM).

The broadcast area seemed most ripe for expansion, both because of its investment potential and because it was an important way to spread church influence. Leaders, such as Harold B. Lee, were fascinated by and fearful of television's ability to influence family and society and were more than willing to give the green light to expansion.

Tanner's first move was to create a new corporate entity, Bonneville International Corporation, to serve as the overall structure for broadcasting acquisitions. Arch L. Madsen, a broadcasting executive who had been hired to run the KSL operation, was named chief executive officer of Bonneville.

Bonneville, under Madsen's leadership, went on a buying spree. Radio stations were acquired in Los Angeles, Chicago, Kansas City, Dallas, San Francisco, and New York, and a production facility was created with headquarters in Los Angeles to produce commercial TV or film packages, while a second facility was established to produce commercials and public-service announcements. Bonneville also established a communications-satellite system with more than 550 stations for beaming messages and programs, particularly to countries south of the border.

Madsen's own inclinations about Bonneville mirrored some of the debates inside the church about the appropriate role of the financial arm of the Kingdom. On the one hand, Madsen, sharp-tongued and acerbic, was an active, ideological member of his church, who railed against the "trash" on radio and TV and defined broadcasting as a key tool for "building the Kingdom." On the other hand, Madsen, like Tanner, was strongly motivated by bottom-line considerations, particularly since the amount of operating and investment capital required for Bonneville was far greater than any of the church's other media, even the *Deseret News*, which during this period was going through a major upgrading of its facilities. Further,

Madsen was aware—and sensitive to—FCC regulations, particularly regarding cross-ownership (having newspaper and broadcast facilities in the same market) problems in Salt Lake and accusations of church intervention in the area of news and public affairs.

The intervention and censorship issues were particularly sensitive at KSL, CBS's Salt Lake outlet. Through the 1960s and 1970s, the TV station was rocked by a series of crises regarding the church's role, stemming from the staff's attempt to develop a reputation for professionalism, management's desire to keep the FCC at bay, and the church leadership's desire to protect its own interests.

In one scathing internal memo, written at the height of a controversy over a KSL documentary on "Mormon Women and Depression," a KSL producer declared that there had been a long precedent at the station "of handling stories sensitive to the Church in an arbitrary manner. I'm aware of many stories which were axed or modified because of either direct pressure from people outside the KSL management who were in the Church leadership hierarchy or because of fears of such pressure." KSL news director Spencer J. Kinard, soon after this incident, resigned his position, telling AP reporter David Briscoe that he had been "under long-time constant pressure in the news director post" and that the pressure "came both from news sources and from station management." Kinard concluded that "station management in the past has been concerned about the impact of news stories on its business and ideological concerns."

Yet Madsen and Bonneville were able to avoid FCC scrutiny and keep KSL's staff in line. The FCC situation was helped by the work of Rosel Hyde, himself a former FCC commissioner and later a Bonneville attorney at the church's Washington law firm, Wilkinson, Cragun, and Barker. The cross-ownership problem was ostensibly reduced when Bonneville sold its KSL-FM radio outlet to Roy W. Simmons, the Mormon businessman who had earlier been the key figure in the sale of Zions Bank. This "new" FM station kept the same staff, format, and overall direction, hiring a Bonneville subsidiary to advise the station on programming. And the staff problems at KSL-TV were ultimately reduced when some of the more difficult staff members moved on to other jobs and former news director Kinard came back to his old job. Kinard declared that the days of church intervention had passed and had, in fact, been quite insignificant all along.

The tension between bottom-line considerations and church control also cropped up in a variety of other ways. In musical programming for the radio stations, for example, Bonneville management desperately tried to avoid hard rock, as Madsen, along with other church and Bonneville officials, complained of the "filthy, suggestive lyrics." Further, Madsen was aware of the musical sentiments of Apostle Boyd K. Packer, the General Authority who made music and the arts his sphere of influence. "Learn to control your thoughts," Packer warned Mormon youth, declaring that hard rock was akin to pornography. Yet Madsen realized that by the 1970s, hard rock programming was among the most profitable. Even those stations owned by Mormon businessman J. Willard Marriott, such as KFMY in Provo, Utah, were dishing out the "heavy metal sound," as one church p.r. man put it. Madsen and Bonneville managers played with compromise formulas, such as the introduction of disco on some of their stations, while others, particularly Bonneville's Los Angeles outlet, tried experimenting with a mix of soft and harder sounds, which was labeled the "brite life" formula.

Ultimately, the managers and financial people emerging in Tanner's new bureaucracy pushed Bonneville toward a bottom-line position. While Tanner and the church leadership spoke internally of Bonneville and the other media as "businesses which assist the church in carrying the gospel message," they declared to those outside the church that Bonneville, in fact, was designed primarily as a money-making operation.

As with the Bonneville situation, Tanner needed to sort out a number of conflicting interests and objectives in the economic sphere. The Moyle period left a legacy of overlapping bureaucratic structures and a lack of clear procedural methods regarding expenditures and investments. Tanner set out not only to restructure the lines of authority and the role of the bureaucracy, but to provide a new direction for investment and expenditure decisions.

Despite Moyle's draw-down of reserves, Tanner could rely on a significant asset pool to undertake his program. The church still maintained a number of independent businesses, some dating back to the early twentieth century, such as the insurance companies, among them Beneficial Life, and agricultural companies, such as Utah-Idaho Inc. The church also owned a great deal of land, including a 300,000 acre ranch in Florida, a purchase engineered by Moyle.

There were several problems with the existing setup. On the one hand, there was no central structure for both tax and management purposes to handle all the church's income-producing assets. Further, many of the business decisions were being made by General Authorities who had neither the background nor the understanding to implement an effective investment policy. Without some kind of centralized structure to give the new and growing bureaucracy greater freedom to operate, Tanner's strategy would never get off the ground.

To move in this direction, Tanner in 1967 created the Deseret Management Corporation to serve as the umbrella for all the income-producing properties. These included Bonneville and the Deseret Book Company, the Hotel Utah, the ZCMI department store, several of the agribusiness entities, and the real estate and investment arms of the church—Zions Securities and the Beneficial Development Corporation. Other independent entities were established, such as a new trust company to handle an expanding investment pool generated by a greater accumulation of trusts and endowments. Tanner also consolidated the church's financial position in several of the independent businesses, such as the insurance companies.

Aside from all the structural changes, Tanner pushed heavily in the direction of "professionalizing" the growing bureaucracy and providing a more businesslike environment for day-to-day operations. Tanner established an in-house law department that quickly expanded into the areas of tax, real estate, and other financial matters. Such companies as the Hotel Utah and ZCMI became more "modernized" in their marketing techniques and sought out ways to identify themselves and their marketing area as more cosmopolitan and no longer cast themselves in traditional church garb.

Despite the changes, Tanner continued to have troubles with the changing bureaucracy because of a lack of checks and balances and the need, among other things, for a centralized and computerized accounting system. He was able to make his move in this area after a 1969 embezzlement scandal. An employee of the Building Division, with an accomplice within the church, was able to write and steal checks, ultimately embezzling $600,000 and giving away twenty-eight color television sets and twenty-seven cars. This feat was made possible by the church's archaic and overlapping bureaucratic structures. Tanner immediately set up a computer network and created a new computer company, which he placed under the Deseret Management umbrella.

Tanner's biggest hurdle was resistance at the top. Individual General Authorities had over the years carved out their own fiefdoms, such as the newspaper or the church schools or even some of the businesses, and were reluctant to part with any of their power. "There was criticism from members of the Twelve," Tanner would later comment, "because they couldn't see why the First Presidency would hand that [power] over to the Deseret Management Corporation."

With sniping from other General Authorities and uneven results in the transformation of the bureaucracy, Tanner's imprint on church economic policy by the late 1960s was, at best, incomplete. His work had been further hampered by the continuing battles within the top leadership as David O. McKay became incapacitated. Tanner's uncle, Hugh B. Brown, an early supporter of the Tanner revolution, had his hands full with his archnemesis, Ezra Taft Benson. Tanner's problems were further compounded when the easily manipulated McKay added new counselors to the First Presidency, especially a former assistant to the Twelve named Thorpe B. Isaacson, who was known for his wheeler-dealer activities in business and politics.

Thorpe Isaacson represented a very different kind of business figure than Tanner. The two, in their own ways, symbolized the 1960s' contrasting approaches toward economic matters. Tanner was methodical, organizationally oriented, conservative in accounting and budgeting areas, and consistently looking to establish corporate-style chains of command.

Isaacson, on the other hand, was a deal maker. His rapid rise within the church hierarchy stemmed in part from his attempts to curry favor with higher-ups, at times by working out lucrative, if questionable, deals. His relationship with Apostle LeGrand Richards, according to one church insider from an elite Mormon family, was key to Isaacson's success, as Richards became Isaacson's backer within the hierarchy. With Isaacson constantly looking to cash in on his connections and exploring deals in everything from insurance to Las Vegas real estate, he became, by the mid-1960s, a power in his own right.

To many of the new Mormon money managers and bureaucrats, as well as to many of those outside the bureaucracy, Thorpe Isaacson's business deals fell into a shady area. His promotion to presidential counselor confused and upset many of them. One church employee at that time recalled that when Isaacson had a heart attack a few months after assuming the counselor's position (thereby removing him from decision making), Harold B. Lee remarked to the employee that the "Lord works in his own mysterious ways."

By 1970, Tanner had weathered the challenges and moved to further consolidate his changes. He was now aided by Lee, who began to dominate church organizational matters through his Correlation program. Like Tanner, Lee was interested in a professionalization of the church bureaucracy, and though his efforts were in organizational matters, he was sympathetic to Tanner's direction. When Lee became president of the church in 1972, he created, at Tanner's urging, a study group that was mandated to analyze how the church should organize itself and utilize its resources. The group was headed by the chairman of Nabisco, Lee S. Bickmore.

The Bickmore study became a pivotal event in Tanner's attempt to restructure the church's economic arm. Bickmore was one of several extremely influential Mormon businessmen, such as Nixon Treasury Secretary and Chicago banker David Kennedy and Washington hotel man J. Willard Marriott, who functioned outside formal church structures, yet through their advisory capacity and knowledge of the business world became critical participants in church policy matters.

The Bickmore group met once a month to look at church procedures and then related them to management principles. The group argued that the church's organizational problems were related to its "stick organization," in which all decisions went straight up and down until they reached clear up to the First Presidency. That not only put an intolerable burden on the decision-making apex, but also meant extraordinary delays in getting things approved and led to a bureaucracy that failed to innovate or function in a flexible manner.

With Tanner's blessing, the Bickmore group came up with a number of recommendations. The key proposal was that a major bureaucratic division of labor should be established: All ecclesiastical functions of the church would fall under the purview of the First Presidency and the Quorum of the Twelve, and all temporal matters, which included the building programs, welfare, real estate, the production of materials, and much of the international activities, would fall under the supervision of the Presiding Bishopric's Office (PBO).

By the mid-1970s, the PBO had come fully under Tanner's influence. The top figure in the PBO, Presiding Bishop Victor L. Brown, fifteen years younger than Tanner, had also been born in Cardston, Alberta, Canada. Like his mentor, Brown had also developed a nonchurch-related business career as a top executive at United Airlines. He later served on the board of Western Airlines at the same time as Tanner.

With Brown in charge at the PBO, major structural shifts occurred, with the last main organizational divisions between ecclesiastical and temporal activities established by 1977. The reorganization of the 1970s also included a divestment of some long-standing church properties, such as the church hospital system, which had been established after World War II. As church properties, the hospitals were perceived to be a financial drain, given their future capital needs. Further, there existed some political liability, given the hospitals' growing dependence on federal funds and problems that were developing with unions and consumer groups.

By the late 1970s, the Tanner reorganization had made a profound impact on the church and the way it conducted its business affairs. In the process, enormous curiosity was generated both inside and outside the church about its economic activities. Unlike the Moyle period, when finances were perceived to be part of the extraordinary missionary expansion, the Tanner period brought a focus on the church as an autonomous financial institution, an economic power rivaling the major industrial and financial corporations. And nowhere did the church become more visible and more controversial in this area than with its real estate holdings.

REAL ESTATE BROKER

Control of the movement of real estate, particularly as it affected the downtown area of Salt Lake City, had long been a concern of the Mormon leadership. The bitter Mormon-Gentile rivalries of the 1880s had spilled over into competition to establish the downtown hub either adjacent to the Temple or further south on Main Street.

When the church first developed the properties around the Temple in the late nineteenth and early twentieth centuries, it immediately clashed with competing Gentile interests. Non-Mormon interests had long sought to create a downtown locus around the Mining Stock Exchange, four blocks south of the Temple. For several decades, Gentile and Mormon interests waged a fierce real estate battle to control the commercial center of the city, a battle ultimately won by the church. Today, some of the area around Exchange Place has an abandoned look, with stately old buildings, such as the Newhouse Hotel, having been demolished.

As the church expanded its real estate holdings around the Temple and throughout the city, it was soon obliged to establish a real estate holding company, Zions Securities Corporation. Zions Securities gathered under its corporate umbrella a number of related corporate entities that were defined as income-bearing, as opposed to ecclesiastical properties that were supposed to be used directly for church purposes. The change, instituted by Heber Grant in 1923, was designed to head off a tax investigation of the church.

Through the 1950s, Zions Securities continued to function as the church real estate holding company and, along with the bank, a source for investment-related acquisitions. When Tanner took over the financial domain, the approach toward real estate development changed considerably, with the church getting more directly involved in the "actual management operation," as long-time church real estate figure J. Howard Dunn put it. This new orientation, as Dunn defined it, meant that the church would now be "improving properties and trying to act as businessmen and get a return on investment wherever possible—not that we're looking for maximum return in any respect, but then we shouldn't be just sitting and holding a piece of property without utilizing it to the fullest extent either."

As Tanner established control over the church's economic sphere, he attempted to juggle two key concerns. He felt the church had to scale back some of the ambitious plans developed during the Moyle period, and he was most concerned in establishing sound business-management principles, including a more active stance regarding the disposition of the real estate.

In the 1960s, Tanner was also responsive to the efforts of development-minded politicians, among them Utah's Democratic Governor Calvin Rampton, to attract new corporations to settle in the Wasatch Front. Tanner welcomed the idea as being in the best interest of the church, despite some fears among General Authorities that such a development could potentially dilute Mormon influence, particularly in the Salt Lake area.

Part of this approach was the plan to build a new civic auditorium and convention center for the region, a project that came to be known as the Salt Palace. Further, the downtown business community was concerned that the area adjacent to the Temple was being overrun by the poor and the transient, thus losing its appeal as a commercial center and headquarters to potential relocating companies.

The church was also concerned about the downtown area. The Temple, for one, had long been a tourist attraction, and the church's Visitors Center was considered to be an important proselyting tool. It presented the proper image and frame of reference for the church for curious tourists, and attendants collected names and addresses for missionary follow-up. The church had already embarked on an expensive revamping of the Visitors Center, relying heavily on visual aids and other media devices.

Disturbed by the growing number of transients and poor people who had made the area their home, the church leaders, so conscious of their image as a mainstream *middle class* church, began to create what Dunn called a "proper buffer" between the church and low income areas in the late 1950s. Henry Moyle suggested a mall with the ZCMI department store as its centerpiece, but plans moved slowly due to fears that any development might turn out to be a drain on funds.

At the same time, the church leadership had become involved with the Salt Palace project. When Tanner became Second Counselor, McKay put him in charge of overseeing church involvement with civic and business figures whose task was to select a site for the project. The site eventually chosen was southwest of the Temple. The church owned about six and a half acres of land—one third of the site—and any development in the area obviously required church property. There was still a considerable amount of opposition to the project, primarily from Mayor J. Bracken Lee and members of the multiethnic community who would be displaced. The possibility that public funds would be earmarked for acquisition of church property intensified the fear of conflict of interest, the delicate issue of Mormon-Gentile, church-state relations, which was always just below the surface.

The use of church property for the Salt Palace also ran into some church resistance. For a time, the church, with its growing membership, had been considering building its own auditorium, possibly on the same site. Plans included construction of a building to hold 30,000 people for use during the semiannual conference and for other occasions. By 1963–64, when Tanner began to consolidate his position, it was clear that such ambitious building plans had to be shelved temporarily because of growing costs.

As the issue came to a head, Tanner devised a plan that satisfied church needs while avoiding negative publicity. The church decided to hold onto its property, thereby eliminating the need for a costly and politically charged sale. Instead, the church would lease the land to the county until the year 2000 at a nominal fee. In turn, the church would be allowed to use the Salt Palace facilities for up to twenty-four days a year.

Most important, the construction of the Salt Palace turned out to be the first risky step in the redevelopment of the area. With the Salt Palace going up, Tanner felt more confident about plans for the ZCMI mall, which catapulted the church into an active role in downtown redevelopment. With the Salt Palace symbolizing Salt Lake's bid for business relocation, N. Eldon Tanner had established himself as a pivotal figure in the increasingly intersecting worlds of the church and the downtown business community.

In this period, Tanner worked closely with Franklin D. Richards, a onetime Mormon lawyer, real estate investor, and commissioner of the Federal Housing Authority during the New Deal. Richards became an assistant to the Twelve on the same day that Tanner did and later rose to a position in the presidency of the First Quorum of the Seventy. Both men symbolized the move by the David O. McKay administration to tap prominent Mormon businessmen and public officials in an attempt to deal with the church's expansion. Richards, with his background in real estate, immediately established himself as a key figure at Zions Securities.

With Richards's approval, plans to construct the church office building were reactivated. During the Moyle period, plans had focused on a forty-two-story office tower. These plans generated a great deal of internal debate, particularly with respect to the scale of the project. The office building, to be located on a site east of the Temple and adjacent to the church-owned Hotel Utah, would clearly overwhelm the Temple, as would another church construction project, the Beneficial Life building to the southeast of the Temple. Completed in 1972, the church office building represented a triumph of the new order, a monument to an economically and institutionally reorganized church and a changing downtown Salt Lake skyline.

Nevertheless, church leaders remained sensitive to charges that it was using its enormous capital pool to shape the new Salt Lake center city. Church leaders were concerned about the church's image, particularly with their growing reputation as an economic power. Several General Authorities, including Harold B. Lee, even advised that the church sell some of its downtown holdings.

By the early 1970s, this image-conscious church had become an inviting candidate for joint ventures with real estate developers, particularly Mormons. It was asset-rich, management-poor, and clearly desirous of continuing redevelopment around the Temple area. Yet, at the same time, church leaders, led by Richards, remained wary of outside joint investments or active partnerships.

Aware of these internal debates, a couple of Mormon developers approached the church with plans for a mall on the same block where the church had been buying property. Their plan—the Crossroads Plaza Mall—called for the church to lease its property to the developers, who would in turn build and manage the development. The advantage for the church was that it would not be identified as the owner of two major downtown malls. At the same time, the church could influence the nature of the project. "They were attractive plans to us," Howard Dunn recalled. "We were quite concerned that the church image and standards be maintained. What was to be built had to meet church standards. That meant no private clubs, no X-rated movies. If those conditions couldn't be met, Zions Securities would have eventually developed the block."

To complete the Crossroads Mall, the church and its partners were

obliged to demolish the entire block, including Richards Street, which was
a historical landmark. The problem of demolition of landmarks emerged as
a full-blown issue by the early 1970s, when the Coalville Tabernacle, identified by the Utah Heritage Society as "one of the four or five outstanding
LDS buildings," was scheduled for demolition. One year after the building
had been officially listed on the Utah State Register of historic sites, heavy
equipment moved in and completely demolished the building. For economic and organizational reasons, the church Building Committee had
decided to override the objections of local members and tear down this
extraordinary building to create a new facility, in the motel architectural
style now popular in the church. The destruction of the Coalville Tabernacle was controversial. Demonstrations, petitions, and other protest activities had been organized by church members in an extraordinary display
of opposition, given the pressure on church members not to challenge
official church policy. In one protest, fifty-five percent of the Coalville
Saints signed a petition asking for the tabernacle to be preserved. The issue
even became something of a problem at the church-owned media, as one
KSL-TV news report was censored and the *Deseret News* limited its coverage to official statements by church leaders.

In the wake of the demolition of the Coalville Tabernacle, a new Division of Arts and Sites of the church Historical Department was organized
to list buildings owned by the church that appeared worthy of preservation,
a list that was hoped would serve as a guideline for other church departments, such as the economically oriented Building Division. Though the
new division preserved some properties, it never dealt directly with buildings owned by or related to projects of Zions Securities.

Zions Securities, in fact, took center stage in the late 1970s and early
1980s when it proceeded with the demolition of a number of residential and
commercial properties, some of which had been owned by late nineteenth-
century church leaders and had long been identified as historic sites. Some
of the properties also involved low- and moderate-income apartment
dwellings, many occupied by seniors who clearly preferred their proximity
to downtown. For Zions Securities, however, the bottom line remained a
clean, middle-class locus around Temple Square, where highrises and
shopping malls became as much the attraction as the Temple itself.

THE ARAB CONNECTION

One of Salt Lake's key downtown historical landmarks became the centerpiece of a project that ultimately linked the church with one of its most
unusual partners. This landmark, Devereaux House, was an old mansion
located west of the Temple and Salt Palace. It had once been a classic
example of nineteenth-century Salt Lake architecture. The home of one of
the city's earliest millionaires and a center of social life among the Mormon
elite, Devereaux House had by the early 1980s become a lonely, burned-

out wreck denuded of its Victorian trappings and was slowly being engulfed by the steel and concrete of the latest redevelopment project to hit Salt Lake, the Arab-owned-and-initiated Triad Project.

The Triad Project was the second major effort in the Salt Lake area by a consortium controlled by three Saudi Arabian brothers—Adnan, Essam, and Asil Khashoggi. The Khashoggis' economic fortune was based largely on their brokering of arms deals between U.S. and European companies and the Saudi government.

Adnan Khashoggi, the leader of the clan, became a celebrity of sorts in the mid-1970s when a number of his high-powered deals and questionable arrangements, such as an alleged $450,000 bribe involving the Northrop Corporation and rumored illegal contributions to Richard Nixon's reelection committee, became the subject of congressional and Security and Exchange Commission probes. Khashoggi was the constant subject of gossip columnists and a favorite at gambling spas.

Khashoggi got involved in Salt Lake when he received a call one day from F. William (Bill) Gay, then the top man in Howard Hughes's organization and a powerful Mormon, who was directly involved in church projects. Gay wanted Khashoggi to set up a joint venture with Hughes for some property near the Salt Lake airport. "We were very interested in the Salt Lake situation," Essam Khashoggi recalled. "We realized the connection with the Mormon church because of Bill Gay and knew, of course, that that was a positive thing in order to do business in Salt Lake."

Hughes dropped out of the airport deal, but the Khashoggis proceeded nevertheless, creating a Utah subsidiary called Triad Utah and building an industrial park and International Center on part of their property, on land adjacent to that held by the church. The International Center, in fact, whetted the appetite of these Arab arms dealers, and they became increasingly interested in the area, thanks in part to their hiring of a local non-Mormon businessman named Emanuel A. (Manny) Floor. Floor was particularly adept at working closely with Salt Lake's power structure, including the leading money managers of the Mormon church.

Floor succeeded in getting church leaders and other local business and political figures to roll out the welcome mat for the Khashoggis, despite their reputation. Church leaders disregarded the SEC investigations and playboy reputation. They were interested in new capital, and lots of it, entering their community. "We never had negative publicity," Floor said, recalling his introduction of the Khashoggis. "People here were saying, 'Oh boy, here comes a major investment into Salt Lake that is going to get our community to grow.'"

When a local developer facing bankruptcy approached the Khashoggis and asked them to take over a redevelopment project built around a restored Devereaux House, the Arab group jumped at the chance. The Triad group immediately expanded the scope of the project, hoping to transform it into a spectacularly gaudy setting with huge office towers, condominium towers, a bell tower, Omnimax movie theater modeled after one at Caesars Palace in Las Vegas, and a trolley car system linking Temple Square with the Triad complex. Dwarfed amidst these buildings was Devereaux House, which had been the original lure for public funds for the project. Preservationists who had fought to save Devereaux House were appalled at Triad's plans, and one particularly scathing letter from the city's Historic Landmark Committee called Triad's plans "a parody of this significant historic building, a pretense . . . unsuccessful . . . an indulgent architectural element, a gratuitous marketing object."

The Khashoggi money, however, easily smothered these protests, and they quickly received the support of political and business figures. The church, nevertheless, remained the key, not only because of its influence in the community, but also as a major landowner in the area where Triad hoped to proceed.

The Khashoggis saw their chance when they learned of plans of the church's media arm, the Bonneville Corporation, to relocate corporate headquarters as well as the KSL-TV and radio facilities. The Triad group saw a tremendous advantage if it could convince the church to relocate Bonneville at the Triad Center instead. Floor approached church leaders and laid out the Triad plans, arguing that they would upgrade the area. He also raised the possibility of Khashoggi investments helping transform Salt Lake into a sleek, new corporate headquarters city for the Intermountain West.

Floor nevertheless ran into some initial resistance, particularly from those members of the Bonneville board from outside Utah who were concerned about doing business with the Khashoggis and who, as Floor put it, "had heard about all the publicity surrounding the Khashoggis and had big problems because of that." Floor went into action, smooth-talking not only the Bonneville board, but working the General Authorities as well. "Manny is a pro," remarked one church insider with direct knowledge of the Bonneville situation. "He knew which General Authority to talk to, and what to say to get their support. And remember, there's more to it than just Triad. Manny was selling the church on a relationship."

Floor could also count on the support of the money managers and bureaucrats who saw possibilities not only regarding the Triad Center, but the airport property and possibly other joint investments as well. Floor also garnered the support of Tanner and the newest member of the First Presidency, Gordon B. Hinckley, who became increasingly prominent as the most active member of the First Presidency as Tanner's Parkinson's disease began taking a greater toll in 1980 and 1981.

Floor got the Bonneville board to agree to relocate to Triad, and the Khashoggis bought the original site where Bonneville had intended to move. Bonneville's Broadcast House became the first, most visible part of the Triad package. For the Khashoggis, Broadcast House was an incredible coup. "Just think of what KSL and Bonneville locating at Triad does to the whole environment of the project," Floor declared. "Every time they broadcast they will say, 'This is KSL from the Triad Center.' Do you realize what that means? People in Utah find KSL so believable. That concept of believability is so important. And that is going to rub off on us as well."

The deal was further assisted when the church sold six crucial acres to Triad without which the project would not have been viable. And then, with all the deals worked out, Wendell Ashton, the publisher of the *Deseret News* and a longtime church spokesman, added a new dimension to the Triad public relations effort by presenting a slide show on its Salt Lake project to the Cities Congress on Roads to Recovery in Cleveland, Ohio.

In the airport situation, the church also joined forces with the Khashoggis. While exploring the possibility of selling their own land near the airport to Triad, the church also joined the Khashoggis in supporting annexation of the area, which would enhance the value of the properties. Even prior to the Triad deal, the church had maintained an interest in airport development and support of the airlines. The church comptroller, J. Alan Blodgett, had served on the airport commission, and longtime United Airlines executive and Western Airlines director Victor L. Brown, a key church financial figure as head of the PBO, engineered a church First Presidency statement supporting the industry's plea for deregulation. In 1983, Western Airlines relocated its corporate headquarters to Salt Lake City, a successful conclusion to the church-backed relocation strategy.

The Triad relationship brought to the fore both the issue of church involvement in joint ventures and the long-term disposition of its real estate holdings. A number of key church figures, such as Franklin D. Richards, continued to resist an active investment strategy that would rely on outsiders as joint investors. The Khashoggis, in particular, were anxious to expand their relationship with the church, and other developers and investors repeatedly approached the church to do business.

Many of the money managers supported such an effort, and a strong current in the church felt that the church itself was ill-equipped to handle 100 percent owned-and-operated investments. Through the mid-1970s, church leaders still sought to control that aspect of their development program regarding the downtown area near Temple Square.

The Crossroads projects and then, later, Triad offered another route— let others do the planning, managing, and operating. As J. Howard Dunn, Zions Securities president put it, the church just did not have the kind of staff "that can handle sales and promotion." "The main question," Dunn declared, "is do we want to compete with the private sector. We're trying to keep a low profile. We're not here to compete with the private sector.

We want to be part of the community. We don't want to be *the* community."

By the early 1980s, the church was opting for a more passive investment strategy. As a real estate broker, the church resembled in many ways a small-town businessman bedazzled by the plans and schemes of those who offer the attraction of big money, big profits, and a spiffy clean environment.

Still, Zions Securities remained a major operation, with holdings not only in Salt Lake, but in Florida, California, Arizona, Missouri, and substantial holdings in Hawaii. These properties were worth tens of millions of dollars, according to Dunn. The sheer quantity of Zions Securities real estate holdings in Salt Lake City also meant that it had to be the major factor in any future plans for the region.

Uncertainties nevertheless remain. On the real estate end, particularly with Tanner's death and Richards's call to preside over the temple in Washington, D.C., more and more of the day-to-day decisions are made by the middle-level bureaucracy. General Authorities are, at times, even unaware of major investment decisions, let alone engaged in the decision-making process. Apostle Boyd Packer recalled, for example, how he first heard about the church's multimillion-dollar investment in some Kansas City properties: "Someone in Oakland asked me about it."

Despite its ability to operate on a day-to-day level, the bureaucracy feels constrained in dealing with the church's substantial assets. Ultimately, the church operates in a helter-skelter manner, sometimes acting as a bottom-line investor, at other times acting cautiously and reactively to events outside its control. Because of its holdings and the extent of its power to invest or divest, the church remains, in the real estate area, *the* broker to contend with or manipulate.

MORMON ENTREPRENEURIALISM

As the church under Tanner progressed toward a more corporatelike body, church publications in this same period gave increasing attention to the success stories of Mormon businessmen and to the financial achievements of the members in general. Figures such as J. Willard Marriott and the Osmonds, whose financial activities were as well known as their musical work, became individual role models for activities in the temporal world. Mormon entrepreneurialism was seen as a value in itself and one's ability to make money a measure of success. For Mormons, the push for material success almost took on a doctrinal quality, as if progress in this world was defined as success in the business world. George Romney, in discussing the importance of succeeding, put it this way: "The question is the degree of exaltation that a man can win for himself in his life on earth."

By the Heber J. Grant period (Grant himself was a role model as a Mormon businessman), the focus on money matters had become in-

119 THE RISE OF THE MONEY MANAGERS

creasingly prominent in this once radical, communitarian church. Changes in Mormon values, however, were more gradual than sudden, as most church members tended to maintain middle-class and even lower-middle-class standards of living. The Mormon West from the 1920s through the 1940s was still relatively rural, with a focus on community and church needs as much as individual success.

As the church grew in the 1950s and 1960s, the focus on money matters became more direct and pronounced. The contrast between young Mormon missionaries from Utah and other parts of the Mormon West and their potential recruits in the Third World heightened the consciousness of the church as an American church with a middle-class constituency. Financial success became a yardstick measuring leadership capabilities, as the Salt Lake leaders pushed hard to develop a wealthier, more middle-class framework for its international membership base.

In the Mormon West, the boom mentality took hold, and Mormon political and business figures championed the rapid growth of the region, while celebrating individual Mormon success stories, primarily in the business world. While in the 1920s and 1930s, well-known Mormon businessmen seemed few and far between—with some of the best known, such as Marriner and George Eccles, members of the church in name only—the 1950s and 1960s saw the emergence of a larger network of prominent Mormon businessmen. Individual Mormon organizations, such as New York's Lochinvar Club, and the growing use of Mormon businessmen inside the church as consultants or board members of particular church bodies highlighted this new, more visible role of the Mormon entrepreneur. The Saints became increasingly aware of these individuals— almost none of whom held a direct church calling. Not only the more publicized figures, such as Marriott (who was the subject of a biography that he paid the church to publish), David Kennedy, and George Romney, became better known to church members, but also more obscure corporate figures, such as Lee Bickmore of Nabisco, C. Jay Parkinson of Anaconda, Glenn Neilson of Husky Oil, Robert C. Kirkwood of F.W. Woolworth, and Stanton Hale of Pacific Mutual Life Insurance, were celebrated as Mormon achievers.

For individual Mormon businessmen, church membership provided an advantage above and beyond their high status in the church. For one, the church was itself an increasingly important *business* organization, having to deal with other businessmen and corporations in a variety of ways. Frequently, that meant the church developed ties with those individuals that church leaders felt most comfortable with, i.e., Mormon businessmen who knew the language and idiosyncracies of the church's growing economic bureaucracy.

The appeal of Mormons dealing with Mormons extended outside the institutional church and could be found as well among individual Mormon businessmen doing business with each other. One of the most striking examples of this situation was the rise in Las Vegas of banker E. Parry Thomas, who became one of the most powerful figures on the Las Vegas scene by the 1970s.

Thomas, a Utah-born "Jack" Mormon (Mormon in name but not in practice) had built a financial empire in the 1950s and 1960s by making his Las Vegas bank the main conduit for loans for casino construction and acquisition from such sources as the mob-controlled Teamsters' Central States Pension Fund. Despite Thomas's questionable activities, the banker maintained strong ties with Las Vegas's Mormon businessmen and civic leaders. "Mormon businessmen know that he knows them and understands them. He's from Utah. They talk the same language," explained casino executive Shannon Bybee, who is a Mormon himself. Las Vegas Mormons, including those who had direct financial dealings with Thomas, never publicly raised questions about Thomas's activities or the source of funds that Thomas raised as contributions for the local Mormon church.

Another group of Mormon entrepreneurs emerged as key behind-the-scenes Las Vegas figures when Howard Hughes entered the world of gamblers and mob financiers by purchasing a string of casinos in the late 1960s. Hughes's chief of staff, Bill Gay, had systematically created around the drug-stupefied billionaire a *cordon sanitaire* of Mormon aides, security men, and medical attendants, who screened Hughes off from the rest of the world. At Hughes's headquarters on Romaine Street in Los Angeles, Gay set up a quasi-military structure, with his Mormon entourage all expressing loyalty as much to Gay as to the larger Hughes organization. The Mormon ties were so deep, in fact, that, as Hughes biographers Donald Bartlett and James Steele noted, "the nondrinking, nonsmoking Mormons had become so intertwined with Romaine Street that when a job opening occurred notices went up on Mormon church bulletin boards all over Los Angeles."

Cashing in on the "Mormon connection" became, by the 1970s and early 1980s, an increasingly widespread phenomenon among Mormon and Gentile dealmakers in the Mormon West. Prominent Mormon figures were either parties to such actions or lent their names (frequently for financial compensation) to questionable operations. Las Vegas, as one might imagine, given its deal-making notoriety, was a major source of scams and frauds within the large and prominent Mormon community. But Utah was also a source of these types of activities, and by the early 1970s, the *Wall Street Journal* would declare that officials of the Securities and Exchange Commission considered Salt Lake City to be "the sewer of the securities industry."

The scams varied in nature and size, but almost all of them traded on Mormon loyalties, trust, and the growing desire to "make a buck" as a sign of success. In Las Vegas, one group of prominent Mormon businessmen, including the late Devoe Heaton, a former U.S. attorney, created a credit

121

union for Mormons and ended up channeling funds to a fictitious corporation controlled by the manager of the operation. In Utah, a Mormon businessman created a phony corporation that he declared was headed by a stake president. The company claimed it would sell long tubular plastic containers for skis to airlines, and that if investors put up as much as $5,000, they would get a seat on the company's board of directors.

These types of arrangements, including those where the names of prominent Mormons, including General Authorities, were bandied about, became increasingly visible by the late 1970s and early 1980s. From 1980 to 1983, the Utah U.S. Attorney estimated that about 10,000 investors, most of them Mormons, had been fleeced to the tune of $200 million. "We are becoming the fraud capital of the nation," he commented, pointing to such incredible scams as the sale of gold certificates by one enterprising con artist. These certificates had a face value hundreds and even thousands of times the actual investment. When the scam finally collapsed, it was discovered that the financial obligations had an alleged value of $612 billion, equal to about half the U.S. national debt. When the case went to bankruptcy court, the only assets discovered were a few pieces of mining equipment.

By the early 1980s, scam artists began to pursue what one law enforcement official called "the Mormon marketing strategy," referring to the ability to draw in Mormon investors based on their trust if another Mormon, particularly a church leader, was involved. In one particularly damaging incident, the use of the name of General Authority Paul Dunn as a board member became the hook by which a number of individual Mormons decided to invest in a company that went bankrupt. The owner was later investigated for possible fraudulent activities.

The Dunn incident became the occasion for a campaign by church leaders to stop fraud, particularly fraud involving the use of the church's name or the name of church leaders. Already by the late 1970s, church publications had begun to warn that there were "cases where dishonest men have traded on their membership in the Church to create trust in their victims. And many Saints are all too ready to believe a convincing story from a 'good' member of the Church without checking it."

During conference in the spring of 1982, Mormon-related fraud became the topic of several talks by church leaders, including a major address on the subject by Quorum of the Twelve member Marvin J. Ashton. Soon after, the *Church News*, the weekly church supplement of the *Deseret News*, ran a strong warning on the subject. "Beware of smooth talk," it warned, stating bluntly that "claims of endorsement or participation by Church leaders are often false. . . . Some Church members think normal business formalities should be suspended when they are dealing with 'brothers and sisters.' This can lead to fraud."

Several months later, Hugh W. Pinnock of the first Quorum of the

Seventy elaborated on the theme before an audience at BYU. "Years ago, no one would have believed Utah would be labeled the scam capitol of the world. It's bizarre, but it's true," Pinnock went on, pointing out that Utah in 1981 was third in the nation for business-loan defaults and had eleven major business frauds. "In our church many in leadership positions are held in awe," Pinnock concluded. "Just because someone is in a leadership position doesn't mean he can talk about a stock proposal."

The problem, ultimately, was not simply the Mormon disposition to trust and obey their leaders; it had to do, as the *Church News* pointed out, with the celebration of money and wealth, the triumph of Mormon entrepreneurialism. "In my interviews of Church members entangled in allegedly fraudulent investment schemes," the *Church News* writer declared, "I have heard the belief expressed that the accumulation of wealth is some kind of sacred obligation."

The concern with wealth and money had become, by the 1980s, a driving force behind not only individual Mormon behavior and pursuits, but the internal activities and organization of the church as well. The desire to accumulate went hand in glove with the fear of debt and the desire for financial security as well as gain. Within the church, these related attitudes were at the core of the major shift that began to take place in the transitional period of the late 1970s and early 1980s. By the 1980s, a new concept had entered the church bureaucracy, the concept of "a capital crunch," which appeared to define the limits and parameters of activities for a church still preeminently wedded to the idea of permanent growth and expansion.

BUREAUCRACY ON A STRING

By the late 1970s, Eldon Tanner had made his march through the bureaucracy and created the various organizational structures that appeared to enable the church to proceed with a secure, bottom-line philosophy where called for. According to William Kirton, the church General Counsel, who had organized the church Law Department, the Tanner philosophy as it evolved through the 1960s and 1970s was ultimately to create two levels of church activity. One was to be ecclesiastical and the other would include all the varied profit centers.

Another Tanner protégé, J. Alan Blodgett, refined that definition further. According to Tanner, Blodgett declared, the economic reorganization had produced three types of businesses. The first involved "businesses which assist the church in carrying the gospel message," that is, the media-related companies, such as Bonneville, the *Deseret News*, the Deseret Book Company. The second group involved businesses that had played a historical role in the early development of the church in the nineteenth and early twentieth centuries but that are less important—both in economic *and* organizational terms—to the church today. The third group are those businesses that exist directly for investment or bottom-line purposes, such as Beneficial Development and Zions Securities.

By the late 1970s, a multitiered financial bureaucracy had emerged. Its headquarters was the new church office building, which stood right next to the building that housed the offices of the more traditional decision makers, the General Authorities. The General Authorities had their own structures, such as the Committee for the Disposition of the Tithes, the Budget Committee, the Finance Committee, and the Committee on Expenditures. These committees were ultimately the final source of power regarding what church funds should be spent, for what purposes, and how the income would be generated. Despite the fact that each of the separate church businesses—part of the profit centers group—had their own separate board of directors (many of whom were the same General Authorities), the ultimate decisions about overall income and expenses came back to the traditional leadership structures. At the same time, there was a co-mingling of funds from church businesses and tithing.

During the Tanner era, the traditional structures tended, to a certain extent, to be eclipsed by the new bureaucrats. Tanner himself could be seen as an extension of the bureaucracy, the chief executive officer. He was, as well, the chairman of the board, i.e., the most important of the General Authorities dealing with economic matters. Tanner was, at once, the defender of the bureaucracy as well as its leader, insulating it as much as possible from the internal dynamics at the top of the church hierarchy.

He accomplished these changes by his ability to oversee an enormous range of economic activities as well as by his reliance on trusted allies such as Victor L. Brown, the presiding bishop of the PBO. The rise of the PBO in the 1970s as the main church body overseeing the temporal sphere in such matters as church businesses, administration, and such activities as the welfare program, was of critical importance in the reorganization of the economic side of the church. Major decisions about the day-to-day operations of the church went through the PBO, and Brown, more than any other figure, played the critical role in handling the administrative aspect of church money matters.

Despite the development of an extensive bureaucracy and new lines of authority, the change in church economics was, in many ways, an unfinished revolution. So much of what had been developed and transformed rested on the authority and power of Tanner himself within church councils. As Tanner began to decline in health in the late 1970s, the question of his successor became a very real and troubling issue. "No one will be able to keep his fingers on so much as Tanner did," J. Alan Blodgett declared. "He defined the boundaries of the new system. He was the one who made it go."

This transition was complicated by the emergence in the late 1970s of a capital crunch, caused by a reduction in revenues to meet expenditures.

The first public signs of the problem, hardly noticeable, involved a drop in the number of missionaries. Church press releases were at first able to disguise the downturn by pointing to other growth statistics or by charting out changes in five-year stretches rather than by focusing on annual changes.

Within the bureaucracy, the capital crunch, by 1980 and 1981, had become a very real and pervasive phenomenon. The initial clue as to its importance was found in the way some General Authorities, particularly Tanner, began to question the continuing viability of the rapid expansion of the church, particularly in the Third World. "There's a limit to how far you can go," Tanner declared.

The problem was exacerbated by the squeeze on tithe-paying members of the church, who were feeling the effects of the dramatic economic downswing in 1981 and 1982. During the 1970s, tithe-paying members in the U.S. were continually called on to make contributions in addition to their tithes. With the Reagan recession, it was becoming clear that members were not able to keep up with anticipated payments, let alone meet additional requests.

In his last major innovation, Tanner began to deal with this pervasive capital crunch. In 1981 a new meeting schedule, designated the "consolidated schedule," reduced the number of meetings during the week, as a way to ease up on members' financial and time commitments. Church departments in the bureaucracy, such as Education, Welfare, and the Building Committee, were asked to explore reductions in expenditures. New budgeting procedures were instituted, requiring a far more stringent justification for particular items.

The missionary program was also deeply affected. The downturn in the number of missionaries reflected, in part, the difficulties families found in supporting their nineteen-year-old missionary children by paying for two years of room and board. Missionary service time was then reduced from two years to eighteen months, and attempts were made to recruit older missionaries to supplement the long-standing recruitment of nineteen-year-olds. Still the number of missionaries in the field, *despite the time reductions*, continued to drop, creating continuing concern and debate about the problem. Construction of new chapels, temples, and other church buildings, another hallmark of the expansionary period of the 1970s, was either cut back or new designs were instituted that emphasized cost-cutting measures.

Perhaps the most serious and far-reaching cutbacks came in the welfare programs. By the early 1980s, the program had become a major component of the church, perhaps the church's most significant program after missionary work and temple-building. The welfare program was what Arrington et al. in *Building the City of God* called "a reaching back into the Mormon heritage of cooperation and shared burdens to find a solution to pressing modern problems."

The program was built in the spirit of the statement of Prophet Joseph F. Smith that "a religion that has not the power to save people temporally and make them prosperous and happy here cannot be depended upon to save them spiritually and to exalt them in the life to come." It reflected a desire on the part of the Saints to provide cradle to grave security for its members independent of government assistance and was still looked upon by church leaders, such as First Counselor to the president Marion G. Romney, as preparation for the utopian world of the United Order.

Statistics for the program through 1981 indicated an impressive and extensive operation. Church members were involved, mostly through volunteer labor, in 600 food production projects. These projects included 20 canneries and numerous meat-packing and dairy operations that were supplied in large part by church-owned welfare farms that were growing food on 140,000 acres.

Two hundred thousand people, most of them church members, received free food from more than 100 church storehouses and auxiliaries. More than 31 million pounds of commodities were distributed; 533,000 man-days of labor were donated by members and welfare recipients; and 27,000 people were placed in jobs through some 300 church employment offices. Church members were also advised to store a year's supply of food in their homes.

More than twenty facilities run by Deseret Industries provided work and shelter for the elderly and handicapped while providing cheap, secondhand goods for the general public. In addition, professionally trained and licensed social workers provided counseling and services for couples seeking adoptions, unwed mothers, and families under stress while working to place young Indian members in foster homes.

Through this program, the church emphasized self-reliance, the work ethic, and avoidance of debt. The problems arose for poor members because of the church's historical antipathy toward the dole and conservative disdain for the welfare recipient. Some poor members chose to avoid the welfare program because, as one member who has been active in the church for twenty-seven years explained, some of the bishops who administer the program make those seeking assistance "feel that they are begging for it."

The stigma of poverty, according to Jeff Fox, the director of the Crossroads Urban Center in Salt Lake City, was one reason for avoiding the program. According to Fox, whose project provided free food to many Mormons, church leaders impress upon their followers that the welfare program is a way to avoid "the evils of the dole" and "the curse of idleness." Members are also told that "If you are worthy, God's blessings will follow." Thus to ask for help is an admission of unworthiness.

The program has been beset with other problems. In California, for example, the State Division of Labor Standards Enforcement discovered that church employees were paid far below the minimum wage. One employee was fired after going public with the information. The church's tax-exempt status was also threatened by the fact that some food grown on welfare farms was sold outside the welfare program.

Most important, in terms of the program's operation, welfare services were also contributing to the economic squeeze on the church and its members. Some of the funds to support the system were derived from annual cash assignments to local units. But with the recession of the early 1980s putting a bite on church members and the local wards and with the demands on the system growing precisely because of the economic hard times, the church leaders realized that the welfare program had become a serious drain, compounding the problems elsewhere.

During the church's annual spring conference in 1983, major changes in the funding and operation of the welfare program were announced. Financing would now be derived from the centralized collection of "fast offerings," a once-a-month donation derived from a one-day fast. New farms and facilities would be paid for by the central bureaucracy, which, in turn, would evaluate each existing production project—whether farm or industry workshop—and decide which to keep and which to close down. Decisions would be made on a cost-effective basis, and a greater emphasis would be put on individual members doing without welfare service. The cutbacks would provide a reduction in expenditures and reduce the stress on church finances. Yet, the cutbacks also meant a scaling down of the church's most effective public relations program.

These changes, according to J. Alan Blodgett, were the result of a major policy debate that remains unresolved. It had become clear by 1980–81, Blodgett declared, that the rate of expansion had to be lessened to deal with the capital crunch. "Any organization that grows rapidly creates excesses," Blodgett noted. "We have to take stock of what we have accomplished up to now and improve our operations, whether that means in the amount of materials distributed, making buildings smaller than before, or cutting back on the number of missionaries. We can no longer have the geometric rate of increases [in membership] that we had in the past."

Even with the changes of the early 1980s, however, the issue—and the problem—still remained. "We basically have only two real options at this point and for the future," Blodgett declared in a 1982 interview, referring to the possibilities of either continuing or limiting the church expansion. "Can we make our efforts less capital intensive?" he asked. "Can we ease back on the rate of our proselyting? We can't increase our expenditures too much greater than our income. We're still at an early enough stage to look at options. It's not yet a crisis."

Time is clearly a critical factor. Despite the changes related to the capital crunch, an effective continuing strategy for the economic side of the church has not emerged in the wake of Tanner's death. "You can not overstate the importance of Tanner when it came to the church's economic sphere," one church insider noted. "There are no clear successors, not only because you don't have anyone with as much real world experience as Tanner had within the Quorum, but you also have the problem that the bureaucrats, the bureaucracy, is afraid of overstepping its bounds. You have today a bureaucracy on a string."

The post-Tanner transition was further compounded by the general uncertainty that existed within the church in the wake of Ezra Taft Benson's anticipated succession to Prophet. Though Benson had little knowledge of the economic side of the church, the church bureaucracy, including the money managers, were still heavily dependent on the decisions and direction of the top leaders. With the high-level changes, the money managers indeed functioned as if they were on a string. "It used to be a couple of years ago that when I would ask, 'Can we do business with you now?' they would say, 'Why don't you wait?'" one prominent Utah businessman declared in 1983. "Now that Tanner is dead and Franklin Richards's power is passing on to others like Marvin Ashton," the businessman went on, "I would think that I could do business now. But no, I'm hearing again that I should wait, that another transition is taking place. I end up feeling that I might never be able to work out the active kinds of arrangements I'd like to make with the Church. I sometimes wonder whether the power I thought they [the money managers] had is not what they really have."

Today, in the early 1980s, the Mormon church stands as a wealthy and powerful institution. A major portion of the income still comes from tithing. Since the early 1960s, the church has been able to rationalize and expand its investment-oriented side. Though income from church members remains the revenue base, church money managers now handle an extensive and integrated pool of funds combining tithing and investment income.

Whatever their source, the full extent of the church's holdings is protected from public scrutiny and the tax man by the church's tax-exempt status. In 1983, Apostles Boyd K. Packer and Neal A. Maxwell dismissed the activities of Zions Securities, the church's investment arm, as not a big issue. Unlike any other American church, however, the church's economic decisions and the sheer weight of its massive holdings, including its participation in the campaign to bring corporations to the Wasatch Front and its plans for downtown Salt Lake City, have a major impact on large numbers of people, both Mormon and non-Mormon. Familiarity with power in Zion has bred a kind of indifference to its consequences, such as the destruction of low-income neighborhoods to clear the way for church-sponsored development in the downtown area.

While the profit side of the church has grown, and along with it the corporate-style bureaucracy, the more traditional hierarchy embodied in the First Presidency and the Quorum of the Twelve has not been able to keep up with this bureaucratic and economic explosion. Despite the Tanner revolution, church leaders have not fundamentally altered their own roles nor brought in new leaders who could effectively serve as chief executive officers.

The General Authorities remain a group of older men who have spent a great share of their working lives inside the church. They have learned to adjust to the bureaucracy and in fact to count on it to handle economic matters. Some church leaders actually do like to think of themselves as heads of corporations. "We, as leaders, have to control the cash flow," one member of the Quorum of the Seventies declared. "It's a management problem."

With Tanner's death, the uneven nature of the organizational change has come to the fore. On the one hand, the bureaucracy exists, managing and administering a powerful financial body whose decisions impact on a range of areas and people, whether in terms of Salt Lake real estate development, regional industries, such as insurance or agriculture, or the overall economy of the Intermountain West. "I'm not saying that we are *of* the world, but we're *in* the world," declared J. Howard Dunn of Zions Securities, "and I think that our business interests give the impression to the world that we're not set up on some platform above and beyond the reach of everybody else, but that we are integral to the world, that we can't live without it and it can't live without us."

On the other hand, the church, despite the predisposition of its bureaucracy, is not yet a corporate conglomerate in its leadership structures and decision-making procedures. It is, in many ways, a middle-management bureaucracy without an effective top-management layer, a bureaucracy that anticipates more than directs, whose sensitivities are most directed at what is happening at the top and what shifts, trends, or changes can be deciphered. Above all, it is also a temporal structure whose major goal is spiritual—the building of the Kingdom of God on earth in preparation for the millennial reign of Jesus Christ.

And at the top, there is uncertainty and lack of direction, with the economic difficulties, as expressed in the capital crunch, paralleled by the political and organizational turmoil involved in the Benson transition. Today, the church faces a contradiction between its bottom-line considerations and its fundamental purpose—to expand the church. For the future, these contradictions might well intensify as the church's desire to become more like a corporation clashes with its desire, as a Correlated and missionary-oriented church, to spread its message and bring in new members throughout the world as rapidly as it had over the last thirty years.

CHAPTER FIVE

FOLLOWING THE FLAG: THE INTERNATIONAL CHURCH

It was, for nineteen-year-old Sheldon Rampton, a rite of passage. He had come to the Language Training Mission (now called the Missionary Training Center) in 1979 to prepare for a two-year mission to Japan, one of the fastest growing areas in the international church.

"Everything in the LTM is immaculately clean and in order," Rampton wrote in his journal when he first came to Provo. "Upon arriving at the LTM, all missionaries receive a short haircut and are required to wear two-piece suits with white shirts and ties. We are cut off almost entirely from the outside world and from our past experiences."

Rampton's daily schedule, excepting Sunday services and Thursday mornings, when he and other missionaries did laundry and ran personal errands, required him to arise at 5:45 A.M. and retire at 10:30 in the evening. There was one hour of physical exercise, seven hours of classroom lessons, and five hours of intensive memorization. That plus an hour each for meals, fifteen minutes for showering, shaving, and dressing, and a half hour at evenings' end for "free time"—to undress, write in a journal, and read scripture.

The training itself had little or nothing to do with the culture, the politics, the people of the countries these missionaries were being sent to. Language training consisted largely of memorizing a script, called a "lesson plan," that was to be delivered verbatim to every potential recruit, called an "investigator." A typical passage went as follows: "Our Church leaders are all good, honest men who perform their responsibilities in the Church as representatives of the Prophet and the Apostles, providing necessary assistance to each individual member. Because they represent God's Prophet, it is necessary that we listen to their advice and follow it. . . . I testify that your happiness depends on the extent to which you follow their direction."

Like everyone else, Rampton was assigned companions, one of whom would be at his side constantly during the six weeks at the LTM and two years on mission. "We had barely met, but I was told to tell him I loved him," Rampton wrote. "We were told never to separate. Church leaders told story after story of missionaries who had left their companions for as little as fifteen minutes only to return and find them fornicating or dead through some devilish accident."

The LTM program, like the missionary experience that would follow, was all-encompassing. With barely a moment to oneself, the missionary becomes totally absorbed by the program. "We are subjected to 'inspirational' films, reminded to pray continually, and pressured to make constant proclamations of our *faith*," Rampton wrote of the LTM. "In addition, we are kept constantly busy—too busy to gain equilibrium."

It soon became apparent that training meant a transition to a new kind of identity. "We are not allowed to telephone friends or leave the LTM grounds without express permission," Rampton continued in his journal. "And we are urged constantly to put all thoughts of 'worldly things' out of our minds." Rampton wrote at the end of his training, "I was the creature of the LTM. It had created me. Outside it, my existence had no context, no purpose, and no meaning. My family, friends, society, all seemed to have vanished from existence." By the end of the training session Rampton, and more than 25,000 other young men were ready to serve as disciplined troops in the service of the international church.

In the contemporary church, numbers are the key. "In an era of increasing disinterest in organized religion," a 1981 church press release proudly noted, "someone joins the Church of Jesus Christ of Latter-day Saints every two minutes and thirty seconds." More than likely, that new member will be a Mexican or a Brazilian, a Chilean, a Korean, or perhaps even a South Sea islander.

Today, the Mormon church has an international face. In 1951, when David O. McKay became president of the church, membership stood at slightly more than 1 million members, most concentrated in Utah and the neighboring states of Idaho, Arizona, California, and Nevada. Membership outside the United States was small (less than ten percent of total membership) and concentrated in a few areas, such as Mexico, Canada, and the South Pacific, where the church had maintained a presence in the first half of the twentieth century. More than thirty years later, the international church has skyrocketed to more than 1.5 million members at a rate far outpacing the steady growth in the States, which has been partly a function of the extremely high Mormon birthrate.

What the figures do not reveal, however, are the realities, conflicts and tensions associated with that growth. The Mormon church is preeminently an *American* church. Church General Authorities speak of a *domestic* church when referring to the U.S. church, and an *international* church when referring to any place outside their country's borders. Domestically,

Mormons belong to a middle-class church. Internationally, they belong to a lower-middle-class and, in certain areas, even a poor church. Despite the "deliberate attempt," as one church General Authority put it, to have Mormon missionaries seek out middle- and upper-class recruits in Europe and the Third World, the church has been singularly unsuccessful in appealing to the elite.

The Mormon success in the Third World in such areas as the South Pacific and most especially Latin America is partly a function of the church's own mythology. The Lamanite people of the Book of Mormon are a chosen, though cursed, people. Their conversion, according to prophecy, will set off a chain of events, a prelude to the millennium. Once they have embraced Mormonism, the dark-skinned peoples of the continent will find that the "scales of darkness" can now "begin to fall from their eyes," transforming them into a "pure and delightsome people."

The Lamanite conversion, similar to conversions throughout the international church, means not only becoming purer but more Americanized as well. The American presence is felt everywhere throughout the international church. Mission presidents, temple presidents, area supervisors, General Authorities, are all almost exclusively American, presiding over local leaders, some of whom come from that particular country. Young boys from Utah, Idaho, or Arizona, with all their American naiveté and kindly arrogance, are sent abroad to do missionary work, supervised in turn by Utahns and Idahoans of their father's and even grandfather's generation. Dressed in their dark jackets and white shirts, they have, over the years, frequently obliged the international recruits to participate in such events as July Fourth celebrations, Halloween parties, or, as occurred in several instances, July Twenty-fourth Utah Pioneer Day celebrations.

Mark Grover, an analyst of the international church, commented, "The idea becomes for the new members that when they change their religion they no longer know what's American and what's Mormon. They mimic the elders. Part of their being a Mormon is changing their clothes: looking Mormon, i.e., looking American. Wearing a white shirt becomes a kind of badge. Members of the international church, particularly young Third World members, join the church saying they want to be like the American missionaries, that they want to go to BYU and become middle class and become church leaders. The cycle is then complete."

Today, the church's two most clear-cut nemeses abroad are nationalism and Catholicism. To church leaders they have become negative buzzwords, signifying loss of control, doctrinal dilution, and radical politics. Nationalism, which takes on an anti-American dimension, is seen to be, *ipso facto*, anti-Mormon. In Latin America, Catholicism, with its ability to adapt to national and cultural conditions radically different from Rome, has become a direct point of contrast with the Mormon church's doctrinal and organizational centralization. And the emergence of liberation theology—service and advocacy for the poor—is in marked contrast to a conservative Mormonism, with its attempt to project an apolitical character. The Catholic church on the other hand is moving in a more and more overtly political direction and has its own radical wing.

As a consequence, the Mormon church finds itself in a political squeeze in the Third World. Unlike the new Catholics, the Mormons are increasingly supportive of and favored by right-wing governments. It is in these countries that church growth has been most rapid, providing the numbers of new recruits crucial to the Mormon emphasis on missionary activities.

Yet the numbers are deceptive. In the politically charged atmosphere of places like Chile, Guatemala, and the Philippines, the situation is fluid and volatile: Today's recruit could become tomorrow's apostate or even revolutionary. Despite the problems, the church leaders still do love to come back to the numbers. The numbers game—numbers of baptisms, missionaries, translations of the Book of Mormon, temples, the list goes on and on—is a central dynamic of the international church.

THE GATHERING

Mormons are well acquainted with two essential church doctrines. One is the tenth Article of Faith, which states: "We believe in the literal gathering of Israel and the restoration of the Ten Tribes; that Zion (the new Jerusalem) will be built upon the American continent." At the same time, missionary activity *throughout the world* was central to Joseph Smith's own thoughts when he declared in 1831, "This Church, brethren, will fill the whole earth."

As early as 1837, Smith sent top aides, including Brigham Young, to serve as missionaries abroad. By the 1850s, the missionaries had visited the British Isles, Scandinavia, Italy, France, Germany, Australia, New Zealand, India, Chile, and South Africa, with the greatest success in England and other northern European countries.

Critical to the missionary effort was the establishment of Zion in America. The massive migrations to Zion, particularly from England, paralleled the overall migrations from the old world to the new, caused by the economic and social dislocations in Europe in the mid-nineteenth century.

When Mormon missionaries reached the United Kingdom, England was in the toils of its own social revolution, inspired by the People's Charter of 1838. Mormon missionaries, such as Orson Hyde, were highly successful in England's industrial districts, where religion and politics mixed freely. "Those who have been baptized," Hyde wrote his wife, "are mostly manufacturers and other mechanics . . . They are extremely poor, most of them not have a change of clothes decent to be babtized [sic] in, but they have open hearts and a strong faith." America clearly held great appeal for England's impoverished. An abundance of land appeared to be readily available, and the Saints insisted that the millennium was about to begin. The first three decades in Utah became, in effect, an era of immigration, as thousands of poor people—destitute laborers, farmers, craftsmen, traders—made their way to the gathering place in the Great Basin. The Mormons saw this as bringing together the select of the world, the "elect of God," who were the descendants of Israel.

By the 1880s, with Mormon Utah under severe political and economic attack, the gathering took a back seat to the survival of the church. The Perpetual Emigration Fund, which had provided the organizational and financial means for the immigration, was seized by the federal government and was ultimately abolished by the church. Prior to the accommodations of the 1890s, Mormon colonies were established in northern Mexico and western Canada as outposts of the polygamy underground. In the 1890s, the gathering was suspended, with the Mexican and Canadian colonies remaining the only significant concentrations of Mormons outside the U.S.

By World War I, what had been a temporary injunction against gathering became a policy that urged foreign members to remain in their own countries and establish their own Zion abroad. The policy remained vague at best, since some members abroad continued to immigrate to the "real" Zion in Salt Lake. Missionary work abroad remained limited, although hundreds were called each year. The one significant exception was the South Pacific and Hawaiian Islands. In Hawaii, the church purchased an island with a sugar plantation and combined recruitment with its role as chief employer.

Between the world wars, the international activity of the church continued to be largely circumscribed, as the cautious church leadership under Heber J. Grant and his First Counselor, J. Reuben Clark, focused on maintaining the financial solvency of the church while upgrading its image as a stable, conservative religion. The limited missionary work was also subject to the political difficulties involved in coping with an increasingly tense and turmoil-filled international scene.

After World War II, the church was once again poised for growth.

EVERY MEMBER A MISSIONARY

David O. McKay looked like an *American* prophet. Tall, husky, with flowing silver hair, he was clean-shaven, unlike earlier bearded patriarchs. His nineteen-year tenure as president of the church coincided with the church's first great expansionary burst abroad. As early as 1920, McKay had developed a strong interest in international expansion when he embarked on an extended worldwide tour that took him to China, Japan, India, the Hawaiian Islands, New Zealand, and several countries in Europe. McKay spent most of his working adult life inside the church, as president of the European mission, General Sunday School superintendent, a member of the Quorum of the Twelve, Second Counselor of two presidents, and then Prophet, Seer, and Revelator.

During his eighteen-year service as counselor in the First Presidency, McKay functioned in the shadow of J. Reuben Clark. Despite Clark's celebrated diplomatic career, it was McKay who emerged as the primary spokesman for an international church. Where Clark had been an America Firster prior to World War II and a critic of the United Nations and American economic and military expansion abroad in the postwar period, McKay was an internationalist, a strong anti-communist who was attuned to the parallel possibilities of American and Mormon international expansion.

By 1951, when McKay became president, the church was ripe for growth, and ample funds were available. Within months after assuming the presidency, McKay went to Europe in the first of numerous world tours as Prophet that took him to Asia, Latin America, New Zealand, and the South Sea and Hawaiian Islands, where the church had remained strong.

The South Pacific was also the setting for the initial development of one of McKay's most interesting innovations, the labor missionary program. By the early 1950s, several related problems had come to the attention of top church officials regarding their construction of chapels, schools, and meeting halls required to accommodate anticipated growth. In such areas as Tonga and Samoa, the church discovered a shortage of experienced craftsmen, such as electricians and carpenters. Even work requiring unskilled labor was proceeding slowly, at a "characteristically tropical pace," according to one member.

Furthermore, the financial arrangement between Salt Lake and the local church organizations required the locals to contribute at least thirty percent of funds for any construction project. None of the South Pacific branches could afford the required donation, given the fact that many of the new members of the church were poor or lower middle class.

To deal with these problems, a number of construction projects in the South Pacific began to experiment with a volunteer labor program. In Tonga, church members were quickly trained and then used as a voluntary labor force to help complete construction of a school. In Samoa, conflicts with an existing group of workers caused local church leaders to recruit volunteer Mormons from other South Pacific Islands, who then displaced the paid labor force.

Thus the labor missionary program of the church was created. It provided a huge reserve of free labor that was at once flexible and mobile. This labor pool could be moved from place to place at a moment's notice. The church could undertake far more building projects by ordering materials in larger quantities at a lower cost with a set timetable for delivery. And it allowed low-income branches in such areas as Tonga or Samoa to contribute their financial share to the building fund by contributing *labor* rather than cash.

By the late 1950s, the program was responsible for a tremendous expansion in church building activity. Heading up the program, Wendell Mendenhall, a California businessman and contractor, developed a tight-knit managerial group consisting primarily of other California businessmen.

Mendenhall reported directly to the First Presidency and operated with a degree of authority and financial autonomy unheard of in the church. His position was further strengthened when his closest ally in the church hierarchy, Henry D. Moyle, became the top finance man in the church.

The McKay-Moyle-Mendenhall leadership combination provided a tremendous impetus for international expansion. McKay, who made his slogan "every member a missionary" a favorite church epigram, was constantly visible during the 1950s, touring countries, meeting with dignitaries, and becoming the most widely known Mormon since the days of Brigham Young.

Like McKay, Henry D. Moyle also preached the possibility of expansion. His reorganization of church finances was essential to the program, as he pushed church leaders and missionaries to continue to outstrip previous increases in baptisms and construction. By the late 1950s, the church had indeed expanded dramatically. The number of chapels built had increased from only a handful to 150 a year by 1958. The building program expanded beyond the South Pacific to Europe and then Latin America, where the church anticipated rapid growth. More and more emphasis was placed on baptisms and recruitment. Entire mission groups competed with each other to see how many "collars" they could recruit and whether they could obtain the best per capita ratio of new members to missionaries.

This urgency created contradictions in the program that ultimately put a brake on early expansion and affected the careers of both Moyle and Mendenhall. It soon became apparent to some church leaders, particularly to Harold B. Lee, that international expansion was getting out of hand. Rumors circulated within the church about recruiting abuses.

One of these stories was about the so-called baseball baptisms where missionaries in the late 1950s had used the church's recreation programs in England to lure new members. The "apostasy" of nearly a dozen young missionaries who left France in 1958 to join a polygamist sect in Mexico sent shock waves through the church. Most important, the diversity of new recruits, many of whom had little inkling of Mormon doctrine, threatened to create a more decentralized church that would diffuse church beliefs and practices. Soon, church leaders, among them Lee, decided it was time to slow down the rate of growth. At the same time, organizational structure had to be reinforced and doctrinal instruction emphasized, a program that culminated in Lee's move to correlate the church.

There were also financial concerns centered around the labor missionary program. Moyle's draw-down of reserves was perceived to be dangerous by a number of church bureaucrats. Tithing funds were coming in slower than anticipated due to the low income level of new members. Much of the support for international work had been provided through the disposal of assets, such as the sale of Zions Bank in 1960. A financial crunch appeared likely to the bureaucrats and Lee.

Unforeseen political troubles had also arisen. In Santiago, Chile, the church had been forced to arm members to drive away squatters who had settled on church grounds, and in Lima, Peru, hostile Catholics sat on the board that granted building permits.

After Moyle became incapacitated by a heart attack in 1963, the labor missionary program lost its champion. Two years later, Mendenhall was relieved of his position as head of the Building Committee. The labor missionary program was itself replaced by a new system that provided for contract labor. The change, according to Mendenhall's assistant, J. Howard Dunn, was due to a greater need to monitor costs.

With a change in the building program and the Correlation program in place, international expansion did slow down in the middle 1960s, although overall membership continued to grow. By the end of the 1960s, the church, thanks to the Tanner revolution, maintained a substantial financial base. And with Correlation, a large force of obedient and motivated young missionaries was available. The conditions for a second great expansionary drive were set, but this time the focus would be primarily on Mexico and Latin America.

RESTLESS NATIVES

In a 1975 tour of Mexico, President Spencer Kimball visited a church school in the southern part of Mexico City. While shaking hands and chatting with a group of the Mexican schoolchildren, the president was asked where he came from. When he answered Salt Lake, a Mexican child replied, "Oh, I thought you were from heaven." He was quickly corrected by the Mormon Prophet. On leaving the school, however, the Kimball party overheard one of the children whispering to another: "Don't you believe him. He's *not* from Salt Lake; he's from *heaven*."

Unlike most other countries where the church has only recently emerged, the Mormon presence goes back more than 100 years in this land "so far from God and so close to the United States," as a Mexican president once put it. Missionary efforts date back to the 1880s, when a besieged Mormon nation began to locate large numbers of American settlers, many of them polygamists, in recently acquired lands in the northern Mexican states of Chihuahua and Sonora.

The "Colonies," as they were called, were quintessential Mormon communities. They were the new frontier of Mormonism, where the primitive living conditions reinforced the attempt to maintain key Mormon beliefs, such as polygamy, economic cooperation, and authoritarian theocratic rule. For more than two decades, they flourished under the protection of Mexican President Porfirio Díaz. Díaz, a strong supporter of foreign investment, hoped the Colonies would both strengthen the regional economy and ultimately provide "a model of industry to be imitated by native Mexicans," as one Mormon observer put it.

When the revolution broke out in 1910, the Colonies backed the Díaz dictatorship, assuming that the rebellion would be crushed with dispatch.

Once Díaz had fled, the Colonies became targets of various revolutionary groups who saw them as a source of funds and equipment. The Mormon settlers faced a "restlessness among the natives which found vent in a sudden disrespect for law . . . a challenge of authority [that] grew into overt acts of insolence," as Colony resident Nelle Spilsbury Hatch put it.

As the raids increased in tempo, the attitude of the colonists changed from scorn and missionary indulgence to fear and hostility. In July 1912, Junius Romney, the Colonies' highest ranking church official, ordered members to leave the area and temporarily resettle in communities north of the border. This departure, known in Colony folklore as "The Exodus," recreated earlier forced Mormon migrations from Missouri and Illinois. Only this time the departure was temporary, and Colony Mormons almost immediately began to return to the area to reclaim their property. By 1916, a sufficient number of Colony Mormons had returned to not only re-establish their communities, but to play a role in supplying and housing the Pershing military excursion into northern Mexico.

By the 1920s, the Colonies had once again become fully operational. They were well-to-do compared to the surrounding communities. Though a number of Mexicans (many of them fieldhands or house servants working for the Anglos) joined the church, the American Mormons dominated the community and the church. "The whole concept of the Colonies was very British," one Colony Mexican recalled. "We were always referred to as 'natives' and any kind of intermingling was frowned upon."

As the Colonies prospered, the church decided to establish a Mexican mission and develop a presence in Mexico City and other parts of the country. Heading up this effort was Colony Mormon Rey L. Pratt, who guided the church through the continuing political ferment in Mexico. Both Pratt and then ambassador to Mexico J. Reuben Clark developed ties with Mexican authorities that proved critical. Even after foreign missionaries were forbidden from operating in the country, Pratt was able to keep the church organization going.

After Pratt died in 1931, a number of issues for the Mexican Mormons began to come to the surface. Because of the ban on missionaries, the church had been forced to rely on Mexican members to sustain programs and recruit members. The top leadership of the church, however, remained American, with Mexican mission headquarters established north of the border, first in Los Angeles and then in El Paso. Mexican Mormons, who had gained their first taste of leadership and decision making, began to lobby for a Mexican to be named as mission president and for a greater say over leadership selection in general.

Mormon theology also played a role in this bid for leadership by Mexican nationals. One of the top local leaders of the church, Margarito Bautista wrote a radically different Mexican interpretation of the Book of Mormon and its implications for the destiny of Mexico and its people. Bautista speculated about the location of the great cities described in the

Book of Mormon and their importance in providing a link to Mexico's future. The Lamanites were, according to Bautista's interpretation, the chosen people of the Americas, descendants of the House of Israel. These Lamanites were indeed Mexicans with Indian blood and capable of leading a revived Mexico to become a mighty nation-empire. The American Anglos and even those of pure Spanish blood were, on the other hand, a "lesser people," even those fortunate to become Mormons "by adoption." Bautista labeled the Anglo church leadership "Gentile," and interpreted the prophesies of the Book of Mormon as signifying the eventual passing of the leadership of the church from the "Gentiles to the Lamanites." The problem, Bautista concluded, was that the current Anglo-Gentile leadership was resisting this transfer of power.

Bautista was unable to convince church authorities to publish his book or to finance its publication in Mexico. Despite the hostility of the Salt Lake authorities, Bautista published it on his own in Mexico City in 1934. The impact of the publication was extraordinary. Immediately, the book passed through the membership and took hold as a special text. One Anglo missionary remembers that Mexican Mormons in that period quoted from Bautista's book as if it were scripture rather than using the Book of Mormon.

As Bautista's book circulated, the local Mexican leadership organized convention gatherings to put together their demands. Their foremost concern was the naming of a Mexican as mission president. When Harold Pratt was named mission president, his appointment, according to Mormon historians LaMond Tullis and Elizabeth Hernández, "reached Mexico City with fire-storm fury."

In 1936, at the height of the national sentiment that led to seizure of American oil companies, Mexican Mormons met for a third time to reiterate their demands. This gathering brought the split between Salt Lake and Mexico City Mormons to a head. Eight Mexican leaders were excommunicated by Salt Lake, but the new group defiantly pushed ahead, creating a new *Mexican* Mormon church called the Church of Jesus Christ of Latterday Saints (Third Convention).

The Third Convention group quickly established itself as a serious counterforce to Salt Lake City. Six hundred of the 1,800 Mormons in Mexico joined, despite the threat of excommunication. Many of those who didn't become formal members were nevertheless sympathetic to the effort. An early dispute over doctrine was quickly resolved with the departure of Margarito Bautista and the emergence of Bautista's nephew, Abel Páez, as the key leader of the Convencionistas.

Bautista had wanted the new group to reorganize itself along the lines of nineteenth-century Mormonism, with United Orders and a polygamous leadership. Instead, the Páez group emphasized doctrinal similarity with Salt Lake, defining their central complaint as the lack of Mexican leadership in the church. After Bautista's departure, the Convencionistas organized their own infrastructure. They continued missionary work, built new meeting houses, and produced religious literature, including a magazine called *El Sendero Lamanita* (The Lamanite Path), with such articles as "How the Gospel Came to Mexico."

At first, the actions of the Salt Lake leadership only intensified the split. Ignoring the initial success of the Convencionistas, in 1938, Salt Lake authorities brought in a new mission president who was widely known for his racial blinders and characterizations of Mexicans as "inferior" people. He was dubbed "El Domador de los Salvajes Mexicanos" ("The Tamer of Mexican Savages").

Finally, a shift began to take place in Salt Lake. In 1942, a new mission president, Arwell Pierce (also a colonist), was selected. He was much more adept at dealing with the complicated sentiments dividing Convencionistas from the American-run church. Pierce, who also had connections in the Mexican government, was an effective maneuverer who spoke with a "soft voice" to the Convencionistas. He implied that the spirit of their demands could be met through the strengthening of Mexican-run stakes at the heart of the leadership structure rather than by controlling the Anglo-dominated mission presidency. Then, after issuing these conciliatory statements, Pierce's counselor, a colonist by the name of Harold Brown, would storm about doctrine, the primacy of the Prophet, and excoriate Convencionistas for defying the words of the Salt Lake authorities.

Pierce's hand was immeasurably strengthened with the death of Mormon President Heber J. Grant and his replacement by George Albert Smith. Smith was a more conciliatory figure than Grant. With the encouragement of his Second Counselor, David O. McKay, he provided Arwell Pierce with additional power to work out a "face-saving" solution. Pierce, among others, arranged for the excommunicated Convencionistas to reenter the church. In May 1946, with George Albert Smith presiding, 1,200 members of the Third Convention returned to a reunited church, now based on Salt Lake's continuing centralized authority. The "disaffected" Mexicans, who had been "out of harmony" as the *Church News* put it, had come back to the fold.

The reunited church had also become a thoroughly re-Americanized church. A "two-Mexico policy," as church Commissioner of Education Kenneth Beesley called it, emerged, distinguishing the powerful, Anglo-dominated Mormon Colonies from the Spanish-speaking members in the south. Along with the church in Mexico City, the Colonies expanded in the 1950s, both in numbers and influence.

Brown became the first stake president in Mexico City in 1961, despite Arwell Pierce's promise fifteen years earlier that a Mexican would be named to that position. First and second generation leaders, such as Harold Brown, grew up in the Colonies and cut their teeth on containing the Convencionista troubles. Brown was particularly sensitive to what he considered the dangers of Mexican nationalism. The Mormon leadership in

Mexico, according to Brown, had to be discreet and knowledgeable about Mexican affairs since the risk and/or threat of another Third Convention was always present. Brown recognized that the postwar church had become "a transplanted American institution because some of the characteristic values of our society have been incorporated." The trick, as he saw it, was to present and support those values as Mormon rather than American. In the process, a new culture would emerge, based on both Mormon doctrine and a contemporary Anglo-Mormon world view.

Such a hybrid culture did indeed emerge in the expansion of the church in Mexico in the 1950s and 1960s. Mormon missionaries promoted key Mormon—and American—values, such as upward mobility, corporatelike attitudes, and the bureaucratic, managerial style that became so prominent in Salt Lake by the postwar period.

Though the church had experienced only modest growth in the 1950s and early 1960s in Mexico, this re-Americanization process found a receptive audience among the displaced urban population. The Mexican government had instigated economic policies that led to a massive migration from the traditional farming areas in the northwest and central parts of the country to the rapidly growing urban centers, such as Mexico City and Monterrey. Mormonism was attractive to those poor and newly proletarianized urban dwellers to whom upward mobility and an all-encompassing cultural and religious organization were appealing.

The postwar years also saw a subtle interplay between the church and the Mexican state. In the 1940s and 1950s, Mormon chapels in Mexico, according to the head of the building program in Mexico, Ray McClellan, were designed to not look like chapels, since chapels were then being nationalized by the government. In the early 1960s, to get around restrictions regarding "foreign" missionary work, the church built up a large-scale church educational system, where a discreet yet effective form of proselyting could take place. Similarly, the church worked out a system whereby many of the land transactions or other acquisitions were ostensibly carried out by the church's Mexican second-level leadership, though in reality, such decisions still ultimately flowed from Salt Lake.

The Mormon church, through its employment of Mexican members, was able to create a middle-class leadership cadre. These Mexicans were dependent on the range of jobs generated by the church itself, such as those connected with the church educational system.

Apostle Neal A. Maxwell sees this new Mexican leadership in terms of a Mormon "priesthood style": the busy, disciplined life of top- and middle-level bureaucrats so prominent today in running the day-to-day activities of the church. "If I arrive there today, get off the plane," said Maxwell, "the stake president hands me a book with the schedule and agenda for the various meetings. He's picked up on that spirit in a way that maybe our stereotype of a mañana image would not let us believe. . . . The upward mobility is there and it seems to fit to a great extent with our management style."

That process has been aided by the development of a middle-level bureaucracy within the Mexican church as well. The school system, the Presiding Bishopric's Office (where financial decisions are made), the Visitors Center, all have developed a paid bureaucracy that has become a key component of the re-Americanization process.

The power of the church to control its Mexican members as employer has come up in a number of settings since the days of the Third Convention. During the mid-1960s, for example, a mini–Third Convention was nipped in the bud, thanks in part to control from Salt Lake. The stake leadership in Mexico City, headed by Harold Brown, functioned as "gatekeepers" for Salt Lake, assigning jobs, creating secondary leadership positions, and using the large church educational system to provide a kind of socialization into the Mormon hybrid culture.

The Brown leadership group was not completely successful in keeping the peace. A few Mexican Mormons, including Guillermo Gonzales, who had been a mission president in the northern part of the country, and Mario Arando, who worked in the church seminary program, had become disturbed at what Arando called "racist statements by some in the Anglo leadership who were not able to accept diversity and had only one cultural standard for the church."

Arando and Gonzales, as northern Mexicans (Arando was in fact a third-generation Colony Mormon), had been largely unaffected by the trauma of the Third Convention, which had been almost exclusively a southern–Mexico City affair. As northerners, Gonzales and Arando appeared more defiant than some of their counterparts and felt that the Mexican Mormons should not tolerate any kind of subservience to an overbearing Anglo leadership.

As the Gonzales-Arando group became more vocal in their criticisms, other Mexican Mormons became more fearful and tense. "It can't be good for us if you rock the boat," they declared, implying that criticism could imperil their membership and their jobs. "We were confused and upset at the reaction," Mario Arando recalled. "And then suddenly it hit us. As northerners we were not familiar with those feelings about the Third Convention. There was real terror there. And the job situation was at the center of it. It became impossible to sort out church and employer. I realized the tremendous power in keeping people in line."

Soon after, Gonzales and Arando left Mexico City with some bitterness though both men remained dedicated, practicing Mormons. "The day I announced I was going to leave, I got a call from my bishop, who was Mexican," Arando recalled. "'I know why you're doing this,' the bishop told me. 'I commend your integrity. It is absolutely right. But you have to understand my situation. I can't do what you are doing. I have eight children. I can't take a stand. My church membership is the basis of my employment.'"

Despite the tensions over leadership, and the continuing problem of nationalist sentiment running up against the Mormon hybrid culture, the church remained a growing force in Mexico through the 1960s and especially in the 1970s and early 1980s. The "two-Mexico policy" enabled the church to grow in the northern areas and in Mexico City and other southern urban centers. The growing push under Spencer Kimball to baptize the Lamanites led to an increased missionary presence in the state of Chiapas and along the Mexican-Guatemalan border, with their high concentration of Indians. From the first Spanish-speaking stake organized in Mexico City in 1961, ten more stakes were added in 1975, then more than fifty within the next six years. By the 1980s, the Mexican Mormon population had grown to 250,000 members.

Some of the growth statistics remain a bit deceptive. Though no clear membership-participation statistics are available, Mormon experts on the Mexico church estimate that at least thirty percent and possibly as many as fifty percent of the Mexican Mormons are "revolving door" members; that is, they attend a single meeting, are counted on the membership rolls, but never return, for reasons ranging from doctrinal restrictions (e.g., abstinence from alcohol) to unmet expectations concerning church financial support.

Despite the re-Americanization of the church, the training of a local leadership stratum loyal to the hybrid Mormon/Anglo culture, and the continuing role of the Colonies in providing the top leadership in the Mexican church, the nationalist issue refuses to go away.

LaMond Tullis, a BYU professor, recently completed a volume on the church in Mexico, originally designed to be part of an official sixteen-volume history of the church. Tullis's manuscript was circulated among the Mormon leadership in Mexico, particularly the more conservative and Americanized part of the leadership group. "Don't publish this," was the feedback from Mexico, "or else we'll have a Fourth Convention on our hands."

There is a continuing attempt among the Mexican Mormons to maintain national sentiments and aspirations while drawing on Mormon traditions and religious mythology. In 1981, a bishop in the Zarahemla (the name is derived from the Book of Mormon) ward in Mexico City decided to draw on one of those traditions to serve his members who were poor and unemployed. The bishop applied to the government for some land to establish an *ejido*, a cooperative farm, in the state of Tamaulipas. For the bishop and his members, this *ejido* symbolized a Mexican nationalist re-creation of the Mormon United Order.

After the land became available, the *ejido* group quickly established links with sympathetic American Mormons, who attempted to provide material and financial support to the fledgling enterprise. An Anglo missionary from Mesa, Arizona, did some preliminary fund raising, and help was procured at BYU through the Indian Studies Center and the schools of management and organizational behavior. The Salt Lake General Authorities gave initial approval, looking favorably upon this attempt to reduce the potential financial drain caused whenever poor people joined the Mexican church.

Still, the *ejido* experiment remained, at best, tentative, an isolated attempt to provide a model of cooperative work and living. Unlike other *ejidos*, it had the advantage of drawing on American skills and material support, so it stood a fair chance of success. Its danger lay in its becoming a model of national identity, which church General Authorities might see as undercutting centralized, organizational control. Ultimately, its fate rests with Salt Lake, which could make or break such an experiment, by providing or withdrawing support.

The conflicting themes of nationalism, Americanization, and centralized control are not just limited to Mexico. In Brazil, for example, two distinct leadership factions have emerged—the "greens" and the "yellows." The greens are the Americanized leaders, those who came into the church precisely because they were looking for an American way of life and identified with Mormonism's American appeal. Several of the younger Brazilian greens became missionaries and resembled their American counterparts with their white shirts, suits, and even some Americanized mannerisms.

The yellows, on the other hand, are more nationally inclined. They tend to be older. Many of them don't speak English and have no intention of learning to. Yet, they operate with relative freedom within the church since many of the missionaries and church leaders who preside over Brazil do not speak Portuguese and remain unaware of the different tendencies among the locals. It remains an ironic twist to this continuing problem of national identity in a centralized church.

CHURCH AND STATE

In Latin America, the growth of the Mormon church and other Protestant fundamentalist groups has had a direct relationship to the fortunes of the Catholic church. Through much of the nineteenth and twentieth centuries, the Catholic clergy identified with and became part of the different elite groupings on the continent. Catholic bishops blessed the activities of Latin dictators, counseled their parishioners to accept the status quo, and dined at the tables of the landed elite.

By the 1960s, divisions within the Catholic church began to emerge. Starting with the Brazilian church but then spreading rapidly throughout the continent, a number of Catholic priests and even, occasionally, bishops began to preach a "theology of liberation." They created what were called *comunidades de bases*, that is, communities of faith struggling to overcome inequalities and injustices for the poor. This advocacy for the poor deeply affected the church, at times splitting the Catholic hierarchy and in some instances, such as Nicaragua, causing Catholic priests and Catholic orders to ally with the Sandinista revolutionaries who were challenging an entrenched political and economic elite.

As the Catholic church began to change, many of the governments in Latin America, primarily those maintaining dictatorial rule, such as the southern cone states of Argentina, Brazil, Chile, and Uruguay, responded to the situation. While not always attacking the Catholics directly, these governments began to play their "Protestant card," looking especially to favor conservative, progovernment, pro-American churches as a way to weaken Catholic influence.

This shift took place precisely at a time when the Mormon church, under Spencer Kimball's direction, made a major move in the 1970s to expand the church in Latin America. The Mormons were immediately drawn into the tug of war between church and state. James E. Faust, a General Authority who had been in charge of church activities in several South American countries during the mid-1970s, told a church interviewer in 1977 how government leaders in countries such as Paraguay and Uruguay constantly brought up the subject of "communist infiltration" of the Catholic church. President Alfredo Stroessner of Paraguay, Faust remarked, "looks upon the Catholic Church as being Communistic and therefore his arch enemy." As the Mormons, who are historically antagonistic to the Catholic church, began to receive more favorable treatment in Paraguay, it became clear to Faust that it was not a matter of Stroessner liking the Mormons; it was "just that he disliked the Catholics more."

The Mormons had several advantages in dealing with these governments. Several of the top Mormon leaders in Latin America during the 1970s and 1980s had strong business and political ties with Latin elites. These included such men as J.F. O'Donnal, a rubber-plantation owner and the Goodyear Tire and Rubber representative in Guatemala; William Bradford, who represented a food-processing company in Latin America before becoming a General Authority; and Robert Wells, an executive and Latin American representative for First National Bank prior to his rapid rise within the church hierarchy.

During the last fifteen years, leaders such as Wells, Bradford, and O'Donnal have helped the church establish friendly relations and obtain organizational privileges on the continent, particularly with the most conservative or right-wing governments. They represented the Mormon church not only as an American-based, conservative church, but as one that stresses, in doctrinal terms, the *depoliticization* of its membership. "If you'll stay out of politics, you'll have a great harvest in Uruguay," that country's military ruler told James E. Faust.

Terror has become an instrument of government policy in Latin American dictatorships. For the Mormons, staying out of politics also means providing implicit and, at times, explicit support for the terror. Church General Authority Wells, who has functioned as area supervisor for the southern cone countries, acknowledged that terror and "disappearances" in countries such as Argentina did exist before the demise of the military government in 1983. He also declared that those who have disappeared, "deserved it." "This is war," Wells declared in a 1982 interview about the tactics of the Argentinian junta. "I've had friends killed or kidnapped by the underground," he went on, referring to his banking days. "It's a different ballgame. They shouldn't deserve to have freedom over there. The press shouldn't have the freedom to criticize. People will elect the dumbest people; they're not prepared for general elections. They've got to have a strong hand to control."

There are even Mormon *desaparecidos* (disappeared ones), but Wells feels that these are "inactive" Mormons, which then solves the problem regarding their "disappearance." There was, nevertheless, one instance, according to Wells, where an active Mormon "disappeared." The Mormon was tortured for three days by the police, until they discovered that they had been looking for someone else with the same name. "The police apologized afterwards and asked us not to tell anyone," Wells declared. In another instance, Wells described how a Salt Lake church "liberal" arranged an interview with a Utah senator for an Argentinian Mormon living in Salt Lake whose daughter had been imprisoned in Argentina. The senator phoned Wells to inquire into the matter. Wells in turn got in touch with the Argentinian local branch. Yes, the branch leaders told Wells, she was in jail but was an inactive member who had a boyfriend who was a communist terrorist. The branch leader then told Wells that the church leaders had "suffered over the girl," tried to warn her of her associations and get her back into the church, but all to no avail. Wells then got back to the senator, and they agreed that the senator no longer needed to intervene. "Thanks for keeping me out of trouble," the senator told Wells.

The ability of church leaders to rationalize government terror is not limited to Argentina, with its well-publicized "disappearances." It extends throughout the continent and is most pronounced in the pivotal country of Chile, where the Mormons have experienced their most rapid growth since the military coup that brought General Augusto Pinochet to power in 1973. Robert Wells called General Pinochet "one of the great leaders of Latin America" and his military coup an act that "served the purpose of the Lord."

Chile plays a special role in the Mormon effort in Latin America. Parley Pratt, the first Mormon missionary on the continent, landed there in 1851. More than 100 years passed before the Mormons officially reentered Chile. In 1961, under the urging of Henry D. Moyle, who took special interest in spreading the church in Latin America, the first Chilean mission was established out of the previous "Andes mission."

From the outset, the mission's first president, A. Delbert Palmer, recognized several serious problems for missionary work, such as class divisions in the country and the lack of opportunities and leadership skills among the lower middle class. The local church was heavily dependent on its North American leaders, and according to Palmer, locals had no input regarding the key school programs and construction projects. The school programs were established in the early 1960s just before the election of Salvador Allende, the presidential candidate of the Chilean left in 1964.

After Allende's loss by a narrow margin, the political polarization intensified. Significant numbers of members, according to one mission president, became sympathetic to the Allende coalition. By the time Allende came to power in 1970, the country was on the brink of civil war. A U.S.-supported military coup seemed a real possibility in this country with a long-standing democratic tradition.

In the three years that Allende held power, the Mormon church had problems maintaining membership. The church also had some difficulties over its school system with the Allende government because the government feared that the church seminary system remained at least covertly antigovernment.

The church was explicit about its "apolitical" character. "Don't talk politics" was the rule laid down to the missionaries, according to Mission President Royden Glade. Political divisions between church members nevertheless had increased, and the anticommunist, anti-Allende attitudes of the American missionaries became even more pronounced.

When the coup occurred on September 11, 1973, the American leadership and missionaries in Chile were ecstatic. Rex Carlisle, the assistant to the mission president, later declared that "The Lord played a great part in the overthrow of that communistic government, as he had many children ready to hear the gospel and the communistic government didn't by any means provide the atmosphere in which the gospel could effectively be preached. So I think the new government deserves a big hand."

After the coup, several church members, including a few local leaders who had supported Allende, disappeared, many to the national stadium where prisoners were held prior to their disappearance. Church leaders immediately preached support for the government *and* noninvolvement in politics and tried to depoliticize former Allende sympathizers, while substituting the church as a source of identity. The church, as Carlisle put it, would help the Allende sympathizers "give up their political communistic opinions by now turning them to the gospel." New leaders were rapidly recruited into the church ranks, as the American leadership promoted those "priesthood brothers" who, according to Glade, "had a certain political leaning or affiliation," i.e., support of the military junta. Within a couple of years, a new Mormon church had emerged whose members, according to Carlisle, now "overwhelmingly" favored the present government, which "fell in line, of course, with the teachings of the gospel."

The key to Mormon succcess was the leadership's application of the twelfth Article of Faith, about "being subject to Kings, Presidents, rulers, and magistrates." To the leadership, that meant support for the military junta and *at the same time* an admonition that the membership not become involved in radical political activities.

The junta in Chile responded favorably, lifting restrictions on Mormon missionary activity, construction programs, and the church school system. According to General Authority Robert Wells, the Chilean junta was still concerned about its image in the United States and sensitive to negative press coverage of its police activities. "If he had to shoot anyone," Wells said of Pinochet, "the great majority deserved it since they were terrorists. The U.S. bleeding heart press doesn't understand the local situation. They are malintentioned. Papers like the *New York Times* and *Washington Post* have a socialistic-communistic point of view rather than a free agency–democracy point of view."

Aware of Wells's and other church leaders' sympathies, junta members suggested a quid pro quo. We have treated you well, they told Wells, now we would like you to help, referring specifically to the press problem. We would like you to tell your members in Utah and the United States, the junta leaders declared, about the religious freedom that exists in this country. A *Church News* article about the rapid growth of the church subsequently appeared.

Another tacit understanding developed over the American copper industry. The most prominent Mormon in the copper industry was C. Jay Parkinson, the chairman of the board of Anaconda. Parkinson had been active in the campaign against Allende in the 1964 election, working with the Business Group of Latin America, which had been organized by David Rockefeller. In the 1970 election he was part of a group of businessmen that attempted to funnel $500,000 into the campaign of Allende's opponent. Parkinson was also a member of the "40 Committee," and heavily involved in many covert efforts to overthrow Allende. According to former *New York Times* reporter Seymour Hersh, Parkinson was also under investigation, though never indicted, on felony charges for perjury, obstruction of justice, and conspiracy, concerning his testimony over the events in Chile before a Senate subcommittee.

The junta also knew that the church had a special relationship with Kennecott Copper. Kennecott, with major mining operations in Utah, had, for many years, a General Authority on its board. "Just recently," Rex Carlisle told a church interviewer in 1976, "relations with the top officials of the country have developed in our favor, because the government leaders have recognized the power of the Mormon church in the controlling of several copper corporations throughout the world. And in trying to get their [the copper companies] influence back into the country, they've tried to make very good friends with not only the Chilean Mormons but with the top officials and quorums of the church in Salt Lake." Although Carlisle has overstated the church's influence at Kennecott, this go-between role for church officials contributed to the junta's positive feelings toward the church.

By 1980, the Mormon presence in Chile had escalated dramatically, with the baptism rate in the country the success story of Latin America. From a membership base of 20,000 during the Allende regime, church conversions grew astronomically during the 1970s, reaching 121,000 in less than a decade. In 1980 alone, 20,000 baptisms were recorded, making Chile the country with the highest per capita rate per missionary.

For the international church, Chile was a success story and their efforts there became a model for the church throughout the turbulent continent.

CAUGHT IN A CIVIL WAR

Julio Cesar Macias was not a typical Mormon. Although inactive at the time he assumed command of one of the key guerrilla groups in Guatemala in the late 1970s, he still was an heroic figure among local Guatemalan Mormons.

To the Mormon leadership, particularly American supervisors, mission presidents, and young missionaries, Julio Cesar Macias was anathema. He had helped organize strikes at Coca-Cola plants. This activity, one Central American Mormon wryly noted, did not go over well with one of the American church leaders for Central America who had been in charge of Coca-Cola in Costa Rica prior to his church role. A member of the church high council in Guatemala and another Mormon who belonged to the American diplomatic corps reportedly had gathered information about the Macias family, which was later used to help bring about the deaths of some of those same family members.

Yet the Mormon leadership was afraid to excommunicate Macias for fear of retaliation, given the guerrilla leader's support among local Mormons. When Macias was finally killed by the military government, the church leadership breathed a sigh of relief. Macias was then quickly excommunicated by the church *posthumously*. The embarrassment of a Mormon guerrilla, the church leaders hoped, would be a thing of the past.

There's the story of Feliciano Acevado, a founder of the Social Democratic Party in Guatemala, the mayor of his hometown, and also a member of the church, who left Guatemala for political reasons to come to Chicago. There, he learned the jewelry trade. When he later returned to Guatemala he opened the Liahona Jewelry Store, named after an instrument of guidance in the Book of Mormon.

In Guatemala, Acevado resumed his political activity as general secretary of his Social Democratic Party. He too became a victim of the civil war. One day, in front of his jewelry store, with his wife and children present, his throat was slashed. His replacement as SDP general secretary, also a Mormon bishop, was soon after gunned down in an ambush.

In contrast, there is the role of Raphael Castillo Valdez, the foreign minister of the Romero Lucas government in the late 1970s. Castillo was a graduate of BYU; though, as another BYU Mormon from Central America recalled, "he was only a Mormon in Provo, not in Guatemala." Nevertheless, Castillo was a big feather in the Guatemalan church's cap. He, like other successful Guatemalans who were Mormons either in name or in practice, identified with this *American* church and believed, as one report on the church in Central America put it, that "because the Church is an American Church, you have to protect the interests of Americans, especially the Mormons, who have investments in Central America."

In Central America today, the Mormons are dealing uneasily with a regionwide civil war, a civil war that has polarized their own followers. Much of the missionary work in Central America is a recent phenomenon, accelerating in the early 1970s, precisely at a time when social and political conditions began to deteriorate seriously throughout the region. Central America offered what appeared to be a special opportunity for the Mormons: large Indian populations throughout the region, mostly in rural areas. In Guatemala, in fact, Indians represent fifty percent of the population.

J. F. O'Donnal is a key church figure in the heavily Indian countries of Central America. O'Donnal, who grew up in the Mexican colonies, settled in Guatemala in the 1940s and married a Guatemalan woman. His wife became the first Guatemalan convert. After World War II, O'Donnal became involved in the Guatemalan rubber industry, first for the U.S. Department of Agriculture and later as Goodyear's local representative. He was also a rubber-plantation owner in his own right.

When a U.S.-backed coup overthrew the democratically elected government of Jacobo Arbenz in the 1950s, O'Donnal, who considered Arbenz a communist, said he had worked closely with the U.S. ambassador to help undercut the Arbenz government. He was also suspected by a number of Central American Mormons to have worked with the CIA, which had orchestrated the coup. During the 1960s and 1970s, while O'Donnal was mission president and then regional representative, the church leader remained a staunch anticommunist, bitterly attacking the Catholic church in Guatemala as being "very leftist in their thinking." For O'Donnal, Guatemalan Catholic priests had "instigated considerable agitation among the Indians against the government and those who have property."

While O'Donnal and other church leaders attacked Catholics and other "leftists," they tried to keep the church focused on its primary mission—proselyting and recruitment. Numbers remained a key, and all missionaries were pushed hard to keep the baptism rates high. Even situations such as the 1976 earthquake in Guatemala became opportunities for recruitment, as church care packages were designated exclusively for members. In an incident after the earthquake, Cordell Andersen, a Mormon living in Guatemala, recalled how 500 Indians in a rural village came to a Mormon chapel because they had heard that relief supplies were available. "These people went for help," he recalled, "but were told they couldn't get help because they weren't LDS. They left, cursing the church."

The O'Donnal approach is best summed up by his statement, "We don't want literacy campaigns, we want collars [conversions]." According to a number of returned missionaries who come from a different generation than O'Donnal, church leaders have little appreciation for the culture and customs of the Indians.

Andersen, who has spent fifteen years in Guatemala as a missionary and plantation owner, divides his life between his father's home in Provo, Utah, and his ranch in Guatemala. He helped to write a book on his experiences and is a critic of the church's missionary program. He notes, for instance, that missionaries are sent to work among the Indians in the standard white shirt and tie. "The first impression is bad," he said. "The tie is hated as a symbol of the conqueror."

Andersen has been trying another approach to missionary work that bears certain similarities to the methods used by Catholic adherents of liberation theology. Andersen called his program the "Good Life" approach. He told the Indians that they are "descendants of a great people who were progressive" and that they can again become like their ancestors. Then combining "the spiritual and the temporal," he emphasized keeping a clean, healthful home, home improvement and construction, nutrition, family unity, education, and work through vocational education. To help the Indian converts support their families, he assisted them in setting up a number of cooperatives on his ranch.

Andersen's experiment drew attacks from church leaders in Guatemala, including accusations that he was a communist. "I went down there to fight communism," Andersen responded. To placate church leaders, he stopped describing the cooperative as a Welfare Vegetable Work Farm because the name implied church support for his work with Indians. Finally he asked to be released from his job as a missionary so as not to cause divisions in the church community. Andersen said other missionary officials have been released because they would not follow injunctions to avoid working with the poor.

Andersen persisted with his experiment, however, and would like to try it with Indians in Utah. He felt that the church creates expectations of a better life among the Indian population but then cannot follow through. "They have a welfare program that hasn't happened in Latin America," he said. "The church is afraid to mention it for fear that there will be an avalanche of conversions."

As the guerrilla movements in Central America gained in strength and violence increased, Mormon missionary work in the region became increasingly problematic. In 1979, the church pulled its American leadership and missionaries out of El Salvador after being told to leave by the guerrillas. That same year, the church witnessed a serious decline in its fortunes in Nicaragua in the wake of the Sandinista overthrow of the Somoza regime. Within three years, the Sandinistas would accuse the Mormons of ties with the CIA. Mormon facilities were closed down despite denials from Salt Lake. In Guatemala, missionaries had to withdraw from several Indian communities after guerrilla movements penetrated the area.

By the 1980s, the church found itself in serious trouble throughout the region. Its position of political noninvolvement, though praised by the right-wing military governments, was under attack by the guerrillas, who called it a way of disguising promilitary and pro-American sentiments. While the church operated more effectively with a passive and quiescent population, in Central America, it encountered major difficulties with political passions at their height.

When church leader Ezra Taft Benson spoke at a recent church conference in Salt Lake about reestablishing the Monroe Doctrine in Latin America, this speech, for a number of Central American Mormons, only added fuel to the fire. "You could see the smoke coming out of the earphones [of the Latin American members]," LaMond Tullis recalled in a 1982 interview. "In Central America, our church might be on the losing side of history."

A Latin American student at BYU tells a story that speaks of the tensions and conflicts facing the Mormon church in Central America. "Liberation theology has been happening in my country, and in Guatemala, Nicaragua, Mexico, and other places," the student declares. "To me it is the idea of helping the poor, but it is not a simple thing to do."

The student recalled how his mother always liked the Mormons because they spoke of the poor and how to share things together so that the poor would no longer be the poor. The Catholics, on the other hand, his mother would say, had ignored the people and seemed to be for the rich. "But today, my mother says that has all changed," the student declares. "By serving the poor, the Catholics, she says, are now practicing the gospel. And what are the Mormons doing? The Catholics are doing what we should be doing. So now we have a situation where the government in El Salvador knows all about our doctrine that says we Mormons uphold governments and laws. Yet it is a government that breaks laws and murders its people, a government that most of us Mormons do not support. So when we hear a General Authority evoke that doctrine, we say, yes, it is true for you, but it is not true for us."

FOLLOWING THE FLAG

Like Latin America, Asia offered some distinct advantages for a church best understood as American in character and middle class in aspiration. Unlike Latin America, several countries in Asia offered distinct disadvantages in terms of the foreign nature of any Christian doctrine in countries where Buddhist, Shinto, Moslem, or Hindu cultures are predominant. The church has been most successful in Japan, Korea, the Philippines, and, for a time, Southeast Asia, where the overwhelming American presence until the fall of Vietnam provided a successful backdrop for Mormon proselyting.

Instead of simply following the flag, Mormonism in Asia followed the troops, as early proselyting was directly linked to U.S. military actions in Korea and Vietnam. In Japan, some of the first substantial proselyting activity was also undertaken by American troops either stationed in Japan or on leave from Korea. American military personnel baptized a number of their Japanese domestic help. A similar situation developed in Korea, where the church began to establish itself shortly after the armistice. Korean Mission President Robert Slover spoke of those joining as people who "wanted to be friends with the Americans and this gave them an opportunity. They were looking for all kinds of opportunities, for food and whatever they could get."

Fully aware of its attraction because of its American character and the role played by young American missionaries, the Mormons, even well into the Spencer W. Kimball period, constantly sought members by evoking the American connection. They taught English for proselyting purposes (using the Book of Mormon as an English text), allowed health or welfare service missionaries to provide aid while simultaneously recruiting potential members, and ultimately held out the dream that by joining the church one could achieve an economic change for the better.

The expansion in Asia, linked as it was to the American presence overseas, culminated in the late 1970s with a growing fascination with the People's Republic of China. From the outset of his presidency, Kimball expressed a deep interest in working out a relationship with the Chinese. In the church magazine *The Ensign*, the church president praised the Chinese for having similar values to Mormons: a strong work ethic, family-centered life, and perhaps most important, a dislike of permissive, sexually explicit, western values.

In 1979, a group of musical performers called the Young Ambassadors arranged a quick tour of the People's Republic. According to a church publication, the BYU performers were well received but only got permission to go after a careful screening process. "The Chinese government had been reluctant to schedule performances," the publication reported, "possibly because of negative experiences with other United States performers whose shows had been embarrassing to the *conservative Chinese people* [our italics]."

The Mormon attempt to penetrate China, following as it did Nixon's opening to China, was not as quixotic a move as it might seem at first glance for this anticommunist church. In the early days of the Cold War, church leaders, such as J. Reuben Clark, had dismissed suggestions that the church become active in socialist countries. In one letter, Clark explicitly stated, "When the time comes that this [socialist] control is thrown over or changed, there will probably be a great field for conversions." As the United States began to influence the economies and cultures of communist-bloc countries, particularly in Eastern Europe, so the Mormons, taking advantage of the political opening, changed their approach and successfully sought to establish missionary efforts in such countries as Poland and East Germany.

In an interview with church radio station KBYU, David Kennedy, the church's ambassador at large, spoke of the delicate negotiations that took place with the Polish government prior to the establishment of a church mission in that country. The Mormons, Kennedy promised, would not only stay out of opposition politics, but would provide, at least indirectly, support for the government. "There is nothing that says you have to be a democrat (with a small d) in order to be a Mormon," Kennedy declared. Explaining to the Polish government the significance of the twelfth Article of Faith, Kennedy told the Polish authorities that Polish Mormons would be taught to be "good citizens," to uphold their government and sustain the country's work ethic.

Kennedy was the key figure not only in penetrating communist countries but in negotiating a range of other sensitive Mormon "foreign policy" matters. Appointed in 1974 by Spencer Kimball to be the church's "special consultant for diplomatic affairs," Kennedy had just the right background for the church. A successful banker (chairman of the Continental Illinois bank) and member of Richard Nixon's cabinet (Secretary of the Treasury), Kennedy had established over the years a vast number of political and business contacts throughout the world. In his last years in public office, he had functioned as United States ambassador at large, while simultaneously establishing contacts for the church, sometimes with some of the same people he dealt with as government representative.

Reporting directly to the First Presidency, Kennedy was at once diplomat and troubleshooter during the Kimball era of rapid international expansion. He would visit with heads of state, such as Philippine President Ferdinand Marcos or Latin American military junta leaders, as well as leading business figures. He would use his financial connections, as he told one church reporter, to establish quid pro quos, such as his suggestion to one Asian minister that in exchange for Kennedy's help on a loan, the minister might use his good office to help maintain and support the Mormon presence in that country. Most important, David Kennedy represented a *personal* link to power, with his ability to recall earlier visits, remember the names of wives and family, and utilize his own extensive business and political associations.

For the Mormon hierarchy, the dangers of international expansion lay not only in the political arena but in the way politics or culture translated into what are seen as doctrinal challenges. As early as 1946, when Ezra Taft Benson was sent to Europe to reestablish Mormon missions on the continent, he was obliged to deal with "new practices" at variance with approved procedures from Salt Lake. Brazilian members' flirtation with spiritualism, Mexico's Third Convention, the existence of a matriarch-dominated church in parts of Africa are all only the tip of a potential volcano that church authorities fear could explode without Salt Lake's intervention. Marion G. Romney, General Authority and counselor to two church presidents, stated in a 1972 church interview that "if it were not for the frequent visits of the General Authorities to the missions and the stakes, we'd have many different churches." Further, Romney went on, "if we didn't send the General Authorities to supervise and direct and bring about harmony in procedure, we'd soon have apostate practices all over the Church."

In describing the non-American Mormon churches, Mormon philosopher Sterling M. McMurrin referred to a "degree of standardization in the Mormon Church [that] is beyond the belief of those who have not seen it for themselves—standardization in local Church policies and procedures, in artistic tastes, in reading and sermonizing, in thought and behavior, even in such mundane matters as the scheduling of meetings."

The issue for McMurrin was at once religious and cultural. "The Church tends to move its people toward a common pattern that often destroys native diversity and creativity," McMurrin declared. "Who will determine what to tamper with and what to leave untouched? Will Dravidian congregations in India open Sunday School by singing 'Utah We Love Thee,' as was not uncommon in some European missions in the past?"

Standardization and centralized control from Salt Lake in a church now active in eighty-one countries created interesting dynamics as the church expanded. The extremely high dropout rate was only the most obvious manifestation of kinks in the system. To meet these problems, church leaders spoke of developing a procedure that would redefine what constituted a "minimal Mormon," given the enormous set of requirements (meetings, the cultural adaptation, tithing, and so on) facing a practicing member. "Leadership training" seemed the most immediate need, as the revolving-door phenomenon also extended to the key leadership cadre, who were often drafted as soon as they indicated a willingness to participate in overall church activities. Unlike Utah, where church leadership positions are primarily reserved for the middle-aged (and older), the international church draws heavily on those in their twenties and thirties to fill even the top spots in the local hierarchy.

Yet even these cultural and organizational tensions are today outweighed by another concern that came to the fore by the end of the decade, a concern that would ultimately cause a slowdown in the expansion rate and a fear that the stresses of growth were straining the very resources of the church itself.

SLOWDOWN

The first sign, hardly noticeable, was a slight drop in the number of missionaries in 1980, although no one yet spoke of slowing down. Press releases were still churned out, proclaiming that the Mormon church was indeed one of the fastest-growing domestic churches and that internationally its rate of expansion was phenomenal. Plans were underway for seventeen new temples outside the United States (only six had been built as of 1983), most of them to be located in Third World countries such as Mexico, Chile, and Korea. During the 1970s, the Kimball era was synonymous with explosive international growth.

For the church leadership, the buzzword was "decentralization," yet the reality was further centralization and direction from Salt Lake. One of the key leadership groups, the Quorum of the Seventy, was expanded in the mid-1970s to accommodate international expansion and to integrate a handful of non-American Mormons into the leadership hierarchy.

American church leaders claim that non-American leadership has finally emerged in the international church, asserting that in some countries "we're almost totally local," as Apostle Neal A. Maxwell put it. Yet the top leadership in the church remains totally dominated by Americans, especially by those from Utah, Idaho, and Arizona. In one church study, cited in the *Church News*, eighty percent of all mission presidents, most of whom were stationed in the Third World, were found to be from this area.

The Salt Lake bureaucracy, the vast organizational apparatus that grew rapidly in the 1960s and 1970s, also had *functional* control in key areas such as expenditure of funds, construction of new chapels, and the church educational and literature systems. This centralized decision-making not only affected the type and content of materials produced (i.e., the Mormon-American culture syndrome), but how much was spent as well. That issue, the allocation of resources, became by the 1980s the real sleeper in determining the future direction of the international church.

In class terms, the church, though growing, was still primarily recruiting poor people, with members looking to the church as a basis for potential economic mobility. Similar to the period when the labor missionary program was first instituted, the local churches were finding themselves increasingly pressed to come up with even a token portion of their share of the range of contributions required. By the late 1970s a de facto system of nearly 100 percent financing by Salt Lake was taking place. As some observers in Salt Lake saw it, a massive drain of funds out of Salt Lake had developed. International missionary work was the key reason for the church's new capital crunch.

Thus, in order to expand, the church's domestic base had to be squeezed. By 1980, every one of the eighty-one countries where the church had established operations, with the two exceptions of the United States and Canada, was short of funds. In some areas, Chile and Brazil for example, where the church was expanding at an exponential rate, the financial drain was serious, so serious that church financial reserves for the first time since the changes of the mid-1960s were being affected.

By the early 1980s, the crunch was taking its toll. The number of missionaries decreased in 1981 and continued to fall over the next years, even after the church changed its policy and reduced the length of mission from two years to eighteen months. Cost-cutting policies instituted in Salt Lake greatly affected the international church. Not only were the number of chapels and other church buildings cut back, but those now built no longer were constructed in a way that reinforced the notion that Mormons were wealthy and powerful. "We had to look at situations in countries like Chile or Argentina," key financial money manager J. Alan Blodgett said, "and ask ourselves, how long could we deal with these rates of success?"

Though church leaders fret about the capital crunch and insist that such phenomena as the drop in missionaries will only be temporary, they see the problem as only reinforcing the *doctrinal* justification of Mormonism as an American-centered church. "We see it as part of the Lord's design putting the church here [in America]," Neal A. Maxwell declared, "because it does have to bankroll the church in the rest of the world."

The financial situation has, to a certain extent, forced the issue of what kind of Mormon church will emerge throughout the world in the next two decades of this century. One route, which Mormon liberals hope will be followed, involves the development of *any kind* of diversity and cultural pluralism. The likely route, however, involves a further strengthening of the hybrid Mormon-American culture based on a narrow and centrally defined reading of doctrine, with all decisions and power still flowing from Salt Lake. Those who favor diversity hope to see the development of a greater number of *national* churches, which could be the means for creating more *universality* within the church. The second route, and the one favored by the church hierarchy, foresees the reinforcement of the standardized, American-influenced character of the church, an ostensibly *international* church that simply stresses the church's *parochial* nature.

Church General Authorities speak of two churches: the domestic church based in America and the international church outside the borders of the United States. To church leaders, the international aspect of church activity involves a kind of foreign policy. Its ultimate measure of success is when people "over there" begin to resemble the people "over here." The model of the successful Mormon in the international church, in fact, is the transplanted middle-class American, a member of the priesthood outfitted in his dark suit, white shirt, and tie.

Today, political, social, cultural, and doctrinal policies are at stake when discussing the future of the international church. With the Mormons continuing to follow the flag as an American church and with the United States in this post-Vietnam era facing the possibility of becoming a declining power in the 1980s and 1990s, the church finds itself at a crossroads. This highly centralized organization, fearing loss of control and subject to worries about finances and nationalist-inspired apostate movements, might ultimately find itself on the "losing side of history."

CHAPTER SIX

FALLEN ANGELS AND
LOST BROTHERS:
THE CHURCH AND RACE

OUT OF SPIRITUAL DARKNESS

On a late fall day in 1982, Ralph Crane and Keith Crocker were sitting in their basement office at Brigham Young University discussing *Eagle's Eye*, the university's newspaper for native Americans—or Lamanites as the Saints call them. Crane, a Canadian Indian whose ancestors were Sioux, Cree, and Assiniboine, was the editor of the paper, and Crocker, a White Mountain Apache from Arizona, was one of his reporters. Their discussion turned to the possibility of a debate in the paper about the impact of the church's Indian Placement Service on traditional Indian culture.

The Indian Placement Service is the centerpiece of the church's native American program. Through it, the church recruits young Indians between the ages of eight and eighteen (changed to ages eleven through eighteen in 1984) to live as foster children in white homes. Most of the Indians at BYU, including Crane and Crocker, come out of this program. Within the Indian community at BYU, there has been an ongoing debate between those who went on Placement and those who did not over the impact of the program on their culture. "We are trying to get away from the fact that the BYU paper is pro-Placement," said Crocker. "It has always been pro-Placement. I think Placement teaches values: family heritage, family unity. Others say it destroys traditions."

When these two young Indians approached one of their faculty advisers with the suggestion, he told them that the discussion would be nonproductive, like beating a dead horse. Another adviser warned them that the subject was too sensitive for the paper. Not surprisingly, the discussion, so central to any appraisal of the church's Indian work, never appeared in the *Eagle's Eye*.

Whether BYU Indian students are allowed to debate the program or not, Indian Placement has been one of the church's most controversial and most successful programs over the years. Numerous Indian critics have castigated the church for "kidnapping" their young, for skimming the best of Indian youth from the reservations to which they have never returned, and for targeting certain tribes, particularly the Navajos, for eventual take-over. A number of traditional Indians, including leaders of the Hopi clan system, make little distinction between the church and a handful of prominent Mormon attorneys and politicians who have set up and manipulated tribal governments, pressed for cash buy-outs of contested Indian land claims, arranged for the exploitation of Indian mineral resources, and generally worked to impose the values of the white world in Indian country. To these Indians, the church and Mormon lawyers and politicians are one and the same, part of a dominant white society that has used and manipulated native Americans for its own purposes.

Loyal church members, such as Ralph Crane and Keith Crocker, have themselves questioned the impact of the church's Indian program. Even Golden Buchanan, the Saint who began the Placement Service, wondered about the consequences of the church's aggressive benevolence. After more than two decades of work with Indians, he questioned if the program merely integrated a handful of Indians, successful by Anglo standards, into white society while leaving the rest caught in some tragic middle ground between the white and Indian worlds.

The church's response is that the Indians are, in fact, their lost brothers, the Lamanites, to whom Joseph Smith dedicated the Book of Mormon, which is their history. Once part of a great American civilization that received the gospel from Jesus Christ Himself when He visited this continent soon after His resurrection, the Lamanites became a fallen people awaiting the arrival of their white brothers who would once again redeem them and make them a great people. To the Saints, traditional Indian culture is really a reflection of a people that once followed the gospel but then lived in "a spiritual darkness which came upon their fathers through disobedience," as the late Apostle Mark E. Petersen wrote.

"There are many promises which are extended to the Lamanites," says the Book of Mormon, "for it is because of the traditions of their fathers that caused them to remain in their state of ignorance. . . . And at some period of time they will be brought to believe in his work and to know the incorrectness of the traditions of their fathers, and many of them will be saved . . ." That time has come, proclaim the leaders of the church, and President Spencer W. Kimball has been the major instrument of this great work.

The church's view of the American Indian is part of a larger racial mythology that takes in blacks, Latinos of Indian extraction, and Pacific Islanders as well. This mythology was born of the primitive archeology and, ironically, the abolitionism of the American frontier. It was nourished through the Utah Indian wars, the first missionary forays into the Pacific Basin, and the construction of an all-white Mormon society in the Great

Basin. But it has finally reached its dotage as a result of the church's rapid international expansion and the rise of a new cultural identity among the Americas' racial minorities.

In 1978, Spencer Kimball, missionary to the Indians and critic of Mormon racism, announced the first revelation in modern times. Henceforth, all eligible males would be granted the priesthood, ending two decades of controversy that had centered on the Saints' practice of denying blacks the priesthood. The Mormon presence in the Third World, particularly in countries such as Brazil, had necessitated this change, a change that seemed to indicate a change in the church's racial views. But in terms of Indians, whose history and fate are central to the prophecies of Joseph Smith and the Book of Mormon, the Saints still cling to most of their peculiar views, which are tinged with the racial arrogance of white society.

The conversion of the Lamanites is the fulfillment of prophecy. As the church expands in this contemporary period, red, black, and brown peoples have become primary missionary targets. For the Saints, modernizing efforts notwithstanding, are determined to set these racial groups, particularly the native peoples of the Americas, on what they consider the right path. And when it comes to race, this path is a special one, for it leads these potential recruits toward a higher, whiter, or, in the recently revised terminology, a purer state of being.

IN SEARCH OF THE LAMANITES

A visit to the North Visitors Center on the Temple grounds at Salt Lake City has to be one of the more unusual experiences offered to students of the Mormon church. Here one is exposed to a startling propaganda barrage, at once racial and doctrinal, titled "Christ in America." As the lights dim and pseudoclassical music pours into the room, a figure dressed in a safari outfit appears on the screen to explain that "the Indians of North and South America are descendants of a great people who occupied this hemisphere many centuries before Columbus." The problem, says the narrator, is that no one has been able "to discover the secret of who they were and from whence they came." The narrator then tells of how both the natives of Hawaii and Mexico greeted the first whites to arrive among them with great fanfare because their legends told them of "a Great White God who once appeared in the Americas, who ministered to their people, who preached of peace, and who promised one day to return." The Great White God, called Lono by the Hawaiians and Quetzalcoatl by the Indians of Mexico, is Jesus Christ, says the narrator, and his appearance in the western hemisphere is recorded in the Book of Mormon, which is an account of the native people's voyage to the western hemisphere centuries before the birth of Christ.

While the Visitors Center film focuses on the appearance of Christ in the western hemisphere, the Book of Mormon tells how the sons of the prophet Lehi, who led his followers from Jerusalem across the Pacific to the new world, fought over their father's prophecies. Two of his sons, Laman and Lemuel, broke with their brother, Nephi, and came under a curse. According to Nephi, who tells the story in the Book of Mormon, "Wherefore, as they were white, and exceeding fair and delightsome, that they might not be enticing to my people the Lord did cause a skin of blackness to come upon them," and they became "an idle people, full of mischief and subtlety, and did seek in the wilderness for beasts of prey."

Ultimately the split between the Nephites and the Lamanites led to the great conflagration in which the Nephites were wiped out by the Lamanites near the Hill of Cumorah. Then according to prophecy, the Lamanites were smitten and scattered and their land was taken from them by the Gentiles, who had come to the promised land from the land across the ocean.

The idea of Indian missions is as old as the church itself. As soon as he founded his new church, Joseph Smith sent missionaries to preach to the native peoples of the middle border. One diarist tells of a meeting between Smith and members of the Potawatami tribe in Nauvoo in 1843. When the Indian's spokesmen told of how their numbers had been reduced and their lands taken in numerous wars with the whites, Smith shed tears. When Smith spoke, he told them of "the book which your fathers made" and promised that if they stopped killing each other and the whites and prayed to the Great Spirit, "it will not be long before the Great Spirit will bless you, and you will cultivate the earth and build good houses like white men."

There are no records of any significant number of Indian conversions in the pre-Utah days of the church. And when the Saints fled to Utah, for a time there was little talk of their lost brothers as the Saints became bitter competitors with the native peoples of the Great Basin, the Utes and Shoshones, for the land and resources of their homeland.

Once the Utes had been defeated by the Mormons and confined to a reservation in the Uinta Basin and the Shoshones had been driven into Nevada and Idaho, the Saints could afford to pursue a more benevolent policy. Brigham Young, who for a time served as Indian agent for the Utah territory, began to emphasize feeding and clothing the natives and the establishment of a model farm project at Spanish Fork, Utah. And as the Saints pushed their settlements southward into the lands of the Paiutes, Hopis, and Navajos, missionaries were dispatched among these people.

In their dealings with the Indians, the Mormon missionaries traded on two facts: their oppression at the hands of other Americans and the unique place ascribed to the Lamanite/Indians by the Book of Mormon. When the Indians told of the horrors suffered in their conflicts with the whites, the Mormons matched them story for story with their own tales of murder, dispossession, and plunder. Also, there were the remarkable similarities between the Book of Mormon's saga of wandering and racial conflict and the oral traditions of numerous Indian tribes. These traditions told of similar wanderings and of the central role of a lost white brother or three prophets (known to the Saints as the three Nephites), whose return heralded the beginning of a new era. Indeed the fascinating mythic system of the Mormons had sprung from the same native soil as the Indians.

In one encounter in 1876, described in David Kay Flake's *History of the Southwest Indian Mission*, a missionary was traveling through Navajo territory in western New Mexico when he and his companions were stopped by a Navajo who asked about "a history of our forefathers" and pleaded with the Mormons to wait for his people to gather so they could hear about it.

"We know that what you say is true," the missionary reported the Navajos saying, "for the traditions of our good old men who never told a lie agree with your story." Older Navajos still use a word for Mormons, *gomolii*, that describes them as another tribe, rather than *bilagana*, which means white.

Early contacts with the peoples to the south, however, were highly volatile, particularly with aggressive Navajo raiders. A number of Saints were killed as the Navajos continued to raid southern Utah well into the 1870s. Finally Jacob Hamblin, the famous apostle to the Lamanites, brought peace with the Navajos by enticing them to trade with the Mormons rather than steal their livestock.

The Saints' contacts with the Hopis were of a different and more peaceful nature. The Saints, for one, considered the Hopis more civilized, given the nature of their farming system, their rock homes built high on the mesas of northern Arizona, and their sophisticated religious beliefs and practices. After numerous expeditions to the Hopi, the Saints managed their first convert when they baptized chief Tuba and his wife in 1871. The Hopis appear to have valued their contacts with the Saints, but they disagreed about whether they were the representatives of the three prophets or the white brother spoken about by their elders.

Brigham Young was so impressed by the Hopis that he was convinced that their language was really Welsh, further verification of their status as a lost tribe from another continent. He tried often to persuade the Hopis to move to Utah. They declined to move but predicted that the Saints would soon join them in Arizona. Others, such as the Zunis of New Mexico, at first welcomed the Saints but then began to worry whether they would steal their land and water.

When the Saints built their line of settlements along the godforsaken Little Colorado River, south of the Hopi mesas in Arizona, they found themselves literally in the midst of the Lamanites. Efforts to make Mormons out of these Lamanites proved very frustrating. Many were baptized, but only a handful remained in the church. David Kay Flake suggests that some baptisms were really a free ticket to the accompanying feast. Although Brigham Young considered the northern Arizona settlements an important base from which to work among the Apaches, Hopis, Navajos, and Zunis, John Taylor, his successor, lamented, "Thus far we have been content simply to baptize them and let them run wild again."

By the turn of the century, most of the missionary efforts had been terminated. For one thing, the Mormons found themselves squeezed out by other churches who, through their contacts with the United States Indian Service (the predecessor of the Bureau of Indian Affairs), had divided the reservations among themselves, leaving no room for the Saints.

For another, the Saints, like other whites, were generally hostile to the Indian people. "Most people looked at the Indians as their enemies," recalled Golden Buchanan, the founder of the church's Indian Placement Service. "There were very few of the old pioneer families that hadn't had a brother or a father or an uncle or maybe an aunt that hadn't [sic] been killed by an Indian in some of the raids." These Saints, said Buchanan, felt "the Indians were uncivilized. They didn't know how to take care of themselves. The way they lived was atrocious. You couldn't be friends with an Indian and keep your self-respect."

Although a number of Mormons, including some reservation-based Mormon traders, asked permission to do missionary work among the Indians, the church was content to leave the work of civilizing the Indians to the government.

The Saints' interest in the Hopis was again stirred in the 1930s when traditional leader Dan Kotchongva came to Salt Lake City after traveling across the country speaking of the lost white brother. "This is the time to which we have looked for generations," Kotchongva told some of the leaders of the church. "We were told that His time was when a road was made in the sky [i.e., the airplane]." Soon after, missionary work among the Hopis and Navajos was resumed.

This gradual renewal of missionary work in the 1940s finally gained the support of Apostle, soon-to-be President, George Albert Smith. Its greatest advocate was Spencer W. Kimball, who championed Golden Buchanan's efforts to start the Indian Placement Service.

Through his father's reminiscences about his work among the Cherokee of Oklahoma in the 1880s, Kimball had developed a powerful, if paternal identification with the plight of native Americans. He often spoke movingly of the brutal forced removal of the Cherokee from Georgia during the time of Andrew Jackson. He was also urged on by his patriarchal blessing, received as a young man, in which he was told, "You will preach the Gospel to many people, but more especially to the Lamanites."

Two years after a new Navajo-Zuni mission was established in 1943, Kimball, recently called as an Apostle, began to assist in supervising Indian missionary work.

In 1947, Golden Buchanan, a rancher from Sevier County, Utah, who was part Indian and whose father had learned a number of Indian languages and had befriended numerous Indians, contacted Kimball about a new idea for an Indian program. Buchanan's idea for the Indian Placement Service grew out of his friendship with a young Navajo girl named Helen John, who was living in a tent on Buchanan's ranch while working in the sugar beet fields. After one harvest, Helen John asked to spend the winter so that she could attend the local schools. Buchanan wrote Kimball for advice, and Kimball encouraged him to take the girl into his home.

"I could see," recalled Buchanan later, "that if a program of this sort were undertaken by the church that literally hundreds of Indian children would have the privilege of living in LDS homes where they could not only be taught in school, but they could be taught the principles of the gospel." Beyond this, the Saints hoped to produce a new Indian leadership that would influence their people to fulfill the prophecies of the Book of Mormon. "Your sons will compete in art, literature, and medicine, in law, architecture, etc.," Kimball told a conference of Indian members in 1959. "They will become professional, industrial, and business leaders, and statesmen of the first order. Together you and we shall build in the spectacular city of New Jerusalem the temple to which our Redeemer will come."

Buchanan and Kimball's greatest problem to begin with was the attitude of their own people, who feared that "the neighbors wouldn't understand." Mormon families had retained Indians as servants since the earliest days of their settlements, and in recent years, Indians had harvested the sugar beet crop. "You would furnish your livestock, your chickens, your pigs," Buchanan told one stake conference, "better accommodations than you force these people to live in because they've come up here to work."

These attitudes changed quickly, according to Buchanan. In a short time, the church was flooded by requests from members offering their homes to young Indians. The program was small at first. In 1958, there were 253 Indian children in Mormon homes, but by 1969, there were almost 5,000. In 1983 there were 2,463 Indians living in Mormon homes, while another 350 attended BYU. In all, some 70,000 young Indians have participated in the Placement Service.

With the development of Indian leadership its ultimate goal, the church first established a seminary program adjacent to the Indian boarding schools run by the Bureau of Indian Affairs (BIA) and then an Indian educational program at BYU in the 1960s. In 1983, Indian students at BYU took courses at the Student Life College in a special program designed to help them cope with the cultural distance between the reservation and a college campus. In this program, about half the students were from the Placement Service, and they attended classes with Anglo and foreign students. "The emphasis is on integration into the mainstream," said sociology profesor Arturo de Hoyos, a member of the BYU staff.

As the Placement Service moved more and more young Indians, particularly Navajos, off the reservation into Mormon homes, missionaries from other churches began to challenge the program. Before the return of the Mormon missionaries in the 1940s, the various churches with missionary programs on the reservations had carved out their little spheres of influence, and there was general agreement about respecting each other's turf. "Each church respected the other's integrity," said Wayne Lynn, who was president of the Holbrooke-based southwest mission in 1983. "Then the Mormons came and proselyted all the people. In large number our membership came as a loss to someone else." Mormon Indian trader Charles McGee remembered opposition to the Mormons so strong in Catholic-controlled pueblos, such as Jemez in New Mexico, that a man was whipped publicly in the early 1950s for allowing a Mormon missionary into his home.

Soon, a number of government agencies, including the Bureau of Indian Affairs and the U.S. Children's Bureau, began receiving complaints about the Placement Service. In 1956, for instance, the BIA office in Phoenix received a number of complaints from the Hualapai Indians in northern Arizona that the church was encouraging mass baptisms on the reservation, was alienating parents' affections, and was removing children from the community.

At a meeting with a number of government agencies in 1957, the church agreed to greater supervision of the families involved and more contacts with BIA officials. The church also agreed not to use the program for proselyting purposes. This was a meaningless concession given the reasons for starting the program in the first place and the nature of Mormon family life, with its constant emphasis on the teaching of correct doctrine. "I think maybe that's been done [i.e., preaching to Placement children]," Buchanan admitted in 1974, "although basically we agreed with the government that we would not use it as a proselyting tool." The church also had its own contacts and influence in these agencies, so much so that a Utah congressman engineered a change in the 1960s in the Internal Revenue Service code to allow Mormon families to receive tax exemptions for taking foster children.

In the 1960s, a dispute over Indian fishing rights in the Pacific Northwest triggered a new Indian rights movement, and inevitably, the Mormon church became a target of the numerous young Indians who became involved in the fight for self-protection and self-determination. Since at least twenty-five percent of all Indian children were either in foster homes, adoptive homes, or at government boarding schools, the Mormon's Placement Service, as well as other adoption schemes, became a constant subject of discussion and criticism at meetings of Indian organizations.

The Indian critics of the church focused on a number of related problems. One charge often encountered was that missionaries entice young

Indians off the reservation by contrasting the material benefits of living in a middle-class Mormon family with the poverty on the reservation. A young Navajo attorney who has represented Navajo families in disputes with the Placement Service felt that Mormonism appeals to Indians who want upward mobility, two cars, and a good salary. "That is what they use to get the kids off the reservation," he said. "And they make it sound like what is out here is not so great. Then they make them feel bad when they go up there, you know, no Jordache jeans, that kind of thing." A Navajo mother spoke of how she resented the way in which missionaries had approached her son without her knowledge and had tried to interest him in Placement by emphasizing the glories of life in Salt Lake City.

Others, including Claudeen Arthur, the head of the Navajo Department of Justice, argued that the program was taking the best Indian students away from their homes and families, draining the reservation of its most precious resource. "It's a disservice to the community," said Evelyn Blanchard, a Zuni social worker, "to remove students with the highest potential who come from the strongest families." Blanchard, like many others, questioned how a church that believes so strongly in the family "can involve itself in this program that causes separation" at a time when "it is vitally important to be around your family." Ultimately the Indian critics felt that the intense indoctrination experienced by Indian students living in Mormon families left them in a potentially destructive cultural limbo.

The only scientific study of the impact of the program was conducted by Dr. Martin Topper of the Indian Health Service. He followed twenty-five Indian students through their Placement experience. Eventually twenty-three of the students dropped out of the program, and most of them rejected their adopted Mormon parents. Topper found that "undergoing a cultural change in family environment at this point in psychological development . . . is a traumatic experience." The problem of returning to family life on the reservation after leaving the program contributed to emotional conflicts that were sometimes intensely acted out. A number of young women experienced hysterical seizures and the delusion that their dead ancestors were pursuing them. For young men, it could mean adolescent binge drinking.

BYU's Dr. de Hoyos claimed that he has done the only critical church study of the Placement Service, but it is not available to the public. In response to the growing criticism of the Placement Service, the church hired a Salt Lake research firm to question Indians about the program. According to the survey, eighty-eight to ninety percent of the former students, parents, and tribal leaders contacted were in favor of the program.

Church officials connected with the Indian Placement Service argue publicly that criticism of their program and their church is almost always inspired by other churches who do missionary work among the Indians.

Privately their own concerns have echoed their critics'. In a remarkable oral history interview deposited in the church archives, Golden Buchanan found that the question of how a family-oriented religion could sanction a program that took children away from their real parents was "the most valid criticism, in my opinion, that has been raised on the program.

"We've not reached the point yet," Buchanan went on, placing the service in the context of white society as a whole, "that we've got enough of these people in our society that they can completely go their own way and become completely white-oriented . . . My fear is that we neither make fish nor fowl out of them. They're neither white nor Indian, and we take them out of their own culture and their old way of thought. Then we don't give them enough of ours that they're happy, that they can make a living and that they can adjust. Then they become outcasts. They can't go back to their old way because they've enough of the new way in them that some of the old way is repulsive and not good. They don't have enough of the new way to fit in completely. Therefore, they're in no man's land in between, and I think we have a thousand drunkards and a thousand prostitutes in between, a people who have lost their way . . . I just don't think we go far enough. I don't think we should either. They've got too many good things we ought to keep. I don't think we should bring them over. But some way, somehow, we've got to help them bridge the gap and we're not doing an entirely good job."

Buchanan, the man in the church who perhaps knew more than any other Mormon about the Indian people, was deeply divided over the program he had intitiated. But Buchanan was too much of a Mormon to let his sympathies temper his beliefs. Later in the interview he concludes that because of the prophecy about the Lamanites' role in building the temple in the new Jerusalem, "they *have to be trained* [our emphasis] in the white world in preparation for this task . . . I see no way they can remain as they are now with their traditions and their superstitions and their more or less easy-going way of life."

While publicly denying most of the criticisms of Placement, the church made a number of changes in the program that church leaders hoped would eliminate some of the problems. For a time in the 1970s, they even reduced the number of enrollees because of the wave of criticism. Prospective children and their families were screened more carefully, for example, and greater efforts were made to maintain ties between the natural and adopted families.

At the same time, the church resisted all efforts to bring its program under government supervision. Abuses in the adoption and placement of Indian children led to the introduction in Congress in the 1970s of the Indian Child Welfare Act. The church, through the Washington law firm of Wilkinson, Cragun, and Barker, lobbied successfully to get Placement excluded from the act.

Despite opposition, the program continues to appeal to the parents of many Indian children. Reservation schools are substandard at best and often inaccessible during the winter months. The BIA-run boarding schools, a number of which have recently been shut down, are often worse. Life in a Mormon home and the opportunity to go to BYU or some other educational institution is obviously preferable to the poverty, alcoholism, and lack of opportunity on many reservations—whatever the cost to the individual in terms of cultural identity and to the tribe in terms of potential leaders.

Keith Crocker, the Apache reporter for *Eagle's Eye*, spent ten years on Placement beginning in the fourth grade. Crocker was encouraged by his sister and father (a nonmember), both of whom wanted to get him away from life on the reservation. "My sister wouldn't let me stay home on the reservation," he explained. "She chased me back to the bus and said she didn't want me drinking around down there."

Crocker said he went through "cultural shock" because of "the organized life-style of a Mormon home." Both Mormon and Indian tradition, however, can exist side by side, he argued. "Some of the knowledge of Indian ways was lost," Crocker went on, "but was replaced by more organized care for my tribe. If I hadn't gone on Placement, I wouldn't care about the tribal leaders and issues like water rights. In the long run, when I settle down, I am going to settle down in White River. For me that is my home, my family, my heritage, my childhood memories."

SAINTS IN INDIAN COUNTRY

In 1983, Wayne Lynn presided over Indian missionary work from Holbrooke, Arizona, on the southern border of Hopi and Navajo country. His headquarters was the modern mission home dedicated in 1963 by Spencer Kimball and located where the paved road becomes a dirt track that disappears into the sagebrush toward the Hopi Mesas. Lynn, stocky, affable, with thinning dark hair and black-rimmed glasses, grew up on a ranch in Wyoming near the Crow reservation.

At the ward house on a gently sloping mesa with a commanding view of the spacious surrounding country, the local Saints were gathering for morning services. Only one Indian sat in the congregation, the rest of them preferring to meet at the Indian branch in another part of town. It is not that they are segregated, explained Lynn, it is just that they are more comfortable with their own people.

Sacrament meeting was followed by Sunday School, which was followed by priesthood meeting. Lynn took his guest to the meeting of the high priests' quorum, where Charles McGee, a retired Indian trader who had been tapped by Spencer Kimball and Golden Buchanan in the early days of the missionary revival, led the discussion of healing, or the laying of hands.

To the Saints, the gift of healing is a clear demonstration of both their godliness and their spiritual affinity for their Lamanite brothers, particularly the Navajos. During a smallpox epidemic at the Zuni pueblo in 1877–78, one Mormon missionary is alleged to have cured 406 Indians. "This incident, if true," wrote David Kay Flake, "could stand on record as one of the most miraculous supernatural healing episodes in all Mormondom, Christiandom [sic], or in all recorded history for that matter."

After services, President Lynn discussed the church's Indian program in his office at the mission home. "We feel a responsibility," he explained, "to share the Book of Mormon with the people whom it originated from." In the past, missionaries emphasized the strong parallels between Mormon teachings and a number of Indian beliefs. These parallels, they claimed, demonstrate that the gospel has been on the earth since the beginning. This approach is no longer as effective, Lynn felt, because Indian religions are changing radically. "It is a great challenge to separate religion from culture," he went on, "and where culture is in conflict with the Bible, it is wrong."

Today the church presents Indian converts with the inevitable manuals, which are such a standard feature of Mormon life. These manuals are designed to help new members live as faithful Mormons where they do not have full access to church programs. President Lynn participated in the writing of this latest set of manuals. "We struggled hard to eliminate material that reflected our culture and customs to get to the doctrine," he explained. "We found that if we stayed with basic principles of the gospel there weren't any differences."

Despite this effort, the manuals are a striking testimony to the cultural blind spot of the Mormons. They explain in simple English how to remake the Indian family in the image of the typical Mormon family. They reflect little knowledge or awareness of the realities of Indian culture, such as the matrilineal clan systems of the Hopis and Navajos. Instead, they are a naive bid to remodel Indian life according to the cultural precepts of the Saints.

The church's missionary work has brought gradual and continuous rather than dramatic growth in Indian membership. "It's often quite discouraging to missionaries who come out here for short periods of time," Lynn went on. He estimated that the church baptized about 1,300 Indians a year; 700 of these were Navajos. In 1983, there were a number of totally Indian-led-and-administered wards and branches, which is the church's ultimate goal. Among these was the branch in Page, Arizona, site of a giant power plant fired with coal dug from lands leased to the Peabody Coal Company by the Hopi and Navajo tribal governments. "The church has been successful in Page," said Lynn, "because the power plant is there and is a good source of income. People who join the church become more successful because of the motivation to improve."

On the remote parts of the reservation, the church is less successful because the church lacks the leadership to carry on programs. Many Placement students returning to the reservation find it difficult "to be accepted unless they fall back into the old mold. Their image of themselves changes," Lynn explained. "They want to achieve but come back and can't excel. So they move away, and this has depleted their strong leadership." To Lynn the loss of strong achievers is typical of rural life. As in the ranch community he grew up in, those seeking opportunity had to move on.

Lynn found that the Navajos were more responsive to the church's teachings than were the Hopis, partly because Navajo culture, known to be fiercely adaptive, is "like a sponge." "The ideal," said Lynn, "is for the Navajos to meld with other groups and lose their identity." In contrast, Lynn has found the Hopis, particularly those living in the mesa-top villages, to be "very traditional and very resistant to missionaries."

Former Hopi tribal chairman Abbott Sekaquaptewa threw some light on the Hopis' resistance to outside religions. His mother, Helen Sekaquaptewa, is perhaps the most famous Hopi convert to Mormonism, and his late brother, Wayne, served as stake president on the reservation before his death in 1982. Although Abbott Sekaquaptewa has found that the Mormons are not dogmatic about restricting Hopis from participating in cultural activities, such as their elaborate cycle of dances and ceremonies, Christianity in general "does not offer anything substantially new or different from our traditional religion. There is not a great need that people have for another religion. Our traditional religion is strong enough and offers the life support and cultural strength that a highly organized religion can offer. Christianity revolves around a creator and a life before and a life hereafter in a pure state and that's what Hopi religion revolves around."

For the Saints, recruiting leadership remains the key. Window Rock, the capital of the Navajo nation, presented a striking contrast to the more remote parts of the reservation, where life is primitive and sheepherding and some cattle raising are still the dominant activities. Here, as the tribal government has grown into an elaborate bureaucracy, the tribe over the years has wrested control of many programs and government functions from the old bureaucracy headed by the BIA.

Until the 1960s, the Navajos successfully resisted the church's efforts to construct even a small church building on the reservation. Now graduates of the Indian Placement Service, new converts, and members of a few old Mormon-Navajo families have found a niche in tribal life, and one encounters numerous Navajo Saints, a number of them holding influential positions in the new tribal government of chairman Peterson Zah, elected in 1982.

Ray Baldwin Louis, Zah's press secretary, is the descendant of an old Navajo-Hopi-Mormon family that kept Spencer Kimball at their home while he was recuperating from one of his numerous illnesses. Mike Allison, the bishop of the Window Rock ward, is the director of economic development. Loren Tapahe is the publisher of the tribal newspaper, *Navajo Times*. George Lee, the highest-ranking Indian member of the church as a Seventy, once expressed a desire to be tribal chairman. And as many as fifteen tribal council members are also members of the church. The church is particularly influential in the so-called Aneth Extension, an oil- and gas-rich part of the reservation in southeastern Utah, where church members virtually control the Utah Navajo Development Corporation.

Mike Allison was introduced to the church by his wife, an inactive member who spent a year on Placement. Allison, who described himself as formerly "a real lost sheep," was impressed by the church when he visited Salt Lake City for the high school graduation of some Placement students in his wife's family. Allison found that the church appeals to more educated Navajos. "I don't think there is really a clash in cultures," Allison explained, "because everything the Navajos believe came from Christ in the beginning."

According to Allison, non-Mormon Indians are already against Mormonism because they are anti-white to begin with. "We know how our ancestors were treated," he continued. "We see open discrimination and different standards of living."

A number of Navajos expressed concern that Mormon Navajos are now in policy-making positions in the tribal government, but most everyone agreed that church members keep a very low profile. There is a long tradition of resistance to Mormon encroachment upon the reservation, some of which was undoubtedly inspired by other missionaries, as the church claims, but not all of it.

Symptomatic of the church's problems in Navajo country is a church farm project being set up in Many Farms, Arizona. Rex Furness, a Utah businessman who had given up some of his own businesses to assist with the project, was helping a group of Navajo would-be farmers apply for tribal funding to set up a cooperative to grow hay and alfalfa. The tribe, which had reversed an earlier decision to support the project, told Furness that he should seek outside funding for the plan since the tribe was already committed to its own large farming project. Even though Mike Allison, the director of economic development and a Mormon bishop, is in a position to help the project, other influential members of the administration of chairman Peterson Zah were determined to block it because of the church's role.

MORMON LAWYERS AND INDIAN LANDS

Beyond the question of the Indian Placement Service and Indian recruitment in general lies the larger problem of the aggressive encroachment of the white world upon Indian country, with an eye particularly to the exploitation of Indian resources. Here too Mormonism, deservedly or not, has gotten a bad name because of the activities of a handful of Mormon politicians and lawyers, some with official connections to the church, who have played a central role in the manipulation of tribal governments and resources, particularly the Indians' precious land base, since World War II.

Just before the renewal of missionary activity in Indian country in the 1940s, Ernest L. Wilkinson became involved in an attempt to redress an old Indian grievance, the taking of their lands by the federal government. Wilkinson, who was a Washington, D.C., attorney and who later became BYU's most famous president, had developed an interest in Indian law as a member of the firm of Charles Evans Hughes, once Secretary of State and later Chief Justice of the Supreme Court. Working during the Roosevelt New Deal with the reformers who ran the U.S. Indian Service, Wilkinson helped write the Indian Claims Act of 1946. Under this law, an Indian Claims Commission (ICC) was set up to establish the legitimacy of Indian claims against the government for the seizure of tribal lands. The commission was to set the date at which the land was taken and then establish the amount owed the Indians based on the value of the land *at the time it was taken.*

After the courts interpreted the new law to mean that the Indians could only receive money, not land, to redress their claims, it became clear that a successful claim really meant acquiescence in the government's long history of seizing Indian lands. Although large sums of money were involved, the Indians ended up receiving only a tiny fraction of the land's present value since it usually had been taken sometime in the nineteenth century, when land that was presently worth $50 to $100 an acre was worth as little as $1.50 an acre. By filing a claim, the Indians acknowledged that the land had been taken from them, and by accepting a cash settlement, they gave up any attempt to regain their land.

Wilkinson had already established himself as a prominent Indian claims attorney through a multimillion-dollar suit on behalf of the Mormons' old antagonists, the Ute Indians. He was also instrumental in having several hundred thousand acres restored to the Utes before the ICC spelled out a new way to settle land claims. At the same time, the title to many a Mormon ranch throughout the Intermountain West was cleared by the efforts of Ernest Wilkinson and his protégés. When Wilkinson settled the Ute claims, he also legitimized the acquisition by Mormons and others of the best lands promised to the Utes by the U.S. government.

Right after the act was passed, Wilkinson and his partners, soon to be known as Wilkinson, Cragun, and Barker, the official Washington representative of the Mormon church, became the country's foremost claims attorneys. They filed claims on behalf of the Shoshones, the Goshiute, the Paiute, the Klamath, the Hopis, and a number of other Indian tribes, many of which were located within the Mormon sphere of influence in the West. "In the end we represented more Indian tribes than any other law firm," said Wilkinson's partner, Robert Barker, in 1983.

With the rise of the Indian rights movement in the 1960s, numerous
traditional Indian leaders, assisted by bright, young Anglo attorneys sympathetic to the Indian cause, began to challenge the buying out of Indian
land claims. According to John Vance, who was appointed chairman of the
ICC in 1968, the ICC "has not accomplished its purpose, but rather has
become part of the problem it was created to solve."

Knowing that they would never control the land again, traditional
Hopis, for example, opposed the efforts of tribal attorney John S. Boyden,
a former Wilkinson partner and another lawyer who had worked for the
church, to arrange a cash settlement for a Hopi claim. In one case, that of
the Western Shoshone of Nevada, Wilkinson's partner, Robert Barker,
continued to insist that he represented the tribe and was even accepted as
tribal attorney by the Bureau of Indian Affairs after he was fired by the
Shoshones.

While Wilkinson was working to settle Indian land claims, another
prominent Mormon, then Utah Senator Arthur V. Watkins, was working
to terminate the tribal status of a number of Indian tribes, including many
of those represented by Wilkinson and Boyden. Saying that he wanted to
free the Indians from the toils of the socialistic Indian bureaucracy in
Washington, Watkins pushed for termination of tribal status as the best
way to deal with the Indian problem.

According to Robert Barker, the Wilkinson law firm opposed termination. "We did everything we could to oppose it," said Barker in 1983.
"There was a climate in Congress for termination. So the problem became
how to make it most palatable. . . . [Later] we worked to get termination
reversed." In all, some twenty tribes were either terminated or started
along that disastrous path with results that are still being felt today. De-
prived of their ancestral lands and with some ready money in their pockets
either from claims cases or from termination, numerous Indians were
forced into urban ghettos, where they suffered from alcoholism and widespread unemployment.

John S. Boyden, who eventually set up his own law firm in Salt Lake
City, became the Utes' tribal attorney, while Wilkinson continued as their
claims attorney. The Utes were really three different groups of Indians.
One, the Uintahs, were forced out of central Utah by the Mormons. The
Uncompahgres were driven out of Colorado after the Meeker Massacre of
1879, and the White River Utes were the original residents of the area.
Many Uintah Utes were of mixed blood, having intermarried with whites
and Indians from other tribes.

In 1951, Wilkinson and Boyden engineered a vote among the Uintah
Utes, despite widespread opposition, to accept part of the $32 million for
the Utes' Colorado lands and to drop their own claims. Senator Watkins
saw this as a necessary precondition for the termination of the Uintah
Utes. "He considered it important," wrote Parker Nielson, attorney for a

number of mixed bloods, "to have a tribe from his own state terminated first to serve as a model for the other Indians in the country."

Wilkinson, Watkins, and Boyden pressed the Uintah Utes to come up with a long-term program for the use of their funds. In 1954, Wilkinson virtually seized control of a Uintah meeting and forced through a vote in support of termination after many of the Utes had stalked out in protest.

Shortly thereafter, Watkins introduced a bill into Congress calling for the termination of all Utes with less than fifty-one-percent Indian ancestry. Even the Uncompahgres, who resisted sharing "their" money with the Uintahs, opposed the termination vote, saying it came from "undue influence and pressure exerted by tribal attorneys." Meanwhile Boyden held up payment of the cash settlement for all three bands until termination was completed.

Next, Boyden created a new Ute organization. Boyden was representing both the Ute tribe and the mixed-blood Utes whom he was arranging to have terminated, a clear conflict of interest. Then he arranged to sell off the mixed bloods' lands to his other client, the Ute tribe, at a bargain price that failed to take into account valuable timber on the land.

At the same time, George Eccles, head of Utah's First Security Bank and a close associate of Wilkinson's, approached the Commissioner of Indian Affairs after learning from Boyden that termination was in the offing. Eccles wanted First Security to become the trustee for the funds that would be distributed as a prerequisite to termination. In 1956, Boyden and Eccles arranged for First Security to become the trustee for the terminated mixed bloods.

"Though the rationale advanced for termination," wrote Nielson, "was that the mixed bloods were individually competent to manage their own affairs, including in particular their financial affairs, they had not been involved with the negotiations in any way." Ultimately, First Security, through Boyden, gained control of the financial destiny of the mixed bloods. They were prevented from setting up a cooperative ranching operation and many of their assets ended up in the hands of Boyden's client, the Ute tribe, or of local whites.

In Hopi country, Boyden took it upon himself to set up a new tribal government. The tribal government imposed on the Hopis by the federal government during the 1930s had been resisted by the traditional Hopi leaders who felt that their village and clan systems were adequate. But Boyden was eager to open the Hopi reservation for mineral exploration, and he needed a compliant tribal government to accomplish this. Eventually, Boyden, in return for millions in legal fees, arranged for the Hopi tribal council to lease at bargain prices sacred lands on Black Mesa to the Peabody Coal Company for a massive strip mine.

For a time in the 1960s, the traditional leaders who were resisting the Boyden tribal government and his efforts to file for a land claim settlement saw themselves surrounded by hostile Mormons. Secretary of the Interior Stewart Udall, a willing ally of Boyden and Peabody, came from an old Mormon family in Arizona. And Boyden had even hired a Salt Lake public relations firm that explained that Mormonism was the dominant Hopi religion.

"The child must be taught a proper concept of money," a church manual instructed foster parents in the Indian Placement program in the 1960s. Boyden, Wilkinson, and Watkins had done just that by persuading numerous tribes to swap their land for cash. Wilkinson and the other Mormon claims attorneys saw themselves as working to benefit the various tribes they represented. Instead they had helped strip numerous tribes of the land base that they would need to guarantee their future. The Wilkinson law firm opposed termination, but the land claim business and termination ended up complementing each other as the two most destructive episodes in modern Indian history. These two episodes also furthered the notion of assimilation embodied in the Mormon doctrine of the Lamanites.

FROM WHITE TO PURE

John S. Boyden died in 1981. Ernest L. Wilkinson had died years earlier. The passing of Boyden appeared to mark the end of an era of all too often arrogant paternalism that had grown out of the church doctrine of the fallen tribe and was encouraged by the postwar drive to convert the Lamanites.

Spencer W. Kimball, whose devotion to the Indians was unquestionable and whose criticisms of Mormon racism were poignant, would speak of "those little redskins." He also believed, as the Book of Mormon once promised, that once converted, the Indians would literally become "white and delightsome."

The belief in the actual change of skin color resulting from conversion was widely shared by many of the leaders of Kimball's generation. For example, Belle Spafford, the longtime president of the Relief Society, claimed that in her experience the predictions of the Book of Mormon were true. "I've seen some of those dark-skinned Indian children who had been in the [Indian Placement] program," Spafford declared. "After a few years, [they] look as if they were more white than Indian."

Beliefs and paternalistic attitudes such as Kimball's became an embarrassment to the church. Then in 1981, the church announced that in an 1840 edition of the Book of Mormon Joseph Smith had changed the words "white and delightsome" to "pure and delightsome." But there was no modification of the passage in Nephi where the Lamanites were punished for their transgressions by being turned "dark and loathsome."

And there have been other changes. In 1980, Utah Congressman Dan Marriott, a Mormon, introduced legislation to restore the Paiutes, one of the victims of termination, to tribal status and to create a 15,000-acre reservation for them.

It was not clear by the early 1980s, however, whether the days of termination had really passed, particularly with the rise of then Secretary of the Interior James Watt as the government official responsible for the trust relationship between the federal government and the Indian tribes. Although the Paiutes' tribal status was restored, the Sevier County Commission, the county where Golden Buchanan lived and where the Indian Placement Service got its start, was working with a major coal company to prevent the Paiutes from acquiring 400 acres of sacred lands on Fish Lake as part of their reservation. Stephen Boyden, John S. Boyden's son and a member of his old firm, Boyden, Kennedy, and Romney, was working with the Zuni tribe to press a land claim that would eventually legitimize numerous Mormon land acquisitions near the Zuni pueblo. And John Kennedy, a member of the same firm, was representing the Hopi tribal council, a Boyden creation, in its efforts to push numerous Navajos off of disputed lands north of the Hopi villages, to clear the area, some suspected, for more coal leasing.

In 1982, James V. Hansen, a Mormon member of Congress representing Arthur V. Watkins's hometown and the Ute reservation, again raised the spectre of termination. In a "Dear Jim" letter, he wrote to Watt, enclosing a copy of legislation introduced in 1977 calling for an end to all treaties between the U.S. and Indian tribes, the termination of all special federal services, and the placing of Indian tribes under state jurisdiction. Hansen felt that the federal government was treating Indians "as mentally retarded children," and that Indians, in short, "are the worst example of what a welfare state can do to individuals. . . . We take away their opportunity for advancement, they become perpetual recipients of welfare, they live in squaller [sic], they have no incentive for betterment and their personal habits have declined at a rapid rate." Describing the Ute reservation in terms of "broken down houses, beat-up pickup trucks, and junk stacked in the yards," he felt that the Utes "are more interested in shooting two deer a year than they are in their grazing, water, and mineral rights. . . . Possibly," Hansen went on, "it is because of my religious background, belief in work, self-sufficiency, and belief that welfare without work is a grave sin, which brings me to these conclusions."

As Hansen suggested, church doctrine and Mormon attitudes were at the heart of the church's and individual Mormon's inability to deal with the realities of Indian life, to see the native people as they were and as they are. Their literal belief in the mythology of the Book of Mormon reinforced by their small-town business ethic meant that they suffered from a blind spot in their attempts to understand their Lamanite brothers. In the ongoing debate over the clash of white and Indian cultures, the Indians, according to the church, do not have a culture. Their culture was once the culture of the Book of Mormon, and then after the fall, it became a deformed thing.

"Most people in the church do not understand and appreciate the good things about Indian culture and life," said Bob Angle, a Concaw Maidu who converted to Mormonism in the army and has since become inactive. "They are part of a culture that came into this country and saw everything as bad. They are more materialistic and individualistic. It is hard for them to see Indians as human beings. They see Indians as fallen people and a lot of that culture is because of that fall."

This attitude, reminiscent of most nineteenth-century missionaries, meant that Indian people were lost souls, poor unfortunates who have to be shepherded by the Mormons with their superior understanding of how they *must* develop in order to fulfill the prophecies of Joseph Smith. For Mormons such as John S. Boyden, James V. Hansen, and Ernest L. Wilkinson, it meant that the native people had to be coerced by whatever means into accepting the ways of the modern world as defined by the federal government, the banks, the energy companies, and the Mormon church.

Despite the church's concern over the plight of the Lamanites and the rhetoric about building leadership on the reservation, the church has done little to help non-Mormon Indians. The church was willing to accept BIA funds for BYU Indian students, despite its strictures against federal handouts, and it was willing to apply to the Navajo tribe for funds to start a model farm project, but Salt Lake City, according to Bob Angle, who is director of the local Indian Health Center, is sorely lacking adequate health and recreational facilities for its large Indian population.

"I think they could do a tremendous good," said Angle, "if they would change the policy and support programs that are Indian-directed. They expect all community leaders to be LDS. Anyone who falls short of that they do not want to support, and they withdraw support. As a result, they are stifling progress."

Doctrine, the myth of the tribe fallen from grace, has shaped church programs and Mormon attitudes toward the native people of the Americas. As more and more native people enter the church, there have been small changes in these programs and attitudes. The idea that Indian converts will turn white is no longer widely believed. The church no longer instructs its foster parents, as it did in the church guides in the 1960s, that their new charges "may not be able to understand the principles of honesty," that "natural parents should be encouraged not to visit the children for the first year and only infrequently thereafter," that "phone calls may be made *only* in the presence of foster parents," or that "the natural parents should not call their children too often; it makes them homesick." But the church, with its own ideas about the Lamanites, will continue to foster conflict as it challenges the new cultural identifications born of the Indian rights movement.

While the destiny of the Indian people is central to the Book of Mormon and the church's sense of prophecy, the destiny of black people, an equally controversial issue in the church, is not. And in this area, the church has made major changes that have eliminated one of the most agonizing problems in its current history.

THE MARK OF CAIN

On June 9, 1978, the church announced that Spencer W. Kimball, "after spending many hours in the upper room of the temple supplicating the Lord for divine guidance," had a revelation. The church, after barring black males from the priesthood for 130 years, was now extending the priesthood to all worthy male members without regard to race or color.

In probably the most significant change in the church belief system in the twentieth century, Kimball eliminated one of the gravest problems facing the modern church. Because blacks were banned from blessing or baptizing children, from church leadership positions, from fulfilling a mission and from participating in most of the sacred ordinances, the church had suffered through more than a decade of confrontations with civil rights activists and critics within the church itself. Ultimately, the church's worldwide missionary program had been hindered by the problem of sorting out the racial background of prospective members, particularly in countries such as Brazil, where race mixing has been common.

The church became embroiled in the issue of how to relate to black Americans at an early date. Most of the original Saints were from a New England background and many of them shared the sentiments if not the exact views of the abolitionists. In the 1830s, Smith responded to the charges of Missourians that the Saints were interfering with slavery by bringing freedmen into the state by claiming that the church was barring blacks from membership. There is some speculation that this statement was made under pressure, since Smith ordained Elijah Abel as a member of the priesthood in 1836. Abel remained the only recorded black member of the priesthood until Kimball's revelation in 1978.

Smith, like many Americans, was preoccupied with the slavery question and its implications for the young nation, but his attitude was ambivalent. In 1832, saying that "slaves shall rise up against their masters," he predicted a war between North and South. At another point, he wrote that blacks, as the sons of Ham, were cursed by "a decree of Jehovah." He also warned his followers not to convert slaves until they had converted their masters. Later calling himself a "friend of equal rights and privileges to all men," Smith urged the Saints to bring slaves to free states and free them. Finally, in his 1844 presidential campaign, he came down squarely on the side of the antislavery forces. "Break off the shackles from the poor black man," he proclaimed, "and hire him to labor like other human beings for an 'hour of virtuous liberty on earth is worth a whole eternity of bondage.'" He called for an end to slavery in the states bordering the Mason-

Dixon line and for the compensation of slaveholders with funds from the sale of public lands.

By the time the Saints reached Utah, Smith's earlier ambivalence had been reduced to a crude racial doctrine, typical of the ideas espoused by many other nineteenth-century white Americans. This doctrine was based on some vague passages in the Book of Abraham, the text that Joseph claimed was the lost writings of the Old Testament prophet Abraham. According to this theory, blacks were the descendants of Cain through Ham and his wife, Egyptus, and Cain had been cursed with a black skin for killing his brother Abel—the so-called mark of Cain.

Although blacks are never directly mentioned in Smith's translation of the Book of Abraham and the doctrine was only clearly spelled out by church historian Brigham H. Roberts in 1912, Brigham Young had proclaimed as early as 1849 that "any man having one drop of the seed of [Cain] . . . in him cannot hold the priesthood." In 1859, he told newspaper editor Horace Greeley that slavery was a "divine institution . . . not to be removed until the curse pronounced on Ham shall have been removed from his descendants."

In Utah, the Saints encountered slavery in a different form. Both the Mexicans and a number of Indian tribes, including the Navajos and the Utes, were involved in the sale of Indian slaves. At Young's urging, the Mormon-controlled legislature passed a law legalizing slavery in 1852. The intent of the law was to provide for the purchase of Indian slaves in order to free them or at least to make them indentured servants.

Throughout the nineteenth century, church publications described blacks as "the lowest in intelligence and the most barbarous of all the children of men." Elijah Abel, a living testament to Smith's willingness to allow at least one black into the priesthood, was denied entrance into the Temple and died on a mission in the 1890s while appealing this decision.

Although the church was pursuing missionary work among dark-skinned Indians and Pacific Islanders, church leaders in the twentieth century began to advance a new theory to account for the denial of priesthood to blacks. According to this theory, which was spelled out by the Apostle Joseph Fielding Smith in 1931, blacks in the preexistence had either remained neutral in the war between Jehovah and Lucifer or had sided with Lucifer and become fallen angels.

Race, at least the black race, remained an insignificant issue in Utah however. The small number of blacks worked mostly for the railroad and lived in Ogden, a city with a large non-Mormon population.

The issue was first raised in the post–World War II era, when the church asked the eminent Mormon sociologist Lowry Nelson his opinion about the possibility of doing missionary work in Cuba, particularly whether there were groups of "pure white blood" on the island. Nelson responded that the church's position on blacks was a possible problem for missionaries since they would be preaching a "doctrine of white supremacy" and stirring up racial conflicts. The First Presidency then wrote back, spelling out their position on blacks in the preexistence and warning about the dangers of miscegenation. Blacks, the First Presidency explained in its first statement on the issue for many years, had been barred from the priesthood since the days of Joseph Smith. Two years later, the First Presidency in its first official public pronouncement, added the curse of Cain to its list of reasons for barring blacks from the priesthood.

In 1953 Senator Wallace F. Bennett described the status of black Utahns in an article in the *Utah Law Review*. He found a small but dispersed population working for the railroads and copper smelters. Black women were denied the right to teach in the Salt Lake City school system; blacks could not swim or dance at the local resorts, the Lagoon and Saltair; they were barred from membership in social clubs and fraternities and had to sit in the balcony at local theaters. This was against the Utah statutes, he concluded, but they were not enforced.

By the mid-1950s, there were signs that the church's racial position on blacks might be softened. The new Prophet, David O. McKay, was, unlike many of the General Authorities, "remarkably free of traditional notions about marks, curses, and the like," according to Mormon sociologist Armand Mauss, who has written extensively on the Mormon race issue.

McKay, in a long conversation with Mormon philosopher Sterling M. McMurrin in 1954, emphasized that the priesthood restriction was a practice, not a doctrine of the church, and that it would be changed "some day." It was at this time that the first rumors began to circulate that the church was reevaluating its racial restrictions. The public knew little of these changes since the reevaluation and the discussion with McMurrin were kept secret for many years.

In the early 1960s, the civil rights movement began to catch up with the church, but not until a strange international development led to more internal discussion of racial matters. In 1959, the church discovered that a group of Nigerians, who had been writing the church and receiving materials since 1946, had built a local Mormon church of several thousand members. In 1963, McKay decided to send missionaries to Nigeria, but when the government found out about the church's racial restrictions they were barred from entering. In the aftermath of this development, Hugh B. Brown, McKay's Second Counselor, with the support of First Counselor Henry D. Moyle, urged that blacks be allowed to receive at least the Aaronic, or lesser, priesthood. As local civil rights activists began to challenge the church, it became clear that Brown's suggestion was the subject of serious internal divisions within the hierarchy.

In 1963, Steve Holbrook, a young Mormon from a prominent family, was working in Washington for Utah Congressman Sherm Lloyd. Holbrook had left his mission because he had been instructed not to work with the poor and to tell blacks that they should attend the church of their choice, not the Mormon church. One of his jobs in Washington was to deal with the Utah delegation of the National Association for the Advancement of Colored People that showed up for the massive march on Washington for civil rights. Moved by the march, Holbrook returned to Utah and began to work with the NAACP to pressure the church to take a position on civil rights.

When Holbrook and other members of the NAACP met with McKay's new counselor, Hugh B. Brown, and his nephew, Nathan Eldon Tanner, they were told that civil rights was a political issue and that the church only took a stand on moral issues. Brown did ask the group to send him material about what other churches were doing. In response, the NAACP and students from the University of Utah scheduled a demonstration to coincide with the church's semiannual conference. When they called Brown to tell him about their plans, he warned them that McKay was a Scot and did not like to have a gun held to his head. Despite the leadership's apparent resistance, the day before the scheduled demonstration, Brown made a public statement on behalf of the church in support of civil rights. Neither the NAACP nor the church mentioned the priesthood ban at this time.

Two years later at the national NAACP convention, the Salt Lake and Ogden chapters secured the passage of a motion condemning the church's "doctrine of non-white inferiority" saying that it "fosters prejudice and . . . perpetuates the contention that Negroes deserve to be the subject of disadvantaged conditions during their lives on earth." In Salt Lake, the NAACP organized a number of demonstrations, one with 500 participants, to pressure the church leadership to throw its weight behind civil rights legislation that was bogged down in the state legislature. The church finally supported a watered-down version of the legislation, which included an exemption—for the Mormon church.

With such a small black population—one percent in 1967—and a civil rights movement that was heavily influenced by whites and largely ignored by national civil rights organizations, the protest movement never went very far in Utah. Ezra Taft Benson, the most politically outspoken member of the Quorum of the Twelve, saw the 1965 demonstrations, though, as a sign that there were traitors in the church and that communists were "using the civil rights movement to promote revolution and the eventual takeover of this country."

It was often thought that McKay would change the priesthood ban during his lifetime. But exponents of change, such as Hugh B. Brown, were apparently blocked by Benson and his allies, who, according to Mauss, probably included Joseph Fielding Smith and Harold B. Lee. Smith, the exponent of various racial doctrines, still referred to "darkies" as wonderful people, and Lee once told Ernest L. Wilkinson that "If a granddaughter of mine should ever go to BYU and become engaged to a colored boy there, I would hold you responsible."

Benson's views touched the deep-seated fears of a number of Mormons about the black threat to Utah. Rumors ran rife that armed Black Panthers were going to invade Utah, that assassination squads were headed for prosperous neighborhoods, and that black children were selling candy bars filled with broken glass. Some spoke of a prophecy attributed to John Taylor that blood would run in the streets of Salt Lake City.

In his diary, Hugh B. Brown reported that he repeatedly had to quell these kinds of rumors, including one about four carloads of machine gun–toting blacks who were headed for the city to start a riot and destroy property on Temple Square. Returning from Washington, D.C., to visit his family, Robert Bennett, the son of Senator Wallace F. Bennett, recalled having to explain that all his neighbors were not black, that crime was not rampant, that children were not mugged, and that there was a black middle class. When Jerry Rubin announced that the Black Panthers and the Yippies were going to move their headquarters to Salt Lake to join Eldridge Cleaver, who was already hiding out there, in a war against the Mormons, many took his statement seriously.

William E. Koerner, a Mormon convert and a retired army officer, decided that neighborhood emergency teams were the only way to prevent a revolution. The takeover, he explained, would be triggered by rioting that would break out in every major city at ten A.M., when children were in school and separated from their parents. The children would then be held hostage until their parents complied with the takeover. Salt Lake would be attacked first, according to Koerner, because of the church's position on blacks. "Revolutionary teams are already in the valley," he warned. Church leaders, at the suggestion of Harold B. Lee, decided that Koerner's efforts were an attack on the existing civil authorities, and when Koerner refused to back down, he was excommunicated.

Once the black issue was raised by activists, the discussion was carried on by prominent Mormons, such as Sterling M. McMurrin, who served as Commissioner of Education under President John Kennedy, and Kennedy's Secretary of the Interior, Stewart Udall, who used the pages of a newly published independent Mormon publication, *Dialogue*, to criticize the church. "The very character of Mormonism," Udall wrote, "is being distorted and crippled by adherence to a belief and practice that denies the oneness of mankind."

McMurrin in a speech before the Salt Lake NAACP in 1969 argued that Salt Lake "could have been a model city where full human dignity and full social justice would be realities in the lives of all its citizens. . . . The tragedy here is that in its early decades the Mormon church was alive with social, moral reform. It had a vital, prophetic, revolutionary message that called for a just society and it was willing to run great risks in advocacy of its principles. Now it is quiescent and conservative and has lost much of its capacity to dream new dreams and chart new paths."

The church again responded with a statement signed by Brown and

Tanner supporting civil rights. In a new departure, the statement explained that blacks were barred from the priesthood "for reasons which we believe are known to God, but which He has not made known to man." In a defensive tone, the statement went on to say that the whole issue of blacks and the priesthood was of no interest to nonmembers of the church anyhow.

Meanwhile, student activists throughout the West began to turn their attention to the issue of Mormon racism by attacking BYU's athletic teams. There was a riot at the University of Wyoming when a group of black athletes were dismissed after wearing armbands to protest BYU's presence. During halftime at a Colorado State University basketball game, students fought police, and eggs and Molotov cocktails were thrown. Stanford University and the University of Washington canceled all sporting events with BYU. And some coaches suggested breaking up the Western Athletic Conference because of BYU. In response, a *Deseret News* reporter wrote that the protests showed "what can happen when you are granting minority groups special concessions."

In time, the student protests died out, and the church appeared to have weathered one of its worst crises. There were scattered protests in the 1970s, including opposition to the construction of a new church building in an interracial neighborhood in New York City and an NAACP suit against the church for barring blacks from leadership positions in Boy Scout troops.

After its new public relations operation was set up in the 1970s, the church began a campaign to improve its image in racial matters. A number of blacks were admitted to BYU, mostly on athletic scholarships. Black speakers, including Alex Haley and Massachusetts Senator Edward Brooke, were invited to BYU, and black singers appeared regularly with the Mormon Tabernacle Choir. In Salt Lake City, the church agreed to let a small number of blacks set up an organization called the Genesis Group for black members.

While pressures for change were mounting within the domestic church, the most significant pressures were building in the international church. Here, the question of racial lineage had become, in the light of the church's expansion in the Third World, particularly in countries such as Brazil, increasingly important and, at the same time, a major obstacle to the church's missionary work.

THE LINEAGE PROBLEM

In Brazil, more than any other country, the race factor was critical. The church was established there in the late 1920s among the German-speaking communities of southern Brazil. Many of the early members of the church were pro-Nazi, and the church was noted for its anti-Latin, prowhite attitudes. Shortly before the outbreak of World War II, the Brazilian government became wary of its German-speaking citizens, including the Mormons, because of the growth of pro-Nazi sentiment. Subsequently, the government banned German-language meetings and finally shut down the German branch of the church for seven months. When the church reopened, the missionaries shifted their focus to the darker-skinned Portuguese-speaking community.

From the outset, the missionaries, who were particularly concerned about the racial origins of their new recruits, experienced enormous difficulties in sorting out "pure-blooded" descendants of the Portuguese from "mixed-bloods," who were the products of intermarriage with Brazil's former slave population. In order to bar those with African ancestry, the church issued instruction sheets for missionaries, describing methods for determining lineage. Missionaries were told to get potential converts to look through their family photo albums in their presence, to carefully question family members, and to be particularly sensitive to skin shading. At times, baptisms did not happen because of a convert's Negroid appearance.

"If there was any question," recalled Mission President W. Grant Bangerter, "you could not get the priesthood." The problem, according to Bangerter, was that so "many Brazilians [were] not either black or white but a shade of brown, and it would be impossible to distinguish clearly between those who have Negro blood and those who don't." Intermarriage, he went on, was more the rule than the exception, though "white people of stature and status do hope to keep themselves free from a mixture of Negro blood."

In 1954, David O. McKay undertook a trip to South Africa for a personal look at the church's missionary problem. Before his visit, it was the responsibility of the potential priesthood holder to demonstrate his non-Negroid racial background. Upon his return, McKay, according to Mormon sociologist Mauss, shifted the burden of proof to the mission president and the priesthood leaders in the mission. The church did, however, set up a select group of genealogists to review complicated lineage questions that were referred to it. This group was active into the 1970s.

By the early 1970s, as the church grew in Brazil, with potential priesthood holders now numbering in the thousands, the problem of sorting out pure from mixed-bloods had become an impossible tangle. During the 1950s, the church had initially shown signs of altering its racial policies because of the problems of building an international church. David O. McKay had reclassified the people of the Fiji Islands and New Guinea in the Pacific as Israelites rather than descendants of Ham. The church, however, still seemed resistant to change through the 1970s.

When Spencer W. Kimball became Prophet, the church's renewed missionary effort abroad again brought the racial factor to the fore. As part of this effort, Kimball in 1974 announced plans for the construction of a new temple in Brazil. This new temple would compound the existing difficulties involved in preserving the church's racial criterion for priesthood. Since the focus had largely shifted from lineage determination to skin coloration as the main criterion for evaluating potential members, it was apparent that a number of light-skinned blacks or mulattoes would eventually, or had already, been granted the priesthood. Once the temple was built, these nonwhite members would then enter that most holy of Mormon places.

By 1978, as the temple neared completion, it had become clear that the policy had reached a crisis point in terms of the church's own internal dynamics. James E. Faust, the General Authority in charge of Brazil, began to be called the Apostle for the Blacks, parallel to the way Kimball was referred to as the Apostle to the Lamanites. More and more information about the Brazilian situation began to reach the pages of church publications, and a well-orchestrated public relations buildup seemed under way. The groundwork was being laid for a change of policy that would hopefully rid the church of one of its most embarrassing features.

According to an interview with Apostle LeGrand Richards two months after the revelation, Kimball was worried because of the impending dedication of the Brazilian temple. "All those people with negro blood in them have been raising money to build the temple," said Richards, "and then if we don't change, then they can't even use it after they've got it." Kimball, explained Richards, interviewed each Apostle personally and asked them to present him with arguments for and against granting the priesthood. After the leaders discussed the question as a group, they held two prayer circles asking for divine inspiration. Finally, Kimball arrived at the weekly meeting of the Twelve "with this little document written out, to make the announcement [of the revelation]." After some minor changes were made, the Twelve all voted in favor and then members of the Twelve were dispatched to interview the other General Authorities.

REVELATION

For thousands of members of the church, Spencer W. Kimball's June 9, 1978, revelation was the greatest moment in the modern church. It was a thunderbolt to those who knew little of the public relations campaign that preceded the revelation, and a dramatically unifying act, particularly for church liberals and intellectuals who could now reassert their ties to the church and recapture their testimony.

As the news spread along the Wasatch Front, people embraced each other, tears of joy fell freely, and cars drove through the streets of Provo honking their horns and flashing their lights. Many Mormons recall the moment they heard the news, much in the way they recollected major events of global import, such as the assassination of John F. Kennedy or the first landing on the moon. "It was the happiest, most joyous day in my life," recalled church public relations man Jerry Cahill, whose department had borne the brunt of the media attacks on the church.

Not all Mormons were joyous. There was concern among church leaders that significant numbers of right-wing Mormons, followers of Ezra Tast Benson and others, would quietly, or loudly, leave the church or protest the change despite Benson's own approval of the revelation. In light of these fears, the issue of the *Church News* that carried the text of Kimball's revelation also had an article warning against interracial marriage. General Authority Bruce R. McConkie, a conservative and doctrinaire theologian who was also the son-in-law of Joseph Fielding Smith, the earlier exponent of the so-called Negro doctrine, responded in his own way to the revelation. McConkie announced that Mormons should forget those doctrines expounded earlier by himself and others who had spoken with "limited understanding," as McConkie put it. Then, according to Armand Mauss, McConkie chose to "retain virtually all the old Negro doctrines in the 1979 revision of his authoritative reference book" on church doctrine.

Even in Brazil, church leaders showed some signs of skittishness. Missionaries at first were instructed not to make substantial efforts to recruit blacks, particularly in the interior of the country, where some of the poorest black Brazilians lived. Nevertheless, by 1980, that policy was giving way to a general policy of expansion as thousands of black Brazilians joined the church. The lifting of the black priesthood ban also enabled the church to expand into the Caribbean, where, ever since the Lowry Nelson exchange with the First Presidency over the racial makeup of Cuba, the church had held back from missionary work. The church also moved ahead in Africa, though with far less success.

Aside from the tremendous value in strengthening their efforts in the Third World, the admittance of blacks to the priesthood had great public relations value for the church, both internally and externally. The Kimball revelation was headline news throughout the nation, and it seemed to demonstrate that the church during its years of modernization and professionalization had renounced its earlier misguided views. For church liberals and intellectuals, who had mounted both private and public campaigns against the Negro doctrine, it eliminated their most essential difference with the church—at least until the issue of women's roles in the church surfaced.

Right-wing Mormons took the revelation in stride. They had been carefully prepared for the eventuality of a revelation. Unlike their liberal counterparts, these more orthodox Mormons maintained a nearly absolute belief in church leadership and obedience to the General Authorities. Furthermore there was sufficient recognition, even among the most right-wing Mormons, that the policy on blacks was not central to Mormon mythology and doctrine. As in the past with polygamy, a belief that left the Saints isolated from the American mainstream had been gradually changed to reach a new accommodation with the outside world.

New storm clouds, however, were gathering over Zion despite the Kimball revelation. In the late 1960s at a Boston gathering for church members, General Authority Boyd K. Packer, then working with Harold B. Lee to correlate the church, was asked about the black priesthood ban. He responded carefully, explaining that he too had a black friend who was disturbed by the Mormon position. Then just as Packer was ready to leave, he wheeled around and dramatically declared: "If you think this is a problem, the greatest problem the church will face in the coming years will be women." With remarkable prescience, Harold B. Lee, in preparation for his Correlation revolution, had diagnosed in 1960 the problems that the church would face in the next two decades. Now one of his protégés, Elder Packer, was himself accurately predicting the future.

CHAPTER SEVEN

THE PRIESTHOOD AND THE BLACK WIDOW SPIDER: WOMEN AND THE CHURCH

She liked to think of herself as doing battle for both the church and the family, as if, or rather, *since* they were one and the same cause.

Jaynann Morgan Payne looked the part. A fifty-year-old one-time beauty queen (she had been a runner-up in a Mrs. America contest), she was handsome under her well-coiffed hair and heavy makeup. She was a proud woman: full of pride for her church, for her organization, the Center for Family Studies, for her family, for her participation in such groups as the Utah Association of Women and the Daughters of the American Revolution. The picture of her twelve children and her husband was prominently displayed.

She was proud of the fact that her church had asked her to present her point of view as *their* point of view. She had spoken on behalf of the church to youth and women's groups on such subjects as "The Joy of Being a Woman," "Beauty for Keeps," and "To Fulfill Her Promise," all titles of books she had written.

Now she was being asked to answer questions about the family and the church. She wanted to show by the strength and righteousness of her position, her charm, and the derived power she received from her church and the Freemen Institute (with which her center was affiliated), that she could explain the value of the church for women.

"We women don't need the priesthood," she explains. "I have all I can handle as is." She talks slowly, not exactly out of memory but from nervousness and a certain kind of repetition. "A woman holds the priesthood through her husband," she continues. "There are all these outside forces that are attacking the family, though we have suffered less because the Mormon family has not eroded. Out there, the divorce rate is up. Women are working outside the home. All of this has affected the family. It's a struggle to keep our families together."

She has fears too, especially about the things some women who call themselves Mormon have been saying and doing. These people, call them what you will, feminists, liberals, whatever, have created problems. Even some of the General Authorities have said this, warning that if these women keep on saying those things, they could cause those new to the church to falter. It would be faith destroying. "We Mormons," she declares, "have much in common with the rest of the nation in what we're subjected to: secularism, humanism, institutionalism, hedonism, the pleasure-seeking, popularity things."

She's not sure she's been convincing. The phone rings. It's the head of the Freemen Institute, W. Cleon Skousen, calling from the Holy City, Jerusalem. She describes the interview, asks if she is giving the right answers, and then pauses. "Oh," she exclaims, "I guess I shouldn't have said those things."

She pauses again, the phone conversation over. "We know there are those who would like to split the church by focusing on our so-called disputes," she says carefully, having been coached over the phone as to the *correct* answers. She refers back to her discussion of *those* people like the feminists. "We are not divided. We are one church," she proclaims.

The discussion is over. "You know," she says, "I'd much rather stay at home than do all this. I respect our family. The church has shown me the way. After all," she sighs, her charm making a comeback, "we Mormon women have always been emancipated."

A WOMEN'S DIALECTIC

Mormonism is a religion of the family. As a frontier religion, the family (or families, during the polygamy period) was the central organizing unit of production. It was also the key to the organizational unity of the church. As a doctrine, family concepts were critical, not only regarding the ability of the faithful to enter the Celestial Kingdom but in relation to the very nature of the Mormon God. In heaven, according to one Mormon folk tradition, there are both our Father *and* our Heavenly Mother, parents of us all.

For Mormon women, their tensions, identities, misfortunes, and opportunities center around this omnipresent culture of the family. Women have been placed on the pedestal and have functioned as de facto heads of households, as frontier wives of polygamous husbands, and as the wives of church leaders who live on the road. They have been both dependent and to a lesser degree autonomous, celebrated as mothers, yet constituting the organizational backbone of the church.

The church has always experienced a kind of women's dialectic: an interplay of dependence and independence that is today creating new tensions and challenges to the status quo. Still, throughout the 150-year history of the church, women have always been subject to the dominant, male power of the priesthood.

Mormonism, as has been increasingly pointed out by both contemporary critics *and* advocates of the church, is a patriarchal religion. The term patriarchy is a positive one in the Mormon culture. The patriarch is the head of the household, at once provider, priesthood holder, and part of a line of authority that extends from God through man to woman. "The patriarchal system provides a basis for government in the Kingdom of God," writes Dean Larsen, a leading member of the Quorum of the Seventy. "It places parents in a position of accountability for their own direct family, and it links these family kingdoms in a patriarchal order that lends cohesiveness to the greater kingdom of God of which they are a part."

As priesthood holders, members of the lay hierarchy, men have a direct role in the contemporary organization of the church. As patriarchs, they not only have a direct line of authority in overseeing this key temporal institution, but as Mormon doctrine makes so amply clear, they are preparing to occupy their *permanent* roles in the Kingdom of God.

That permanent role is established through a temple marriage, when a man and woman in good standing in the church can get "sealed" for eternity. The temple marriage is the *sine qua non* for entering the Celestial Kingdom, where the patterns and structures of Mormon daily life get reduplicated for eternity.

The Celestial Kingdom is the highest level of heaven in the Mormon division of terrestrial, telestial, and celestial orders. "The patriarchal order has no relevance in the eternal worlds except for those husbands and wives and families who have entered into the covenant of eternal marriage," declares Larsen. Larsen, whose remarks appeared in a church magazine, warned that couples who do not qualify for temple marriage or single members who do not marry "are as unwise as if they avoided the covenants of baptism or of the priesthood. It matters not that they may have been endowed or that they regularly attend the temple and fulfill other responsibilities in the Church. All of these things are preparatory and preliminary to the ordinance of celestial marriage."

Through a temple marriage, men and women are eligible to enter the Celestial Kingdom. In the Celestial Kingdom, men progress to be like God himself. "As man is, God once was; as God is, man may become," is one of the most famous of all Mormon doctrinal statements. There are marital and sexual differentiations, however, even in heaven. Man becomes like God and a king and is promised all the blessings of Abraham and Jacob (meaning that there is polygamy in the Celestial Kingdom, whatever its legal status on earth). His wife becomes *his* queen, while a divorced woman cannot aspire to be any more than "a ministering angel," a servant to the God-King. She can, if worthy, link up as a polygamous wife to a man-God.

The Celestial Kingdom is a reflection of the church's male hierarchy and a reflection of the doctrines of the nineteenth-century church. (Church leaders would say that the hierarchy is a reflection of the Celestial Kingdom.) There is also a Mormon concept of a Mother in Heaven that provides a particular place for women in their understanding of themselves as having been created in the image of God.

> *In the Heavens are parents single?*
> *No, the thought makes reason stare!*
> *Truth is reason, truth eternal*
> *Tells me I've a mother there*

says a popular hymn written by Eliza R. Snow, a plural wife of Joseph Smith and the most important leader of women in the nineteenth-century church.

This idea of a Mother in Heaven, despite general Mormon familiarity with the concept, "is a shadowy and elusive one floating around the edges of Mormon consciousness," according to Mormon historian Linda Wilcox. The concept, says Wilcox, was likely generated by Smith, who passed the idea on to Eliza Snow. Though never developed into doctrine as such, it was referred to by church leaders into the early twentieth century in part to demonstrate Mormon commitment to women's rights. Apostle and theologian James E. Talmage, for instance, declared, "The church is bold enough to go so far as to declare that man has an Eternal Mother in the Heavens as well as an Eternal Father, and in the same sense 'we look upon woman as a being essential in every particular to the carrying out of God's purposes in respect to mankind.'"

During this period, Mormon leaders, male and female, constantly pointed out the church's commitment to sexual equality and the early granting of women's right to vote in Utah. In 1870, Mormon Utah was, in fact, the second state to pass a suffrage law. Yet that early commitment was an attempt in part to offset the protracted national campaign against the Mormon practice of polygamy.

Unlike the popular misconception at the time, which spoke of such alleged Mormon horrors as white slave trading or libertinism, Mormon polygamy was, in fact, a strict, sexually restrictive practice. It was tied instead to Mormon leadership patterns and frontier needs. Polygamous relationships extended the concept of the Mormon family, and sexual activity was for procreation rather than pleasure. Male leaders often took several wives as a mark of distinction and power, with the practice limited to only a small percentage of church membership. Polygamous wives were not happy women by and large, as several accounts have pointed out. Their men were off on missions or between households, and the women suffered from long bouts of isolation coupled with insecurities generated by the antipolygamy campaigns. Nevertheless, plural wives were still able to maintain a level of solidarity and relative autonomy created in part by the very nature of that isolation. Polygamous women effectively ran their households and were often obliged to develop a variety of skills in order for their families to survive.

Polygamous women were often the backbone of the church's varied women's organizations and publications, helping generate a significant number of organizational and political skills for women in late nineteenth-century Utah. During the polygamy attacks, these women organized many of the most important public demonstrations, linking their support of polygamy to the struggle for women's suffrage and equal rights. Such organizations as the Relief Society (first created in Nauvoo in 1842) and publications as the *Woman's Exponent* (founded in 1872) eventually became at once semiautonomous institutions for women in the church *as well as* defenders of the male-dominated hierarchy.

The protracted campaigns against Mormonism in the 1880s only strengthened that dialectic of independence and submission to authority, as a heightened sense of solidarity and Mormon unity existed among both polygamous and nonpolygamous families, men and women alike. Women had a definite role and a real identity, albeit both radical and contradictory in nature.

Yet, with the subtle and not so subtle shifts that took place in the aftermath of the Great Accommodation of the 1890s, Mormon women began to see that sharp definition fade. In its place emerged a new, hazier identity, still tied to the family yet without the sharp contours generated in the years before the Accommodation.

A *READER'S DIGEST* SENSIBILITY

"Home life, home teaching, parental guidance, father in leadership—these are the panacea for the ailments of the world, a cure for spiritual and emotional diseases, a remedy for problems," declared church President Spencer W. Kimball in 1978. The statement can also be found in the Family Home Evening manual, an instructional guide for Mormon families with suggestions for lessons and events for their once-a-week gatherings.

When you visit the church's Visitors Center at Temple Square in Salt Lake City, there is a special media presentation devoted just to this heavily encouraged church activity. Sitting in a plastic tree house in a suburban backyard, a ten-year-old plastic puppet named Johnny talks to the audience. His knees move happily up and down, as he relates to the audience how his family—Mom and Dad Brown, two older brothers, Mike and Don, younger sister Susie, and dog Butchy—engage in this weekly mix of family happiness and togetherness, sprinkled liberally with Mormon religious homilies and hymns. A film presentation follows, which includes a typical Family Home Evening of the Browns, interspersed with comments from Johnny who continues to point out the advantages of this form of family get-together.

Though the film is obviously more graphic and "real" than Johnny, the most striking and dominant image of the presentation remains Johnny in the tree house, who, more than anything else, is a kind of throwback to an earlier, less turbulent era of suburban homes and *Reader's Digest* sensibilities. The Brown family provides a good example of an idealized Mormon home—the one presented in the manuals, at church service, and throughout the intricate organizational web of the church.

It is an image that weighs most heavily on Mormon women. They have learned, through more than half a century of accommodation and change, that their special role is to establish and orchestrate this Mormon home life and to act less and less as independent agents with their own set of networks and organizations.

This transition took on many forms. With the Relief Society organization, women had an independent, semiautonomous organization that they, rather than the men of the priesthood, controlled. Independence was always tempered by the fact that the women's organizations still saw themselves as following the dictates of the priesthood in doctrinal matters and in relation to broad church policy and hierarchical organization. Leaders active in women's organizations placed a heavy premium on motherhood roles and were frequently obliged to reinforce dominant notions of male superiority in matters both doctrinal and temporal.

Yet the Relief Society and a number of the other auxiliary organizations for women, such as the Young Women's organization, functioned on their *own* more than any other church auxiliaries. That relative autonomy was expressed through their day-to-day activities, fund raising and expenditure of funds, internal educational programs, and social service activities.

In 1892, the Relief Society was, in fact, legally incorporated under a separate name, The National Woman's Relief Society, to conduct business on its own, with its own set of trustees separate from the church itself. Relief Society meeting halls were, until the 1920s, physically separate from church chapels. Fund raising drives for particular projects, subscription drives for publications, bake sales, bazaar sales, handiwork sales were all regular events, with a high degree of enthusiasm and participation among women members.

The Relief Society and some of the other women's auxiliaries became places apart, similar in ways to women's cultural clubs in the late nineteenth and early twentieth centuries. The ideal Mormon woman, such as Susa Young Gates, a daughter of Brigham Young and one of the most prominent Mormon women in the early twentieth century, was someone who could combine her priesthood-defined role of mother of twelve children with her better-known activities as writer, musician, suffragist, teacher, and church worker.

Another key aspect of women's organizational work involved service activities that became most prominent in the 1920s and 1930s. Through World War I, the Relief Society participated in a variety of service activities, particularly in crisis situations where additional labor became a necessity. Relief Society activities ranged from Red Cross volunteer work to the sale of its entire inventory of 200,000 bushels of wheat to the U.S. government to use for war relief.

By 1919, this approach was consolidated under the leadership of Amy Brown Lyman, who helped create the Relief Society Social Service Department. Lyman was an important figure within the women's organizations, symbolizing the transition from the suffrage-oriented leadership of the late nineteenth century to the service-oriented group that emerged between the wars. With an impressive background in social work, she had been one of Utah's earliest female legislators and the main supporter of legislation providing for public protection of maternity and infancy. Her key organizational role within the Relief Society lasted several decades and included stints as both general secretary and president of the organization. Over time, Amy Brown Lyman became recognized and applauded as an effective, indomitable woman's leader. Yet, ultimately, events outside her control impinged on the recognition of her as a symbol of a strong Mormon woman.

For one, service work became more limited when the church, in 1936, created the Church Welfare Program, which incorporated many of the Relief Society projects, such as the grain-storage program.

More important were the events surrounding Amy Lyman's husband, Richard R. Lyman, one of the members of the Quorum of the Twelve. Richard R. Lyman, in an extraordinary and unusual move at the time, was excommunicated from the church in 1943 for engaging in what the church called "a violation of the Christian law of chastity." Amy Lyman, still head of the Relief Society, was then subject to a round of rumors insinuating that she, as an active, powerful, *independent* woman with outside interests, was responsible for driving her husband into an affair. After her husband was excommunicated, Amy Lyman was obliged to step down from the Relief Society presidency.

Nevertheless, by the end of the 1940s, women in the church still maintained a set of semiautonomous organizations, networks, and activities, with a substantial financial base and a popular set of publications. Repeated attempts by the priesthood in the 1920s and again in the 1940s to "take over" and/or integrate auxiliary activities had been resisted. Women were the most active members in the church and the most successful in sustaining not only their own functions, but overall church programs as well.

The women's magazines also remained popular. Similar to their successful resistance to reorganization, the women's groups also resisted periodic attempts to consolidate the magazines as well. "Of course we held on to the magazine," Belle S. Spafford, Amy Brown Lyman's successor as Relief Society president, recalled, "because we saw values for the women having their own publication."

Priesthood attempts prior to the 1950s to refocus women's activities more exclusively toward the home also met with only partial success at best. In the postwar period, church leaders were increasingly concerned about pressures on the traditional family, including the entry of large numbers of women into the work force.

In the early 1940s, newly appointed Apostle Ezra Taft Benson asked the Relief Society under Amy Lyman to reinstitute Family Home Evening. The Relief Society rejected this suggestion, declaring that such a formal program was "incompatible with the informal atmosphere of the home," as well as irrelevant to teenage concerns.

Then in 1946 and 1947, church leaders pushed the program once again, calling for a new approach they entitled Family Get-Together. They talked about the need to stimulate "gospel teaching in the home, unifying the family, and strengthening testimonies." This proposal also never caught on as a major program. Suggestions for activities were printed in the Relief Society magazine, and members were encouraged to review ideas in such publications as *Good Housekeeping*. No set time for the Home Evening was provided, and, similar to other attempts at Correlation up through the 1940s, the women in the organization still essentially set their agendas and defined the scope of their activities, largely ignoring the Home Evening event.

The concern about the impact of social changes on the family continued to grow in the 1950s. The idea of an independent teenager became an initial focus of concern in the postwar years, particularly for church president David O. McKay. McKay warned about the evils of juvenile delinquency and maintained a direct pipeline to the Salt Lake City police department regarding this particular problem. In one 1951 conference speech, he warned church members that "parents who do not know where their children are at night are recreant to the sacred obligation of parenthood, and untrue to the high ideals of the Church regarding home life."

Church conferences also became increasingly devoted to the subject of women's roles and the institution of the family and motherhood. The Mormons' fears and concerns about the family were not so dissimilar to those found in the larger society. National media portraits during the 1950s reflected how, in the eyes of the press, the church had indeed become a solid, family-centered American institution. With Ezra Taft Benson leading the prayers at Dwight Eisenhower's cabinet meetings and *Reader's Digest* and *Time* magazine offering flattering profiles of the church, the reemphasis on the home, with the concept of motherhood virtually equated with womanhood, paralleled the general American reaction to the wartime image of the working woman.

By the early 1960s, church leaders were still not satisfied with the state of the Mormon family. A new program was in the works, a program that would this time effectively undermine the independence of the auxiliaries. The feeling of loss of control among church leaders had grown, as had fears about family dynamics and the continuing changes in the larger society. Conflict was in the air, as the church leadership moved to insulate its members from the outside world and to impress upon its women that their place was most certainly in the home.

SHELTER FROM THE TEMPEST

"The key to the whole Correlation movement," Harold B. Lee told priesthood leaders in 1962, "was given us when the First Presidency, in an important communication some years ago, declared that 'The home is the basis of a righteous life and no other instrumentality can take its place nor fulfill its essential functions.' The utmost the auxiliaries can do is to aid the home in its problems, giving special aid and succor where such is necessary."

For Mormon women, the Correlation movement would have profound significance. Though most church members understand Correlation in terms of its organizational, centralizing impact, they miss its fundamental ideological character, which centered on the newly evolving role of women, the family, and their relation to the overall leadership structures and policies of the church.

That ideological character was understood at the outset by the man most responsible for the Correlation revolution that swept the church in the 1960s and 1970s—Harold B. Lee. "Harold B. Lee had this sense of social breakdown," declared Ruth Funk, one of Lee's key female assistants within the Correlation movement and later president of the Young Women's Mutual Improvement Association during Lee's Presidency. "He saw the breakdown of the nuclear family. Television was also coming into play, and he could see how that might undermine traditional family roles and the danger that television might take us away from the gospel. His premise from the start was that Correlation strengthens the family."

The key to Correlation, as Lee explained it to leadership cadres throughout the church, was the ability to create mechanisms to increase church influence in this most basic unit of society. The father, the husband, must be considered the representative of the priesthood in the home, and through that relationship church attitudes, policies, and doctrines could be reinforced. "Placing the priesthood as the Lord intended, at the center of the Kingdom of God," Lee told one group of church leaders, "[includes] a greater emphasis on the fathers in the homes as Priesthood bearers in strengthening the family unit."

Taking the church directly into the home thus became Correlation's first crucial task. Unlike previous attempts in the 1920s and 1940s, the Family Home Evening concept was presented this time with all the power and prestige of the church First Presidency and its instrument, the Correlation Committee, which Lee headed. As an initial step, Lee pushed for an upgrading of the ward teacher program, by which, among other things, inactive members in a ward were "reproselyted." Calling this new effort the "home teacher" program, Lee declared that home teaching would be the first vehicle to bring Correlation into action. The new Correlated programs of the church would be made available not to errant members per se but to *families.*

Then, within a year after home teaching was introduced, Family Home Evening was reinaugurated with a great deal of fanfare. "For a few years, Family Home Evening was the number-one program of the church," Lee's assistant Ruth Funk recalled. "All the church's resources were geared towards making it happen; everything was beamed at the family. The Family Home Evening almost became scripture. They [church leaders and the Correlation Committee] did everything in their power to make it succeed. You would hear it from the pulpit. It was the focus, the number-one vehicle." With the first Family Home Evening manual produced by the Correlation Committee, the "pipeline of authority" was now established. It ran from "the head of the home [who presided over Family Home Evening], to the home teacher, to the priesthood leader, to the stake president, to the Quorum of the Twelve, to the Prophet, to Christ."

By the new decade, the first phase of Correlation was an important success. Monday evenings were set aside for Family Home Evening, and other church activities were eliminated. Even temples were closed. In 1970, the new president of the church, Joseph Fielding Smith, would declare, regarding the Family Home Evening lessons: "Parents who ignore the great help of this program are gambling with the future of their children."

With phase one a success, the Correlation Committee aimed its fire at another critical target: the auxiliary organizations. For Lee and his most intimate allies, such as Quorum of the Twelve member (and later counselor in the First Presidency) Marion G. Romney, the auxiliaries had grown too independent, too autonomous, both in financial matters and in the range of their activities. As with Family Home Evening, repeated but unsuccessful attempts had been made not only to take over the publications of the auxiliaries but to redefine the nature of their activities as well. By the postwar period, church leaders grumbled that the auxiliaries were taking over more and more church activities and that they had become, as one General Authority put it, "separate churches, to a degree, within the church."

Lee's concern about the role and nature of the family extended to the key role that the auxiliaries played within the day-to-day life of the church. Lee thought, as his son-in-law and biographer, L. Brent Goates, put it, that the "auxiliaries were the scene of the action in terms of time and investment. That had gone on for a very long time." For Lee, it was a matter of "how to get the auxiliaries out of the way to allow the priesthood to take over."

To restructure the auxiliaries, the Correlation Committee first set out to redefine the programs of each component part of the church, most particularly the auxiliaries, such as the Relief Society. By the mid-1960s, the Blue

Book had been developed. It systematically directed the rewriting of the manuals, lesson plans, and other auxiliary programs. Reading Committees, Writing Committees, Review Committees, powerful Coordinating Councils were all established to take over this function. Up to then, the auxiliaries, principally the women's groups, had boards that selected the authors for their publications or wrote the lessons themselves, and oversaw all publishing decisions, down to picking the typeface, the cover design, and the formats.

With Correlation, that power was placed in the hands of a new Lee-directed bureaucracy. Content of the programs also changed dramatically. For example, Relief Society courses, which had, during the Amy Brown Lyman period, dealt with such subjects as social welfare, were transformed during the Correlation revolution of the 1960s to such topics as "The Place of Woman in the Gospel Plan," and "Teaching the Gospel in the Home," with literature classes on "Ideals of Womanhood in Relation to Home and Family."

The revamping of the auxiliaries was by the late 1960s in high gear. For the leadership of the women's organizations, the restructuring process had already begun to take its toll, even before the most substantial changes were laid out in 1969–70. Lavern W. Parmley, the president of the preteen Primary organization, recalls how the initial thrust of Correlation "made us feel more confined." "When you work through the Correlation Committee," Parmley declared, "you go through Curriculum Development, and then you go through Correlation. You go through editing. You go through publication. You go through printing, publishing, distribution, and you work with so many people. It's quite different than when you had the complete responsibility of it and when you had questions, you'd probably go only to your two advisors."

Frequently, Parmley and other auxiliary leaders would try to bypass this new organizational maze and go directly to Lee and other General Authorities in order to get their way, often without success. The overall process was draining, particularly for a leadership group used to controlling the general, day-to-day life of its organization. "We did everything," Parmley recalled, "and then all of a sudden [we were] put under such strenuous directives."

"For so many years," Ruth Funk declared, "the auxiliaries had maintained this attitude of 'possessiveness.'" Funk recalled that even while program activites were being restructured, auxiliary leaders, such as Belle S. Spafford, then president of the Relief Society, literally would say about Funk, the emissary of the Correlators, "Who's that little young punk telling *me* what to do."

By 1969–70 these issues were coming to a head when the Correlators made their most significant and controversial move to date: the taking away of the magazines and the elimination of the women's organizations' financial autonomy. Henceforth, the priesthood would run the magazines.

The Relief Society publication, in fact, was formally suspended, and a new overall church publication, *The Ensign*, was created to take up Relief Society concerns, as well as priesthood-related matters. Further, all monies would now flow outside the auxiliaries to the centralized, priesthood-controlled financial bureaucracy, which would have the power to also decide how the women's funds would be spent. It was nothing less than a structural revolution in the operation of the women's organizations.

The change came suddenly and directly. In 1970 the women leaders were summoned to the office of Apostle Mark E. Petersen, where Harold B. Lee announced the new decisions. This time there was no recourse, no lobbying to try and change the decision.

The change came as a shock not only to the leadership group, but to women throughout the church. Sonia Johnson, who was excommunicated for supporting the ERA, recalled that her first serious moment of doubt concerning the church's male leadership involved the decisions about the magazines, finances, and a related decision taking away women's right to lead prayers at sacrament meetings. Rodello Hunter talked of the change as the "arbitrary slicing away of the Relief Society magazine and the Church bazaars by which the women of the Relief Society stayed financially independent. The women no longer have any financial control—the greatest part of any control—over their affairs," Hunter bitterly concluded in 1971.

Letters were exchanged in the *Salt Lake Tribune*. Mormon women throughout the world wrote to their auxiliary leaders. Even talk of some kind of protest, an incredible rarity in the Mormon culture, filled the air, but to no avail. Initially, there was a big drop in circulation for such publications as the Primary's *The Children's Friend Magazine*, since among other reasons there were no longer women members canvassing for subscribers. Yet the Correlators stuck with the changes, insisting that they were absolutely necessary to provide full implementation of Correlation goals.

Though some important women leaders continued to criticize the shift for a time, all the leaders ultimately went along, and some, like Belle S. Spafford changed from opposition to support. A sense of *inevitability* accompanied the change, for Mormon women had by 1970 been subject to an intense campaign about *their* role, which cut at the heart of their ability to operate as an independent force. "I just knew there was no use when they'd instigated all these programs," Parmley said of the changes. "I don't know why they need a president [of the Primary] now. We're just told what to do and when to do it and how to do it."

The Correlation revolution paralleled the Mormon counterattack about the role and definition of women in society—a counterattack that not only stressed the power of the priesthood and women's roles as homemakers and babymakers, but also included a revival of certain kinds of themes and images from the 1950s, placed in the context of the turbulence of the late

1960s. The bouffant hairstyle was fashionable, while miniskirts, shorts, and strapless evening dresses became "an abomination in the sight of the Lord."

Nowhere was this approach as strikingly presented as in *Fascinating Womanhood*, a popular book of the 1960s' counterrevolution against the budding women's movement written by a Mormon woman named Helen Andelin. Though not officially sponsored by church leaders, Mormon women, with the informal blessings of church leaders throughout the country, organized groups to read and study the book.

The central theme of Andelin's book is that women should "revere your husband and honor his right to rule you and his children." In listing a set of "do's'" and "don'ts,"Andelin evokes the idea that women should use artifice and subterfuge as part of their attempt to corral and then hold on to their husbands. Examples included: "acquire a child-like manner" and "express yourself when your husband mistreats you by child-like sauciness." Andelin, in effect, provided an entire behavioral package to complement the church's own view of women's roles.

Through the 1960s, the Correlation revolution had the further effect of infantilizing women by creating instructions through manuals and other publications that treated women as childlike innocents who had to be led step by step through the church emphasis on chastity and motherhood. Church leaders—sixty- and seventy-year-old men (ninety-year-olds in the case of David O. McKay and Joseph Fielding Smith)—were shocked at the changing mores of the 1960s. They moved forcefully to prevent such attitudes and behavioral displays from infecting Mormon women, many of whom were the age of the leaders' granddaughters.

Despite the attempt to create an idealized version of a Mormon woman, whether through church manuals, Family Home Evening programs, or informal behavioral tips, church leaders, by the beginning of the 1970s, were becoming more anxious than ever. Women were witnessing and participating in changes in life-activity that Harold B. Lee could scarcely imagine when he fretted over these problems in pre-Correlation days. "The charge to bear children, which the Lord gave to Eve, and to women, generally, is, by many, flouted today," Lee ally and Correlation leader Marion G. Romney exclaimed at a Relief Society meeting. "The sordidness of our society, which, on the one hand tolerates, encourages, and even condones such abominations as unchastity and other types of licentious debauchery, and, on the other hand, legalizes abortions, encourages, and in some cases attempts to enforce birth control, is a prostitution of the functions of life."

The warning signs were ominous. "These are the last days," thundered then church president Joseph Fielding Smith at a 1972 conference. "They are the days of trouble and sorrow and desolation. They are the days when Satan dwells in the hearts of ungodly men, when iniquity abounds, and when the signs of the times are being shown forth."

CONSCIOUSNESS RAISING

The Boston-area church community always had a reputation as a breeding ground for intellectuals, liberals, and, by the 1970s, feminists. It was at a Boston-wide gathering of church members that a new member of the Quorum of the Twelve named Boyd K. Packer made his remarks about women being the greatest problem the church would face in the coming years. The remark startled the people who heard it, and one of the women there recalled how striking it had been for her. "All of a sudden it became clear to me why the Brethren were becoming so uptight," recalled the woman, who later became prominent in church women's organizations. "Here was a man who had grown up in Brigham City [a small town north of Salt Lake City], who had little contact with the world outside Utah and the Church, and then he runs smack into the middle of the women's movement in the Boston area."

To Packer and other church leaders, the women's movement represented their worst fears: lesbians, women questioning male authority, women attacking the nuclear family. The women's movement, more than any of the social movements of the time, frightened the church leaders and quickly led them on a route that would dramatically thrust the church into the public spotlight.

By 1970, despite the extraordinary, systematic attempt to insulate women and the family from the perceived evils of the larger society, slowly and hesitatingly, small numbers of Mormon women began to explore the new world of feminism. Boston, in fact, was fertile ground for some of these earliest attempts at consciousness raising among Mormon women. Small groups got together to talk about their lives, their Mormonism, and the demand by church leaders that a woman's place was not only in the home, but to be the mother of a very large family.

In June 1970, a handful of these women got together to explore what would turn out to be a pivotal moment in the development of their consciousness. Many members of the group had been involved in Relief Society projects so they had a fair degree of organizational experience. Contacted by the male editor of the independent Mormon publication *Dialogue*, the group was asked to put together a special issue about women and the church, which came to be known as the "Pink issue" because of its jacket color.

For the women who produced the issue and for women who read it, the Pink issue was a rite of passage. "A certain amount of turmoil is probably characteristic of any group project, as most Mormons know," Laurel Thatcher Ulrich, one of the Pink *Dialogue* participants, wrote about the project ten years later. "Yet in a church context, both our pain and our achievement were different. We had called *ourselves* to the task. Without a confirming priesthood blessing and without any clear historical precedent, we had taken upon ourselves a project which would neither build buildings nor win converts and which by its very nature would disturb the equilibrium of our lives."

In the context of the women's movement of 1970–71, the Pink *Dialogue* was a very mild affair. One of the group editors referred to the issue as *Ladies' Home Dialogue*, which, as Ulrich put it, "even tongue in cheek says much about our insecurity and self-conscious conservatism at the time." Nevertheless, the women were acting independently, autonomously, and they experienced "the usual queasiness about countering the brethren, a genuine fear of being wrong, of being caught out of bounds."

The group, as well as several others throughout the country, including Utah, continued to emerge and grow. In 1974, the Boston group produced the first issue of *Exponent II*, which it called the spiritual descendant of the *Woman's Exponent*, the first publication of the Relief Society. Even some of the leadership of the auxiliaries felt they had to respond in some way to the growing interest in consciousness raising, which was primarily centered around a minority group of educated, professional women in the church.

Ruth Funk, Harold B. Lee's Correlation emissary during the 1960s, was in the early 1970s president of the Young Women's Mutual Improvement Association and got caught in just such a situation. An informal gathering of about twenty-five women, most connected in one way or another with the Young Women's group, began meeting, initially to discuss the work of that organization. "Those meetings soon became kind of consciousness-raising sessions," recalled one of the participants, a member of a prominent Mormon family. "Yet less than a third of the people there would have called themselves feminists. We had incredibly open and honest talks. There was some griping about the way some General Authorities treated women, and we also talked about the overall relations of men and women in the church."

When word of the meetings drifted back to the General Authorities, the reaction was swift. The meetings were immediately terminated, and Funk's position became less secure, despite the fact that she had always remained a loyal defender of the church line on women. Not too long after, Funk was released from her position, primarily for other reasons. Nevertheless, it was clear that even such tentative, informal, unofficial gatherings as these threatened church authorities, compounding their growing fears about what they perceived to be attacks on church authority and the priesthood.

By the mid-1970s, the church leadership began to focus directly on this new phenomenon of Mormon feminists. When a small group of Utah women began to organize to select a Utah delegation for the International Women's Year Conference scheduled for 1977, church leaders not only took note, but made what turned out to be the first systematic attempt to intervene on a large scale in a women's event.

Those planning the IWY affair hadn't given much thought to possible church hostility. The event, after all, was government-endorsed, and unlike some other activities of the women's movement, such as those concerning the ERA or abortion, the IWY affair seemed tame and respectable. Without much forethought, the IWY organizers sent an invitation to Barbara Smith, the president of the Relief Society, to attend the Utah selection meeting. They inadvertently set in motion a chain of events that would have a lasting effect on both the Mormon feminists and the church leadership.

Within a matter of days after the Smith invitation, church leaders mobilized their own forces to take over the Utah IWY delegation. Beginning with a letter sent out on church stationery over the signature of Quorum of the Twelve President Ezra Taft Benson, an organized Mormon network was put into motion. Word was put out through both the ward structure and the local Relief Society organizations. The Relief Society itself sent out a letter that called for at least ten women to attend from every Utah ward. Smith, the Relief Society president, worked through both the Priesthood Executive Committee and the Public Communications Department of the church to orchestrate the entire affair.

Expecting at most 3,000 Utah women, the IWY organizers were startled to discover when they convened their meeting at the Salt Palace that over 13,000 Mormon women had been mobilized to attend. Suspicious and hostile, perceiving the "feminists" who had put together the meeting to be doing "Satan's handiwork," as church leaders had said time and again from the pulpit, the 13,000 became an incredible force that literally swallowed up the meeting. Functioning as a tightly disciplined voting block, they followed particular leaders, many of them men, who were strategically placed throughout the meeting site and who signaled how to vote. Rightwing groups had also been brought in for briefing. The church-directed women voted down resolution after resolution put forth by conference organizers, including those not related to such topics as the ERA. Some of the defeated resolutions included those attacking racism, supporting child care, and even one for providing support for incest victims.

To the IWY organizers, the church-directed onslaught was a traumatic affair. "I was terribly shocked by what happened at the Utah IWY meeting," one of the conference organizers recalled. "At first, I cried for days I had so much pain. I couldn't forget the faces of those women the Church had mobilized. So full of hate, so hostile to me without knowing anything about me. But then my pain began turning into anger, and I knew what I had to do. I had to organize."

For the church leaders, IWY offered parallel lessons, particularly for those in the leadership who wanted to move more aggressively on women's issues such as the ERA. For the IWY meeting, church leaders had brought in a number of women to take active roles, such as Jaynann Morgan Payne. "I was called by the church to participate at IWY," Payne said. After IWY, Payne and others helped create a number of anti-ERA, antifeminist organizations, such as the Utah Association of Women, to work closely with church leaders.

After IWY, both sides mobilized. And for the first time, an issue emerged that would place the Mormon church in the forefront of an explosive national campaign and subject it to the most intense media scrutiny since the days of polygamy. With the Equal Rights Amendment, the church, as one Mormon journalist noted, would "meet its Vietnam."

LET THE HEATHENS RAGE

The Public Communications Department official looked around furtively to make sure that nobody could hear his lunchtime chatter while he downed his Little America hamburger special in a crowded Salt Lake motel restaurant. As he ate, he continued his analysis of current church policy. Within the month, the ERA would be dead, and a milestone for the church would have passed. "What's the church going to say about the ERA now that it's over?" he asked rhetorically. "Do we take a low profile, downplay what we've done, or do we, as will likely happen, broadcast to everyone that *we* did it, that we flexed our muscles and brought the amendment down?"

On the other side of downtown, at a coffee shop near Temple Square, a Mormon journalist, a critic of church policy, was noting the same situation. "Take a look at a map," the journalist noted. "Mark out where the church has political influence. It's not just Utah, there's also Nevada and Arizona. Those were your three states needed for ratification, but it doesn't end there. The church has influence elsewhere and played a direct, even critical role. Illinois, Florida, Oklahoma, and even Georgia; all states that needed to ratify."

When the ERA was first making its way through Congress in the early 1970s, few anticipated that the Mormon church would play such a crucial role in the fortunes of the amendment. Early readings of the Utah legislature, where more than seventy percent of its members belonged to the church, indicated relatively easy passage, according to then Governor Calvin Rampton. The women's movement was cresting throughout the country, and even in places such as Utah and Nevada, Mormon women were awakening.

Even as late as 1974, the church appeared to provide no clear direction on the issue. Barbara Smith, the newly named president of the Relief Society, tells of how Phyllis Schlafly came to visit her in November 1974 to discuss the amendment. "I was impressed with her feminine appeal and her determination to accomplish what she believes to be right in spite of strong opposition," Smith said of Schlafly. The Relief Society president felt she could not act without church sanction and said to Schlafly that she did not think that the church could take a stand against the ERA because it only took stands on moral issues.

Smith then relayed her conversation to Thomas Monson of the Quorum of the Twelve, who informed her that she was wrong: The church was, in fact, preparing to take a stand. Church officials had decided that the ERA might well be a suitable vehicle to promote more aggressively the church's position on women and the family. With advice on the ERA from church lawyer Oscar McConkie and BYU law professor Rex E. Lee (who later became Ronald Reagan's Solicitor General), the church decided to make the ERA the first major test for the newly created Special Affairs Committee.

In December of that year, two members of the committee, Gordon B. Hinckley and James E. Faust, met with Smith to inform her about how to proceed. "They felt it was appropriate for me," Smith recalled of the meeting, "as the leader of the women of the church to announce my stand against the ERA if I felt so inclined." The Special Affairs staff then instructed Smith on what to say at a speech at the University of Utah, where the church was arranging extensive press coverage. The campaign against the ERA was launched.

At first, the anti-ERA effort was limited to editorials in the *Deseret News* and statements by the First Presidency that proclaimed the church's commitment to women's rights while attacking the ERA as legislation that would destroy the family and "stifle many God-given feminine instincts." The impact in Utah was immediate. Mormon public opinion and Mormon politicians literally changed overnight from a position of support to opposition. By 1977, church leaders decided to move into high gear, thanks to the impetus of IWY and partly in response to what it perceived to be a favorable national climate as a result of the rise of such phenomena as the Moral Majority.

The first important test was Florida, where in 1978 a referendum on the ERA was on the ballot. The Florida election was extremely close as it came down to the last month, and among other factors, the availability of last-minute campaign funds was of crucial significance. At this point, church leaders swung into action. Special Affairs Committee members systematically began to approach local church leaders outside Utah, a number of them in the Sacramento area of northern California. They requested that the Sacramento leaders, through the local bishops, assess their membership, a common practice for raising funds for official church projects. Then the money that was collected—disguised as small, individual donations by church members (some of whom were even unaware that their names were being used)—was forwarded to the Mormon-connected anti-ERA forces in Florida. More than $30,000 entered the referendum campaign and, according to many observers, helped tilt the election against the ERA.

When the information began to filter out to the public, thanks to investigative stories in the *Miami Herald* and *Sacramento Bee*, church spokesmen, instead of denying involvement, took credit for the Florida defeat as part of their new, more aggressive posture. New campaign tactics came to the fore, among them the creation of Mormon-dominated front groups, in states such as Nevada and Virginia, and informal coalitions with other right-wing anti-ERA forces, such as the John Birch Society and Schlafly's Eagle Forum in Arizona, Georgia, Oklahoma, and other states. In both Nevada and Arizona, ERA legislation was blocked by pivotal Mormon legislators, including James Gibson, a high church official in Nevada who also happened to be the powerful state senate majority leader.

In southern Idaho, an area of Mormon influence, another church regional representative, U.S. District Judge Marion Callister, struck down the 1979 ERA extension law late in the ratification campaign. Callister's action, though never implemented since the amendment died before any appeal of the ruling could be made, nevertheless had a strong impact in undercutting passage of the amendment during the final months of the ERA battle.

In Illinois, Special Affairs member (and later counselor in the First Presidency) Gordon B. Hinckley called an Illinois church official "to coordinate the anti-ERA efforts in the state of Illinois," as a local church newsletter put it. Those efforts included lobbying legislators, fund raising, handling legal matters, and dealing with the news media.

Perhaps the most blatant intervention involving the formal use of church facilities was the campaign in Georgia during the winter of 1982. As a vote in the Georgia legislature neared, public opinion polls showed a surprising plurality for ERA. Once again the church hierarchy swung into action with instructions from Salt Lake conveyed through top figures in the Georgia hierarchy that the anti-ERA message was to be taken *inside* church services. Priesthood meetings, Relief Society meetings, and even sacrament meetings included appeals from church leaders to undertake letter-writing campaigns and other lobbying activities with key legislators. In several wards, material handed out during services contained information on "How to Write Your Legislator," with the names and addresses of targeted representatives. Entire church meetings were turned over to the letter-writing and lobbying efforts, and at one Sunday School meeting, the session was canceled to not only discuss the anti-ERA campaign, but to present as well the Eagle Forum slide show, "Facade of Feminism."

Since the topic was raised at church meetings, the pressure to participate in the anti-ERA campaign was obvious, given the importance of the message coming from the top. A Mormon bishop in one of the Atlanta wards, according to one ward member, constantly evoked the anti-ERA effort as the "prophet's wish," referring to President Spencer Kimball's position as a "revelation," which it was not. In wards outside of Atlanta where Mormon members tended to be more conservative, the anti-ERA lobbying effort quickly turned into an activity for the entire ward.

As the anti-ERA efforts grew in intensity and scale, many of the same Mormon women who had been involved in early consciousness-raising activities were joined by new recruits angered by the church's ERA activities in a loose, pro-ERA Mormon network. A pamphlet entitled "Another Mormon for ERA" was published in 1976 and circulated throughout the country. A tentative new organization called Mormons for ERA was established, and a newsletter eventually was published on the group's activities. Pro-ERA networks developed in nearly every state where the church was active, and as the church grew increasingly bold, so did some of these new activists.

Nowhere did this become more striking than in Virginia, where a handful of Mormon women started going to the press about the church's role in creating an anti-ERA front group that was actively lobbying legislators and possibly violating laws regarding the church's tax-exempt status. By the time one of the four leaders of this network, a forty-year-old teacher named Sonia Johnson, got catapulted into the spotlight after a confrontation at a senate hearing with Utah Senator Orrin Hatch, the Virginia group had become a common point of reference for the national press regarding the church's anti-ERA activities.

Sonia Johnson was by the late 1970s at once thoroughly Mormon and representative of a new type of professional Mormon woman. "Ex-Utahn Sonia Johnson," declared *Utah Holiday* magazine, "was that combination of traditional Mormon (she had laid in her two-year supply of food, had completed her four-generation genealogical records, had taught her Relief Society cultural refinement class as recently as the week before the trial) and tradition-breaker that confused and irritated many Mormons (especially those in Utah) who got to know her through continuous but fragmented press coverage."

Johnson was a practicing Mormon, holding down three church positions, paying her full tithing, and regularly attending ward meetings. By the late 1970s, she increasingly experienced a sense of contradiction between her church status on the one hand and her beliefs and attitudes, particularly regarding the ERA, on the other. Johnson and other professional Mormon women, many of whom lived much of their adult lives outside Utah, were strongly committed to the ERA as a symbol of the need to develop more equal roles for women both in Gentile society and in their church. In their manners, habits, training, and socialization, these women all remained, at the least, cultural Mormons.

For Sonia Johnson and others in the Mormons for ERA network the tension between those two roles was becoming more severe by the end of the decade. After her confrontation with Senator Hatch, Johnson became increasingly bold and visible on behalf of the ERA. She and other Mormon ERA activists began to act as well to oppose their church, staging a series of events designed to draw attention to their point of view, such as the flying of a banner during the church's semiannual conference proclaiming, MOTHER IN HEAVEN SUPPORTS THE ERA. Church leaders ignored the protests, assuming that Mormon women universally accepted and backed the position of leadership, as they were expected to do.

At first, Johnson and other ERA supporters had attempted to meet with church leaders to have them explain their growing anti-ERA campaign, but to no avail. Church leaders remained unresponsive and instead escalated their own anti-ERA tactics, exacerbating the divisions between the male priesthood organization and those Mormon women who felt strongly not only about the ERA but also decried the virtual elimination of any independent role for Mormon women and their organizations within the church.

Increasingly, Johnson, an effective speaker, took to the lecture circuit declaring the existence of what was more and more perceived as a feminist opposition in the patriarchy's midst. She not only vigorously criticized the church's anti-ERA role, but began to raise more general issues of male-female relations in the church. In one famous speech at the American Psychological Association in New York City, Johnson declared: "The very violence with which the brethren attacked an amendment which would give women human status in the Constitution abruptly opened the eyes of thousands of us to the true source of our danger and our anger. This open patriarchal panic against our human rights raised consciousness all over the church as nothing else could have done."

The press quickly became the best weapon available to the Mormon ERA supporters, who were successful in presenting themselves—in dramatic contrast to an increasingly paranoid church hierarchy. The activities and remarks of Johnson and other ERA activists had finally unnerved the leadership, causing indeed a kind of "patriarchal panic." The more the ERA activists ran into a brick wall at the church, the more intense became the conflict, the more the ERA supporters turned to the press. The church hierarchy now began to see plots everywhere, especially ones stirred up by the press.

The intervention of the press fundamentally altered the way the pro-ERA networks were perceived by the church hierarchy. At the outset, Mormon ERA supporters had been seen as a vocal nuisance. Now, talk of excommunication was in the air, talk that culminated in December 1979, when the local leadership in Virginia, in a move that has been widely understood to have been sponsored and blessed by the Salt Lake hierarchy, moved against Johnson.

Sonia Johnson's trial was an extraordinary moment. The national press was out in force. Various issues seemed to drift in and out of the proceedings, such as the "Mother in Heaven question" and several of Johnson's speeches, including the one on "patriarchal panic," but no definite charges were leveled, and no defense, as such, could be used. The local church leadership—and the Salt Lake hierarchy—seemed at first to move rigidly, almost catatonically through the affair, preparing to rid themselves of this perceived-to-be hostile agent who was fast becoming a celebrated figure to millions of non-Mormons.

Sonia Johnson had an incredibly striking appeal. Appearing on network television with her Mormon mannerisms and sincerity, Johnson was able to bring the ERA back onto the front pages in the early months of 1980. Once excommunicated, she became a champion of non-Mormon feminists and was herself increasingly pulled away from the debates and issues of Mormon women and into the world of national feminist politics. The publication of her book, *From Housewife to Heretic*, became a cathartic act, a freeing of herself from the constrictions of her Mormon past. "Her autobiography," one Mormon woman writer declared, was "the most graphic, weighty, literary example of change and confrontation in the life of a Mormon woman to appear in the literature."

Sonia Johnson's excommunication had a traumatic impact inside the church. Pro-ERA Mormon women began to wonder whether they too might be excommunicated, and many felt that further public activities could lead to such actions. The pro-ERA Mormon networks were also split between those who had become fully disenchanted with the church and others who still wanted to change the church position on the ERA and even alter the definition and limits of women's roles in the church.

The excommunication of Sonia Johnson also generated backlash against Mormon feminism. The gates were closed, shutting off once again the Mormon community from a hostile outside world. "When the Prophet speaks, sisters, the debate is over," declared Elaine Cannon, the new head of the Young Women's organization, paraphrasing a long-standing Mormon precept. Until her anti-ERA statements, in fact, Cannon had been considered something of a moderate. The tension level increased dramatically in Salt Lake and throughout other Mormon communities as a sense of deep insecurity began to pervade the feminist networks.

Dallin Oaks, then president of BYU (and later on the Utah Supreme Court, and in 1984 named to the Quorum of the Twelve), symbolized the polarization that was taking place. At a talk given shortly after the excommunication, Oaks, considered by many Mormons to be a leading moderate, declared that the controversy over the excommunication was an example of evil forces conspiring in the world at large against the church. It is time, Oaks declared in his talk, to "close our ranks, and let the winds howl and the heathens rage."

By the time the ERA had finally died and the Sonia Johnson affair had faded from the pages of the press, the church leadership began to take stock of the consequence of the Johnson and ERA affairs. A few church insiders were critical, such as one influential Washington Mormon who is also a member of an old church family. "The Sonia Johnson incident was a public relations disaster," the critic declared two years after the event. "Everything they [church leaders and church public communications people] did was designed to pull up the drawbridge and prepare for the state of siege."

The clearest lesson for the church hierarchy was, in fact, the need to handle their relations with the press more adeptly, a project they focused on over the next couple of years with limited success. Despite the attempt to reorganize its public relations effort by making Special Affairs director

Richard P. Lindsay director of Public Communications, it had become clear that by the early 1980s the attitudes and policies of the church had only hardened in the wake of ERA and the Sonia Johnson affair. The church counterrevolution against feminism remained at fever pitch, with the battle now expanding to deal with every aspect of a woman's daily life.

FAMILY RETRENCHMENT

At first it was hard to tell who was more frenetic, the camera or Michele Meservy. Following her through the course of a day's activity, the film-makers wanted to record the texture of her life. She was a woman who had been Utah's Young Mother of the Year, was an active member of her local ward, and she and her husband had five children under seven. In short, she was the ideal of the New Mormon Woman.

Michele and her husband were young, under thirty, relatively orthodox Mormons. They had a nice suburban home with all the modern conveniences and a house full of kids. There is a certain frenzy that rules the Meservy situation—feeding the kids, cleaning the house, taking care that the children behave, doing the shopping, preparing for the evening meal, doing the laundry, and even attempting to give her kids religious instruction. The pace is dizzying, but everything moves according to the clock. Michele is organized, efficient, patient, and, despite the fatigue, thinks of having more children. "In many ways," one Mormon writer declared, "Michele epitomizes what some think a good Mormon mother 'ought' to be doing."

The filmmakers Diane Orr and Larry Roberts called their documentary *The Plan*, and they based the title on an organizational chart with the same name that the Meservys had come up with in deciding how to spend their time during the week, a term also related to the doctrine of the Divine Plan. Michele Meservy tells the filmmakers that she wants to have as many minutes occupied and set down in the plan as she can. Each day is charted out, with the minutes crammed together. Menus for meals are prepared a month ahead. During the day, she plots out her housework and child care. Weekends and evenings are also planned this way, many of them reserved for church events.

When *The Plan* was shown in Utah, the reactions were striking. Michele Meservy liked the documentary and felt it accurately presented her day-to-day life, though she complained to one publication that she would have also included her flower shop business, practicing the violin with a daughter, holding the children, and the moments when she took a break. For some Mormon women, it was a wrenching film that was too close to home and too painful. For some other Mormon women, particularly feminists, it demonstrated the internalization of Mormon values and life-style associated with the church-approved-and-sponsored emphasis on large families and idealized mothers. And for the church public relations people, it was a bit unfortunate that Michele Meservy on camera went through her day the way she went through it off camera. The image had come back to haunt the image makers.

The internalization of church-promoted values around such issues as large traditional families runs very deep in Mormonism, particularly in the home-base areas of Utah and the Mormon-influenced West. A study by three BYU professors on large Mormon families in 1982, where the mothers selected were all college-educated and the families moderately well off, described that socialization process in relation to the mothers' decision to have large numbers of children. The main criterion for the choice, the study noted, was "religious" and included such sentiments as: A family has its number of children assigned by God; church leaders tell their members to have big families; birth control is wrong, and so on.

In conference after conference session, in ward after ward, Mormon women are instructed, as Ezra Taft Benson put it at an October 1982 conference, that "in an eternal sense, salvation is a family affair." "Homemaking is the highest, most noble profession to which a woman might aspire," Benson told a Relief Society audience in 1980. "Support, encourage, and strengthen your husband in his responsibility as patriarch in the home. A woman's role in a man's life is to lift him, to help him uphold lofty standards, and to prepare through righteous living to be his queen for all eternity."

The contemporary attack on the family, or as Benson put it in a 1982 conference talk, "the deliberate efforts to restructure the family along the lines of humanistic values," has placed the church at the center of other political battles aside from their ERA involvement. "Today we are aware of great problems in our society," Benson said at this same conference speech. "The most obvious are sexual promiscuity, homosexuality, drug abuse, alcoholism, vandalism, pornography, and violence. These grave problems are symptoms of failures in the home—the disregarding of principles and practices established by God in the very beginning."

Family politics, as the church defined them, became by the early 1980s all-pervasive in the tenor and content of church messages to its membership. New Mormon-dominated family and women's groups, such as United Families of America and the Utah Association of Women, came to the fore in the battles over the "social issues," providing links to the New Right and keeping Mormons at the center of the conflicts around women.

Even as the church continued to flex its muscles, the women in the church, it was becoming clear, no longer represented a solid monolith, particularly in relation to the behavioral requirements the church continued to emphasize. Divorces in Utah were at a record high; teenage pregnancies had become a serious social problem. Perhaps even more striking was the dramatic increase in spouse and child abuse, an increase serious enough that church leaders began to address the subject during conferences. But no statistic was more striking in Mormon Utah than the continuing and dramatic rise of the number of women in the work force.

"You are the provider and it takes the edge off your manliness when you have the mother of your children also be a provider," Ezra Taft Benson told BYU male students at a point when the working-woman issue started to be publicized. One internal church study, completed just prior to the Reaganomics recession of the early 1980s, pointed out that thirty-one per-cent of all Mormon women were in the work force. By 1984 that figure had risen to forty-eight percent. In 1956, the *Church News* had declared that working mothers were "one of the greatest threats we have to stable home life in America." Twenty-five years later, the rhetoric level had been re-duced, but church opposition remained as great. Even as the number of Mormon women entering the work force increased, church leaders, wed-ded to an economic and social environment long since passed, could not believe that women actually needed to work for financial reasons. Women should, as one leader put it, "read stories . . . to a little girl in a faded blue hand-me-down dress [rather] than have her entertained by a color TV because you are away working to make the payments."

Even with the retrenchment, the Mormon push for a large reinvigorated nuclear family had become a point of contention in the wake of the con-flicts of the late 1970s and early 1980s. While Sonia Johnson's excom-munication had created a kind of chill factor among Mormon feminists for a period of time, Mormon women continued to write about and expand on some of the themes that had emerged during the 1970s. A shift in emphasis and priorities had gradually taken place, reflected for example in the differing tone and content of two issues of *Dialogue* published ten years apart—the Pink *Dialogue* of 1971 and a Red *Dialogue* (also the color of the cover) published in 1981.

New themes were raised, responding to the retrenchment of the church and added pressures on professional Mormon women seeking to maintain their Mormonism in the face of a changing social environment. One essay, by Salt Lake therapist Marybeth Raynes, talked about the issue of "Get-ting UnMarried in a Married Church." Partly autobiographical and partly based on her counseling work, Raynes presented a powerful picture of the pressures and tensions of a marriage breakup in a church advocating the family retrenchment. "My perspective now is that being married or being single are both simply circumstances," she wrote. "Both are conducive to growth. Neither is easy. Both require us to face the same basic dilemmas of life: survival, spiritual growth, balancing our own needs with others. The question now seems not 'When will I get remarried?' but 'Which circum-stance is currently best for me?' "

In the same issue of the magazine appeared a discussion concerning a long-standing church policy—whether women, as with blacks before them, ought to hold the priesthood. The author, an ERA activist named Nadine Hansen, explored the concept in doctrinal terms, analyzing positions in the Old and New Testaments, and how other churches have approached the issue. Hansen concluded with a passionate plea that an "empathy" similar to that developed by church leaders in finally granting blacks the priesthood should "be evoked on behalf of our faithful sisters."

The Hansen plea touched a deep nerve among Mormon male leaders. Dissident Mormon women have frequently referred to a statement by Hartman Rector, Jr., a church General Authority who in response to Sonia Johnson's 1979 encounter with Utah Senator Orrin Hatch wrote: "In order to attempt to get the male somewhere near even, the Heavenly Father gave him the Priesthood or directing authority for the church and home. Without this bequeath, the male would be so far below the female in power and influence that there would be little or no purpose for his existence, in fact [he] would probably be eaten by the female as is the case with the black widow spider."

Rector's analysis is echoed by an influential Mormon, W. Cleon Skousen, head of the right-wing Freemen Institute and a longtime ally of Ezra Taft Benson. "The reason we have priesthood only for men," Skousen declared in a 1982 interview, "is the division of labor that exists to make men equal with women. Men need to have this leadership capability in order to balance their existing inequality with women who have historically determined the development of the society because of their influence over children."

The question of women receiving the priesthood is, for the Mormon leaders, fundamental in nature. "There will be no change regarding women and the priesthood," declared Apostle Neal A. Maxwell forcefully in a 1983 interview. Even church liberals, such as University of Utah President Dr. Chase Petersen, one of the founders of the B. H. Roberts Society (a liberal discussion group) and a longtime champion of the cause of blacks seeking the priesthood, questions the idea of women in the priesthood. "Women want the public power and the flexibility of roles that comes with the priesthood," Petersen said, "but I'm not so sure. We have to ask what is the priesthood. Grethe [his wife] has it with me and we share it. She doesn't need it. She can accomplish the same by sharing it and being part of it with and through me."

By the early 1980s, Mormon women wishing to change the church were at a crossroads. Their critique of church leaders, however limited, continued to generate a harsh and intemperate reaction. Raising such issues as women in the priesthood or changing sexual roles and perceptions intensified the divisions rather than leading to any kind of dialogue.

Ironically, Mormon women, who have an extraordinary range of organizational skills and training in group dynamics, resisted the development of any kind of organizational challenge to the leadership. Women counseled developing "charismatic gifts of the spirit," as one leading Mormon woman historian put it. This meant, in effect, sticking with the system and trying to influence and change it on the local level in whatever small ways one could.

A smaller number of Mormon feminists had made a stronger, more defined break with the church leadership and the retrenchment policies.

These women, frustrated over the lack of challenge to church authority and the enormous power that church leaders held over their membership, found themselves increasingly in search of individual solutions to their desire for change, solutions that included an eventual shift of loyalties away from the church itself. Finally, a few opted for the most radical break, calling directly for their names to be lifted from the church roles and actively joining cause with the women's movement in the larger society.

Yet even these relatively timid and unorganized challenges to the church continued to be seen as a threat by the leadership and, most important, as a threat to the organizational and doctrinal thrust of the contemporary church. With the tentative exploration of the women-priesthood issue, with the trend toward women joining the labor force in greater numbers in the future, and with the political clash over such issues as ERA likely to intensify, the church continues to face a protracted crisis regarding the role of women.

The church has always maintained a central concern for women and the family as crucial to the definition of the role and nature of the priesthood. That concern intensified in the post–World War II period, culminating in the 1950s' celebration of the American Mom. It took on an added organizational and ideological component in the Correlation revolution of the 1960s and early 1970s and reached a certain fever pitch in the family retrenchment policies of the Spencer W. Kimball years.

The issue of women's roles remains central to the future of the church. What happens in the coming decades will tell us much about whether increasing numbers of women will be driven out of the church or whether they will wait and develop their "gifts of the spirit," hoping that the church will make one of its painfully slow accommodations to the outside world.

CHAPTER EIGHT

CULTURES OF ZION: MULTIPLE SIDES OF THE CHURCH

THE MAINSTREAM CHURCH

The bustle and noise level are all-pervasive. They are, of course, related to the fact that there are so many children inside the ward meeting hall. There are the infants, terrible twos, antsy four- and five-year-olds, newly baptized eight-year-olds, young Aaronic priesthood members, *very* scrubbed twelve- and thirteen-year-old boys in their first suits, white shirts, and ties, who will pass the sacrament aisle to aisle.

This ward in the West Jordan area consists primarily of young, suburban families, the base of Mormon membership in the Salt Lake Valley. In Zion, young couples who are practicing members, as in West Jordan, are also embarked on the road to large families. They will usually have no less than four children, often as many as six and seven, and in a few, though not all that rare, instances, as many as eight, nine, ten, even eleven and twelve children. That is particularly true for those who take seriously the advice of church leaders that good members should strive to have large families. The Mormon birth rate is in fact 28.1 per thousand, higher than any equivalent religious group in the country. These Mormon families on the west side of the valley are a good reason why.

Sacrament meeting in a west side young couples' ward offers a distinct yet mainstream portrait of the culture. Ward activities remain the center of the community and the very presence of such large numbers of kids adds to the informality of the occasion. A Mormon church service is not your traditional Sunday ritual. In some ways, it has the feel of a peoples' church, with its high level of participation in activities and the enormous number of meetings that an active church member attends each week.

On Sundays, you sense that so much of what will be brought up will be *practical*, and you end up feeling that when you go to church, you haven't exactly left home.

At this Sunday sacrament meeting in West Jordan, the bishop reads off the list of weekly events, who's sick and couldn't come, who's moving out of the ward, who's moving in. New duties are assigned. Events, such as the chorus group or the Mormon-dominated Boy Scout troop, are scheduled and rescheduled. Today's speaker, in fact, is the scout leader, who has a hard time stretching metaphors and finishing his awkward speech. A second speaker is a returned missionary, a Donny Osmond look-alike, who is talking about perfection, a favorite Mormon buzzword. This man is full of self-conscious enthusiasm and has just the right touch of ambitiousness to make him a good-enough speaker to talk over the continuing rustle of kids who are either in the process of being escorted in or out or being hushed.

This obviously is not high mass or low mass. The distance between bishop and ward is not extreme but more like that of a successful Mormon, a prominent uncle, if you will, who is looked on fondly, as well as with respect.

On the one hand, you are struck by the *sameness* of it all. The services at this ward and the inner-city Tongan ward, for example, will not only be largely identical in structure and design, but the Mormon dress code of basic brown, blue, or gray for men's suits and prim dresses in subdued colors that are a couple of inches below the knees remains *de rigueur*, no matter what the setting. Yet the activities and events at the ward level, including Sunday sacrament meeting, are also special and crucial to that sense of *distinctiveness* of the culture, to that all-important feeling of community that binds the members of the ward together into a powerful social force.

This is the mainstream church, and young couples like those of West Jordan are its backbone. For many of the West Jordan couples, the mother stays at home and the father looks to succeed at his lower- or middle-management position or at a similar job that brings him just enough to make the payments on the new washing machine and dryer and on that crowded three-bedroom frame home that abuts the neighbor's fence. This type of Mormon family is the centerpiece of the culture.

To a non-Mormon, it appears that the ward is where the action is, and here at West Jordan, as the bishop stumbles through the last of his announcements and the last notes of "Come, Come Ye Saints" fade into the distance, can be found the glue that holds it all together. For at West Jordan, as in so many other wards where the mainstream church comes together, they say that an orthodox Mormon is one who is either at a meeting, coming to a meeting, or leaving a meeting. And, one might add, with a large family in his or her wake.

Not far from this wardhouse in West Jordan, a tall white spire topped by a gilt-painted statue of the angel Moroni reaches up from the valley floor above a massive, stone-faced structure. A non-Mormon's first inkling of the truly unique character of this home-grown American religion comes inside a temple, such as this one in West Jordan, which was open for a time in the fall of 1981 to all visitors.

Ordinarily, one might expect to find a large central room comparable to the nave in other Christian churches. But from the front door where the guide demonstrates how a computer system checks each member's plastic temple recommend card to see if admittance has been authorized, visitors are gently but firmly steered through a nursery and then into elaborate changing and anointing rooms for men and women. From there the tour proceeds through a series of ordinance rooms and sealing and endowment rooms, past a huge baptismal font mounted on the backs of twelve oxen, and then into the richly furnished Celestial Room where the Saints gather to get a sense of what life promises in the Celestial Kingdom.

In contrast to the informality and bustle of the wardhouse, the temple is the solemn dwelling place of the Lord, the site of the Saints' most important and secret rituals, and the place where the full meaning of their religion is explained. Here the Saints are ritually cleansed and anointed, and are given their white temple garments, which they wear inside and outside of the temple for the rest of their lives; and here men and women are sealed to each other in matrimony "for time and all eternity." Here also the unique practice of baptism for the dead takes place as members of the church are immersed in the giant font in the name of those who never experienced this sacred ordinance because they died before Joseph Smith's restoration of the true church. This ordinance explains the church's obsession with genealogical work that has led to the amassing of perhaps the greatest genealogical collection in the world. More than an interest in family history, genealogical work provides the names of those persons to be baptized vicariously. This ceremony assures that a member's entire family stretching back into history and ultimately the entire family of man will gather in the Celestial Kingdom.

The temple is also the site of sacred rites that Joseph Smith adopted from the Masonic Order in Nauvoo. These rites include the giving of a new name, the teaching of secret signs and handshakes, and the reenactment of a kind of folk play that portrays the creation of the world by Elohim, Jehovah, and Michael while it explains church doctrine. This ceremony concludes with a ritual passing through the veil, which symbolizes the Saints' entrance into the Celestial Kingdom.

Temple work, more than any other church ritual, reinforces the sense of the Saints as a people apart. "It has the effect," wrote sociologist Thomas O'Dea in *The Mormons*, "of increasing the loyalty of the church member by initiating him into secrets and thereby making him a privileged sharer in holy mysteries and by his promising in impressive ceremonial circumstances to be loyal to the church and obedient to its priesthood."

When Wallace Stegner wrote *Mormon Country* in 1942, he described a square dance in a small town in rural Utah. The community was the Mormon Village, the base unit of the church, evoking images of Lowry Nelson's classic about Mormon rural life in a cohesive, cooperating community. Forty years later, Mormonism has definitely shifted from a rural to an urban setting. Rural Utah still remains a significant force in Mormonism, since seventy percent of the state's members still live in a rural setting. Yet the people of the rural areas of the Intermountain West are today being buffeted by forces outside their control—energy development, the squeeze on small farmers, high levels of unemployment—all of which are causing migration toward regional urban centers at a rate greater than the days of the 1920s and 1930s, when economic decline hit the region hard. The migration is not just to the big metropolises, such as Salt Lake City or Las Vegas, but to smaller, growing regional centers. St. George, in southern Utah, for example, acts like a magnet, drawing young people away from home and village. Even the small towns of the Mormon West have become more "urbanized," with fast-food franchises, chain stores, and highway-oriented businesses. The Mormon Village has given way to the Mormon Suburb, and the West Jordan ward is a 1980s embodiment of the basic Mormon community.

To describe the culture of the contemporary Mormon suburbs, appearance is a starting point. The church's four-page handout for its employees, "A Style of our Own," spells out the appropriate "personal appearance that reflects the image of the Church." For men, "extreme hair styles are discouraged. Long hair, beards and sideburns below the earlobes are not acceptable. Hair must not extend over the shirt collar. . . . Clothing should not be extreme in any way." For women, "pants and immodest clothing are not acceptable," with shoes "always worn with stockings. . . . Whatever our work may be," the brochure goes on, "we should be sure that our appearance befits that of individuals engaged in the Church's important work, that we add to and not detract from the positive impression the Church communicates everywhere."

Public relations and image making become key in the contemporary church. Mormon leaders have placed a high premium on their media campaigns and overall public relations activities. The description of Mormon life and the mainstream Mormon is the center of this effort. In *Reader's Digest* ads for the church, for example, the "typical" Mormon family is presented: white, middle class, mother in the home and not at work, kids not engaged in drugs, sex, or other modern excesses, the entire family as self-reliant, good-natured, dynamic, achieving, and, as the ad puts it, "always smiling, always happy."

For mainstream members, who are themselves constantly subject to a stream of image-conscious sermons, stories in church publications, and comparative models at the ward level, the appearance becomes a goal to strive for. The talk of "perfection" is in part the desire to achieve such self-conscious status and resembles those portraits that are constantly held up in the various weekly and monthly publications of the church.

In a controversial KSL-TV documentary, "Mormon Women and Depression," made in 1978, this theme of striving for perfection is presented as a substantial cause of depression among mainstream Mormon women, who become terribly isolated in their quest to be the ideal Mormon mother and church participant. In the documentary, Jan Stout, a Mormon psychiatrist, speaks of how some Mormon women "feel they have to reach this kind of idealized, crystallized, beautiful Mormon woman whom I term the Mother-of-Zion syndrome. This is a woman who is really a myth, a mystic. She doesn't exist at all, in fact. But yet every Mormon woman in almost any ward you wanted to go into would tell you they knew a woman who is like that, who's got it all together, whose children are well-groomed. She bakes bread every day. She has wonderfully clean things in the house. Her husband is happy and whistles off to work. She never complains at any of the church meetings she goes to. She's supportive and loyal, and not only that, she gets up and reads her church scriptures at six in the morning. She's got it all together. And that's a very intimidating thing for the average Mormon woman."

Ironically, the sense of isolation that comes from a quest for perfection is compounded by the *pervasiveness* of the community, which functions both as a support system and as Big Brother. Every mainstream Mormon has an equivalent story to tell about community support. The family has moved, the story goes, perhaps just to a new ward in another suburb in the same city, perhaps to a new city or town, perhaps to another country. The moment they arrive at the new home a delegation from the new ward or branch is there to greet them. Help is immediately offered and accepted. The new family feels as if they never left home in the first place. For home preeminently is the culture, and the security that comes with it is the feeling of sameness that permeates the church, like a blanket that stays with you wherever you go.

Community participation is extensive and intensive. Children, for example, engage in a myriad of church-related-and-sponsored activities, everything from sports, which include interward, interstake, and interstate tournaments, to homemaker activities for the girls, to seminary programs (for which in Utah one receives release time from the public school system, despite the fact that they are entirely church-related functions), all in addition to Monday Family Home Evenings, scout activities, and on and on.

Ward activities are indeed the lifeblood of mainstream Mormonism. They provide a full sense of identity and belonging, of participation without democracy, of a self-absorbing community. It reinforces the perception of Mormons as a peculiar people, in the sense that they are so self-contained in their community. Yet at the same time, particularly in terms of the contemporary church, Mormons stand out as a people who are prototypically American in a 1950s style.

The community is also an exacting force, demanding a certain conformity not only to doctrine and organizational requirements, such as tithing, but to behavioral and life-style patterns as well. For example, strictures against alcohol, tobacco, tea and coffee, known as the Word of Wisdom, have changed from a guideline in the pre–World War II church to a strict requirement in recent years. Countless church members have stories of a grandfather who cussed and drank coffee and yet was a mainstream Mormon as it was then defined. No longer; today the restrictions are explicit. Behavioral restrictions are the most visible and telling signs of the community's presence. With the Word of Wisdom, violators are admonished and told not to continue violating this code. In this area, unlike some other behavioral restrictions, positives rather than negatives are emphasized. Church press releases, for example, constantly point out how practicing the Word of Wisdom is likely to lead to, as some studies have shown, longer life expectancy.

While the Word of Wisdom is important, other life-style issues, such as sexuality, are far more essential in identifying church behavorial standards. When such standards are violated, excommunication is the rule not the exception, and the community peruses you with its watchful and wary eye. "Not only is Big Brother watching you," declared one prominent Salt Lake Catholic, "but little brother is watching you. Your neighbor is watching you. The community is watching you. Excommunication is a community action." For mainstream Mormons, the behavioral bottom line is sexual.

A DENSE FOG OF SENSUALITY

Church-defined sexual norms are a key component of the Mormon culture. During much of this century, Mormon attitudes toward sexuality evolved two modes: a more moderate appeal to uphold the standards of premarital chastity and of monogamy, and stronger, harsher strictures that include the famous Mormon precept of the 1940s, "Better dead clean, than alive unclean."

When David O. McKay became president in 1951, he promoted the moderate approach, emphasizing, as he did in other spheres of Mormon activity, that this was a mainstream, contemporary, American church. Though McKay continued to promote the concept of chastity, he focused, as Mormon social analysts Marvin and Ann Rytting have pointed out, "on the positive reasons for remaining virtuous and made chastity seem romantic." In conference speeches during the 1950s, McKay would conjure up images of classic chivalry: "The flower growing by the roadside is covered with dust; the young man passes her by and risks his life to scale the perpendicular cliffs in search of the sweet and lovely flower that grows in the high mountain meadow, untouched by human hands."

McKay's views set the tone regarding morality and sexuality in the 1950s. Though chastity was brought up numerous times, it was never singled out as the most critical issue involving Mormon self-control or behavioral definition. Themes of "deviation" that became so prominent in the late 1960s and 1970s, such as masturbation, homosexuality, necking and petting, pornography, and abortion, were hardly touched on, let alone made the subject of major pronouncements.

The harsher, more negative approach toward sexual matters, nevertheless, still found a substantial following among the church leadership, including members of the Quorum of the Twelve, such as Spencer W. Kimball and Mark E. Petersen, who were assigned morality questions as a key aspect of their work.

By the late 1960s, the church adjusted to the emergence of the youth culture and women's movements with the ideological hardening and organizational centralization brought about by the Correlation revolution. As a result, attitudes toward sexuality began to change. Brigham Young University President Ernest L. Wilkinson instituted a tightening of dress and behavior codes, paralleling the harsher tones concerning these subjects used during conference and in church publications. The father of Correlation, Harold B. Lee, who was recognized in the church for his stern demeanor and no-nonsense approach, contributed to this shift, lashing out at conferences at the "engulfing waves of permissiveness which seem to be moving over the world like an avalanche." Even such a moderating figure as N. Eldon Tanner was caught up in this maelstrom of invective and assault against what was perceived to be a Satanic revolution in sexual and other behavioral mores. "Twenty years ago, there was much public support for the principles you and I believe in, despite some occasional straying from those principles," one church leader wrote in *The Ensign*. "All that is different now. We are almost suffocated by a dense fog of sensuality. Pornography and moral permissiveness are so widespread that there is nothing to compare with in the last several centuries in any civilized society; not since Rome, not since Sodom and Gomorrah."

This change in rhetoric was ultimately most influenced by the calling of Spencer W. Kimball as Prophet in 1973. Kimball's involvement in sexual issues dated back to 1947, when he was first assigned to interview members who had violated church sexual rules. He broadened his concerns to such issues as modesty and dress, sexual practices among teenagers, pornography and sexual imagery in the media, and homosexuality. Kimball repeatedly brought up these issues, admonishing members not to stray in even the most limited ways from what were now presented as strict and absolute behavioral codes.

"What, may I ask you, is like unto adultery if it is not petting?" Kimball asked in a special message to all church members, published in 1980. "Did not the Lord recognize that this heinous sin is but the devil's softening process of the final acts of adultery or fornication?" Kimball then went on to suggest that early teen dating was "most hazardous" and should be eliminated, and that those involved in dating after the age of sixteen should avoid "close contact," at least until the young man returned from his mission, presumably at age twenty or twenty-one. At this point, marriage would be the recommended step.

One of the key changes from the David O. McKay to the Spencer W. Kimball period was the church's reaction to the shift in values and practices in the larger society. The Mormons' idealized conception of chastity appeared to fit within the dominant cultural themes of the 1950s, and it helped establish the church as a mainstream religion, with a sturdy American character. The cultural tensions and changes of the 1960s changed all that. The church, now drawing on ideas from the period a half century earlier when most of the General Authorities were young, developed a siege mentality. At first, church leaders attacked what they perceived to be the decadence and moral dissolution of the period, trying to safeguard and isolate younger members from what was characterized literally as an infection, a kind of social disease run rampant. By the Kimball era of the middle and late 1970s, church leaders, particularly those most in tune with societal trends and conflicts, such as Apostles Gordon B. Hinckley and Neal A. Maxwell, detected that the conservative backlash and the rise of the Moral Majority provided, in the areas of behavior and sexual mores, an opportunity for the church.

Church leaders began to promote coalitions with other morally oriented groups, and they took the leadership of the conservative backlash, particularly around such themes as pornography and birth control.

Despite the identification with the conservative backlash, the church by the 1980s still spoke in defensive tones, albeit with harsh and at times virulent rhetoric. From the images of romantic chastity and positive self-control of the 1950s, church leaders now spoke of young people needing the church as a restraint against the culture of the larger society. Self-control became a battle between Satan, who held sway in the larger society, and the church, which was both the champion and the enforcer of the necessary behavioral codes.

Men and boys were primarily the focus of this sexual battleground, since church leaders tended to characterize women and girls as peculiarly asexual objects when left to their own devices. Men and boys, on the other hand, were by and large inclined to act on negative sexual drives without the guidance and discipline of the church. And nowhere was this problem of male drive more striking for church leaders than with masturbation.

"Masturbation, a rather common indiscretion," Spencer W. Kimball wrote in 1980 in a special message to all church members, "is not approved of the Lord nor of his church, regardless of what may have been said by others whose 'norms' are lower." Urging church members to give up this "weakness," particularly before going on mission or entering the temple, Kimball went on to say that masturbation, in the analysis of church leaders, could be the "introduction to the more serious sins of exhibitionism and the gross sin of homosexuality."

The importance of this subject for church leaders was evidenced not only by its frequent mention during discourses on sexuality and morality, but by the emphasis placed on direct counsel of members to avoid this practice. During the 1960s and 1970s, the church offered to young men stern advice on the subject, as indicated by the pamphlet written by Mark E. Petersen called "A Guide to Self-Control: Overcóming Masturbation."

Asserting that "masturbation is a sinful habit that robs one of the Spirit and creates guilt and emotional stress" and "separates a person from God and defeats the gospel plan," Petersen went on to catalogue more than twenty steps to overcome masturbation. These included the more obvious ("Never touch the intimate parts of your body except during normal toilet processes"); the more obscure ("If the temptation seems overpowering while you are in bed, GET OUT OF BED AND GO INTO THE KITCHEN AND FIX YOURSELF A SNACK"); some unusual suggestions ("Reduce the amount of spice and condiments in your food"); some religious ("Pray. But when you pray, don't pray about this problem, for that will tend to keep it in your mind more than ever"); and some harsher prescriptions ("In very severe cases it may be necessary to tie a hand to the bed frame with a tie in order that the habit of masturbating in a semi-sleep condition can be broken").

The masturbation issue weighed heavily on young Mormon boys (all of the advice was directed at boys, not girls). At times, the issue had its lighter side, such as when a biology textbook used on the BYU campus in the late 1960s that contained information on the subject of masturbation had a page literally removed at the urging of the administration. When some students discovered the page missing, it circulated as a premium item in the campus underground.

The issue had its darker side as well. A number of young men suffered deep scars in trying to control their tendency to masturbate, and the use of the "bedpost method," among others, was not unusual. In 1983, a young Idaho Mormon boy, obsessed with a sense of guilt because of his sexual fears, committed suicide. His father, bitter at church advice on sexual matters, including the bedpost method, sued the church for damages.

The amount of intrusion into members' sexual lives by local church leaders varies greatly from ward to ward and depends heavily on the attitudes and approach of the local bishop and his advisers. It is common practice, nevertheless, for bishops to question teenagers once a year about all their sexual activities. The framework established by the central leadership also offers a range of opportunities to intercede.

In a January 1982 missive from the First Presidency to all local leaders, for example, the leadership declared that "married persons should understand that if in their marital relations they were guilty of unnatural, impure or unholy practices, they should not enter the temple unless and until they repent and discontinue any such practices." The instructions went on to catalogue those kinds of problem areas, including child and spouse abuse and oral sex. "If a person is engaged in a practice which troubles him enough to ask about it," the statement went on, "he should discontinue it."

On sexual matters, Big Brother and little brother are both alert, because behavioral attitudes go to the heart of what defines an orthodox or a straying Mormon. In areas such as masturbation and marital oral sex, violation of the taboo can lead to denial of "temple recommends," the annual recommendation by local bishops as to whether members can enter the Temple. This is a serious matter, since the temple rites are critical to one's ability to be a faithful Mormon and enter the Celestial Kingdom. More important, for church leaders, such unnatural acts can lead to one of the worst sexual sins of all, the one that has emerged to preoccupy the leadership at every level and that causes them to summon forth the harshest rhetoric and most severe penalties.

THE GAY FACTOR

To church leaders, homosexuality is a multiple sin. In a widely circulated pamphlet on the subject, several reasons are listed for why "homosexuality is of grave concern to the Church." At the head of the list is the fact that "it violates the Lord's eternal plan for man's progress by perverting the proper use of procreative powers and loving relationships."

"Eternal increase is the greatest blessing in the Celestial Kingdom," an earlier pamphlet on homosexuality declared, pointing to the fact that one entered the Celestial Kingdom through a temple marriage and that the *purpose of such marriage*, as Harold B. Lee declared, "is to build the bridge from the eternity of spirits to mortality, over which God's spirit children might come into mortal bodies. Your failure to remember that revealed truth will be your failure to attain the highest bliss in married life." Thus, homosexuality, with its forgoing of temple marriage, is also a violation of the requirement to procreate, a doctrinal transgression.

The second great concern over homosexuality, the church pamphlet declares, is that "it deprives God's children of the happiness and fulfillment possible only in family life." Homosexuality is seen as threatening this most crucial Mormon institution. Homosexual relations are seen by church leaders as the most severe and extreme form of attack on the family, the culmination of the revolution in values of the 1960s, which brought with it "powerful forces seeking to establish this sinful practice as an acceptable way of life."

Prior to the 1970s, church leaders relied heavily on counseling techniques. Church leaders evoked the doctrinal principle of free agency as a means of reversing behavior, while threatening heavy disciplinary action, including excommunication, if cooperation was not forthcoming. Cooperation, in part, meant providing the names of sexual partners and other known homosexuals, as well as demonstrating some clear behavioral change, such as getting married.

By the 1970s, additional techniques came into play, as the practice only seemed to be getting more extensive. Instead of simply offering advice, church leaders began to encourage practicing or would-be homosexuals to undertake a new type of therapy introduced at BYU in the 1970s. This method, known as aversion therapy, involved the use of electric shock treatment to change behavior. Oriented once again toward male rather than female homosexuals, the therapy utilized electrically induced shock (usually to the genitals) at a point when the subject became sexually aroused through pictures or film clips of naked men. The shock was then withdrawn when *Playboy*-like pictures of naked members of the opposite sex were presented.

Along with aversion therapy, the church also stepped up surveillance and spying, particularly at BYU, which became a focal point of the attack against gays. In one famous incident, an undercover agent for the BYU security department placed an ad in a gay newspaper asking to meet gay students. A student responded to the ad, an advance was made, and the student was arrested.

The BYU and church security networks were crucial to the church campaign. Files were compiled, and whenever a BYU student was thought to be gay, or even when a student went to his bishop for help, that individual was called in to talk to University Standards, the security people who upheld BYU's behavioral codes on everything from sexual behavior to haircut regulations. Surveillance of gay bars in Salt Lake City was commonplace, and lists were drawn up that identified "persons involved in lewd behavior."

At the peak of the campaign against gays, the BYU security force was granted statewide power by the Mormon-dominated legislature, an action that was widely interpreted as directed against gays. Soon after this authority was granted, BYU security joined the Utah highway patrol in a raid at a rest stop on highway I-15 between Provo (where the BYU campus is situated) and Salt Lake City. Acting on a tip that the rest stop and its bathroom were a gay hangout, several people were rounded up, including, as it turned out, a BYU instructor. That night, according to members of the gay community, the instructor hanged himself in jail. Though hushed up publicly, word about the incident quickly spread on the gay underground with devastating effect. Fears about discovery, already deep, further intensified.

By the late 1970s, a number of individual gays began to counter the church campaign. Several BYU students put together a fifty-three-page statement in response to BYU psychologist Reed Payne's attack on homosexuals. The letter, entitled Prologue and written anonymously, provided a detailed critique of the church position on homosexuality, including Payne's own role in aversion therapy. "The day of passive acceptance of humiliation and discrimination are over," the letter stated. "As the homosexual becomes less and less willing to submit to this damaging influence and the rest of the world comes to realize the plight of the Mormon homosexual, the Church stands to face a very serious and embarrassing blow to its integrity."

The Prologue letter had a strong impact both on the church and Mormon gays, particularly the much larger, tortured group of "closet gays," who existed throughout the church. Aversion therapy was suspended, although a less intensive practice, described by a psychologist in the BYU Comprehensive Clinic as "coversive therapy," that is the association of negative thoughts with pictures, was employed. Soon after, Apostle Boyd K. Packer delivered a talk at BYU on the subject that was somewhat milder in tone but remained as stern and foreboding in its analysis and conclusion. Once again, Packer emphasized the importance of procreation, calling the failure to utilize that physical power a "spiritual disorder."

The Prologue letter helped stimulate the first organized attempt to provide a network and home for Mormon gays. Initiated by a former BYU student in Denver, the group, Affirmation, soon spread to Los Angeles, San Francisco, and eventually Salt Lake, Provo, and even London. It became a magnet, particularly for closet Mormon gays who needed group support. Encouraged by the growth and open activities of non-Mormon gay organizations (the gay newspaper, *The Advocate*, was the first to publish the Prologue letter), Affirmation grew slowly, with a small paid membership but a much larger number of individual Mormons attending the monthly therapy sessions.

From the outset, according to Affirmation coordinator Paul Mortensen, the group had two major goals: to help gay Mormons deal with the fact that they were both gay and Mormon and to attempt to educate the church leaders and help them either change or at least soften their attitudes. Affirmation organizers felt the most critical problem facing Mormon gays was the question of self-worth, a problem even more extensive than among non-Mormon gays, given the powerful hold of the church on its members *and* the nature of the church attack. Even Mormon gays who had been subject to aversion therapy or excommunicated still defined themselves as Mormon. Closet gays were particularly tortured by the situation. Some Mormon gays did leave the church, particularly those that had been converts. But those who were born into the church had an enormous need to somehow reconcile 150 years of doctrinal, organizational, and cultural identity with a church that *The Advocate* called "one of the most viciously homophobic denominations."

Affirmation attacked the church assumption that sexual behavior could

be changed at any time, asserting instead that "sexuality is largely determined by the time one is two or three years old." In fact, some Affirmation
leaders utilized church doctrine to give legitimacy to their condition, declaring for example, that Mormon gays were this way in the "preexistence," a Mormon doctrinal concept. Most important, Affirmation wanted
to demonstrate to Mormons that they were, as Mortensen put it, "happy
people, contributing to society, leading decent lives. We want to show we
are gay and still have a testimony."

The attempt to change the position of the church leaders, however, did
not make a dent. If anything, the position of the church hardened in the
early 1980s, as the campaign against gays once again picked up momentum. An editorial in the *Church News* cited a biblical reference to homosexuals being stoned to death. Though the reference was used as an
allusion, it intensified the already substantial paranoia among Mormon
gays in Utah.

There is little possibility that the church will change its position on
homosexuality in the foreseeable future. Even more than with women and
the priesthood, the church view of sexual practices, tied as they are to
procreation and temple marriage, precludes any shift unless major doctrinal changes occur. Given church sensitivities about marriage and family
roles, hostility toward gays will continue, and future conflicts between the
authority of the church and this disenfranchised underground part of the
culture will only continue to grow.

MORMON FUNDAMENTALISM

The young, intense woman holding her child to her breast spoke of how
she was always attracted to the early church, "I have a certitude about
John Taylor's meeting in 1886 where the prophet spoke of his revelation to
continue the practice."

She was not an ordinary polygamist. She didn't wear long skirts though
other polygamists felt such dress was "divinely inspired." She was a little
more "modern" in her thinking and attitudes. Yet, like other polygamists,
she had suffered from the strict, disapproving standards of the Mormon
community. Once it became known that she had become the third wife of a
known polygamist, she lost her apartment, thrown out by a landlord who
didn't want "one of those people" living there, though she had paid her
rent on time and kept the house tidy.

To become a polygamist had been an act of faith. She had fasted off and
on during a six-month period prior to making her decision. At a critical
moment, she went out with her husband-to-be and his two wives to the
desert. There they fasted for three days. She had visions, including her own
reconstruction of the 1886 meeting when five men were ordained to keep
plural marriage alive. And now she was being called to do the same, nearly
100 years later. "I am a kind of radical," she spoke softly, "for this is the
radical thing to do."

Everyone in the Mormon community has a friend, an acquaintance, an incident, a similar story to tell. It could be that house next door where the women and children keep to themselves, or the quiet family—the mother and the children without the father—sitting in the back aisle during sacrament meeting or the kids at school with their awkward mannerisms and dress, especially the girls, where the flesh is almost completely covered up. Polygamy, the most prominent form of Mormon fundamentalism, lives on alongside contemporary Mormonism, despite the powerful hostility of the institutional church.

For nearly eighty years, particularly since the Second Manifesto of Joseph F. Smith in 1904 calling for the excommunication of anyone continuing the practice, polygamy has been both an embarrassment and an unresolved doctrinal and organizational riddle for the mainstream church. Unlike the original Wilford Woodruff manifesto of 1890, which defensively attempted to distance the church from the practice, Smith's action, coming in response to the Senate hearings on the seating of Senator Reed Smoot, placed the church affirmatively within an accommodationist framework.

Even after such decisive action, however, the embarrassment lingered and eventually grew, as numerous attempts to create polygamist colonies continued to plague the church and cause what leaders perceived to be negative publicity about the entire church. Even after the Smith manifesto, polygamy remained a practice for several years among certain top- and middle-level leaders of the church, most notably John W. Taylor and Matthias F. Cowley, both members of the Quorum of the Twelve Apostles.

John W., as he was known, had six wives, the last one being wed after the 1904 manifesto. Given the publicity generated by the Smoot hearing and ever-vigilant attempts by anti-Mormons to harass the church by pointing to continuing polygamy, Taylor was obliged to resign from the Quorum and was later excommunicated. Though the first wave of polygamist groupings that emerged in this period failed to enlist Taylor's support, the one-time church leader never publicly renounced the practice and died a symbolic hero to the hundreds of families that still were part of the faith.

Within a few years after John W.'s death in 1916, polygamist groupings began to come together to create a more solid organizational network in the face of growing hostility on the part of the church. In contrast to John W.'s open espousal of polygamy, church leaders, such as Heber J. Grant, who assumed the presidency in 1918, publicly attacked the practice, while discreetly hiding the fact that they too had been polygamists and that out of the public eye their plural wives and children lived their separate lives.

To the polygamists, the church, through revelation, had never abandoned plural marriage. The key to this belief was a famous incident in 1886 involving John Taylor. According to the story, Taylor, while living underground, had a vision one night after he had retired to bed. As a brilliant light streamed under his bolted door, he was heard talking to two people. When Taylor appeared the next morning, he informed his hosts and bodyguards that he had spent the night talking with Joseph Smith and Jesus Christ. As his body hovered a foot off the ground, Taylor told the assembled Saints that he had received a revelation from the Lord stating that "All commandments that I give must be obeyed by those calling themselves by my name." Taylor, in the presence of Smith, who appeared to the group, then "set apart" and granted authority to five men who "would see to it that no year passed by without children being born in the principle of plural marriage," as one of the five polygamist leaders, Lorin C. Woolley, described it in 1929.

The Woolley statement soon became the founding document of the twentieth-century polygamists. Woolley himself was supposed to have passed on the ordination power to the first organizationally oriented polygamist leader, Joseph Musser, who in turn passed it on to a number of other, younger figures, who became the male patriarchs of what was turning out to be a persistent and sizeable network within Mormondom.

By the 1930s, the polygamists had become enough of a threat to the church that it began to issue statements from the First Presidency denying that the 1886 meeting ever took place. Church leaders also cooperated with Utah and other law enforcement agencies to try to eradicate the practice. In 1935, 1944, and 1953, police raids against polygamist colonies and family groups were designed to break up the polygamist network.

One of the objects of these raids was the colony of Short Creek in the all but uninhabited desert lands on the Utah-Arizona border. Short Creek had major significance within the polygamist world, insofar as it existed as an open community. It became a kind of "lambing ground," as one fundamentalist leader called it, where women could give birth quietly and without fear and where visiting polygamists could practice their religion openly. After the 1953 raid, which generated enormous publicity (it later became the subject of a television movie), the Short Creekers discreetly regrouped, changed the community's name to Colorado City, and continued to provide a fundamentalist home away from home.

Divisions among the polygamists, from the 1940s on, became extensive and protracted and prevented the emergence of any kind of serious organizational threat to the church. These divisions extended to polygamist groups who established settlements not far from Mormon colonies of northwest Mexico. One of the key groups in Mexico centered around the LeBaron brothers, Joel, Verlan, and Ervil. Their father, the LeBarons claimed, had been given priesthood authority to keep the practice alive.

For a number of years, the LeBaron brothers flirted with the early ideologue of the Third Convention, the Mexican nationalist Margarito Bautista, who had attempted to put into practice his interpretations of polygamy and the United Order. As with the Short Creek community and several other polygamist groups, fundamentalism, with its celebration of the nineteenth-century church, promoted the concept of the United Order.

This concept worked best, fundamentalists argued, in self-contained, isolated communities outside the temptations of the larger society. Margarito Bautista attempted to connect those issues with his nationalist celebration of Lamanites, or Mexicans, as chosen people. The LeBarons, on the other hand, eventually drifted away from Bautista's influence and attempted to create a separate and isolated community, as removed from Mexico, where they continued to practice their religion, as from the Mormon church, in whose name they still defined their mission.

The LeBarons, led by brother Joel, originated their own Church of the First Born and began issuing materials laying out their particular version of fundamentalist doctrine. Though the group remained small, just one of several polygamist sects that had emerged in the 1950s and 1960s, it nevertheless came to the attention of the church in 1958 when nearly a dozen young missionaries stationed in France left the church to join the LeBarons in Mexico. Their action shocked General Authorities and became one of the precipitating factors in the development of the Correlation movement and its attempts to tighten the church's organizational apparatus.

By the late 1960s, the LeBarons had also split apart. Ervil LeBaron created his own Church of the Blood of the Lamb and vowed to destroy his brother's church. Ervil put together a group that not only celebrated his status as the One Mighty and Strong (that is, a leader who would usher in the millennium), but also proclaimed a number of nineteenth-century Mormon concepts, most particularly blood atonement (the use of violence as a sacrificial and cleansing act), as central to his new church.

For Ervil, violence soon became a means to accomplish his goal of emerging as the chief fundamentalist leader. Beginning with the murder of his brother Joel, LeBaron's followers went on a spree that included the murder of several other fundamentalist figures, as well as issuing threats against Mormon leaders, including Spencer W. Kimball. The violence culminated in 1977 in the murder of Rulon C. Allred, perhaps the best known of the fundamentalist patriarchs, whose family included eight wives, forty-eight children, and hundreds of grandchildren and great-grandchildren.

The Allred murder badly frightened the already fearful fundamentalist community and caused the church to intensify its efforts, which included active collaboration with Utah and federal law enforcement agencies, not only to put an end to the Ervil LeBaron sect, but to undercut the influence of the fundamentalists as a whole.

LeBaron was caught, jailed, went on trial and then died, apparently of a heart attack, in jail. Other fundamentalist groups were clearly relieved when LeBaron died and attempted to regain some semblance of order and continuity in their efforts. Another incident, the killing of polygamist John Singer by Utah police officers (Singer refused to send his children to public school), reinforced fears about polygamist actions and further frightened an already disoriented fundamentalist community. Yet, by the early 1980s, the fundamentalists had largely regrouped and stabilized, with new patriarchs in charge.

For much of the twentieth century, polygamy has remained an extraordinarily sensitive issue for church leaders. On the one hand, the church is concerned about its image and views any effort to publicly link the contemporary church with polygamy as seriously undercutting its attempt to portray itself as a modern Christian church. Polygamy evokes images of nineteenth-century patriarchs, press persecution, and Mark Twain put-downs, where today a clean-shaven man in a business suit is *de rigueur*.

Sensitivity about the church's image reached to the highest levels of the church, as witnessed by their intervention in 1970 with the entire Utah congress delegation. The church leaders wanted to get the census bureau to change the wording on a line regarding marriage that included the category "more than one wife of American Indians, Mormons, etc." In a letter to Senator Frank Moss, the First Presidency wrote that they wondered "whether the error represents a deliberate attempt by someone to embarrass the Church or to arouse antagonism toward it."

Even more than the image issue, the church was concerned about the impact of the fundamentalists on its own membership. The shift of position by the church at the turn of the century was largely in response to outside pressures. Yet the change never included a doctrinal shift as such.

Though the church had abolished the *practice* of polygamy, it had never renounced *belief* in the practice, particularly since it was clear that plural marriages would continue in the afterlife of the Celestial Kingdom. "The more deeply immersed a Mormon becomes in his religion," Rulon C. Allred had declared thirty years ago, "the thinner the line may become between belief and practice. The threat of Fundamentalist doctrine is to the most devout. Among extremists, the line can disappear. This is the threat. Some Mormons may deny it, furiously—too furiously."

Fundamentalists potentially represented a threat, capable of snapping the thin line between belief and practice, particularly among the most orthodox or doctrinally pure members. To undercut that possibility, the church had long undertaken efforts to destroy polygamy in Utah and throughout the Mormon-influenced areas of the West. Polygamy investigators at the city, county, and state levels in Utah, for example, had long maintained a relationship with the church, including the swapping of information and the monitoring and surveillance of polygamist activities, as one government official pointed out. In the late 1970s, in the wake of the LeBaron incident, the church escalated these activities and intensified efforts to keep members immune from the polygamist infection.

Still, the problem remained. In 1983, a lawsuit was filed by a Murray, Utah, policeman that challenged antipolygamy federal statutes. He brought his action after he had been fired on the basis of the statutes.

The Murray suit adds a whole new dimension to the situation. If the law is overturned, the question arises: Would that eliminate the reason for the church to continue forbidding the practice of polygamy? The obvious answer, as both Mormons and their fundamentalist counterparts understand, is no, since the church, as a contemporary institution, would never agree to such a change.

Yet a victory by the Murray policeman could strengthen the polygamists. Though harried by the events of the late 1970s, they still remained in the early 1980s a minor but significant group. Estimates of polygamy adherents ranged from 10,000 in Utah (by a Salt Lake County investigator) to more than 30,000 by some polygamists themselves. Most important, polygamy remains that potential threat, the doctrinal riddle that fails to go away. Its persistence compounds the problems facing a church that dislikes any uncertainty and sees ambiguities as a challenge to its authority.

KNOWLEDGE GAINED BY OBEDIENCE

While the mainstream church has always placed a high premium on orthodoxy and belief in leadership, particularly in relationship to the Prophet, there is a part of the culture that is even more rigid and authoritarian than the attitudes and values of much of the membership. It is a strand of the culture that flourished as a reaction to the social dynamics of the 1960s, and it has been reinforced in the 1980s by the anticipation that its moment in the church will come.

For many both inside and outside of the church, the distinction between orthodoxy and authoritarianism is at best a fine line. The strict behavioral codes; the willingness and desire to internalize and obey leadership signals, even in the name of free agency; and the strong identification with patriarchy in the home and hierarchical rankings in the church all reinforce an authoritarian culture.

Through the 1960s, there were numerous clashes between the milder and more intemperate styles of leadership in the church. Ezra Taft Benson clashed with Hugh B. Brown. The early presidency of David O. McKay contrasted with the later years. N. Eldon Tanner served as a marked contrast with Thorpe B. Isaacson. One of the most influential figures who joined with the authoritarian style was BYU President Ernest L. Wilkinson. Wilkinson, who locked horns with some in the leadership and was supported by others, was himself one of the church's most controversial figures, ending up at the center of one of the church's more embarrassing incidents.

When Wilkinson assumed the presidency of Brigham Young University in 1950, it was a relatively small religious school, known more as a training ground for continuing church participation and possible leadership roles than for its academic reputation. In 1911, the school had been racked by a major controversy regarding three faculty members who had been teaching evolution, contending that it was consistent with Mormon belief. The professors were ordered either to alter their teaching or resign, since their teaching was conducted in a way that would "disturb, if not destroy, the faith of the pupils." Two of the faculty resigned, and the incident caused BYU to develop "an anti-intellectual reputation that persisted for several years," according to church historians Leonard J. Arrington and Davis Bitton. "To many Saints," Arrington and Bitton wrote, "the academic world became suspect."

Up through the 1950s, intellectuals remained a relatively small yet tolerated minority, which functioned largely outside the centers of power in the church. In the late 1940s, when George Albert Smith was president, and through much of the 1950s, when David O. McKay maintained control, Mormon intellectuals and academics were able to expand their modest influence through the church's religion institutes and seminary programs, where several key intellectuals played a prominent role.

At BYU in this same period, Ernest L. Wilkinson emerged as a strong advocate of expansion, and buildings appeared to spring up on campus overnight. One Mormon academic recalled how the short, excitable BYU president became an eccentric if energy-filled figure on campus, leading cheers at sports events and doing pushups in the center of the court during halftime at basketball games. Wilkinson used his enormous energy to sway the General Authorities to support BYU expansion financially.

Wilkinson also intensified efforts to make sure that expansion did not mean a broadening of attitudes toward intellectual matters. He was instrumental in establishing church organization by creating wards and stakes directly on campus and pushing the faculty to demonstrate their church loyalties through tithing and other related actions. In the academic area, particularly in the sensitive subjects of philosophy, economics, and religion, Wilkinson intervened in such matters as textbook selection. According to a key Wilkinson aide, Robert K. Thomas, the BYU president was "deeply committed to the adversarial approach, which the faculty did not understand. They thought he was countering them, and that led to some tensions."

The issue came to a head in the wake of Wilkinson's unsuccessful run for a U.S. Senate seat in 1964. The BYU president had by the early 1960s made direct cause with the Ezra Taft Benson wing of both the church and the Utah Republican Party. Wilkinson launched a vitriolic attack against moderate Republican Congressman Sherm Lloyd in the primary and Democratic incumbent Frank Moss in the general election. Several BYU faculty members openly supported Lloyd in his loss to the fiery Wilkinson, while a handful cautiously backed the successful Moss.

In the middle of the campaign, Wilkinson, through a key aide, set up what eventually became a celebrated spy ring to monitor statements of certain BYU faculty (one of whom was Richard Wirthlin, who later became Ronald Reagan's pollster). The students involved were recruited from a local chapter of the John Birch Society. For ten months, they proceeded to monitor classroom discussions, prepare reports that ultimately went back to Wilkinson, and, on some occasions, actually tape-recorded conversations.

Quite by accident, word of the monitoring came back to some of the faculty who had been spied upon. Political science professor Ray Hillam was brought before a hearing held by three BYU vice presidents on charges that his political leanings were too far to the left, as witnessed by his support for admitting communist China to the United Nations. Rumors of purges of faculty liberals and that the Wilkinson-led campus would more directly sponsor right-wing political views and conservative church doctrine were in the air.

Some faculty members turned to the General Authorities, specifically presidential counselors (and known moderates) Hugh B. Brown and N. Eldon Tanner, as well as the influential Harold B. Lee. Tanner urged the faculty to keep careful, duplicate files of all their information on the spy ring, and Lee expressed concern that the matter had become "morally wrong." Still, Wilkinson refused to retreat and only backed down after two of the students decided to fully confess the entire affair.

Although the spy ring was suspended and an administration report was filed that identified the sequence of events, including Wilkinson's participation, the incident entered a kind of gray area for nearly fifteen years, as the report of the incident got filed away in an uncatalogued and unused portion of the BYU archives in the basement of the library. The official version of the incident, contained in Wilkinson's own church-sanctioned history of BYU, only refers to the spy ring in passing, while ignoring his own involvement. The story soon became a part of Mormon underground folklore until a BYU alternative paper, the *Seventh East Press*, discovered the file and published a full account of the incident in the summer of 1982.

Wilkinson stepped down as BYU president in 1971 to be replaced by a more moderate, though orthodox, Mormon, Dallin Oaks, former acting dean of the University of Chicago law school and later a member of the Quorum of the Twelve. The Oaks period paralleled the growing concern for professionalization that characterized the institutional church in the 1970s, as the new BYU president slowly and quietly tried to modify some of the stricter behavioral and academic restrictions of the Wilkinson era. This was the period when the church Historical Department flourished, when evolutionists could be found in the Life Science Department, and where some major innovations took place on campus. Even occasional feminists and, in church terms, would-be radicals, obtained teaching positions and created a modicum of diversity for a campus still heavily oriented toward conservative orthodoxy.

When Oaks stepped down in 1980, the issue of a direction for BYU remained an open question. Oaks's attempt to relax the dress codes had only been moderately successful, and some of the more controversial faculty had ultimately drifted away. Further, the authoritarian strain associated with Wilkinson still had a major following at BYU, some of it associated with the authoritarians' most important advocate within the church hierarchy, Ezra Taft Benson. Bensonites, led by Benson's son Reed and by Richard Vetterli, a former Pasadena, California, school-board member who had been a controversial opponent of school integration, had regained influence and positions on campus, leading the charge against liberals and promoting strong right-wing views.

Oaks's replacement, Dr. Jeffrey Holland, had risen through the church educational bureaucracy and, like Oaks, was considered a moderate in church terms. It quickly became apparent that Holland needed to move even more cautiously than Oaks, as shifts within the church hierarchy continued to be reflected in the campus environment.

The notion of the little brother watching over others' shoulders was indicative of the authoritarian point of view in the church. In part, the little brother attitude had its roots in the celebration of a certain type of Americanism, which, by the 1970s and early 1980s, was most associated with W. Cleon Skousen and his Freemen Institute.

BYU students, young missionaries, and employees of the church, several of whom were being encouraged by church leaders to poke their nose into the attitudes and behavior of their fellow students, faculty, missionaries, and employees, became prime candidates for spying roles in the larger society. Thanks to this authoritarian strain in the culture, the FBI and CIA have continually found young Mormon missionaries or students to be a major source for recruitment.

What then distinguished the mainstream from the authoritarian point of view was the extent and zeal with which such activities were pursued, not whether the activities might or might not be legitimate. In a culture that encouraged informing and spying, the issue became not whether but to what extent and in what context the deed should be done.

By 1980, the authoritarian point of view had several advocates within the church hierarchy, including but not limited to Ezra Taft Benson. In the area of doctrine, Bruce R. McConkie, a son-in-law of Joseph Fielding Smith, took it upon himself to set the standards for doctrinal orthodoxy. McConkie particularly lashed out at Mormon academic liberals, whom he saw committing heresy in their more open analysis of church history and doctrine. "Please note that knowledge is gained by obedience. It comes by obedience to the laws and ordinances of the gospel," McConkie declared at BYU in 1980 in a speech that outlined what he called "Seven Deadly Heresies," including that old bugaboo, the notion that evolution and Mormon doctrine could be harmonized.

About the same time that McConkie outlined his views on heresy, another key authoritarian in the church leadership, Boyd K. Packer, was spelling out his views for church employees on the question of "keeping confidences." Warning of leaks of information from church headquarters to the outside world, Packer emphasized that the duty of the church employee was to tell on others, if any cause for suspicion warranted it. Packer explained that "there is a place to quietly report lapses of security, in the proper channel," while warning that any employee should make sure to avoid contact with any "apostates and excommunicants [who] have a perverse interest in what's going on at Church Headquarters. . . . The war with the adversary goes on," Packer exclaimed. "When you are at war (and we are), security is crucial."

The concern with security among church leaders had grown by the 1970s and 1980s into major proportions. The church security apparatus, which had developed into one of the key operations aimed at maintaining a tight, leakproof church bureaucracy, also came to symbolize the more authoritarian approach among key church leaders. The growing media interest in the church, heightened by the excommunication of Sonia Johnson in December 1979, created an even stronger sense of a siege mentality that seemed to take hold of the church bureaucracy and its leadership. The appointment of L. Martell Bird as head of security in 1981 furthered that process even more. Bird, considered a Benson follower, was a longtime FBI agent who had served around the same time that W. Cleon Skousen had worked for the bureau. He later served on a number of church assignments, most especially as the head of the Missionary Training Center, then called the Mission Home. His appointment strengthened the Benson forces within the bureaucracy and encouraged the tendency of employees to spy on others in the bureaucracy as a means of gaining favor and demonstrating loyalty.

Soon after the Bird appointment and the Packer speech, the number of incidents involving informing, spying, opening interoffice mail, and overall security surveillance began to escalate. One longtime employee was dismissed for supplying information to an independent Mormon publication; another for writing for a nonsanctioned publication. A chill was in the air, particularly with regard to the bureaucracy, as the long-anticipated ascendancy to the presidency of the champion of the authoritarians, Ezra Taft Benson, appeared just a fragile heartbeat away. With the siege mentality prevalent, and the security apparatus maintaining order, the authoritarians saw the 1980s and beyond as the triumph of their point of view.

THE NEW RENAISSANCE

About the time of the Wilkinson spy ring, a onetime BYU faculty member, who had been one of the original targets of the spying, gave a talk at his new ward in Palo Alto, California, where he had recently moved to take a teaching position at Stanford University. The professor, Richard Poll, spoke on the subject "What the Church Means to People Like Me," and he described two types of practicing Mormons, Iron Rodders and Liahonas. Using metaphors from the Book of Mormon instead of the more traditional terms "orthodox" and "liberal," Poll defined an Iron Rodder as a Mormon who "does not look for questions, but for answers," secure that "in the Gospel—as he understands it—he finds or is confident that he can find the answer to every important question." The Iron Rod, as Poll pointed out, referred in the Book of Mormon "to the person with his hand on the rod [for whom] each step of the journey to the tree of life was plainly defined."

In contrast to the Iron Rodder, the Liahona Mormon, according to Poll, was "preoccupied with questions and skeptical of answers; he finds in the Gospel—as he understands it—answers to enough important questions so that he can function purposefully without answers to the rest." The Liahona, Poll pointed out, was also a Book of Mormon symbol, a compass pointing to a destination, but not fully marking the path. "Indeed," Poll declared, "the clarity of its directions varied with the circumstances of the user."

The Iron Rod–Liahona imagery provided an essential tool for those Mormons in the 1960s who, frightened by the Benson wing and fearful of the church's tightening and centralization, wanted to give definition—and legitimacy—to their continuing participation in the church. "It gave me a place in the Church I didn't know I had," recalled Kathryn MacKay, a women's historian, who at the time was a student at the University of California at Los Angeles. Others responded in a similar manner when the first issues of *Dialogue*, a new magazine for Mormon intellectuals and self-defined Liahonas, began publication in 1966. A liberal reformation had begun. Though tentative and uncertain at times, it was able, nevertheless, to mobilize and begin to give definition to this disenfranchised part of the culture of the church.

The liberal Mormon was certainly not a new phenomenon. For the first thirty years of the twentieth century, B.H. Roberts had come to symbolize the inquiring, liberal-minded Mormon leader, a champion of the intellectuals, who was less conservative than many of his contemporaries among the General Authorities. Another church leader, J. Golden Kimball, a freewheeling, down-home Mormon cultural rebel, developed a tremendous popularity by his off-the-cuff conference talks and aphorisms. Yet, through the Heber J. Grant period, such figures as Roberts and Kimball, despite their popularity, became far more the exception than the rule, as the conservative church leadership attempted to mobilize against outside forces, such as the New Deal, which they thought were undermining the strength and belief system of the Saints.

After the war, Mormon intellectuals, who saw themselves as independent agents influenced by secular and religious trends outside the church rather than by intellectual developments inside the church itself, began to create loose networks, sharing with each other their scholarship and analyses. The 1940s and early 1950s, when this network emerged, was a kind of cultural renaissance for the independent Mormon intellectual. Novelists, such as Maurine Whipple, Vardis Fisher, and Virginia Sorensen; historians, such as Fawn Brodie, Juanita Brooks, and Samuel Woolley Taylor; philosophers and religious thinkers, such as Sterling M. McMurrin, T. Edgar Lyon, and Lowell Bennion; and sociologists and cultural anthropologists, such as Lowry Nelson and William Mulder, provided an insightful look at the Mormon experience that far overshadowed any official sanctioned material on the same subjects.

That cultural renaissance was at first resisted strongly by church leaders. Fawn Brodie was excommunicated for her biography of Joseph Smith and became the most abused and celebrated apostate of her generation. Both Vardis Fisher and Maurine Whipple, though not excommunicated, became church outcasts, and in the social sciences, history, and philosophy, such independent thinkers as Lowry Nelson, Juanita Brooks, and Sterling M. McMurrin became targets of suspicion rather than subjects for accolades.

Nevertheless, by the early 1950s, as the church began its first moves toward expansion and modernization, certain of these intellectuals found themselves with occasional defenders among the leadership. The protection afforded Sterling M. McMurrin at first by David O. McKay and later by Hugh B. Brown was a case in point.

Through the late 1940s and early 1950s, McMurrin had become a target for Joseph Fielding Smith, the church historian, next in seniority after David O. McKay within the Quorum, and, since the passing of B.H. Roberts and his more conservative counterpart, John A. Widtsoe, the official theologian of the church. McMurrin was anathema to Smith, particularly for his refusal to accept church doctrine as a literal belief system. In an extraordinary 1952 session with Smith and Harold B. Lee, for example, McMurrin, who had been summoned to explain his position on various doctrinal matters, directly presented his views to the two General Authorities. McMurrin stated that he believed that Adam and Eve were not real people but part of a culture myth, that he did not believe in the Fall of Man, and that Joseph Smith's first vision had to be placed in a contextual framework in order to properly understand and analyze it, all beliefs that further incensed the church theologian.

Yet Smith failed, after repeated attempts, to get McMurrin excommunicated. To Smith, McMurrin was a heretic—and worse. In one 1960 letter, Smith described the philosopher as a "betrayer of the church and its teachings," who was "destroying the faith of our young people." McMurrin recalled how Smith, at one stake conference in the late 1950s, thundered to his audience, "There are wolves among us, I tell you there are wolves among us." Later, the church leader declared that McMurrin was "the chief wolf." Yet McMurrin, heretic that he was thought to be by Joseph Fielding Smith and Ezra Taft Benson, was able to maintain an open channel to David O. McKay, who recognized McMurrin's value for a growing and increasingly visible church.

While McMurrin was warding off excommunication atttempts, he and other like-minded intellectuals established in the 1950s a more formal setting for their network of Mormon independents. Calling themselves the Swearing Elders, the group explored in critical fashion a number of historical, philosophical, and doctrinal issues directly or indirectly related to the church. Even the excommunicated Fawn Brodie and other outcasts, such as Juanita Brooks, were invited to the sessions, as this high-powered assortment of Mormon intellectuals defined both the strengths and limits of the independent tradition of Mormonism as it existed in the environment of the church of the 1950s.

By the 1960s, however, the optimism and relative openness of the early expansion years had given way to a tighter, narrower mood spawned by Correlation, as the church attempted to isolate its members from the changing cultural and political dynamics of the larger society. It was precisely this isolation, the fact that "Mormon doctrine reinforces individual withdrawal and defiance of conformity in the face of modern convention," as the editorial preface to the first issue of *Dialogue* put it, that provided the impetus to start *Dialogue* and attempt to create a new liberal renaissance.

The key for the *Dialogue* group was that its potential audience would be Mormons living outside Utah. "Los Angeles and New York are as important subsidiary centers of Mormon culture now as St. George and Nephi were fifty years ago," the first issue of the magazine proclaimed. "Mormons are participating freely in the social, economic, and cultural currents of change sweeping twentieth century America." This powerful need to overcome isolation and somehow not "feel forced to choose between heritage and the larger world," as the magazine prospectus put it, became both the purpose and the attraction of the magazine.

Both the emergence of *Dialogue* and the immediate popularity of Richard Poll's Iron Rod–Liahona dichotomy were the most direct expressions of the beginnings of this liberal Mormon renewal in the late 1960s, particularly for a younger generation of Mormons who were caught up in the events of the period. "It was a very exciting time for me," one student at the time recalled. "It's never been like that before or since. We had this sense of openness, of possibility. I felt like I was part of what was happening *as a Mormon.*"

The issues for the young Mormon liberals and the older group of intellectuals that ran *Dialogue* were parallel to the debates in the larger society: civil rights, Vietnam, and, by the 1970s, women's rights and women's roles. Each of the issues in turn had their Mormon component: the denial of the priesthood to blacks, the church attitudes toward the Vietnam war, and, of course, the question of the family.

These new intellectuals and Mormon activists helped create a new presence, a new force in the church, which, though weak and not as well defined and organized as an actual movement, nevertheless played a role in restructuring the debate and at times influencing some subtle yet important shifts in church policy.

Activism, albeit limited and cautious, even touched the BYU campus in the late 1960s and early 1970s, as one antiwar leader was elected BYU student body president at the tail end of the Wilkinson era. And some of the tentative, cautious steps to define an independent women's position, as articulated in the pink issue of *Dialogue*, represented the beginnings of what would later emerge within the decade as a kind of women's underground, with a few women moving outside but most remaining inside the church.

The issue that for many of the new Mormon intellectuals and activists became remarkably compelling and exciting at the time was the new thrust in exploring church history. Nearly a generation after Fawn Brodie was excommunicated and Juanita Brooks was in strong disfavor, a group of young Mormon historians, seeking to further develop a tradition of objective analysis and historical scholarship, formed the independent Mormon History Association.

The MHA became an immediate success, attracting such prominent scholars as Leonard J. Arrington, whose *Great Basin Kingdom* had become a kind of primer for this new approach. It brought together historians from not only the Salt Lake church, but from the Missouri Reorganized Church of Jesus Christ of Latter-day Saints and independent non-Mormon scholars as well. The MHA also worked closely with *Dialogue* and a revitalized, relatively independent *BYU Studies*, which provided outlets for some of the historical studies being generated.

The professionalization that had emerged within the church in the late 1960s and early 1970s—associated in part with Harold B. Lee and his organizational revolution—gave further impetus to the efforts of the Mormon historians. When a new General Authority, Howard Hunter, was named church historian to replace Joseph Fielding Smith, who had become Prophet, the process culminated with the reorganization of the church historian's office. Hunter, with Lee's blessing, decided that professional historians ought to run the office, a suggestion that originated with the Correlation-linked Bickmore study. He turned to Leonard Arrington, who was called to take over the History Division in 1972.

Arrington's appointment electrified the professional historians and many of the young activists who considered church history as the key area for the liberal renaissance. Ambitious plans were laid out and expectations ran high. A Friends of Church History group was organized with the idea of developing communication between the church historian's office and people outside the bureaucracy. At the first meeting of the Friends of Church History, overflowing with enthusiastic scholars and activists, Arrington spelled out some of the new division's initial plans. Proposals included a sixteen-volume history of the church, involving scholars from around the country. The division also wanted to publish documents "important for understanding church history which ought to be brought to the attention of the Church," one of the historians declared. These included studies on women in the church and the completion of a manuscript on the United Orders. An oral history program was designed, articles on church history were to be prepared for various church publications, and an overall effort was to be made to collect minutes, diaries, and other documents of ordinary Mormons to show that history was more than just an exposition of the activities and doctrinal positions of the General Authorities.

For four years, the new History Division flourished. "It was the Arrington spring," one of the new historians, Dean May, recalled. Young researchers became important contributors to *Dialogue* and *BYU Studies* and even influenced such church publications as *The Ensign*. Some went on to create new publications, such as *Sunstone*, an important, feistier, more controversial version of *Dialogue*.

While the efforts of the division continued to be supported by several General Authorities, including some conservatives who were assigned by the leadership to oversee the historians, some leaders, most noticeably Ezra Taft Benson and Boyd K. Packer, were critical of many of the projects. Two of the division's initial book projects—a one-volume history of the church, entitled *The Story of the Latter-Day Saints*, and the history of the communitarian efforts, entitled *Building the City of God*—were bitterly attacked by Benson and then withdrawn from publication after first editions sold out. Benson objected to the "humanistic philosophy" and "contextual history" he saw being promoted by the Arrington group and claimed that the terms "communal life," "communitarianism," and "Christian primitivism" in *Building the City of God* would "offend the Brethren and church members." "The emphasis is to underplay revelation and God's intervention in significant events," Benson concluded, "and to inordinately humanize the prophets of God so that their human frailties become more evident than their spiritual qualities."

As a revealed religion that teaches that God has spoken directly and personally to the Prophet, the issue of historical interpretation was clearly critical for church leaders, who feared that the efforts of the historians, in their attempts to develop an objective point of view would lead to what Packer called "faith destroying" activities. "In an effort to be objective, impartial and scholarly," Packer declared to a BYU audience, "a writer or teacher may unwittingly be giving equal time to the adversary." About the Arrington History Division, Packer was explicit: "Those of you who are employed by the Church have a special responsibility to build faith, not destroy it," Packer exclaimed. "If you do not do that, but in fact accommodate the enemy, who is a destroyer of faith, you become in that sense a traitor to the cause you have made covenants to protect."

To the historians and their allies, the Benson and Packer attacks were aimed at the very heart of the liberal renaissance—to open up the process, to respect the most elemental rules of scholarship, and to seek out, as University of Utah historian James Clayton put it, "true knowledge, [which] is indeed hazardous, just as true faith does indeed require a leap into the unknown." For the historians, it was critical to maintain their Mormon faith and cultural heritage *and* their worldly pursuits and connections, in this case unbiased historical research and analysis.

The Benson and Packer attacks were part of a direct and dramatic shift of policy toward the Arrington group. When a new General Authority, G. Homer Durham, was placed in the late 1970s over the historians, there was a brief flicker of hope based on Durham's own academic background, which included a stint as president of Arizona State University in the 1960s. Yet Durham became a "snake in the grass," as one historian bitterly put it, constantly undercutting the historians and their work.

Systematically, the History Division began to be dismantled. Projects, such as the sixteen-volume history, were officially terminated, and archives were restricted, often in an arbitrary manner.

When the History Division was finally transferred to BYU, Arrington was formally removed from his position as church historian. For the historians, intellectuals, and activists whose work and activities had constituted the renaissance of the 1970s, the Arrington spring had turned into the winter siege.

By 1980, the siege mentality seemed in high gear, as witnessed by the difficulties of the History Division and the excommunication of ERA advocate Sonia Johnson. A speech by Ezra Taft Benson at BYU around the same time intensified that mood. Benson, whom church intellectuals feared most, declared that the president of the church was God's "unerring prophet" and his word was law on all issues. All these events pushed this new generation of Mormon independents to "open things up for debate," as attorney Jon Lear put it. Lear, along with a handful of other Mormon liberals, such as University of Utah medical school Vice President (and later university President) Chase Petersen and his wife, Grethe Petersen (a leader involved in church and women's activities), *Sunstone* editors Peggy Fletcher, Allen Roberts, and Lorie Winder Stromberg, and political science professor J. D. Williams (an outspoken Benson critic), put together a group to sponsor regular forums, called the B. H. Roberts Society. Unlike the Swearing Elders of a generation before, the B. H. Roberts forums were large public gatherings with formal presentations on such potentially controversial subjects as women in the church or whether the church should be involved in political matters.

"The purpose of B. H. Roberts," according to Chase Petersen, "is, for some, to keep people within the church, and for others to try and reform it." Declared Lear of the church leadership, "We are dealing with a group of men who grew up at the turn of the century who believe these things are very threatening. The B. H. Roberts forums show Mormons that it is all right if you question, it is all right if you don't believe the party line."

Like the early impetus for *Dialogue*, the B. H. Roberts forums demonstrated a concern about how the church and its members could learn to interact with rather than be isolated from the outside world. Many of those attending the forums were desperately searching for ways to remain Mormons and maintain their "testimony," given the harsher, increasingly conservative drift of the church. That need was heightened by the fears about Ezra Taft Benson, and the expectation that once Benson became Prophet, there would be no more space for this grouping within the Mormon culture. Ultimately, these Mormons felt they were walking a tightrope between their church and the outside world.

Yet, as Chase Petersen pointed out, there were also others who wanted more than just self-renewal. These Mormons wanted a mechanism by which the church could be changed—whether in terms of its attitudes and policies toward women or in relation to many of the other church behavioral and organizational practices and restrictions. For these more radical, or "autonomous," Mormons, the need to change Mormonism meant connecting with Mormonism's own radical roots. They celebrated the church's communitarian tradition and its early social, economic, sexual, and political critique of the larger bourgeois society. They asserted that the members of the church—not just its leaders—have the gift of revelation. "We are a prophetic people, not just led by a prophet," one of the autonomous Mormons told a sacrament meeting at a university ward. Prophecy, in that context, becomes a form of spiritual participatory democracy.

For liberal and radical Mormons, tightropers and autonomous Mormons alike, the emergence of the B. H. Roberts forums and independent publications, such as *Sunstone* and the *Sunstone Review*, and BYU's alternative paper, the *Seventh East Press* (which ultimately was banned from campus in 1983), were important, self-validating, and at times extraordinarily exciting moments for *their* culture.

Once a church member left Salt Lake and Utah, it became easier to nurture that culture. At the same time, however, the independents remained largely Salt Lake phenomena, and as such, they were continually preoccupied with matters regarding the church hierarchy and bureaucracy. Furthermore, during the 1970s, many of the independents maintained a kind of umbilical relationship to the church, which functioned as their employer, whether through the History Division, church publications, or in the bureaucracy as a whole.

Yet, even with the renaissance since the late 1960s, these independents remained a small, distinct minority in the culture. Wishing to explore the past yet hampered in their attempt, they remained wary of the present and fearful of the future. Their greatest power was in their willingness to air issues and events that other Mormons, whether members or leaders, would rather keep private, and even secret.

An important ally for the independents was the media, which had become during the 1970s and 1980s increasingly interested in the church. The media sought out this group to provide not only information, but an explanation and analysis of the policies and shifts in the church leadership.

For the church leaders, the renaissance was, at best, a mixed blessing. On the one hand, figures such as Chase Petersen (who became prominent as University of Utah spokesman during the Barney Clark artificial-heart operation) and other select independents brought prestige and prominence to the church. Church leaders hoped that these figures would keep the debate within certain parameters. But many in the leadership also mistrusted the renaissance and saw possible conspiracies and other "faith-destroying" work at play. They agreed with Harold B. Lee that there were *only* Iron Rodders in the church; the rest were either straying or on the road to apostasy.

Those attitudes of mistrust were not just limited to the Bensons and the Packers, but in some respects extended to the entire leadership of the Quorum, many of whom were especially mistrustful of the independents' relationship with the media. Gordon B. Hinckley, who became a counselor in the First Presidency in 1981 and who was seen by many independents as a moderate counterweight to Benson, was particularly incensed by some of the media activities and their relationship to the independent Mormons. "In the nineteenth century we had the vigilantes, the mob, the persecutions," Hinckley declared at one meeting shortly after he became counselor. "Today, we have the press."

For both the liberal and more radical, or autonomous, Mormons, an attempt to influence or challenge certain policies, including behavioral attitudes and restrictions, such as the role of women in the church, will lead in the decades to come to a confrontation not only with church leaders but with their interpretation of church doctrine as well. Some will undoubtedly leave the church, hard as that is, given the powerful cultural influence that comes with being a Mormon, at least for those born into a Mormon family. Others will remain, a few to fight, but most to watch and hope that the centralized and authoritarian church will somehow allow a modicum of diversity.

MULTIPLE CULTURES IN ZION

A Mormon journalist recently wrote that when a Mormon asked the question "Are you a Mormon?" it was no longer sufficient to answer yes, if that were the case. The question really ought to have been, "What *kind* of a

Mormon are you?" since the person likely wanted to know, "Are you *my kind* of Mormon?"

There are problems dividing Mormons into different cultures or groups, for there are clearly overlaps. Some will change positions over particular issues, and others, as they grow older or change job or life situations, might well change in approach and attitudes. Yet, it is clear that different sub-cultures do exist in Zion, despite the very real and powerful centralizing forces that have been unleashed by the contemporary church.

To start with, there is a mainstream culture with which many, though not all, church members identify. Even within the mainstream culture, there are distinct tendencies or differences between those more "straitgate" Mormons, or Iron Rodders in Richard Poll's typology, and a less extreme, though orthodox Mormon attitude. The straitgate Mormons see God's hand, through the Prophet, in everything and search for the right way to enter the Celestial Kingdom. They will faithfully follow the Mormon behavioral code, seeking to create a large family and be active in all church activities.

The orthodox Mormons, also mainstream Mormons, remain less concerned with absolute codes. They may shift from the letter to the spirit of the law on occasion, such as when Mormon wives are economically obliged to enter the job market. These orthodox Mormons tend not to be fascinated by questions nor thirsty for information, but remain open, nevertheless, to a variety of answers.

To the right of the mainstream culture are situated the authoritarian Mormons. Many of them are politically inclined, participating in such organizations as the Freemen Institute or the John Birch Society. Their champion is Ezra Taft Benson, who they feel gives a political dimension to the Prophet's role. They also feel that since Mormonism has assigned a sacred role to the American Constitution they must become defenders of the flag as well as the faith. These authoritarian Mormons are activists on such issues as pornography and birth control and try to provide a bridge to the Moral Majority. They do not simply uphold the behavioral code but attempt to make sure that others do so as well.

Then there are the fundamentalists, primarily those who practice and/or believe in polygamy, but especially all those who look to the early church for inspiration. They take behavioral restrictions to an extreme, as witnessed by their dress and sexual conduct. (Polygamists, for example, are the most Victorian of Mormons.) And while church leaders and most members do not consider fundamentalists Mormons (many of them are, in fact, excommunicated), they are nevertheless an authentic part of the culture. Fundamentalists, in fact, understand themselves to be the real Mormons, and others, particularly church leaders, to be the apostates.

The independent Mormons are another key part of the cultural typology, and they in turn can be viewed both in relation to more accommodationist or autonomous postures. The accommodationist, or tightrope, Mormons seek to maintain a delicate balance between the church and the outside world, between faith and knowledge, change and compromise, expectation and reality. The autonomous Mormon, unlike his or her more cautious counterpart, no longer walks a tightrope but proceeds on the basis of inner principle and conviction that redefines the cultural birthright. While the tightrope Mormon tries to figure out ways to stay in the church, the autonomous Mormon thinks of ways to change it.

Finally, to complete the typology, there are ex-Mormons, not necessarily excommunicated Mormons, but all those who have made their break in one form or another, both with the church and with their cultural birthright. The ex-Mormons are de-Mormonizing as quickly and conspicuously as possible, particularly in terms of behavioral codes. They wear their identities on their sleeves and have no patience with doctrine, seeing it as obscure, otherworldly, and peculiar.

For more than a century after the Mormons created their society in the Great Basin desert, the Mormon people have been perceived as a different, peculiar people, as they like to put it. In the process, they have come as close as any nonimmigrant grouping in this country, as sociologist Thomas O'Dea put it, to defining themselves with full ethnic or near-nation status. Yet the shifts that began with the accommodations of the 1890s meant that the church was also attempting to create a mainstream culture identified with a certain type of Americanism, upholding the traditional values of the larger society.

That society, however, has changed during the last thirty years. In the process, there has emerged a certain tension in the Mormon culture, where both the differing tendencies of isolation and accommodation have yet to be resolved. At the same time, there have also emerged subcultures within the culture, tied together by the thread of the church and a common birthright, yet different and at times in conflict with each other.

Today, the tension is manifested openly in behavioral and other conflicts. It promises to intensify in the years to come. The church, as monolithic and as centralized as it appears to be, nonetheless remains diverse, even as its leadership continues to attempt to create a single, stricter, more disciplined organization to prepare for the Great Battle with the Adversary it sees almost everywhere.

CHAPTER NINE

NO NEED FOR INNOVATION: A CONCLUSION

1983: THREE YEARS LATER

It was not a propitious time for the Saints. Their leader, Spencer W. Kimball, who had just celebrated his eighty-eighth birthday, would not attend spring conference. He had survived yet another operation, but the rumor was circulating that he could last only a few more days or weeks at best. The Prophet's sister had told an Associated Press reporter that he was so disoriented and weak that he could hardly eat his breakfast. His nurse, who was on call twenty-four hours at Kimball's new apartment at the Hotel Utah, had to feed him. When the AP reporter asked a church spokesman to comment about the sister's remarks, he limply replied, "You've obviously talked to someone who knows much more than I do."

Kimball's First Counselor, Marion G. Romney, was also unable to attend conference, another casualty of ill health and advanced age, in his case eighty-five years. Nathan Eldon Tanner, who had died the previous winter, was also sorely missed. Even as Tanner had declined in health the previous year, finding speaking increasingly difficult, he had still played a key role in providing a more worldly dimension to the leadership, especially in its business affairs. Now, with Tanner dead, it was unclear just who would emerge to take his place.

There were other problems in Zion as well. The U.S. attorney for Utah was about to announce indictments of twenty-one people in a $32 million fraud plot, one of the biggest for federal investigators. Mormons once again were both the targets and participants in the fraud, and the key to the whole scheme was what the U.S. attorney called "a Mormon marketing strategy."

The press was also on the mind of the General Authorities. The *Denver Post* had recently run an eight-part series on the church that stirred up considerable controversy. In this instance, the church looked particularly inept. First, the church denied the *Denver Post* reporter's request for interviews with General Authorities. Then it turned around and attacked the series editorially in the *Deseret News* because the reporter interviewed primarily well-known critics of the church.

Church leaders had also intervened in another press matter, this time closer to home. The gadfly *Seventh East Press*, the feisty independent student newspaper at BYU, was banned from campus, and some church-related advertising was withdrawn. The action by the BYU administration, which was thought to have been carried out at the order of Ezra Taft Benson, caused a flurry of protests, but eventually succeeded in accomplishing what the champions of orthodoxy had most wanted to do. The *Seventh East Press* suspended publication within a month, and a new, tamer paper, *The University Post*, took its place briefly and then folded.

All of this, along with Kimball's continuing health problems, raised once again the issue of what would happen to the church if and when Ezra Taft Benson took over as the Prophet. Unlike any previous General Authority in recent years, Benson had become a magnet, attracting those who embraced the authoritarian strain in the culture, while repelling others who most identified with the intellectuals and independents in the church. To the independents, Benson was an issue that would not go away, and they could only pray, as Sterling M. McMurrin put it, that "the good Lord takes Brother Benson before he takes Brother Kimball."

It was a cold, overcast April morning when Gordon B. Hinckley opened the first conference session. Hinckley, who had been named to the First Presidency a year and a half earlier, was now the only active member of that leadership body, with Tanner dead and Kimball and Romney too ill to function. He would make a point early in his speech of insisting that all the work of the First Presidency was proceeding according to schedule. But others would report in the months ahead that Hinckley was pushing himself to the limit, carrying the enormous burden of the First Presidency on his shoulders alone while working continuously to head off the conflicts between conservative and moderate members of the Quorum of the Twelve Apostles.

While Benson symbolized controversy both inside and outside the church, Gordon B. Hinckley was the quintessential church organization man, who had spent much of his adult life inside the church, working his way systematically through the leadership ranks. "Elder Hinckley's calling to the First Presidency," explained the *Church Almanac*, "is a natural extension of a life characterized by service close to the heartbeat of the church, often pioneering new areas."

Hinckley was neither a moderate nor an authoritarian. He was primarily public relations conscious, thanks to his work in church media, where he developed early radio and television material and later oversaw the church's media and public relation apparatus. His view of the church was more in line with the bland, nondescript brochures on the church, such as "What is a Mormon," which he authored. And he maintained a view of the membership and the issues facing the church similar to those spelled out in the *Reader's Digest* ads, which he had approved personally. Hinckley had emerged as a potential leader during Correlation. He had been a Harold B. Lee man, one of a handful of leaders overseeing the Correlation Committee. He had been executive secretary of the General Missionary Committee as the church embarked on its major expansion in the international arena. Hinckley had also followed the flag to Asia and Vietnam in the late 1960s, supervising church work among the 500,000 American troops stationed there.

Hinckley, more than some church leaders, liked to think of himself as more worldly and knowledgeable about such things as politics, business, and public relations. He had initially replaced Lee as the church's political expert and had helped set up the staff-based Special Affairs Committee, serving as its first director. Hinckley also served on a number of corporate boards, some church-owned corporations, such as Bonneville International and Deseret Management, and other church-influenced ones, such as Zions First National Bank and Utah Power and Light.

Hinckley had touched all the bases in the contemporary church. He was a fitting leader for a church that had developed a vast organizational and bureaucratic apparatus and yet lacked some of the typical qualities of a corporate or political bureaucracy. Unlike some of the blood and thunder speakers of the past but like most of the other current General Authorities, Hinckley spoke in homilies and *Reader's Digest*ese, liberally sprinkled with doctrinal references. He was a contrast to Benson in that he was not an ideologue, but neither was he someone who publicly challenged that ideology. He was the church's man in the dark blue suit, a leader of men who looked, talked, acted, and thought like his peers.

At conference, Hinckley's theme was continuity. "Some express concern that the President of the Church is likely always to be a rather elderly man," the seventy-two-year-old Hinckley declared, "to which my response is, What a blessing! . . . The basics of our doctrine are now well in place, and we are firmly established as a people at least until the Lord should mandate another move," Hinckley went on. "We do not need innovation. We need devotion in adherence to divinely spoken principles. We need loyalty to our leader, whom God has appointed. He is our Prophet, Seer, and Revelator."

The themes of unity, obedience, and continuity were repeated throughout the conference. In one speech, Apostle Bruce R. McConkie dealt directly with the matter of succession. The senior member of the Quorum of the Twelve succeeds the Prophet, McConkie declared, no ifs, ands, or buts about it. In this case, if Kimball were to die, Ezra Taft Benson would *automatically* be next in line.

Succession has not always been such a cut-and-dried affair. Church moderates, hoping against hope, talked during the 1970s of possible new procedures, or at least of modifying Benson's power by some means. The favorite analogy for church moderates and even some Mormon conservatives, such as U.S. Senator Orrin G. Hatch, was the succession of Joseph Fielding Smith as Prophet in 1970 after the death of David O. McKay. When the ninety-three-year-old Smith became president, "Everybody thought he would be very strait-laced and tough on interpretation of the church gospel doctrine," Hatch recalled. There were fears that Smith would persist in his attacks on evolution and insist on the importance of his belief that the earth was formed 7,000 years ago. But the enfeebled Smith never had any influence over church policies during his brief two years as Prophet. His two counselors, Harold B. Lee and Nathan Eldon Tanner, completely ran the church and continued to implement the reforms begun by Lee during Correlation.

Benson was another matter. Though he was also getting on in years (he was three years younger than Kimball) he seemed more alert and in control of his faculties than the Prophet, despite Benson's own recurring health problems. More important, Benson by the early 1980s had established his own network within the church bureaucracy. He had also created an ideological climate that was becoming more and more dominant within church councils. Several top leaders, including Boyd K. Packer, Bruce R. McConkie, and Mark E. Petersen, shared much of the Benson approach and had begun to adopt some of his techniques of leadership.

Petersen was a pivotal figure until his death in January 1984. He had recently established a committee to undercut and ultimately weed out church liberals and intellectuals. The committee was headed by Roy Doxey, a BYU professor who had been in charge of the Correlation Committee in the 1970s. Doxey, with another pro-Benson ally from the church History Division, was charged with systematically going through independent publications, such as *Dialogue, Sunstone,* and *Seventh East Press,* to identify those independents whom Petersen and his committee had decided would need possible disciplinary action. Petersen then forwarded their names to their bishops, who were asked to call the individuals in, question them about their sex lives, their tithing payments, church attendance, and a range of other behavioral and organizational matters, suggesting that they had been straying and were possible candidates for a loss of temple recommend. The possibility of excommunication also lurked in the background.

With Benson and his supporters trying to establish a new tone and direction for the church, Gordon B. Hinckley was increasingly called upon to challenge that direction. In a dramatic confrontation, he put the lid on Benson and Petersen's efforts to muzzle critics within the church. Of those investigated, only one member, an employee of church security, was terminated or disciplined.

Despite this victory, Hinckley and the moderates found themselves constantly on the defensive. Hinckley's job, it was clear, was to oversee the administrative apparatus, not to implement new policies, to try to keep the church on its modernizing course. Through the early 1980s, however, the ideological dimension of the church was being shaped by others, like Benson and Petersen, who were most identified with a particular authoritarian style and perspective.

During the 1960s, Benson, as he moved to the right, had been largely contained by the First Presidency, led by Hugh B. Brown and Tanner. They in turn had received backing from the Quorum of the Twelve in attempting to rein Benson in, backing that included more conservative Apostles, such as Joseph Fielding Smith and Petersen. The irrepressible Benson, however, could never be held back for long. With his sons and such longtime allies as W. Cleon Skousen providing support, Benson continued to stir things up. Periodically, he would come up with a statement such as how very hard it was to be a good Mormon *and* a liberal Democrat if the person was living the gospel and understood it.

By the early 1980s, Benson had become such a charged political and ideological figure that even the conservative and usually cautious former Senator Wallace F. Bennett would comment, "Are there two Ezra Bensons: Benson, the political philosopher, where he's free to speak out, and Benson, the loyal member of the Quorum of Twelve devoted to the welfare of the church? Well, I'm not so sure that if Benson succeeded to the presidency that the political animal might disappear."

By the spring of 1983 it had become clear that whereas Benson had not yet succeeded to the presidency, he had largely succeeded in defining an ideological mindset to which others in the church were being forced to react. Whatever space existed for church intellectuals and independents in the late 1960s and 1970s was being limited. The conflict around the ERA and the role of women had firmly established a mainstream ideology in the church that was particularly hostile to any approach that placed women outside the home. "The divine work of women," Benson had declared, "involves companionship, homemaking, and motherhood."

Through much of the history of the church and increasingly in the modern period, there has been tension between two key ideological precepts: free agency and obedience to authority. Free agency is central to the culture of the independents, who celebrate the notion of individual choice and self-determination that had long been put forth as church doctrine. "Teach them Correct Principles and let them govern themselves," is a favorite church aphorism, originally coined by Joseph Smith, and it became the framework through which free agency expressed itself.

The other half of the dialectic, obedience to authority, was also a longstanding church concept which gained more prominence in the 1960s and 1970s with the advent of Correlation. As the church expanded, the fear of losing control of its members, particularly in relation to the international church, concerned church leaders. In this context, they reemphasized the notion that the Prophet and the priesthood were at the center of the religion, and that the Prophet's words, as Benson put it, were law. Obedience to authority meant obedience to the organization, policies, and ideology of the church in whatever form they expressed themselves. Free agency, for church leaders, then only worked when those policies and ideologies were effectively and thoroughly internalized by the members. The most complete form of control became, as Boyd Packer explained during his 1983 conference talk, a form of "self-control." "Latter-day Saints are obedient because they know certain spiritual truths and have decided, as an expression of their own individual [free] agency, to obey the commandments of God." And God's commandments are the words of the Prophets.

The Benson succession, in ideological terms, appears at first to contrast with the church's other worldly aspects—its vast business empire, its international dimension, its attempt to develop political reach and sophistication, its public relations apparatus. The business interests of the church have, of necessity, obliged church leaders to create a new source of organizational power—the money managers. Even if they are not of the world, top money manager J. Howard Dunn explained, at least they were in the world. And in the world meant utilizing capital's mandate to maximize profits: to see to it that the end point of the business of the church was the ability to make more money, an enterprise church leaders eagerly back.

Making money, however, also brought with it some constraints, not the least of which were ideological, as well as organizational. It was not only what the church did with its investment, but whom it did business with, whether they were Arab playboys, Mormon real estate developers, or Las Vegas casino owners.

Furthermore, the business of the church—to grow and expand—was becoming a capital-intensive as well as labor-intensive business. The church could no longer simply rely on its member-subsidized missionary system to establish a church presence, particularly abroad, but it also had to create a physical and organizational infrastructure with buildings, schools, bureaucrats, and so on. With the expansion taking place largely in the Third World, that meant more money was going out than coming in. Thus, the money managers' mandate became problematic: either cut back or face a capital crunch.

The money managers themselves were not about to make that or any other major policy decision. When Tanner was alive, he made it for them and at the same time created an operational framework that gave the money managers some degree of independence. Tanner was their leader because he had been of the world, not just in it. Without Tanner's power, the money managers had little ability or inclination to challenge any shift in direction, let alone a hardening of current ideological trends in the church. As Apostle Packer put it, the church bureaucrat was still a member of the priesthood, someone who was part of the ideological and theological system, someone the leaders could trust.

Nor had the growth of the international church established an independent base to challenge the drift toward ideological self-containment. Though church leaders had made some attempt to correct some of the more blatant examples of Salt Lake City chauvinism, the international church remained an extension of the home front in Zion. Missionaries, top local leaders, mission and temple presidents, General Authorities all remained overwhelmingly American, with nearly all of the Americans in turn coming from the small towns and cities of the Mormon West.

The growth of the international church, for church leaders, had transformed them into cosmopolitan men of affairs, spending countless hours living out of their briefcases and on airplanes. Neal A. Maxwell's "priesthood style"—the style of American corporate management—was embraced from the General Authority level on down. Yet that worldly style had little to do with the cultural, social, and economic realities of the Third World countries in which the church had experienced its most rapid growth. The connection ultimately was to the American flag: The priesthood style meant, in effect, recruiting and socializing those who would most readily adapt to and accept the American presence. It was more than just coincidence that the church found that their top leaders came from the ranks of the multinational corporations doing business in those very same countries.

In the area of politics, the church leaders decided in the 1970s to develop its politics around social issues, such as the ERA and pornography. It utilitized its more worldly Special Affairs Committee to develop political alliances with such groups as the Moral Majority and Phyllis Schlafly's Eagle Forum, at a time when the social issues appeared to be moving the country to the right. And while the church move did generate such alliances, it created internal divisions within the church even greater than the problems that grew out of denying blacks the priesthood. The emergence of an oppositional focus within Mormondom against church policies, however limited, created an enormous internal backlash, spearheaded directly by Benson, but with the full and unanimous backing of the entire church leadership. When it came to women and the social issues, Hinckley and Benson were one and the same.

And even in the area of press and public relations, only a thin line separated the professionally oriented, apparently more worldly and modernizing leaders, such as Hinckley, and the hard-line ideologues, such as Benson. In the year prior to the first 1983 conference, church leaders established a Public Communications Council, consisting of church leaders, among them Hinckley and Packer, top bureaucrats in the church Public Communications Department, and a number of prominent Mormons from the worlds of media, business, and politics, such as columnist Jack Anderson, former Michigan Governor George Romney, and Washington lawyer Robert Barker.

The Public Communications Council was established in the wake of Sonia Johnson's excommunication and related events that had generated enormous publicity about the church, much of it negative. Once again, reporters were inquiring into church policies and operations, and the church leadership decided that it needed the help of worldly Mormons to create a more positive image for the church. To do so, council members would, they hoped, intervene, particularly through their contacts and influence with media executives.

Despite attempts to create a more sophisticated approach toward the media, church leaders remained locked into an attitude that perceived the media as an enemy, a new type of persecutor. The Benson ideologues had nothing but disdain for the media. "Most TV and a lot of radio programs are a waste of time, if not corrupters of morals or distorters of truth," Benson told BYU students. And as to newspapers, "usually a few minutes is more than sufficient to read a paper" since, as Benson put it, it is sometimes better "to be uninformed rather than misinformed."

Church leaders, such as Hinckley, were also uncomfortable with the press. These leaders, in fact, were most responsible for creating an attitude of hostility and mistrust throughout the institutional church, with the exception of the church independents, who have used the press to their own advantage. Ultimately, despite all the bureaucracies, press councils, and would-be media sophistication, the ideologues and the modernizers come back to the same starting point: As the one and only true church, Mormons might be in the world, but they are certainly not of the world.

Still, church leaders think of Mormons as a mainstream people, the prototypical Americans that appear in church ads and television public service announcements. "This curious combination of typicality and peculiarity," wrote Thomas O'Dea twenty-five years ago, describing the Saints, and it is still true today as it was 154 years ago.

There are other visions of what the modern church should be. Liberals and independents would prefer a church in the old prophetic, reforming tradition, the church described by Sterling M. McMurrin in his address to the NAACP. These Mormons would like to see less political involvement; greater concern for the poor, whether Mormon or non-Mormon and particularly in the Third World; more autonomy and variety within the membership; an intellectual and cultural flowering; less top–down control; and a church open to interaction with other religions. As maverick University of Utah political science professor J. D. Williams put it dramatically at the 1983 Sunstone Symposium, they simply want, "Freedom, freedom, freedom." But like other visions that are not condoned by the General Authorities, such as fundamentalism, this vision suffers from the timidity of its advocates and the enormous pull of church tradition.

"The child of a Mormon family undergoes what must be one of the most powerful indoctrinations of any society," wrote Mormon writer Rodello Hunter in *A Daughter of Zion*, "so that in adult life, that child is incapable of admitting publicly, and sometimes not even to himself, that he does not believe in some or even in all of the basic teachings of the church. To do so is to drain himself of one hundred and forty years of Mormon blood."

In recent years, the independents have fought for and gained a small measure of autonomy. Still, to challenge the church, no matter how limited the challenge, is tantamount to heresy. And in 1983, church intellectuals appeared more concerned with demonstrating the strength of their testimony and their true Mormonism than the extent of their criticisms or the nature of their alternative visions.

Under Joseph Smith and Brigham Young, the Mormons represented a radical strand of the American culture. Born and bred in the revolutionary hothouse of the "burned-over" district of western New York, the Mormons later developed a frontier society that came close to establishing a separate theocratic empire outside the U.S. This nation-state attempted to build a different type of order in the political, economic, social and sexual spheres. It never achieved full autonomy, however, and much like underdeveloped nations today, it was quickly buffeted by economic and political factors beyond its control. With the accommodations and transformations of the late nineteenth and early twentieth centuries, the Mormon experiment was essentially interrupted, to give way to a conservative acceptance of the mainstream culture and political economy.

Yet through much of the twentieth century, the Mormons maintained their peculiar, idiosyncratic nature, even while their celebration of Americanism reached its peak. That peculiarity was both doctrinal and cultural, as Mormon communities preserved the sense of themselves as a people, and the church as a way of life. During the 1950s, Mormonism came as close as it ever had to seeing its way of life mesh with the American experience.

It was, however, a short-lived honeymoon. Already during the 1950s, church leaders began to anticipate divisions and separations between their culture and the culture of the larger society. Correlation was at once self-protection and a redefinition of the Mormon experience. At first sharply antagonistic to the changes in the outside world then consciously and aggressively seeking to join with forces reacting against those changes, the Mormon church began to show a harsher, more strident aspect of its culture that narrowed the space in which freer-thinking Saints could comfortably live as members in good standing. All the mechanisms for modernizing the church were put at the service of this more ideological organization. Centralization and homogeneity became the way of life.

Today, the Mormon church is not even a pale shadow of its radical past. It is powerful and growing but fraught with tensions, many a result of that expansion and that power. To the world and its members, church leaders present a face of unity, with everything in order. "All is well, all is well," church members sing of their Zion, but all is not well, and the problems appear ready to intensify in the near term.

The Mormon church as an institution has an enormous influence over millions of its members, unlike any other church of its size. It is a fundamental part of their lives, both in the way they perceive themselves and their history. As an institution, it also plays a political and economic role far greater than other equivalent churches. It is a growing church, but the growth is uneven, creating a scale of problems unprecedented in the church's history.

As it faces the future, church leaders and many members are convinced of their mission, with each new development further proof of the church's special status in the divine plan. The future, to modernizers and ideologues alike, is clear; only the terms of the battle are still to be determined. For them, Satan is loose in the land. And it is only the Mormon church, with its onetime radical, millennial ambitions, today transformed into a subculture of reaction, that stands in the way. It is, no matter who the Prophet, a bleak and difficult future.

As more and more non-Mormons are exposed to the realities of Mormonism rather than the myths about the church, they will face a complex and vigorous challenge. Born in the rural Northeast and nurtured in the isolation of the Intermountain West, the church is one expression of a heartland culture that is often very different from what Mormons would call the secular humanism of the country's great cosmopolitan urban centers. In the heartland, religion, family, community, and patriotism are being redefined by Mormons and others less visible and are still the dominant values.

As cultural and geographical distances diminish, phenomena like Mormonism can no longer be glibly ignored as some kind of quaint sideshow. The Mormon church demands recognition because of its growing impact, particularly in an era of increasing interest in religion and of increasing interconnection between religion and politics. For the religious, Mormonism offers the idea of a church that, unlike other mainstream American religions, is all-encompassing, one that requires complete participation and willing obedience and offers an answer to both spiritual and temporal needs. For conservatives, the church is an attempt to preserve traditions and construct a bulwark against change as well as an attempt to provide a nongovernmental solution to social problems that between the

New Deal and the rise of the New Right were considered the responsibility of the government. The church also provides an example of how conservative ideals can be perverted through the construction of an authoritarian bureaucracy and how that bureaucracy can be a potent force in the lives of individual Saints, a force that has often caused great pain in its attempts to shape the lives of individual Mormons.

To liberals, radicals, and true conservatives, the church's rich history offers proof that common folk can dream, can challenge the established order, and can fashion a substantially new community from the native soil. The church also demonstrates what kinds of changes a utopian fringe group must make before it is accepted into the mainstream—changes that involve a denial of those very utopian traditions. These same traditions can then be invoked, as they are being invoked by younger Mormons, to challenge the entrenched order.

Mormonism once again brings us face to face with our own history, with the attempt to strike a balance between the demands of everyday life and the need for a spiritual vision, and with the long struggle to fashion a just society, to build the fabled City on the Hill. Mormonism also brings us face to face with the ways in which this struggle can go astray.

POSTSCRIPT: APRIL 1984

Spring Conference in April 1984 was a marked contrast to Conference a year earlier, when a major theme had been "No need for innovation." In 1983, Gordon B. Hinckley, the man who was clearly running the church, was a lonely figure on the podium who carried the burden of the ailing Prophet and his frail counselor, Marion G. Romney. By 1984 Hinckley and his allies were clearly in charge.

For one, Spencer W. Kimball continued to hang on to life. While several alerts had gone out to the Quorum in 1983 that Kimball was near death, a year later he had somehow sprung back again, even making an appearance at Conference. For Hinckley and his moderate allies, each year that Kimball stayed alive tempered the potential power of would-be prophet Ezra Taft Benson, the ultraconservative whom the moderates—and the bureaucracy—feared most.

At the April 1984 Conference, Hinckley and his allies introduced some of the most far-reaching organizational changes in the contemporary history of the church. New members of the Quorum of the Seventy—those General Authorities who were in large part responsible for supervision of the bureaucracy on a day-to-day basis—had their appointments changed from a lifetime term to a three-to-five-year term. In one stroke, the role and power of the Seventies were circumscribed, the most significant elevation of power for the professional bureaucracy since the changes triggered by Correlation.

Hinckley announced the second big surprise—the appointment of two more "worldly" Mormons to the Quorum of the Twelve—Dr. Russell M. Nelson, a prominent surgeon from Salt Lake City, and Dallin M. Oaks, the former president of Brigham Young University and later a member of the Utah Supreme Court.

The appointment of Oaks and Nelson furthered the aims of the moderates in two critical ways. For one, it lessened the potential power of Benson, who, if he became prophet, would now be able to appoint only one, rather than three members of the Twelve. Furthermore, Oaks in particular was an old Benson antagonist from BYU days. He in fact came out of the liberal wing of the church, having been one of the founders of *Dialogue* magazine. Although Oaks had lost much of his critical edge in recent years, he and his one-time colleague Neal A. Maxwell appeared to be the strongest comers in the Twelve, serving as important counterweights to the ultraconservative Benson faction.

In a final symbolic change, Hinckley announced the appointment of new heads of the Relief Society and Young Women, the two major women's organizations. Those attending Conference who were aware of the significance were startled when, for the first time in the twentieth century (with one exception), women addressed the Saints from the podium of the Tabernacle. Furthermore, Ardeth Greene Kapp, the new head of Young Women, is a professional woman who does not have children, a signal to women in the church who chafe under the constrictions of being told to remain at home and raise children rather than pursue a job or a career.

Benson, however, was still assertive. In his Conference speech, he continued to hammer at the theme that women were called by God to raise children and be "helpmates to their husbands." "Divinely prescribed roles to father, mother, and children were given from the very beginning," Benson declared. This is not inequality, he concluded, but "a matter of division of responsibility."

By 1984, it was clear that thanks to Kimball's longevity, the church was beginning to weather one of the most difficult transitions in its history. With Hinckley and the moderates in charge, and with increased power for both the bureaucracy and the Quorum of the Twelve, it was becoming apparent that the church would continue to strive to stay within the conservative mainstream. Nevertheless, the church, for both moderate and ultraconservative alike, remained committed to its restrictive notion of the family and its campaigns against the ERA and homosexuality, suspicious of its own members who challenged the injunction to believe and obey, and torn by different conceptions of the meaning of modern Mormonism.

Sources

Our efforts to research the contemporary Mormon church were complicated by a number of factors. Among them were the church's interview policies, certain restrictions placed on access to church documents at the Church History Division, and frequent requests for anonymity while interviewing.

We first approached church officials with a request for interviews in 1979, when we were writing a story for *Los Angeles* magazine on the church's Indian Placement Service. We were told that interviews were granted only to writers from family-oriented magazines, and that we should direct our questions to Public Communications, where someone would provide answers to our questions. In time, Jerry Cahill became the person we dealt with at Public Communications. Although Cahill was most friendly and helpful in arranging visits to places such as Welfare Square and the new temple in West Jordan, Utah, he was not in a position to answer many of our questions. For one thing, we were learning things about the church that needed to be confirmed or denied that he knew little or nothing about.

When we decided to write a book about the church, we submitted a list to Public Communications of about twenty General Authorities that we wanted to interview. For the next three years, we heard little that was encouraging. We were told that a file had been collected on us and that our writings, particularly articles in which we discussed the church's political and business activities and influence, explained why it was that church leaders were opposed to being interviewed.

It wasn't just a question of not granting interviews. In some cases, we arranged interviews on our own, only to find soon after that the interviews were canceled, apparently after the General Authority checked with Public Communications. Ultimately, we were obliged to contact General Authorities on an individual basis and only succeeded in interviewing those who would speak to us on background, outside the purview of Public Communications.

Finally, in frustration, we indicated to Public Communications that we had come to the end of our research and that we were giving up on the idea of getting "official" interviews with church leaders. We had seen many of them in action either at press conferences or at church conferences, had read their writings and their speeches, both those that were not publicly circulated and those that were, had talked about their views, actions, and their personalities with friends, relatives, and associates, discovered memos and other private papers that were revealing, and even had several background interviews with General Authorities.

At this point, Cahill indicated that the church was reconsidering its interview policy. We were told that we would likely get all the interviews we had requested, with the exception of President Kimball, who was gravely ill, and Ezra Taft Benson, who was not speaking to the press. Then, in another turnaround, Cahill informed us that we could talk to only one General Authority, G. Homer Durham, the church historian who had replaced Leonard J. Arrington. We explained that this was pointless since we had already interviewed Durham outside of official channels.

Meanwhile, the church was becoming the victim of its own interview policy because of its response to a series written for the *Denver Post*. In this situation, the church had also refused to grant the requested interviews. But then the church went one step further. After the series appeared in the *Post*, an article appeared in the church-owned *Deseret News* criticizing the series for being "weighted in favor of anti-Mormon voices and those critical of the church."

About the same time, church authorities banned the *Seventh East Press* from the Brigham Young University campus, and in response, a *Denver Post* editor canceled a BYU campus appearance. This inept maneuvering, which had resulted in a pointless confrontation with a major western daily, led to yet another round of reevaluating church media policy. In the end, we were granted official interviews with Apostles Neal A. Maxwell and Boyd K. Packer, both rising stars in the Mormon firmament. Those interviews, combined with unofficial interviews of numerous influential members of the church, inside and outside the hierarchy, did provide us with a rare glimpse of church leaders on a one-to-one basis.

Next came the problem of access to the church archives. On the one hand, the church, a supremely history-conscious organization, has one of the greatest collections pertaining to its history relative to any church in the world. On the other hand, it is impossible to get access to numerous important documents in the collection. For example, many of the documents pertaining to the lives of contemporary General Authorities, including their papers, diaries, and so on, are not available to researchers. Information about the economic holdings of the church is also concealed behind a veil of secrecy, reinforced by the fact that the church is a nonprofit entity and therefore has a legal right to keep its holdings confidential. Its for-profit operations are also kept secret since they are 100 percent owned by the privately held Corporation of the First Presidency or the church's holdings companies, such as Deseret Management Corporation. Since 1958, the church has refrained from publishing information about its assets and income.

Sometimes, however, sensitive and revealing papers can be found in the archives. Given the vast amount of material available, including material regarding the contemporary church, a careful and persistent researcher can unearth important documents. What is curious is the arbitrary and often capricious nature of the restrictions, a policy that includes placing some documents off limits that are obviously noncontroversial, while other, more explosive material is not.

For more than three years, we systematically pursued interviews and culled archival material. At first, we thought we might have problems finding enough sources to go *on the record*. For Mormons, especially those in Utah, being identified with Gentile critics of the church, such as ourselves, can be a risky business. Utah is a church-dominated community, and as such, one's church standing often has a bearing on one's employment possibilities, particularly if one works for the church or plans to. The church, after all, is the largest employer in the state. One friend summed up the concern about church employment by asking, "What am I going to do? Go out in the desert and eat worms?" So, all too often people asked to speak off the record and to not be identified as a source. Over time, however, we were able to overcome some of the initial hesitations.

Despite all of this, there is a wealth of information available. For one, we were able to obtain a large number of on-the-record interviews. We interviewed and spent time with more than 300 people, and about half were ultimately willing to go on the record. Similarly, we gathered large amounts of information from a variety of archival and other sources. At the church archives, the oral history program was invaluable and was used extensively. Documents on such diverse topics as Correlation and the economic organization of the church became important pieces of a larger research puzzle.

We also used important collections at the University of Utah and Brigham Young University. In addition, we looked through the *Journal History* at the Church History Division, which is a daily collection of newspaper stories about the church. We also read through a substantial number of internal church commentaries and speeches about and by particular church figures.

We went through the files of the *Deseret News*, the *Los Angeles Times*, the *New York Times*, the *Salt Lake Tribune*, and newspapers in Arizona, Nevada, Idaho, and California. We perused numerous church publications, including various manuals, the *Church News* Sunday supplement, the proceedings of church conferences, *The Ensign* and other monthly publications, and the *Church Almanac*. We also read all the issues of unofficial Mormon publications, including *BYU Studies, Dialogue, Exponent II, Seventh East Press, Sunstone*, and *Sunstone Review*. These publications are an invaluable source of information about history, current events, analysis of church trends, and debates within the church over doctrines and policies. We found *Utah Holiday*, at first glance an innocuous coffee-table magazine, to be a good source of information about the church.

We were also fortunate to obtain certain documents, diaries, letters, and so on, from anonymous sources. Several key pieces of information ranging from Ernest Wilkinson's diaries to Mark E. Petersen's masturbation guide, came to us through this route.

We also used many traditional investigative techniques to obtain information on economic, political, and social matters. These included: court files, SEC documents, FCC materials, papers from the Utah insurance and utility commissions, and several other government regulatory agencies. Ultimately, we discovered that the problem in researching the contemporary church was not the lack but the surfeit of information we obtained and tried to digest and compress into a comprehensible and readable manuscript.

CHAPTER ONE: THE CHURCH AT 150 YEARS

The description of the 150th anniversary conference is based on our personal observations. The *Denver Post* series appeared from November 21 to 28, 1982. Descriptions and information about Spencer W. Kimball's family, background, and career comes from his speeches, his book *The Miracle of Forgiveness*, and his biography, by his son and his nephew, Edward L. Kimball and Andrew E. Kimball, Jr., *Spencer W. Kimball*. Gordon B. Hinckley's statement on *The Today Show* is taken from a tape recording of the April 7, 1980, show provided by the church.

CHAPTER TWO: THE TRANSFORMATION

Since B. H. Roberts's highly detailed, seven-volume *The Comprehensive History of the Church*, which was written under church supervision in the 1920s, the church has produced no official extensive history. James B. Allen and Glen M. Leonard's *The Story of the Latter-day Saints* is the best one-volume history. It was published by the church but is now out of print, a victim of the bleak autumn that followed the Arrington spring. Other general works on the church we found helpful include: Leonard J. Arrington and Davis Bitton, *The Mormon Experience*; Gordon B. Hinckley, *Truth Restored: A Short History of the Church of Jesus Christ of Latter-day Saints*; Klaus J. Hansen, *Mormonism and the American Experience*; Mark Leone, *The Roots of Modern Mormonism*; Marvin S. Hill and James B. Allen, editors, *Mormonism and American Culture*; John S. McCormick, *Salt Lake City: The Gathering Place*; Thomas F. O'Dea, *The Mormons*; William Mulder and A. Russell Mortensen, editors, *Among the Mormons*:

Historic Accounts by Contemporary Observers; Robert Mullen, *The Latter-day Saints: The Mormons Yesterday and Today*; Lowry Nelson, *The Mormon Village*; Wallace Stegner, *Mormon Country*; Wallace Turner, *The Mormon Establishment*; and William Whalen, *The Latter-day Saints in the Modern Day World*.

For an understanding of Mormon theology, our starting point was *The Book of Mormon, Doctrines and Revelations*, and *The Pearl of Great Price*. These comprise the writings and sermons of Joseph Smith. They have been extensively revised, and the King Follett Sermon, one of Smith's most important works, is available in a nonchurch pamphlet. We also read James E. Talmage, *The Articles of Faith; The Discourses of Brigham Young*, compiled by John A. Widtsoe; LeGrand Richards, *A Marvelous Work and a Wonder*; B. H. Roberts, *Mormon Doctrine of Deity*; Sterling M. McMurrin, *The Theological Foundations of the Mormon Religion*; and Thomas G. Alexander, "The Reconstruction of Mormon Doctrine: From Joseph Smith to Progressive Theology," *Sunstone* (July-August 1980).

The two best biographies of Joseph Smith are Fawn M. Brodie, *No Man Knows My History*, a psycho-history that led to her excommunication, and Donna Hill, *Joseph Smith*. Fawn Brodie's 1970 American West Lecture, "Can We Manipulate the Past?" was also helpful. The descriptions of Smith are taken from Samuel Woolley Taylor, *Nightfall at Nauvoo*, and Lucy Mack Smith, *History of Joseph Smith*. Whitney R. Cross, *The Burned-Over District*, is a classic work on the region of western New York that produced Mormonism and other religious experiments. Equally important is the little-recognized comparative study of experimental communities, Lawrence Foster, *Religion and Sexuality: Three American Communal Experiments of the Nineteenth Century*.

There are numerous biographies of Brigham Young. We found his daughter Susa Young Gates, *Life Story of Brigham Young*, to be helpful. Other important books on the nineteenth century include: Leonard J. Arrington, *Great Basin Kingdom*; Richard Burton, *The City of the Saints*; Parley P. Pratt, *The Life and Travels of Parley P. Pratt*; Bernard DeVoto, *1846: The Year of Decision*; and Samuel Woolley Taylor, *Nightfall at Nauvoo, The Kingdom or Nothing: The Life of John Taylor, Militant Mormon*, and *Rocky Mountain Empire*.

Leonard J. Arrington, Feramorz Y. Fox, and Dean L. May, *Building the City of God*, is the most comprehensive description of the church's cooperative experiments. Juanita Brooks, *Quicksand and Cactus*, is a memoir of the Mormon frontier in the post–United Order period. In addition to the other works cited, the Great Accommodation is dealt with in Frank J. Cannon and Harvey J. O'Higgins, *Under the Prophet in Utah*, and Ronald W. Walker, "Crisis in Zion: Heber J. Grant and the Panic of 1893," *Sunstone* (January-February 1980). The Smoot hearings are found in the Senate Committee on Privileges and Elections, *Proceedings before the*

Committee in the Matter of Protest against the Right of Reed Smoot to Hold his Seat, 1904.

Because the history of the twentieth century appears to lack the drama and excitement of the early church, published material on this period lacks the quality of writings on the nineteenth century. Truman Madsen's biography of B. H. Roberts, *Defender of the Faith*, is useful but limited, skimming over Roberts's conflicts with church leaders. The two-volume biography of J. Reuben Clark by Frank W. Fox, *J. Reuben Clark: The Public Years* (Vol. 1), and D. Michael Quinn, *J. Reuben Clark: The Church Years* (Vol. 2) was most helpful. The story of Heber J. Grant's attempt to change the speaking style of J. Golden Kimball was told to us by Sterling M. McMurrin. We also looked at Jeanette McKay Morrell's *Highlights in the Life of David O. McKay*. Harold B. Lee's writings and important commentaries can be found in the church archives and at BYU, including his most informative "Address to the Regional Representatives," April 3, 1970, and several talks on Correlation such as his July 2, 1961, "An Enlarged Vision of Church Organization and its Purpose" and January 3, 1970, speeches.

The documents concerning Correlation that we pieced together from the archives and at BYU were also helpful. Correlation documents included: "A Review of Present and Proposed Programs for the Adults of the Church" (1965); Dale Mouritsen, "Efforts to Correlate Mormon Church Agencies in the 20th Century: A Review"; Jerry Rose's master's thesis, "The Correlation Program of the Church of Jesus Christ of Latter-day Saints during the 20th Century"; Carol H. Cannon's "Correlation Chronology"; and "Procedures and Outlines for Correlated Adult Curriculum" (1971).

Interviews: Lowell Bennion; Ruth Funk; L. Brent Goates; Neal A. Maxwell; Sterling M. McMurrin; David Lawrence McKay; Boyd K. Packer; Heber G. Wolsey.

Papers and Oral Histories: Paul Dunn; J. Reuben Clark; F. Thomas Fyans; Dean L. Larsen; Harold B. Lee; Marion G. Romney.

CHAPTER THREE: POLITICS: THE SECULAR COMPULSION

The controversy over the political Kingdom of God is discussed in Klaus J. Hansen, *Quest for Empire*, Andrew F. Ehat, "It Seems Like Heaven Began on Earth: Joseph Smith and the Constitution of the Kingdom of God," *BYU Studies* (spring 1981), and D. Michael Quinn, "The Council of Fifty and its Members," *BYU Studies* (winter 1980). An unpublished paper by John R. Sillito and John S. McCormick, "Socialist Saints: Mormons and the Socialist Party in Utah, 1900–1920," provides important information on radical Saints after the fall of the United Orders. J. Bracken Lee is discussed in Dennis L. Lythgoe, *Let 'Em Holler: A Political Biography of J. Bracken Lee*. Frank Jonas's works, including *Political Dynamiting*, and his papers at the University of Utah provide useful information on the 1940s and 1950s.

Ezra Taft Benson's activities as Secretary of Agriculture are described in Wesley McCune, *Ezra Taft Benson: Man with a Mission*. Benson's two books, *Crossfire* and *Red Menace*, as well as numerous of his articles and pamphlets such as "The Book of Mormon Warns America," are also helpful. Benson's statement about his cabinet position fulfilling the prophecy of Joseph Smith comes from the *Deseret News* (December 2, 1952). Richard Vetterli, *Mormonism, Americanism, and Politics*, spells out the Mormon right-wing position. Hugh B. Brown is dealt with in Eugene E. Campbell and Richard D. Poll, *Hugh B. Brown: His Life and Thought*. Several of *The Bulletins of the John Birch Society* dealt with Mormon issues. See especially the February 1963 Bulletin. We were also provided access to the unpublished diaries of Ernest L. Wilkinson, which had fascinating passages on the Benson-Brown split and other quarrels and activities of the General Authorities regarding political matters.

For a discussion of the church and the right-to-work law, see Garth Mangum, "The Church and Right to Work," *Dialogue* (summer 1968). J. D. Williams, "The Separation of Church and State in Mormon Theory and Practice," *Dialogue* (summer 1966), is a good summary of church involvement in politics, as is the J. D. Williams-Edwin Firmage debate on the same subject in *Sunstone* (July-August 1981). Calvin Rampton's discussion of Mormons and politics at an April 20, 1983, University of Utah lecture was helpful. We discussed the role of the Mormon church in Las Vegas in greater detail in "Don't Touch the Dice: The Utah–Las Vegas Connection," *Utah Holiday* (September 1980), and "Zion in Gomorrah," two parts, *Sunstone Review* (July and August 1982). W. Cleon Skousen's best-known books are *The Naked Communist* and *The Naked Capitalist*. A two-part series on "Freemen America" by Linda Sillitoe and David Merrill appeared in *Utah Holiday* (February and March 1981). "Watergate's Utah Connection" by Fred Esplin, *Utah Holiday* (March 28, 1977) was also helpful, as was "God and Man at the CIA" by Dale Van Atta, *The Washingtonian* (December 1983).

Interviews: Jack Anderson; James Andrus; Robert Barker; Robert Bennett; Wallace F. Bennett; Kent Briggs; Robert Broadbent; Mahlon Brown; Richard Bunker; M. McClain Bybee; Shannon Bybee; Samuel Davis; Rod Decker; G. Homer Durham; Frances Farley; Edwin B. Firmage; Jeff Fox; James Gallivan; James Gibson; Mike Graham; Orrin G. Hatch; Ashley Hall; Ralph Hardy; John Harmer; Devoe Heaton; Omar Kader; J. Bracken Lee; Rex Lee; Scott M. Matheson; Frank E. Moss; Elbert Peck; Larry Jensen; Calvin Rampton; L. C. Romney; Harry Reid; James K.

Seastrand; W. Cleon Skousen; Samuel Woolley Taylor; Reed Whipple; J. D. Williams; Ted Wilson; Richard Winder; Richard Wirthlin.

Papers and Oral Histories: Wallace F. Bennett; Ezra Taft Benson; Dean Brimhall; J. Reuben Clark; Frank Jonas; David King; Frank Moss; Sterling M. McMurrin; Ernest L. Wilkinson.

CHAPTER FOUR: THE RISE OF THE MONEY MANAGERS

Although there are almost no public documents describing the church's overall economic holdings, much can be learned by looking at the filings of various public agencies and at government documents, such as the tax rolls or the Utah Insurance Commission, where the church's four insurance companies annually file a list of their assets. Church holdings in such companies as Utah and Idaho, Inc. are detailed in SEC filings. Bill Beecham and David Briscoe, "Mormon Money and How it's Made," *Utah Holiday*, builds on their earlier stories for the Associated Press, which appeared in the Idaho State Journal (September 21, 1975). We also used Neil Morgan, "Utah: How Much Money Hath the Mormon Church," *Esquire* (August 1962). For a look at the church's holdings in California, we were helped by Jeffrey Kaye's article on Mormon money in *New West* (May 8, 1978). Kaye made available to us the transcript of his recorded interview with N. Eldon Tanner. Heber J. Grant's trip to Wall Street is described in Ronald W. Walker's "Crisis in Zion," op. cit. Useful background on N. Eldon Tanner can be found in G. Homer Durham, *N. Eldon Tanner: His Life and Service*.

Though many of our key interviews in this area were off the record, several leading church business advisers, including J. Alan Blodgett and J. Howard Dunn, spoke quite openly with us. For a more detailed description of the church's involvement with the Triad Center, see our "Triad Utah: Angels or Flying Carpetbaggers," *Utah Holiday* (March 1983). The destruction of the Coalville Tabernacle is detailed in a spring 1971 issue of *Dialogue*. For a description of the church's media operations, see our "Static in Zion," *Columbia Journalism Review* (July-August 1979). The most revealing church admonitions on Mormon scam artists appeared in the May 15, 1982, issue of the *Church News* and the September 1983 issue of *The Ensign*. A *Wall Street Journal*, November 9, 1983, article, "Leaders of Mormonism Double As Overseers of a Financial Empire," was helpful.

Interviews: Wendell Ashton; J. Alan Blodgett; Harry Blundell; Michael Chitwood; Stephanie Churchill; Rod Decker; Louise Degn; J. Howard Dunn; Emanuel A. Floor; Sydney Fonnesbeck; Ernie Ford; James Gallivan; Charles Graves; M. McLain Haddow; Joseph G. Jorgensen; B. Z. Kastler; Essam Khashoggi; Spencer J. Kinard; Jon Lear; Ron Little; Arch Madsen; Kelley Mathews; Tony Mitchell; L. Gerald Pond; Bradley P.

Rich; Allen Roberts; J. L. Shoemaker; Roy Simmons; Irv Skousen; Alice Moyle Yeats.

Papers and Oral Histories: J. Alan Blodgett; Edgar Brossard; B. Z. Kastler; Wilford Woodruff Kirton, Jr.; Henry D. Moyle; Franklin J. Murdoch; Merrill Ross Petty; Franklin D. Richards; Douglas Hill Smith; Irwin Tanner; Nathan Eldon Tanner; Charles Ursenbach; Ernest L. Wilkinson.

CHAPTER FIVE: FOLLOWING THE FLAG

There are three key overall studies of the international church: F. LaMond Tullis, editor, *Mormonism: A Faith for All Cultures*; James R. Moss, R. Lanier Britsch, James R. Christianson, and Richard O. Cowan, *The International Church*, and Spencer J. Palmer, *The Expanding Church*. There are also a number of works on the church in specific countries, particularly Mexico. These include: Nelle Spilsbury Hatch, *Colonia Juarez: An Intimate Account of a Mormon Village*; Estelle Webb Thomas, *Uncertain Sanctuary: A Story of Mormon Pioneering in Mexico*; F. LaMond Tullis and Elizabeth Hernández, *Mormonism in Mexico: Leadership, Nationalism, and the Case of the Third Convention*; and Karl Young, *Ordeal in Mexico: Tales of Danger and Hardship Collected from Mormon Colonists*. David W. Cummings, *Mighty Missionary of the Pacific: The Building Program of the Church of Jesus Christ of Latter-day Saints* provided background on the building program and the church expansion in the South Pacific. That part of the world was the subject of Max Edward Stanton's University of Oregon, Ph.D. dissertation, "Samoan Saints: Samoans in the Mormon Village of Laie, Hawaii." The Kimball meeting with the Mexican children is discussed in F. Burton Howard, "An Ordinary Monday Night," *The Ensign* (October 1980).

The following *Dialogue* articles were helpful: Wesley W. Craig, Jr., "The Church in Latin America: Progress and Challenge" (fall 1970); Don Hicken, "The Church in Asia" (spring 1968); and Eldger B. Benson Whittle, "From the Mission Field: Brazil" (winter 1966). Several summary pieces in *The Ensign* on the church in Latin America were also used, the best being "The Church's Cross-Cultural Encounters," by Lavina Fielding Anderson (April 1980). The transcript of a meeting of Spencer W. Kimball and David M. Kennedy with Philippine President Ferdinand E. Marcos on October 18, 1980, was particularly instructive. Sheldon Rampton's account of his stay at the Missionary Training Center is taken from a paper he presented at Princeton University. The discussion of Jay Parkinson's role in Chile is found in *The Price of Power* by Seymour M. Hersh. The oral histories in the church archives were an invaluable source of information. Again, many of the interviews in this area were conducted on a background basis.

Interviews: Cordell Anderson; Mario Aranda; Arturo de Hoyos; J.

Howard Dunn; Rita Edmonds; Mr. and Mrs. Ruben Gomez; Mark Grover; Neal A. Maxwell; Boyd K. Packer; Paul Smith; F. LaMond Tullis; Robert Wells; Werner Woodworth.

Papers and Oral Histories: Angel Abrea; W. Grant Bangerter; Kenneth H. Beesley; William Bradford; Harold Brown; Julian Saville Cannon; Rex Carlisle, Jr.; J. Howard Dunn; James E. Faust; Glen G. Fisher; F. Thomas Fyans; Royden J. Glade; John Groberg; David McClellan; Jasper Ray McClellan; Evelyn Moyle Nelson; John Flores O'Donnell; A. Delbert Palmer; Robert H. Slover; A. Theodore Tuttle.

CHAPTER SIX: FALLEN ANGELS AND LOST BROTHERS

Much has been written in the press about the church and blacks, but there are few studies of the church's overall racial views. Howard A. Christy, "Open Hand and Mailed Fist: Mormon–Indian Relations in Utah," *Utah Historical Quarterly* (spring 1971), describes the realities of early church–Indian relations. David Kay Flake, *History of the Southwest Indian Mission*, was an invaluable source. *Me and Mine: The Life Story of Helen Sekaquaptewa* as told to Louise Udall is about the church's best-known Indian convert. Helen Bay Gibbons, *Saint and Savage*; Arturo de Hoyos, *The Old and the Modern Lamanite*; Dean L. Larsen, *You and the Destiny of the Indian*; and Mark E. Petersen, *Children of Promise: The Lamanites Yesterday and Today*, help explain the church's view of the Indian people. We also used Wallace F. Bennett, "The Negro in Utah," *Utah Law Review* (spring 1953), and Clarence R. Bishop, "A History of Indian Placement Service" (University of Utah, master's thesis). *Navajo Times* did a special report about Mormons on the reservation in its July 27, 1982, issue. Richard G. Oman, "LDS Southwest Indian Art," *The Ensign* (September 1982), argues that Mormon Indians are among the finest artists in the Southwest. Parker M. Nielsen, *Of Worthier Blood: A Chronicle of the Cultural Destruction of the Indian* (unpublished), presents the case of the mixed-blood Utes. John S. Boyden's activities as Hopi tribal attorney are discussed in Indian Law Resource Center, *Report to the Hopi Kikmongwis and Other Traditional Leaders*. Linda Sillitoe, "The Old and the New Come Together on the Ute Reservation," *Deseret News* (September 25, 1983), was also helpful.

Mary Frances Sturlaughson, *A Soul So Rebellious*, is an account of the tribulations of a black convert before the black priesthood revelation. The most important sources for the black issues are: Lester E. Bush, Jr., "Mormonism's Negro Doctrine: An Historical Overview," *Dialogue* (spring 1973); Armand L. Mauss, "Mormonism and the Negro: Faith, Folklore, and Civil Rights," *Dialogue* (winter 1967), and "The Fading of the Pharoah's Curse: The Decline and Fall of the Priesthood Ban Against Blacks in the Mormon Church," *Dialogue* (fall 1981); Newell G. Bringhurst,

Saints, Slaves, and Blacks: The Changing Place of Black People Within Mormonism; Jan Shipps, "The Mormons: Looking Forward and Outward," *Christian Century* (August 16–23, 1978); John J. Stewart, *Mormonism and the Negro*; Stephen G. Taggert, *Mormonism's Negro Policy: Social and Historical Origins*; two papers by BYU Professor Wilford E. Smith, "By Their Fruits," 1975, and "Doctrinal Consistency and LDS Priesthood for Blacks," 1978; and Douglas Monty Trask, *A Rhetorical Analysis of the Rhetoric Emerging from the Mormon/Black Controversy* (University of Utah, Ph.D. dissertation). In their *Black Power: A Study of Black Power, Red Alternatives, and White Alternatives*, with a foreword by Ezra Taft Benson, Wes Andrews and Clyde Dalton argue that the civil rights leadership was "white, led by vermin [who] are without exception members of a communist-socialist, fascist-liberal cartel." William E. Koerner presents the case for the Neighborhood Emergency Teams in *Is All Well in Zion: Neighborhood Emergency Teams*. Jon Stewart provided us with a transcript of an interview he had with Navajo General Authority George P. Lee.

Interviews: Glenda Ahaitty; Mike Allison; Bob Angle; Claudeen Arthur; Harris Arthur; Tom Banyacya; Robert Barker; Evelyn Blanchard; Katherine Collard; Ralph Crane; Keith Crocker; Arturo de Hoyos; Rex Furness; Steve Holbrook; Dennis Irving; Larry Jensen; Cyrus Josytewa; Hayes Lewis; Robert Lewis; Wayne Lynn; Ray Baldwin Louis; Tom Luebben; Charles McGee; Sterling M. McMurrin; Maxine Natchess; Parker M. Nielsen; John O'Connell; Otis Paleoloma; George Pooley; Joyce Pooley; Abbott Sekaquaptewa; Wayne Sekaquaptewa; Martin Seneca; Mary Ellen Sloan; Eric Swensen; Martin Topper; Steve Tullberg.

Papers and Oral Histories: Golden Buchanan; John Flores O'Donnell; Ernest L. Wilkinson.

CHAPTER SEVEN: THE PRIESTHOOD AND THE BLACK WIDOW SPIDER

The colonization of southern Utah in the nineteenth century is described from a woman's point of view in the classic novel by Maureen Whipple, *The Giant Joshua*. The issue of women in the church has led to the creation of two important publications, *Exponent II* (based in Boston) and *The Mormons for ERA Newsletter*. Two special issues of *Dialogue* ten years apart (1971 and 1981) dealt extensively with women in the church. For the church's position, see, among copious material, *The Church and the Proposed Equal Rights Amendment*. Rodney Turner, *Women and the Priesthood*, is a revealing look at the church-inspired attitudes toward women. Helen B. Andelin, *Fascinating Womanhood*, presents a church housewife's view of how women should behave. The proper role for women is spelled out in a number of Ezra Taft Benson's writings; see especially his "The Honored Place of Women," a talk he gave before the Relief Society in 1981. For a different point of view on the subject see Sonia Johnson's account of her life as a Mormon woman and pro-ERA excommunicant in *From Housewife to Heretic*. The ERA and Sonia Johnson's excommunication have been described at some length in a number of publications, but two of the best accounts are Linda Sillitoe and Paul Swenson, "A Moral Issue," *Utah Holiday* (January 1980), and Linda Sillitoe, "Church Politics and Sonia Johnson: The Central Conundrum," *Sunstone* (January-February 1980). The ERA issue was one of several raised in the exchange of letters between Relief Society President Barbara Smith and Doris M. Harker of the law firm Romney, Nelson, and Cassity. The Mormons and the IWY Conference is detailed in a fall 1977 *Exponent II* article. Barbara Smith's January 15, 1977, talk in Coeur d'Alene, Idaho on "The Rights of Women" was instructive. Marilyn Warenski, *Patriarchs and Politics*, touched off some of the more recent debates on women and the church. The Mother in Heaven issue was analyzed by Linda Wilcox, "The Mormon Concept of a Mother in Heaven," *Sunstone* (September-October 1980).

Interviews: Linda Adams; Lavina Fielding Anderson; Mary Bradford; Ruth Funk; Nadine Hansen; Sonia Johnson; Rex E. Lee; Susan Lindsay; Judith Little; Jaynann Morgan Payne; Carol Lynn Pearson; Chase Petersen; Grethe Petersen; Martha Pierce; Alice Allred Pottmeyer; Rene Rampton; Jan Tyler; Lee Ann Walker; Marilyn Warenski.

Papers and Oral Histories: Sonia Johnson; Lavern W. Parmley; Barbara Smith; Marion Isabelle (Belle) Smith Spafford.

CHAPTER EIGHT: CULTURES OF ZION

Dean L. Larsen, "Marriage and the Patriarchal Order," appeared in the September 1982 issue of *The Ensign*. Spencer W. Kimball's position on marriage and sexuality is outlined in "Marriage and Divorce," a talk he gave on September 7, 1976, at BYU. A fall 1982 issue of *Exponent II* was devoted to Mormons and sexuality. Mark E. Petersen's church masturbation guide is called: "A Guide to Self Control: Overcoming Masturbation." The church position on homosexuality can be found in its pamphlet "Homosexuality," as well as in two Boyd K. Packer speeches, "To the One" (1978) and "To Young Men Only" (1976), among others. The anonymous letter written in response to Reed Payne's attack on homosexuals was printed as a pamphlet entitled "Prologue: An Examination of the Mormon Attitude towards Sexuality." An important statement about the Mormon-gay situation is found in the "Solus" article that appeared in *Dialogue* (1976).

The classic study of the extent and practice of polygamy is Stanley S. Ivins, "Notes on Mormon Polygamy," *Western Humanities Review* (summer 1956). Samuel Woolley Taylor, *Family Kingdom*, is a wonderful account of his father's polygamous family, and his *I Have Six Wives* is an account of polygamy from the 1930s to the early 1950s through the thinly disguised biography of the Rulon Allred family. A more recent account of the Allreds is found in Rulon's daughter Dorothy Solomon's memoir in *Good Housekeeping* (April 1979). There are a number of nineteenth-century feminist attacks on polygamy, the best-known of which is Ann-Eliza Young, *Wife Number Nineteen: A Life in Bondage.* Kimball Young also discusses polygamy in *Isn't One Wife Enough?* There are two accounts of the activities of the LeBaron polygamist cult: Ben Bradlee, Jr., and Dale Van Atta, *Prophet of Blood: The Untold Story of Ervil LeBaron and the Lambs of God*, and Verlan LeBaron, *The LeBaron Story.* The description of the lost revelation upholding polygamy comes from Samuel Woolley Taylor, *The Kingdom of God or Nothing: The Life of John Taylor, Militant Mormon.* The unofficial church response to the polygamy issue can be found in J. Max Anderson, *The Polygamy Story: Fact or Fiction.*

Boyd K. Packer's talk on "Keeping Confidences" was delivered at the Church Employee's Lecture Series on January 28, 1980. Bruce R. McConkie's "The Seven Deadly Sins" talk was delivered at BYU on June 1, 1980. Richard Poll's "Liahona and Iron Rod" Mormon dichotomy first appeared in the winter 1967 *Dialogue.* Talks from several of the B. H. Roberts forums have been reprinted in *Sunstone*, which has also reprinted proceedings from both the Sunstone Theological Symposium and the Mormon History Association. The History Division controversy was elaborated on in two articles we wrote: "Shutting the Window on Mormon History," *New Times Weekly* (April 18–May 4, 1982), and "U.C. Choice Raises Issue of Church Education Policy," *Seattle Times* (March 25, 1983). Rodello Hunter, *A Daughter of Zion*, describes church work at the ward level in Salt Lake City in the 1960s. J. Bonner Ritchie, "The Institutional Church and the Individual," *Sunstone* (May–June 1982) was helpful.

Interviews: Linda Adams; James Allen; Lavina Fielding Anderson; Leonard J. Arrington; Lowell Bennion; Gary Bergera; Davis Bitton; Mary Bradford; Jerry Cahill; G. Homer Durham; Peggy Fletcher; Jeffrey Holland; Jon Lear; Neal A. Maxwell; Dean May; Kathryn MacKay; Jerry Merrill; Paul Mortensen; Boyd K. Packer; Elbert Peck; Chase Petersen; Ron Priddis; D. Michael Quinn; Marybeth Raynes; Lewis M. Rodgers; W. Cleon Skousen; Lin Ostler Strack; Paul Swenson; Samuel Woolley Taylor; Robert K. Thomas.

Papers and Oral Histories: James Clayton; Boyd K. Packer; Ernest L. Wilkinson.

ACKNOWLEDGMENTS

Writing a book on the Mormon church is a sensitive and complex undertaking, particularly if it is done critically and without approval of the
church General Authorities. Some of the problems we encountered while
gathering material for this book reminded us of problems we had had while
gathering material for the chapters on Salt Lake City, Las Vegas, and
Phoenix in *Empires in the Sun.* By the time we started our research for
America's Saints, we had already developed a way to deal with potential
sources: we approached people with discretion and tried to establish our
trustworthiness. It took time, but after months of interviews, inquiries,
informal get-togethers, and unobtrusive meetings, we were able to develop
some trusting relationships and even some lasting friendships. People put
up with us and put us up in their homes, breaking bread with us, sharing
holidays in the mountains, attending services together, and making us feel
not only like welcome guests but like part of their community as well.

We were not simply Gentiles experiencing the Mormon world (a strange
notion for Bob, who is Jewish); we were journalists discovering information and analyzing material that the church leadership had no desire to see
made public. Although our relations with the church via its Public Communications Department were proper and courteous, there was nevertheless wariness and suspicion regarding our project. The church
leadership tends to mistrust outsiders doing research and writing about the
church. The tension becomes particularly acute when such research leads
to questions about the economic and political activities of the church, some
of its international activities, and its racial and sexual doctrines and practices.

For our sources, a level of paranoia existed, some imagined, but most
real. We found that people had been fired for passing information or being
suspected of passing information about sensitive church matters to persons
outside the church. During the time we were working on the book, others
were scrutinized by church leaders because of their association with critics
inside and outside the church. The possibility of being fired is particularly
threatening in a community like Salt Lake City, where the church is the
major employer and a person's alleged loyalty can be a factor when he or

she seeks employment in the Mormon business community. In an era of correlation and increased authoritarianism, the space for an independent Mormon has definitely narrowed.

For these reasons, we are unable to acknowledge here all those who helped us. This is particularly true of loyal members who hold respected positions in the church or the church community, but are critical of one or another church practice. It also includes people who felt that there was no real reason for discouraging members to discuss the church critically but were nevertheless hesitant to be associated with us publicly.

We do want to thank those others who read and criticized our manuscript, provided us with information and leads, shared their writings, examined and criticized our attitudes toward the church, and generally guided us through what appears to most outsiders as a self-contained and somewhat mysterious community: Lavina Fielding Anderson, Paul Anderson, Gary Bergera, Aileen Bentley, Mary Bradford, Peter Carlson, Twinkle Chisolm, Kathy Collard, Dr. Everett Cooley, Della Dye, Diane Divoky, Ed Dunn, Fred C. Esplin, Frances Farley, Ed Firmage, Chad Flake, Peggy Fletcher, Emmanuel A. Floor, Jeff Fox, Charlie Gibbs, Mark Grover, Richard Hall, Linda Haslam, Steve Holbrook, Arturo de Hoyos, Helen Johnson, Sonia Johnson, Joseph Jorgensen, James L. Kimball, Kay Kosow, Donald Lefebvre, Jon Lear, Wayne Linn, Leland Lubinsky, John MacFarlane, Katherine MacKay, John McCormick, Audrey McIlwrath, Parker Nielson, Jack Noel, Gladys Noyce, John O'Connell, Chase Petersen, Grethe Petersen, Elbert Peck, Martha Pierce, L. Gerald Pond, Alice Allred Pottmeyer, Ron Priddis, Rene Rampton, Sheldon Rampton, Allen D. Roberts, Ann Schmidt, Richard Schmidt, John Sillito, Linda Sillitoe, William W. Slaughter, George D. Smith, Susan Staker, Lori W. Stromberg, Jan L. Tyler, Lynn Van Dam, Clyde Weiss, Brad Wiley, Brad Wiley II, Linda Wilcox, Heber Wolsey.

We also want to thank Paul Swenson, editor of *Utah Holiday,* with whom we worked on a number of stories about the church; Peggy Jolley, who critiqued and typed our manuscript; and Sam Weller, bookman *extraordinaire,* who guided us in our readings.

Special thanks also goes to Jerry Cahill of the church's Public Communications Department, who showed great patience and professionalism answering (and sometimes not answering) our many questions and for guiding us through the West Jordan Temple and Welfare Square. Cahill, a former journalist and city editor, was a kind friend throughout our research.

We want to thank Howard Bray and the Fund for Investigative Journalism for their continuing support and always helpful comments; our editor, Diane Reverand, for her patience and perseverance; and our agent, Bob Cornfield, for his insights and thoughtfulness. And our families and friends for listening patiently to our endless tales and thoughts about our new experiences.

INDEX